ADMINISTRATIVE DECISION-MAKING

ADMINISTRATIVE DECISION-MAKING

EXTENDING THE
BOUNDS OF RATIONALITY

John W. Sutherland

VNR VAN NOSTRAND REINHOLD COMPANY
NEW YORK   CINCINNATI   ATLANTA   DALLAS   SAN FRANCISCO
LONDON   TORONTO   MELBOURNE

Van Nostrand Reinhold Company Regional Offices:
New York Cincinnati Atlanta Dallas San Francisco

Van Nostrand Reinhold Company International Offices:
London Toronto Melbourne

Library of Congress Catalog Card Number: 77-23594
ISBN: 0-442-28075-0

Manufactured in the United States of America

Published by Van Nostrand Reinhold Company
450 West 33rd Street, New York, N.Y. 10001

Published simultaneously in Canada by Van Nostrand Reinhold Ltd.

15 14 13 12 11 10 9 8 7 6 5 4 3 2 1

Library of Congress Cataloging in Publication Data

Sutherland, John W
  Administrative decision-making.

  Includes bibliographical references.
  1. Decision-making. 2. Management. I. Title.
HD30.23.S9   658.4'03   77-23594
ISBN 0-442-28075-0

*To Susan, Johnnie, and Brenda—
they are the real purpose of
this work.*

Preface

Many years ago, Coventry Patmore made an ominous declaration: "Nations often die of softening of the brain, which for a long time passes as softening of the heart." It is fitting that such a statement lead us into our work in this volume, for we have entered an age where intellectual integrity has become less generally important than matters of personality or character. I frequently hear even well-schooled individuals suggesting that all the world's problems could be solved merely by improving the character of our leaders—by getting the crooks out of government and industry and replacing them with men and women of good intention and benevolent ambition. But the problem is this: as many of the world's problems are caused by inept individuals as by corrupt ones. Good intentions and purity of character are not of themselves sufficient basis for the management of the complex organizations we have evolved. Rather, a good character must be accompanied by a good mind; the telling blows against waste, dysfunction, error, and debacle can only be delivered by men and women of great analytical sophistication and disciplined intellect. So, if the public at large is unwilling to forgive our leaders their faults of character, I am unwilling to forgive them out of hand for their faults of mind.

However, if many decision-makers are simply intellectually unqualified for the responsibilities they hold, the fault is mainly mine and that of my academic colleagues. We have consistently pandered to administrators' own concepts of their jobs, and thus have become more frequently apologists than prophets. Particularly, perhaps to try to pose ourselves as practical men and women of affairs and as realistic consultants, we have applauded—if not posed—suboptimality as a decision criterion. We have told decision-makers that they cannot really hope to obtain optimal solutions to their problems, and so they should therefore rest content with satisfactory or sufficient solutions. This is rather like a track coach telling the runners to quit just as soon as their lungs and legs start to hurt. So, in these pages, I want to restore optimality to its pre-dominance as a referent for real-world decision-makers, and will spend con-siderable time trying to show why such an ambition is not only feasible, but imperative.

Another area in which we academics have failed dramatically is in the type of education we have supplied those entering the world of enterprise. For the most part, we have tended to try to make our students into our own image. But our image is not so promising. In the first place, we are a badly divided house. A majority of management scholars are primarily interested in principles of man-agement, in rhetorical science. They tend to suggest that management is "the art of getting things done through people" or the "distillation of experience." Their concept of the scientific aspects of management training is thus to expose their students to the way things are done, taking great pride in pointing out the "realities" of management. The normative content is restricted to generalizations about the proper span of management or to such prescriptions as "a subordinate should report to only one superior." It is possible for a student to graduate from such a program with virtually no training in mathematics, statistics, or computer science. Such students must rely primarily on wit, charm, connections, or luck to get ahead. And, as such, the positions they occupy tend to be treated primarily as *social* functions, not necessarily as positions of considerable analyt-ical significance.

The foil of the rhetorical management theorist is, of course, the "scientific" scholar. Acting as the agent for operations research, econometrics, mathematical programming, or the like, he tends to see management as an instrumental function—as the application of Markov processes, Bayesian statistics, decision trees, or other technical artifices. But the fundamental problem is this: most of the instruments to which the students of management science are introduced—most of the technical tricks they are taught—are useful only in the face of the problems that emerge at the lower levels of modern enterprise. They may be at home on the plant floor, in the inventory-control office, or in the transportation department. But they will not operate on the issues that emerge in the board-room or the executive suites. The problems we find there simply do not, as a rule, lend themselves to the quantitative tools we have developed; they are too ill-structured, too broad in their ramifications, and too protean to be contained by the kind of mathematical models we are capable of constructing. In short, what we have posed as "scientific" management is really scientific only in the most constrained sense. For the scientific component is really just raw em-piricism, which means the only kind of problems we can recognize or treat are those that are fully observable, susceptible to numerical surrogation, and amenable to manipulation in what amounts to a controlled laboratory environ-ment. And once we rise above the operational levels of enterprise, such prob-lems become rare indeed.

The net result of our educational emphasis is thus a generally unpalatable one: the more trivial and well-contained decisions in complex organizations may benefit consistently and completely from strong (if constrained) scientific discipline, whereas the more significant decisions are left in the hands of individuals who may have virtually no real technological discipline. And, as we will see clearly enough, most of the really dramatic failures and dysfunctions in business and government alike tend to be spawned somewhere in the vast no-man's-land between the rhetorical and scientific decision-maker.

As such, we must broaden the skills and perspectives of those preparing for positions of administrative responsibility. The constrained and somewhat artificial education of the management "scientist" must be elaborated to include the matters of logic, qualitative analysis, and deduction, which are so critical to the disciplined solution of higher-order organizational problems—for matters of basic mission analysis, goal-setting, and strategic planning. By the same token, the rhetorician must be lent some of the precision and instrumental sophistication that is now reserved for the student of administrative science *per se*. For there is really no unalterable dictate demanding that complex problems have to be solved by casual speculation or unbridled trial-and-error. The sweep of proper science is wide indeed, wide enough to encompass *all* the problems that arise within the complex organization, not just the simpler ones.

It is in that proposition that we find the basic ambition for this book. Specifically, it will be the task of these pages to develop a truly generalized decision theory, one that points out the promises of science across all decision domains from the machine shop to the boardroom. Moreover, we will concentrate on how decisions *should* be made, not on the logic and procedures that are currently in force. Some readers might suggest that what we do here—and what we demand of the decision-maker—is unrealistic in light of the constraints that exist on business people and public administrators. I can only remind those readers that the future is the place where all constraints disappear, and it is the future with which I am concerned. And without normative referents—without the "oughts" and "shoulds"—the future is condemned to be little more than a replay of the past. Few, I think, would consider that desirable.

To a great extent, the scope of our inquiry and the level of our argument are conditioned by the fact that this book is the inaugural volume of a new management and decision science series. As such, I will be concentrating on the broad logical and procedural aspects of decision-making, leaving discussion of individual tools and specific techniques to subsequent volumes. Thus, we can deal with issues in a way that won't penalize those readers without much technical or mathematical background. For the logic we develop is, at heart, merely an extension of common sense, somewhat formalized. An intuitive grasp of the mathematical and statistical instruments available to the modern decision-maker is more than sufficient to lend the logical and procedural points some immediate operational significance. All that is assumed of the readers, then, is that they have a quick mind, a professional pride of purpose, and a commitment to excellence in the interest of those organizations or communities they serve.

Of course, any attempt to produce a work that sets out normative criteria—that presumes to tell people how they should conduct their affairs—sets the author at peril. Therefore, this book was written with almost equal measures of enthusiasm and trepidation. The enthusiasm reflects that fact that such a book really had to be attempted by somebody; the trepidation reflects the odds against doing the work really well, of succeeding in what must be described as a somewhat arrogant ambition. So I hope the shortcomings of this book will be viewed in light of the general unfamiliarity of the ground over which we will be traveling. But I do not ask to be forgiven for errors or inadequacies; recrimination for such faults is a price that the normative scholar must be prepared to pay for the hearing that his audience gives him.

As for audiences, this volume was written with three in mind. Initially, I wanted to make some contribution to the many education programs that are attempting to equip students of administration with a broad perspective and a truly catholic set of analytical skills.

Second, there are the practitioners. I am fully aware of their impatience with theoretical or abstract arguments. Any work with theoretical pretentions may be precondemned by individuals of action as "irrelevant." But it is theoretical deficiencies that, perhaps more than any other single factor, prevent the men and women of action from best serving their own interests, to say nothing of the interests of the organizations with which they are entrusted. Etched in stone at the entrance to the Columbia University Graduate School of Business is a quote from Alfred North Whitehead: "A great society is a society in which its men of business think greatly of their function." But what is often overlooked is another statement by this great thinker, which expresses most eloquently the underlying philosophy of this volume: "The paradox is now fully established, that the utmost abstractions are the true weapons with which to control our thought of concrete fact." The more popular expression of this thought is simply this: there is nothing so relevant as a good theory. Therefore, I ask the busy, active, and impatient readers to give some attention to the possibility that one can only become more pragmatic—more useful—to the extent that one becomes more theoretically sophisticated.

Finally, these pages try to answer the questions of my professional and academic colleagues about the immediate potential of a system-based decision theory, one capable of dealing with a wide range of problems rather than being confined to those problems that permit direct quantitative solutions. Many of these colleagues, seeing so clearly the staggering burdens under which our world labors, have become victims of the popular pessimism of these days. They read the learned treatises proposing an immediate—and apparently well-deserved—doomsday for the human race; they are stunned by the simplistic and fatuous analyses of political leaders, and by their sophomoric panaceas for our social, economic, and political quandries; they see the failure of traditional managerial mechanisms to control complexity or contain calamity; every morning their newspapers offer new candidates for the concatenating hit parade of administrative horrors. But I ask my colleagues to take heart. For, a majority of these "horrors" appear to be due more to faults of mind than of character, and faults of mind are much easier to repair than faults of character. Moreover, there is a legion of scholars attacking the faults of mind. And many of these, I am sorry to say, are probably better equipped to launch the attack than I. So, we should not be concerned that the age of rationality has come and gone, died aborning as it were. Indeed, the age of rationality still awaits us, and from this we may take great comfort.

John W. Sutherland
Piscataway, N. J.

Contents

Preface / vii

1. Sources of Suboptimality / 1

    1.0   Introduction / 1
    1.1   The Decision Domains / 2
    1.2   The Problem Contexts / 12
    1.3   The Straw Men: Mechanist and Rhetorician / 24
    1.4   Toward a Resolution / 37
    1.5   Notes and References / 48

2. The Structure of Decision Responsibilities / 51

    2.0   Introduction / 51
    2.1   The Decision Contexts / 51
          2.1.1   Directors and System Integrity / 52
          2.1.2   The Strategic Decision Domain / 60
          2.1.3   The Tactical Decision Domain / 76
          2.1.4   The Deterministic Domain / 85
    2.2   The Decision Configuration / 90
    2.3   Relativistic Decision Criteria / 95
    2.4   Notes and References / 106

3. Decision Performance and Propriety / 108

    3.0   Introduction / 108
    3.1   The Focuses of Accountability / 108
          3.1.1   Propriety and Performance / 110
    3.2   Congruence and Utility / 124

3.3 Efficiency, Return, and Productivity / 140

3.4 Notes and References / 172

4. Aspects of Decision Discipline / 174

4.0 Introduction / 174

4.1 The Method Audit / 174

4.2 The Decision Analyst as Model-Builder / 185

4.3 The Expected Value of Decision Error / 197

4.4 Analytical Congruence / 206

4.5 Dynamics of the Decision Analysis Process / 229

4.6 Notes and References / 234

5. Managing the Decision Function / 236

5.0 Introduction / 236

5.1 The Decision System / 236

5.2 A Generalized Decision Paradigm / 248

5.3 The Structural Trade-off: Decision Scope and Decision Rectitude / 269

5.4 Operationalizing Optimality / 287

5.5 Notes and References / 301

Appendix to Chapter 5: *Ideologics* by Stephen E. Seadler / 303

Index / 313

ADMINISTRATIVE DECISION-MAKING

1

Sources of Suboptimality

1.0 INTRODUCTION

It has long been a maxim of practical management that we cannot obtain optimal results. Rather, we should rest content with adequate or sufficient solutions to the problems we are asked to solve. Popularly, this has been called the concept of "satisficing." But the first problem for any work dealing with administrative decision-making is to try to explain why decision-makers make so many mistakes —why they transgress not only the rules of optimality, but also often fail to meet the much softer criteria of sufficiency or adequacy. The answer that emerges is disturbing: most decision-makers are simply intellectually unqualified for the positions they hold.

To make this clear, we will first take a look at the decision functions that must be performed within any complex organization. Next, we will examine the formal guises in which decision problems emerge, as these set the requirements for decision rationality.

In the process, we shall see that "scientific" decision-makers—those schooled in the technology of operations research and management science—are really equipped to handle only the lower-level, better-defined problems that emerge in enterprise. This leaves the major decisions in the hands of their generally pre-scientific counterparts, the rhetorical decision-makers. They, by default, dominate both commercial and public enterprise. The mid-range between these two extremes is ill-populated. As a result, we shall see that most administrative mistakes are spawned somewhere in the nexus between misplaced scientific arrogance and the rhetorical administrators' general ignorance of scientific potential.

1.1 THE DECISION DOMAINS

As suggested in the preface, our interest in this volume is rational decision-making within the context of complex enterprise. As such, we will be trying to tell the reader how decisions *should* be made. The criterion we will employ is one that has been much maligned in recent decades: optimality. Optimality has been driven from the field by the concept of "sufficiency," where decision-makers are not really expected to obtain any optimal solutions, but merely adequate ones. But unless optimality is the guiding criterion, adequate solutions have a way of quickly turning into inadequate solutions, and rapidly deteriorating into dramatic dysfunctions. Therefore, we here want the decision-maker to search for optimality, although we will not always condemn him if he fails to achieve it. And even at this preliminary point, we might add this central qualification: optimality does not demand that the decision-maker always be right in the actions he takes; it means, rather, that he take pains to reduce, to the fullest possible extent, some appropriate expected error function. Thus, most of what we will do in these pages is concerned with the methodology of decision-making, for the results of decision are not always the appropriate bases for judging decision rationality.

We might begin by taking a look at what constitutes the generalized decision-making process, i.e., what tasks have to get done. In this respect, consider Figure 1.1.

At this preliminary point in our work, we must be very brief in our description of these decision functions. But a decision-making exercise begins, of course, with a decision requirement. This might be imposed on the decision functionary by some higher authority, or the requirement may arise from the environment in which the decision-maker operates (e.g., from some event demanding a considered response). In either case, the decision context is determined by the nature of the problem to be solved, and thus includes some factors at the same time that it excludes others, although the inclusions and exclusions are sometimes not so obvious as the decision-maker might like. Therefore, deciding on a decision context must itself often be an exercise in formal analysis, and not merely a given. The same is true for the formulation of the goal that the decision-maker is to achieve, this goal specifying what it is hoped the decision-making exercise will accomplish. Initially, this decision goal may be stated in quite abstract terms, and only later in the process lent real specificity.

The next major function in the decision-making context is the model-building task. Here we attempt to develop an allegory of the problem context, setting out the structural and dynamic properties of the subjects, processes, or other entities that we must seek to control or modify, or to which we are expected to react. Models of the subjects of decision processes will generally contain some

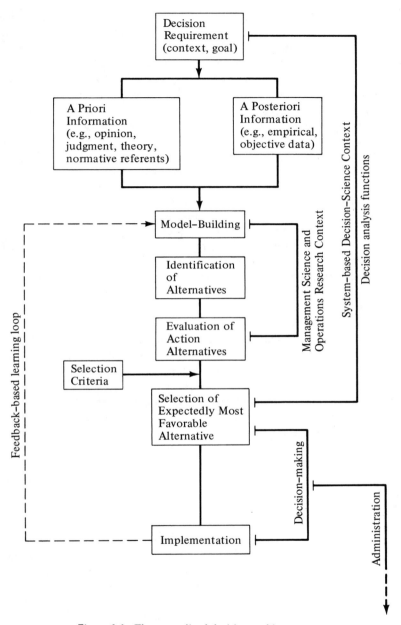

Figure 1.1. The generalized decision-making process.

mix of *a priori* and *a posteriori* information. *A priori* predicates are generally products of assumptions or suppositions, some of which may be scientific, others of which may be irrational. That is, there is a right way and a wrong way to generate *a priori* information. The same is true of the *a posteriori* information that enters into the model-building process. This, generally, is a produce of empirical observation. These observations may be very disciplined, as with those associated with a formal experiment, or they may be quite casual (e.g., impressions based on unordered experience). While *a posteriori* information is generally to be preferred—and, indeed, constitutes virtually the only source of direction for some management scientists—it may sometimes be very inappropriate, especially when the problem at hand is very complex. As we shall see, then, the value of either *a posteriori* or *a priori* information must be taken as a function of the decision context; we can make no generalized proclamations about their respective virtues without specific information on the nature of the problem the decision-makers must attack and contain.

At any rate, the model gives us a more or less complete and accurate portrait of the decision context. Therefore, it may be used to identify the various action-alternatives open to us, i.e., the several different courses of action we might take in attempting to solve the problem. Thus, not only does the model describe the properties of the problem to be solved—and allow us to project these properties toward some future point in time—but it serves as the base against which we will evaluate the expected effects of the different actions we might take. Given this array of action-alternatives, each equipped with some expected outcome, we can then select some particular action for implementation. This involves a consideration of the alternatives with respect to the selection criteria. These selection criteria are generally a precise restatement of the overall goal that was set earlier, and may provide very definite direction (e.g., minimize cost, maximize profit, find the most favorable trade-off between two competitive objectives). Finally, having selected an expectedly most favorable alternative, we move to implement it. In some cases, we will be alert to the emerging effects of the decision action, perhaps setting up some sort of feedback-based learning process. In this case, we will try to gradually improve our solution by taking a step-by-step approach (which usually means that we are adding more and more *a posteriori* information to our "model" of the problem).

Now, all these tasks are integral to the decision-making function. They must all be performed in any decision exercise, even if the decision-maker is not really aware of the steps he or she is taking. That is, models may be implicit in the mind of the decision-maker, and not have any substantive form on a sheet of paper or in a computer program. Selection criteria must exist, even if they are sometimes transparent to those using them. And, of course, all these various decision-making tasks may be performed across an enormous continuum of quality. That is, the rationality of a decision-making process is really a variable, and depends upon the discipline, precision, and ingenuity with which each successive step in the decision-making process is taken. Thus, our work in these pages will direct toward advice on each of the decisions that must be made "within" the decision-making process, e.g., how the various tasks should be performed, what instruments of analysis are appropriate in what contexts, etc.

However, certain aspects of the decision process are already fairly well treated by existing disciplines. For example, a legion of literature is available from traditional management science and operations research scholars on various model-building techniques and evaluation instruments. But, unfortunately, most of the techniques and instruments they offer require that the decision context and goal be specified beforehand, i.e., that the problem definition appear as if by magic. Moreover, much of the model-building advice offered by the traditional management scientists and operations researchers really is pertinent only to the modeling of relatively simple, well-behaved problems. Therefore, we are going to have to treat those areas that are ill-defined or largely neglected elsewhere, which means we will be spending a lot of time on the matter of rational problem definitions and the modeling of the more complex problems we are likely to encounter in the real world. As these are the highest-level tasks in the decision process, they deserve the most attention; however, because they are also the most complex tasks, they have been largely ignored by practitioners and scholars alike. Thus, the system-based decision focus we shall be adopting includes all the analytical aspects of the decision process, from initial problem definition to the commitment of action itself. But we must plan to leave the matter of implementation to the general administrative scientists, for the implementation of a decision demands discipline of a different order than that which we are prepared to offer here. Particularly, the implementation task is "getting things done through people," whereas the decision-analysis tasks constitute the *intellectual* aspects of management. The latter is what we are concerned with in this volume.

It is also important, even at this initiation of our inquiry, to distinguish between decision analysis and decision-making. In the terms of our model, the decision-making responsibility would belong in the selection task, i.e., the actual commitment of the organization to some particular course of action. The decision analyst, on the other hand, may be thought to do all the work leading up to that point, i.e., structuring the various alternatives open to the decision-maker. In some cases, the decision-analysis and decision-making functions may be performed by a single individual. In other cases (and perhaps more frequently), we must distinguish between line and staff. Presumably, the decision-maker is the line functionary, whereas the "scientific" staff performs all the analysis functions, leaving the decision-maker the selection task. As we will try to show later, there are both advantages and disadvantages associated with this type of partitioning of decision responsibilities. On the whole, our inquiry will suggest that the separation of decision-analysis and decision-making functions is usually not to be preferred. Rather, we would much prefer to cross-educate our administrators and technicians, so that there is no artificial separation between the analysis tasks and the selection function.

Such propositions await us later on. Here, we must make explicit a point we have treated only obliquely thus far: that the way in which each decision task should be performed will depend upon the nature of the problem the decision-maker is called upon to solve. Thus, we need some sort of decision taxonomy, one which attempts to set out the broadly different classes of decisions that must be made within the context of any complex organization.[1] For our purposes, this decision taxonomy must reflect the different types of intellectual demands that are associated with the structure of organizational administration (Table 1.1).

This construct is normative, that is, it expresses what we want to see in an organization, and is not intended to reflect the way in which organizations are actually structured. But these appear to be the organizational prerequisites for optimal decision-making, at least from the perspective of the working decision scientist. And the relationships between the decision functions and the administrative functionaries of the organization are probably not too far removed from the reality of most enterprise structures.

At any rate, this typology provides us with a "map" of where we will be going. Here, in this chapter, we will discuss problem categories and the rudiments of the different decision functions. In Chapter 2, we will pay particular attention to organizational significance (the entries in the second column of Table 1.1). Chapter 3 will be concerned with the several focuses of accountability and with the evaluation of decision-making performance on the basis of results. Chapters 4 and 5 will treat the analytical modalities, and try to make the instruments and techniques we develop operational within the confines of real-world organizations.

We may begin by examining the decision functions themselves. In doing so, we will be critical of current practices. The frequency with which decision errors are made—especially in the three higher-level decision domains—demands nothing less from us. Thus, our criticisms are not so much a matter of arrogance as a matter of responsibility that we simply cannot escape. But by way of general elaboration, the goal-setting function is the highest-level intellectual responsibility in the complex organization. It lends the organization its basic character, determining what fundamental mission will be served (e.g., what business it will be in, what service it will provide) and often defining the organization's ultimate destination (i.e., where its directors want it to go). The task of the goal-setters (or mission analysts) is thus to read the future, trying to identify those niches that the organization can hope to occupy with reasonable expectation of success.

Table 1.1. Attributes of the several decision domains.

Decision Function	Organizational Significance	Functionary	Problem Category	Analytical Modality	Focus of Accountability	Selected Responsibilities
Goal-setting	Integrity	Director/Officer	Indeterminate	Normative/Heuristic	Propriety	Mission analysis, extremely long-range planning
Strategic Programming	Effectiveness	Executive	Severely stochastic	Hypothetico-deductive	Utility	Functional structure, major allocations, competitive posture
Tactical Programming	Efficiency	Manager	Moderately stochastic	Inductive/Projective	Return	Logistics, short-term planning, forecasting
Operations Programming	Mechanisticity	Supervisor	Deterministic	Algorithmic/Trial and error	Productivity	Basic production and support functions

Thus, the goal-setter is the prophet of the organization, scanning the future for organizational opportunities, but at the same time being concerned that the organization seek its goals only within certain limits of behavior. In short, it is in the goal-setting process that we decide what the organization *should* be and in part provide it with a certain code of conduct or, perhaps, a "personality."

When we move to the level of strategic analysis, two lesser issues face us. First, if the goal-setters have exercised some sort of prophetic vision in telling us what we should be, it is the strategic analysts who must decide what we *can* be at any given moment. It is they, then, who read the immediate environment, relative to the organization's resources and capabilities, and thus set the nearer-term objectives that the organization must seek in order to reach the destination the goal-setters have visualized. The second aspect of strategic planning is actually a corollary of this first task. Particularly, the strategic analysts are at work trying to devise strategems to achieve the goals. Thus, they not only set objectives (which are generally more explicit and immediate in significance than goals), but they must also generate and/or evaluate means for achieving those objectives. Now, the central implication of strategic analysis is that one does not move unhindered toward these objectives, nor in a straight, safe line toward one's ultimate goals. Rather, there are always factors at work that tend to impede progress, and sometimes hostile elements that must be dealt with. In some cases, these may be actual competitors or enemies, who are trying to predict our moves so that they can blunt them, or who are trying to achieve the same objectives we are, before we do. In the more general situation, however, it is strictly a question that, for any given objective, there may be several alternative approaches we might take. The strategic analyst must then decide among these different approaches, thus committing the organization to a course of action with very significant implications.

Let us take an example from the public domain. Suppose that the directors of our organization (in their role as goal-setters) have looked to the future and visualized a need for a national health care delivery system to be in operation by 1980. They have further decided that such a service must be provided within two constraints: (a) it must be delivered in a way that yields an effectively minimal cost-effectiveness ratio (in short, we want the most bang for the buck), and (b) it must also be delivered in a way that will maximize the dignity of the clients. We now have a desired destination for the organization—a goal—but we also have some limitations on the trajectory by which we may move toward that destination. Both this goal and the constraints are examples of *normative* analysis. This means that the destination and character of the organization have been determined by a presumably free and conscious weighing of various options; they have not been established by imperative (e.g., the organization is not simply reacting to some environmental pressure). For, within a sometimes very wide latitude, the individual organization is something of a sovereign, and may thus become largely what its goal-setters think is desirable. In short, organizations are not always just passive victims of their environment or simple slaves of circumstance.

With a goal and procedural constraints defined, the strategic analysts may go to work. The question they must answer is how best to achieve the goal, within the constraints specified. We can see that the decision latitude of the strategic planners is less than that of the goal-setters, for the former operate within an envelope of constraints provided by the latter. But the strategic planning task is nonetheless a very intellectually demanding one. In the example of national health care, there are several alternative methods for actually delivering health services, and each must be carefully weighed. For example, one might evaluate the expected effectiveness of giving prepaid insurance to every citizen; or of enabling a strict fee-for-service system, where costs are covered by mainstream providers after the fact of service. We might consider developing neighborhood clinics run by public officials, with certain clinics assigned to treat certain types of conditions on demand. As still another alternative, we might employ the health maintenance organization (HMO) concept, which is concerned especially with preventive care. We can see that the strategic planning might involve deciding which of these modalities of delivery should be employed, with the selection criterion being their expected effectiveness with respect to the goal at hand, given the constraints. Perhaps the best strategy is to employ some mix of modalities; perhaps the strategic analysts will have to "invent" some entirely new approach. For our purposes, however, we simply want to suggest that modality-selection problems are relatively frequent strategic exercises in public administration.

Of course, the industrial and commercial worlds have their own examples of goal-setting and strategic planning, and, in many cases, the decision requirements are very similar to those associated with governmental or public service organizations. For example, let us suppose that a set of corporate goal-setters have set a goal that is expressed in terms of some desired share of market, e.g., we want our organization to have a 50 percent share of the widget market by 1980. Now, as is so often the case, this goal may be accompanied by a set of normative constraints, perhaps something like these: (a) the 50 percent share of the market is to be achieved in a way that minimizes the possibility of attracting any antitrust suits, (b) at no time should the rate of return on investment fall below 7.5 percent during any reporting interval, and (c) the strategies employed should not contravene the principles of capitalist enterprise (in short, collusion, voiding competition, and other such practices are proscribed). Now, given this goal and the explicated constraints, the strategic analysts must decide on a strategem that promises to achieve this goal within the procedural constraints. Among the different approaches they might weigh are: increasing advertising for the product without making any structural changes; attempting to make design changes that will make the product perform significantly better than any competitor's; making manufacturing or processual changes that will make the product significantly cheaper to produce, therefore permitting us to enjoy a price advantage and thereby increasing demand. Note, for example, that the normative constraints would prohibit a strategy such as attempting to corner the market through artificial price-cutting or driving out potential or actual competitors through takeovers or acquisitions, etc. At any rate, each of the three permissible strategies (as with those of the national health care example) are "qualitatively" unique alternatives, having little in common other than their orientation toward the same goal.

Now, we might continue with this simple business example in an effort to explain the role of tactical planning, the third of our organizational functions. Like strategic planning, tactical planning involves objectives, constraints, and alternatives, but they are of a different order than those that prevail at the strategic level. In the first place, the tactical planner will be given an objective that is really the specific strategy decided upon at the higher administrative level. For example, let us assume that the corporation in question elected the first strategic alternative, i.e., to increase advertising without making any product changes. The successful implementation of this strategy now becomes the tactical decision-maker's objective (whereas the broader goal—the achievement of a certain market share—was the strategic decision-maker's objective). There will probably also be some constraints passed down that will restrict the tactical decision-maker's means of achieving this objective. For example, he might be given some advertising budget limit, or he might be told that he should not engage in any false advertising or directly criticize any competitors' products. Thus, the tactical decision-maker operates in more certainty than does the strategic decision-maker, who in turn has less decision latitude than the goal-setter. The implication is that, somehow, as we pass down through the organization, the inherent complexity of the decisions that must be made decreases. Later, we will phrase this in more specific terms (and replace the concept of complexity with a more precise variable), but even here we can get some idea of why this is so.

Particularly, we can take a look at the kinds of alternatives among which tactical decision-makers must decide. They may have some latitude in the media to be selected (e.g., radio, television, magazines), and the decision regarding how much to spend on each medium is theirs, given any aggregate budget limitations. We can see, then, that whereas the strategic decision-maker was forced to select from among broadly different alternatives—each with major implications for the organization—the alternatives available to the tactical decision-maker usually have much narrower implicational differences. In fact, for the present case, all the various alternatives may merely be different values for a single variable: promotional elasticity. This is a measure of the real or expected relationship between product sales and advertising expenditures.[2] Now, the usual mandate that passes down to the tactical decision-maker is that the solution arrived at be the optimal one. In this case, the demand is that he or she evolve the promotional program that has the most favorable cost-effectiveness ratio. As such, most of the decision-maker's analytical energies and efforts will be devoted to basic statistical research in an effort to measure the promotional elasticity curves, and then finally to selecting the particular media mix and expenditure schedule that meets the cost-effectiveness criteria.* Thus, unlike the strategic analyst, the tactical decision-maker is at work weighing different alternatives that are all members of the *same* qualitative set (they are all various values for the relationship between advertising expenditures and expected revenue).

We can summarize the administrative process thus far. The directors have given us a goal (share of market) and some normative constraints. These became inputs to the executive-level, strategic decision-making process. Here we lighted on a most favored approach to achieve the goal (increasing advertising), coupled with budgetary and certain procedural constraints. These in turn were passed on to the managerial or tactical level, presumably to the manager of the advertising department. The manager, operating within these constraints and presumably in the face of some near-term, specific objective passed down from the executives (e.g., to increase sales in the coming year by x percent), then set to work analyzing the various advertising alternatives, and selecting that which exhibited the highest expected efficiency or which was thus deemed to be optimally cost-effective.

We are not yet through with the set of administrative functions performed, however, for the problem of actually implementing the tactics still remains. This would fall to what is usually called the supervisor-level. Now, by the time the problem gets to the supervisor, virtually all the uncertainty and risk have been stripped away at the higher levels.[3] In the present example, the supervisor's function is to effect the placement of the advertising. This is an essentially deterministic exercise, for the problem is one for which a single, correct answer is either immediately apparent, or accessible through an essentially mechanical analytical process (e.g., simple trial-and-error).

Now, even at this very preliminary point in our study, two things should be apparent. First, it is *more serious* to make a mistake at the goal-setting level than at the strategic level, and it is more serious to make a mistake at the strategic level than at the tactical, etc. As a corollary, it is usually *easier* to make a mistake at the goal-setting level than at the strategic, and easier to make a mistake

*See Section 3.2.

at the strategic than at the tactical level. It is essentially quite difficult to make a mistake at the instrumental (supervisory) level, for here we are simply following instructions that allow little if any decision latitude. In short, supervisors may largely be considered "instruments" of administration, and may not often face problems that demand formal decision discipline.

The second point that should be apparent is that decision scientists should probably concentrate their efforts at the goal-setting and strategic levels, for it is there that we would find the highest *expected value of decision errors* (a measure taken as the absolute cost of making an error of a given magnitude, times the probability of an error of that magnitude being made). Later we will deal with this variable in great detail, and propose it as the central variable for controlling the quality of decision-making exercises. For now, it is enough to suggest that a situation that is the effective inverse of the desired one holds true more often than not. That is, the contribution of the general administrative speculations is often restricted almost entirely to the domain of supervisory decisions, the lowest-order functions of the organization. And, by the same token, most efforts of decision science are directed at introducing scientific procedures only into the domain of tactical analysis. The reason for this becomes most apparent when we begin to look at the nature of the problems that dominate the various decision domains.

1.2 THE PROBLEM CONTEXTS

Each of the several problem categories listed in our major administrative typology (Figure 1.1) is the basis for defining a particular decision domain. These we noted, but did not define, as four different types of generic problems the complex organization is forced to face: (a) indeterminate, (b) severely stochastic, (c) moderately stochastic, and (d) deterministic. These four entries in the first column of our typology represent the referents against which all decision-making responsibilities must be weighed.

We will make an effort here to define these categories in very precise terms. But before we do so, we should make explicit one of the simpler, more obvious points of our original typology, i.e., we expect that the various problem categories will be distributed across any organization in a very special way, as Figure 1.2 indicates. Now, this simple diagram yields a "map" with very definite implications. It suggests that indeterminate decisions will tend to be concentrated at the highest levels of any complex organization, and appear much less frequently as we move away from this level. Next, it implies that, as we move somewhat lower in the organization, the incidence of indeterminate decisions declines and the frequency with which severely stochastic decisions appear increases. These in their turn begin to tail off as we go still lower in the organization, to the point

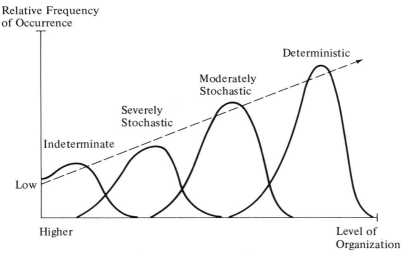

Figure 1.2. Normative distribution of decision classes.

where the class of moderately stochastic decisions dominates. Finally, deterministic problems preoccupy the lowest levels of organization.

There are two corollaries to this model that should be introduced here, even though we have not yet begun to define the categories themselves. In particular, we will suggest that there is an increasing frequency function (a step-function, in fact), so that the aggregate number of indeterminate decisions is expectedly smaller than the number of severely stochastic decisions, which in its turn is expectedly smaller than the number of moderately stochastic decisions, and so on. In short, we postulate a normative frequency distribution like that in Figure 1.3. We can see that this figure represents the situation for what we might call the ideal-type organization, that which appears most frequently in the academic literature and, probably, in the real-world as well.[4] The majority of decisions to be made are of the simpler, deterministic type, concerned with day-to-day functioning of the organization. The more complex decision categories appear with radically decreasing frequency. The obvious secondary implication is, then, that the ideal-type organization will have more supervisors than managers, more managers than executives, and finally more executives than directors. Thus, we would expect that the distribution of decision-makers would more or less parallel the distribution of decision classes.

But the second corollary we want to offer concerns itself with possible departures from the ideal-type organization. Particularly, some organizations may have a different distribution of decision classes and, therefore, a different distribution of decision-makers. For example, an organization that has to face a consistently

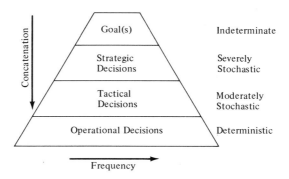

Figure 1.3. Expected frequency of decision classes.

complex, rapidly changing environment may have fewer individuals concerned with moderately stochastic decisions *per se* and more people concerned with severely stochastic issues; in many simple systems, there may be just one chief, with all others subordinate. The variations are almost endless.[5] But, for the moment, we may neglect these exceptions to the organizational rule and return to our examination of the ideal-type organization, which we now know is really the theoretical bureaucracy (with a pyramidal structure and a hierarchical system of decision authority).

There is one final note we should make before we actually begin defining the several problem categories. The typology presumes some relationship between the several administrative functions and the problem categories. That is, we suggest that indeterminate problems dominate at the goal-setting level, that strategic planning activities most often involve severely stochastic problems, that tactical planning is usually concerned with moderately stochastic problems, and finally that supervisors are most often called upon to solve only deterministic problems. To a certain extent, our definitions of the various administrative functions in the previous section give us the clues we need to defend these assertions, but we will give a further explanation of why certain administrative functions tend to be dominated by certain problem types in the following pages.

At any rate, we may now begin to look at the complex organization from the perspective of a decision scientist—as a collection of problems to be solved. And we must look at our several problem categories as highly generalized situations, with a majority of real-world problems expected to approximate one or another. Their formal definitions appear in Figure 1.4.

Initially, these four problem types are defined so that the deterministic case is the simplest, and the indeterminate is the most complex. Moreover, we have a possibility now to be relatively precise about just what we mean by *simplicity* and *complexity*. The way in which we will use these terms throughout this book is available from an inspection of the definitions themselves.

Deterministic. Where, for any given set of starting-state conditions, there is one and only one event which may be assigned a significant probability of occurrence (i.e., as with the finite-state automata).

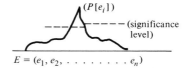

Moderately stochastic. Where, for any given set of starting-state conditions, a limited number of qualitatively similar events must be assigned significant probabilities of occurrence (as with the problem of trying to estimate next-period sales levels for a well-precedented product).

Severely stochastic. Where, for any given set of starting-state conditions, some number of qualitatively different events must be assigned significantly high probabilities of occurrence (as in the area of conflict behavior or game-based analyses).

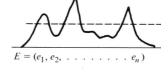

Indeterminate. Where, for any given set of starting-state conditions, there is *no* event which can be assigned a significant probability of occurrence; thus the high probability that some outcome we have not been able to pre-specify will occur (as in extremely long-range forecasting problems).

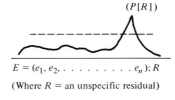

Figure 1.4. Ideal-type problem categories.

First of all, we must think of a *problem* as being an entity or phenomenon that the decision-maker must comprehend, control, manipulate, or otherwise act upon. Now, the starting-state conditions for any decision exercise will likely contain the following information:

(a) The objective the decision-maker is to achieve regarding the problem at hand, along with any constraints that might be passed along.

(b) The information the decision-maker already has about the problem (the set of *a priori* information).

Either of these two sets may be either very well-ordered and precise, or they may be quite vague, ambiguous, or incomplete. Nevertheless, we must think of a problem as having a life of its own, as being an entity (either real and tangible, or merely conceptual) that has a structure, a set of dynamics, a boundary, or other properties we will later introduce. Now, where the starting-state conditions are such that the answer to the problem—the required or desired action—is apparent from these alone, then the problem is deterministic. For example, suppose the problem is what to do when faced with a light switch, a simple binary system.

Now, suppose that the set of starting-state conditions contains the following: (a) the objective is to turn on the light; (b) the information we already possess is that, if the light is off, then it is activated by moving the switch to the "on" position; and (c) we observe that the light is off. Therefore, there is only one action—flipping the switch to the "on" position—that has any significant probability of achieving the objective.

Thus, although it is a trivial example, the problem of the light switch represents an *effectively* deterministic problem. This means that our *a priori* information is sufficient for us to solve it. In some cases, however, a problem may be only *inherently* deterministic. Here, although the problem is capable of being solved completely, we may not have enough information to solve it. In short, we will need to undertake some research and analysis before the problem can be converted to an effectively deterministic one. For example, suppose that instead of being a simple binary machine, the light switch has three unmarked positions. Now, suppose that the room is dark. We know that, to turn on the light, we will have to move the switch to one of the remaining positions. The question is, however, which one? At this point, we have two alternatives, so the problem is not effectively deterministic. However, it is inherently deterministic, for simple, direct, trial-and-error exercise will allow us to determine—with no real probability of error—just which position we want.

Many problems in the real world are of this type. If a decision-maker is asked to optimize some production process, and if the process is one where a single, most favorable state may be found, then this is an example of a deterministic problem. Many machines and other automata (e.g., finite-state machines) are of this type, where there is a single best setting, configuration, or structure that may eventually be located (or that may be obtained simply by having access to the design criteria). Many routing and transportation problems are also of this type, where there exists some single best schedule for shipment or some single routing that will minimize, for example, the cost of servicing or of wasted time on a salesperson's rounds. Many assembly and manufacturing operations are also either effectively or inherently deterministic. Indeed, Frederick Taylor and others of the time-and-motion school sought to find the single best way to perform certain simple tasks, such as loading bricks or assembling some mechanism.[6] Much of the work of industrial engineers is aimed at designing the single best production layout or finding the single most efficient way of performing a set of industrial operations. In another case, one may face the problem of finding the best mix of ingredients for such items as mortar, aviation fuel, fertilizer, and so on. Again, through trial and error, or perhaps through access to preexisting chemical formulas or compositional laws, an unequivocal answer is expected to emerge.* In short, such problems are either inherently or effectively determinis-

---

*Inherently deterministic systems, from another perspective, are those that are observable in entirety, with measurable properties, and that are amenable to controlled manipulation.

tic, or both. In this respect, note that an effectively deterministic problem is always an inherently deterministic one; however, the converse does not always hold.

Now, the indeterminate problem is the opposite of the deterministic in every way. Specifically, the indeterminate entity or process is one that is an utter mystery to us, given the starting-state conditions at our disposal. In the extreme case, we cannot even define what the entity or process might do, either on its own accord or in response to some action we might initiate. In short, the behavior of the entity is entirely unpredictable, given the *a priori* information at hand, and the entity is effectively beyond our control. Therefore, there is no specific, predefinable outcome to which we can assign any significant probability of occurrence; in other words, we don't know what's going to happen. Moreover, we are relatively certain that whatever happens, it probably will not be anything that we were able to foresee. For example, the far-future of weather is sometimes said to be indeterminate, as is the far-future state of high fashion or international relations. Such entities are often said to be inherently indeterminate because their dynamics are such that they are completely unpredictable, irrespective of the amount of information we might have. Other processes or phenomena are effectively indeterminate, but are expected to be ultimately reducible to some more analytically tractable state (e.g., stochasticity or determinacy). The process of cancer growth, and genetic code, and the geology of the Planet Venus, for example, are usually put in this category. The implication is that they are only temporarily beyond comprehension or control, and that additional information will eventually make them more predictable or even totally comprehensible. In summary, effectively indeterminate problems are either those where existing information is grossly inadequate, whereas inherently indeterminate entities have innate structural and behavioral properties that naturally defy prediction or control. Finally, the further away in time its implications, and the greater the number of variables that determine its state, the more likely a problem is to be indeterminate. Therefore, indeterminate problems are most likely to be encountered at the point where the organization meets the world outside—where it is tangent to its environment.[7] And this, for the ideal-type organization, means that indeterminate problems will dominate at the highest levels of authority. For it is here, as we have seen, that we find the responsibilities for long-range planning, for basic mission analysis, and for determining the role the organization will play in the world at large.

If the deterministic and indeterminate cases are effective antonyms, the moderately and severely stochastic cases are very close relatives, but only in the abstract. As suggested in Figure 1.3, the stochastic case occurs when there is more than one alternative to which we must assign significant probabilities of occurrence. As defined, the difference between the moderately and severely stochastic cases is not one of processual significance (both involve multiple-event alternatives), but rather in the nature of the events. A moderately stochastic situation involves events or alternative outcomes that are all members of the same qualitative set, whereas severely stochastic problems involve event alternatives that are members of qualitatively distinct sets. For our purposes, the distinction is important indeed, and we have already used it in the previous section to distinguish between strategic and tactical exercises.

A few more working examples should help clarify both the distinction and the decision implications. Suppose that our objective is to act in a way that will decrease inflation. In addition, suppose that, as part of the starting-state conditions, we have at our disposal the principles of basic macroeconomic theory. Let us even further suppose that the operative principle in our *a priori* repertoire is that one may reduce inflation by reducing the disposable personal income of the population. Finally, let us suggest that the government has elected to reduce disposable personel income by increasing taxes. The "strategy" is this: as the tax burden on the population increases, the disposable personel income falls, and there is less money to spend. Therefore, demand pressure is reduced, and the reduction in the rate of inflation naturally and inevitably follows. Therefore, with economic theory to guide us, the strategic problem is solved *a priori*. In particular, the relationship between a surtax and inflation appears to be deterministic, as an increase in the one implies (with no significant probability of error) a decrease in the other. However, at the tactical level, the problem takes on moderately stochastic overtones, for it is a question of how much of a surtax to impose. This involves the determination of the *magnitude* of the relationship between increased taxes and reduced inflation (with the strategic analysis having already closed the issue of the direction of the relationship by posing the inverse function). Thus, we attempt to solve the tactical problem by developing a function that describes this relationship for all values of the surtax within our domain of consideration. We may try to solve the problem deterministically, searching for a simple unique value for reduction in inflation for every surtax value we propose. In so doing, we should be assuming that, for every incremental tax increase, there is one and only one resulting reduction in inflation that has any significant probability of occurrence.

However, in actual practice, the econometricians who make such calculations tend to treat these measurement and function-building problems as inherently moderately stochastic, and do not expect complete accuracy. Particularly, they use what are called *shock models*, which allow for an error of estimate or for some variance in the relation that is calculated. Now, the difference between this formulation and a deterministic formulation is simply this: whereas the deterministic formulation involved a single value of reduced inflation for every value of the incremental increase in taxes, the moderately stochastic formulation provides us with a *range* of reductions in the rate of inflation for any incremental increase in taxes. In short, we impose a probability distribution in the moderately stochastic case, and it would be the preferred method for trying to generate an answer to the tactical problem of how great a surtax to impose.[8]

To illustrate the differences further, let X be the incremental increase in the tax rate, and Y be the expected reduction in the rate of inflation, given X. The differential implications of the deterministic and moderately stochastic formulations are illustrated in Figure 1.5. Again, in the deterministic case, X implies Y directly, with the implication being that the analysts believe that the relationship between incremental tax increases and inflation rates can be assessed with perfect accuracy. In the moderately stochastic case, however, the analysts consider the relationship imperfect to some extent (indicated by the configuration of the probability distribution and the degree of variance; we will discuss these terms later). They therefore propose that any one of a range of alternative events (different deflation rates) might be the true result of imposing a surtax at any given level. Now, from the diagram of the moderately stochastic case, we can see that certain alternative values of Y are assigned significant probabilities of occurrence, namely, those that fall within the range of $+\sigma$ or $-\sigma$ (i.e., those values that fall within the range determined by taking the mean and adding or subtracting 1 standard deviation, a common statistical technique).[9] In terms of our original definition of moderate stochasticity, then, we have:

(a) There are several different event alternatives that are assigned significant probabilities of occurrence.
(b) All the alternatives belong to the same qualitative set; that is, all are numerical estimates of the rate of deflation (Y) associated with some proposed surtax rate (X).

Now, in this example, the starting-state conditions for the analysts in large measure determine whether or not the problem will be treated as deterministic or

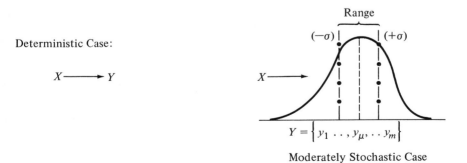

Deterministic Case:

$X \longrightarrow Y$

Moderately Stochastic Case

Figure 1.5. Decision implications.

moderately stochastic. Both the deterministic and stochastic analysts would have started with the same objective: to construct the relationship between tax and inflation rates, presumably so that some decision-maker could decide what particular incremental tax rate to employ, based on the desired rate of deflation. However, the other aspect of starting-state conditions—the *a priori* information sets—must have been different for the two classes of analyst. Particularly, those that treat the problem as moderately stochastic were equipped with the perspectives of modern econometrics, which suggests that we must treat, consider, and explicate the error inherent in estimating economic relations. The deterministic analyst, on the other hand, comes equipped with a much simpler, essentially mechanical view of economic processes, and indeed may not even have any sophisticated statistical skills.

But is the moderately stochastic formulation superior to the deterministic? The reader will agree that, where economic processes are involved, it clearly is. Most economic processes (and therefore problems of treating, controlling, or manipulating them) are not very well-behaved; it is virtually impossible, no matter the scope of our research and analysis, to accurately assess all the variables that have a potential impact and to accurately estimate their magnitudinal characteristics. Thus, the moderately stochastic formulation forewarns the decision-maker that the problem with which he is dealing holds some potential for surprise, and that any action he takes may not work out completely as predicted. Therefore, we expect moderately stochastic problem formulations to engender more caution in the decision-maker. Just as obviously, however, the moderately stochastic formulation is gratuitous (and also an uneconomic use of scarce analytical resources) when the problem at hand is effectively deterministic. We will discuss these matters in greater detail later on.

As it happens, exclusive reliance on the moderately stochastic formulation for the inflation problem was improper. We know this because our example reflects a decision made by President Richard M. Nixon in the late 1960s to impose a surtax in order to dampen the inflation rate. (I believe that a 7.5 percent surtax was eventually decided upon.) And, the real-world result was the opposite of that which had been expected: the surtax was accompanied by an increase in inflation. In short, the fundamental strategic assumption was wrong. It should by no means have been accepted as an invariant and axiomatic matter that increasing tax rates forces a decrease in inflation. Therefore, the problem should not have been treated as moderately stochastic, but as severely stochastic.

The severely stochastic nature of the problem did not occur to the economists or politicians involved, for their *a priori* information sets were critically limited. In the first place, many economists believe that economic problems can be solved by manipulating economic variables alone. Therefore, it is natural that, being concerned with measuring relationships rather than weighing strategies, they would turn to the moderately stochastic formulation. Second, because the *a priori* information base of the economic analyst tends to be dominated by economic principles—by matters of theory, as it were—there was a tendency to neglect any contextual or empirical evidence that might have been available. In short, at the strategic level, inflation (and therefore the problem of reducing it) was considered deterministic—economic theory provided us with an *a priori* answer, one that was not to be disputed or contextually validated. Therefore, the problem eventually reduced itself to the moderately stochastic one we described, a matter of simple statistical estimation of the relationship between X's and Y's. Now, this would have been a proper, rational, and scientific approach *only* if the *a priori* assumptions were indeed correct; that is, that increasing the tax burden must result—and can only result—in a decrease in the inflation rate.

However, were a social scientist of broader thinking given the problem of evaluating the surtax as a strategy for reducing inflation, he or she may have considered the problem severely stochastic, and therefore given more credence to its real complexity than did the economists. In particular, the social scientist would have posed another qualitative alternative to the economists' theoretical assumption: the alternative that the imposition of a surtax might actually result in an erosion of people's expectations for the economy, and lead them to dissave. Dissaving—withdrawing one's savings in the expectation that they will deteriorate in purchasing power—was indeed one of the *real* reactions to the imposition of the surtax. Also, there is the logical probability that the surtax, through its depreciation of expectations, might lead people into increased borrowing and credit, so that they can purchase goods before prices increase. This was also one of the real outcomes of the surtax. In short, rather than the strategically deterministic postulation of President Nixon and his economic advisers, the inflation problem should have been posed as severely stochastic, with three distinctly different qualitative alternatives considered: (1) that consonant with the economic principles, tax increases do positively effect reduction of inflation; (2) that a surtax would cause dissaving and thereby increase inflation; and (3) that a surtax might alert people to economic difficulties and cause them to press their credit, thereby increasing demand pressure and exacerbating inflation.

Therefore, it was only because of the sorely limited *a priori* information set of the analysts that these other strategic alternatives were ignored, and the problem was automatically relegated to the level of a moderately stochastic one. Perhaps the most serious remission of information was the fact that historical data illustrating the real complexity of the problem were available to the economists and policymakers, for the British had previously gone through exactly this same process, with exactly the same unexpected, undesirable consequences.

The tendency to treat effectively severely stochastic problems and processes as moderately stochastic is perhaps the most frequent and serious source of major administrative errors. We can see just what occurs in the forced transition from severe to moderate stochasticity. Our surtax case made this clear. Particularly, the strategic alternatives are disposed of by the assumption—*a priori*—of a particular *direction of influence* between problem factors. In short, for our surtax example, it was wrongly assumed that the relationship between tax rates and inflation rates was invariantly inverse in direction, e.g., increasing the former automatically decreases the latter. We saw that this imposition of a direction of influence was conditioned by the analysts' incomplete *a priori* information set (neglecting the fact that noneconomic variables can enter into economic processes, and also ignoring the historical precedent that the British set). Thus, the decision problem was again reduced to one where only the magnitude of the relationship between X and Y remained to be measured, a task for which the econometricians were well equipped. The experience is rather similar—and effectively just as ironic—as the famous instance of the pre-Copernican astronomers trying to make astronomical measurements under the mistaken strategic assumption that the sun revolved around the earth, and not the other way round.* In either case, the measurement problem may have been entertaining, but absolutely gratuitous. At any rate, our surtax-inflation example should have helped clarify the difference between moderately and severely stochastic processes and problem formulation. But perhaps another example, briefer and from a somewhat different direction, might help even more. So let us now spend a few words on an issue mentioned earlier—the provision of medical services to a broad-based population.

Here, just as with the surtax-inflation example, the basic issue seems to have been disposed of *a priori*, and therefore the issue is reduced automatically to one of moderate stochasticity. And, just as with the surtax-inflation example, this transformation has been performed improperly and thus promises another set of administrative errors and dysfunctions. Particularly, policymakers have largely considered only one strategic alternative for delivering government-sponsored health-care services, i.e., health-care insurance. What this seems to amount to is that every American should be given some sort of prepaid coverage. Thus, matters of contention are largely just tactical: should the government pay for all costs? should the employers pay? should all Americans be required to take the insurance, or should it be optional? The moderate stochasticity of the problem, as currently defined, is now exhibited by the projects under way trying to relate costs to breadth of insurance coverage; in short, the projects are building simple input-output functions. Thus, we are already at the measurement stage, assessing the magnitude of the relationship between costs and benefits, without ever having gone through a proper strategic analysis, where the severely stochastic properties of the problem would have been appreciated.

*Nevertheless, some of their calculations for navigational purposes were useful indeed, and remarkably accurate. Their cosmological assumptions were, however, largely futile.

Just what should have been entailed in a proper strategic analysis is a point we treated in Section 1.1. In particular, we would have assessed the possibility that different modalities are available for the provision of health-care services, and that the insurance modality would not necessarily be the optimally effective one in all instances. For example, would providing insurance be a positive strategy for the very old, the senile, the retarded, or the chronically ill? Obviously not. In the first place, insurance carriers are very selective about their clients. Second, issuance of a Blue Cross card, for example—to be effective—presumes that the individual clients are capable of making their own decisions about health-care needs and are adequately prepared to assess the competence of medical practitioners. It presumes that they won't take the card and sell it for a bottle of whiskey. It assumes that they won't be such a social liability that they will be refused medical service, as often happens with alcoholics or transients. This type of insurance is a modality that gives us only after-the-fact control of the client's medical services, and not the planning control that is required for many elderly or disadvantaged clients.

There may be strictly economic or fiscal deficiencies as well. For example, access to free medical services may inflate medical costs, because so many trivial conditions are brought for treatment. It may—as insurance companies have experienced—lead many medical practitioners into falsifying treatment records. Indeed, there are so many deficiencies with the insurance modality that any objective strategic analysis would find it to be optimal for only a very restricted set of the population, i.e., those who are intelligent, mobile, discriminating, and not chronically ill, aged, or otherwise incapacitated. Should not other coverages be explored? Of course. Among them should be the health maintenance organization (HMO), which stresses preventive medicine, the neighborhood clinic where indigents and acute cases can be treated, and standard fee-for-service arrangements with private practitioners. Moreover, one would think that the managerial aspects of the insurance modality would have to be questioned, because we cannot adequately manage the much simpler and more bounded medicaid and medicare programs that have been legislated.[10]

This, then, is another example of a problem that has been improperly transformed from severely stochastic to moderately stochastic. As such, the analysis being done is restricted to the measurement of the relationship between various levels of insurance coverage (e.g., what should be covered) and the various cost levels. Presumably, then, the real decision will not be whether to implement the insurance modality, but at what level to implement it. The guiding factor in this decision will be the level of congressional appropriation available, which will in turn determine the extent of coverage. These, of course, are tactical matters, as are the percentage that employers should pay or whether there should be a minimum cost to participants based on economic class, and so on. In other words, we have chosen to work with quantities rather than qualities, and with *magnitudes* rather than basic *directions* of influence.

As is evident, legitimate moderately stochastic problems abound in both public and commercial enterprise. But legitimate severely stochastic problems are not nearly so scarce as many would have us believe. Virtually all policy-level problems, as we will see, should be treated as severely stochastic, and bent to the discipline of qualitative and strategic analysis. However, as has been suggested, they seldom are, and this is a prime source of administrative error. On the other hand, we are marvelously adept and enthusiastic in treating moderately stochastic problems. These emerge almost constantly, in the guise of problems in forecasting, logistics, operations planning, staffing, materials provision, demand-and-supply analysis, and the other set of decisions that, when taken, lend the organization its substance as a provider of goods or services.

By now, the reader should have some idea of the differential characteristics of the types of problems that decision-makers must face. We will have more to say about the emergence and characteristics of all four categories of problems as we proceed with our inquiry. In the next section, we will examine why many administrative problems are faced so poorly.

1.3 THE STRAW MEN: MECHANIST AND RHETORICIAN

The basic reason for the lack of rationality in the administration of complex enterprise is the lack of properly qualified administrators. On one hand, we have the mechanist, who is a sort of applied mathematician and statistician, equipped with both the assets and liabilities of those fields. On the other hand, we have the rhetorical managers, products of an educational program that may have given them little if any exposure to scientific procedure or to the instruments of quantitative analysis. In practice, the mechanists are restricted to operations at the lower levels of organization because the kind of mathematical and statistical tools with which they are equipped—and perhaps even their expectations and behavioral referents—do not operate well once we leave the deterministic or moderately stochastic domain. The rhetorical managers, though they dominate both commercial and public enterprise, are really not particularly well equipped to solve with discipline any of the problems that arise within enterprise. Unfortunately, there are few active decision-makers who fall outside these two extreme cases; in short, there are very few administrators who are skilled in quantitative methods yet also sensitive to issues of qualitative significance, e.g., values, norms, strategic analysis. Their lack is sorely felt.

Historically, students of "scientific" management were first of all taught to be *realistic*. But what realism often means, as taught, is that the mechanist should be concerned only with hard facts, not with suppositions, intuitions, or other vagaries. These hard facts are often defined to be only those data that are tangible, observable, measurable, and, ideally, manipulable. In effect, the scientific decision-maker—*qua* mechanist—was *a priori* condemned to the domain of reality as defined by modern empiricism.

Second, the students of scientific management and decision theory were taught to be *objective* in their analyses, that is, they were to ignore any parochial, personal, or emotional factors in their decision exercises, either in themselves or their context of operations. But objectivity, in this instance, is rather narrowly defined, because many students took it to mean that the exercise of imagination, or the reliance on any universalistic principles or generalizations, was to be avoided. Thus, objectivity, following the empiricist clue, was eventually transformed into intellectual myopia, where the decision-maker is asked to approach problems without benefit of any predisposition or apriorities. In certain contexts, this is good advice; in many others, it bodes ill indeed.

Third, students were urged to confine their interests to the immediate problem at hand and to avoid the entrance of extraneous factors into their calculi. In short, they were taught to work only with *well-bounded* problems, the kind that empirical science excelled at solving. In the process, however, mechanists tended to condemn all really significant issues to the realm of rhetoric, because significantly complex problems were, by definition, unconstrained and ill-bounded. Therefore, they became very preselective about the kind of problems with which they would deal, or about the issues they would recognize as legitimate.

Fourth, in keeping again with the predilections of empirical science, they were taught about the benefits of *reductionism*, about the way in which problems or issues could be broken down into smaller, manageable segments. But what was not taught—largely because very few scientists themselves know how to do it—is how to put the pieces back together again without losing substance. This almost guaranteed that the "scientific" managers or mechanists would often invite the very consequence they were ostensibly dedicated to eradicating—suboptimality. In short, they became adept at solving pieces of problems, often without a comprehension of the problem as a whole.

Finally, and perhaps most seriously, students were taught the importance of immediate results. As a consequence, they adopted, often unconsciously,[11] the *instrumentalistic* bias of their empiricist instructors. In practice, this means that the mechanists sought immediate results, and became far more concerned with means than with ends. As a corollary, they tended to court quick, localized effects, often at the expense of long-term or ultimate ramifications. In short, their decision horizon was often very limited, and when they solved one problem, they often created others.

Rhetorical man contrasts with mechanistic man in virtually every respect. For example, where the mechanist is realistic—exclusively concerned with facts and variables that can be observed, measured, and manipulated in what amounts to a laboratory environment—rhetorical man obeys other dictates, many of them abstract, idiosyncratic, and otherwise "irrational" from the standpoint of the modern scientific practitioner. Finally, if mechanistic man takes pride in his instrumentalism, rhetorical man may often be more concerned with means than with ends, and may be reluctant to reach a goal unless the means are consistent with some moral or ideological constraints.

It would appear, at first blush, that mechanistic and rhetorical administrators would make excellent complements. The former would bring the organization discipline, precision, and a preference for actions predicated on facts; the latter would offer breadth of vision, sensitivity to broad contextual issues, and occasionally that spark of real genius that emerges as a hunch that happens to be right. Cautious, mechanistic man—true to his ostensibly scientific origin—might act as a brake on the compulsiveness of rhetorical man. Rhetorical man, in turn, would be there to call a halt to study and research and to initiate action. But the real-world circumstance is that mechanistic and rhetorical man have often become adversaries. Members of these two camps thus tend to compete for prestige, privilege, and authority, and the promises of complementation are lost. And, in this competition, rhetorical man is the consistent victor. In fact, the operations research people and the scientific staff are among the first individuals an enterprise lets go during a downturn. They usually go out the door just a couple of steps behind the human relations experts and the flashy economic consultants. Rhetorical man remains. For this, there are several reasons.

First, although training in quantitative management and decision-making has increased dramatically in the last decades, most senior administrators in both industry and government are products of rhetorical programs. The rhetorical program introduces the student to certain principles of management, which are seldom grounded in formal logical or scientific procedure. Rather, they tend to be *distillations of experience* and are entirely consonant with the traditional management theory view of administration as an art. Second, even where scientific management programs exist, they may be confined merely to recitations of the use of certain quantitative instruments, and have little appeal for those students (a majority, we are sure) who have a fear of mathematics and a distaste for statistical analysis. Unfortunately, those students who do enter the scientific side of management studies may sometimes be the least socially sophisticated, or the least ambitious and alert. As a result, they tend naturally to gravitate toward staff functions, while their counterparts in the rhetorical programs may move into direct line functions.

There are at least two other critical reasons why the "scientific" man is still largely subordinate to the rhetorician. First, the former, with very good reason, resents being considered irrational, for in some contexts, it is rhetorical man who is rational and mechanistic man who is irrational.

There is really no paradox here, but there is a distinct and proper ambiguity. The ambiguity stems from the fact that the criteria for the scientific method are variables and not constants. That is, the concept that science holds of its own behavior and mission changes through time.

The currently popular empiricist definition of rationality is thus rather self-serving or, at best, somewhat parochial. Therefore, it is understandable that rhetorical managers or decision-makers would bridle when told by an empiricist-realist challenger that they are irrational or unrealistic. They might counter with several telling points. First, they might suggest that the mechanist is also a rhetorician, because the very foundations of his beliefs in the rectitude of empirical science are as much products of faith as are another person's belief in God or in the visions of Marx. Second, they might suggest that it is the scientific decision-maker who is unrealistic, because he always takes recourse in such abstractions as numbers, graphs, and formulas, which are not as real as the people or contexts with which the rhetorical manager deals. Or they might suggest that scientific managers and decision-makers have their place, true enough, but that it is at the lower echelons of the organization. And having said this, rationalistic man has advanced his most important argument against management and decision science as it is now constituted. For if the scientific administrator has acceded to the assets of empirical science and the prevailing definition of rationality, he has also, usually unknowingly, courted its liabilities as well. And these liabilities are perhaps the most telling reason why our institutions are still dominated by people whom the scientific manager or decision-maker considers to be anachronisms.

Indeed, it is the very qualities of "scientific" man, those of which he is most proud, which also limit his utility in the real world. In short, his skills and perspectives set constraints at the same time they open opportunities. Recall, for example, that scientific man was supposed to be realistic. What this meant, following the empirical leadership, is that he is concerned only with the tangible, the immediate, the manipulable—with hard facts. In this respect, he mirrors the preferences of the laboratory scientist from whom he gains his basic identity. But in business, government, and organization in general—in the world outside the laboratory—there are many problems that cannot be defined or approached using hard facts alone. The problem may be unprecedented. When this happens, there is no historical informational or experiential base on which to draw. Now, the empiricist-realist will then tell us that the proper approach is to collect hard data. But other conditions may interfere here. There simply may not be time. Or, as frequently happens, there is such great complexity associated with the problem that even what data to collect becomes a matter of bitter dispute. Here, rhetorical and mechanistic man come into head-to-head conflict. The latter, following empiricist ideology, will demand that formal experiments be established. This preference may be granted in some cases, especially where the organization can control its own environment. But in some cases, the organization may have only incomplete autonomy, and thus confoundations occur. For example, a common problem arises with the condition that one must try to predict the behavior of some competitor or other agency. In such a situation, hard data are not usually available, nor does one have the option (as a rule) to conduct a controlled experiment to determine the other party's intentions. Here, then, action must often be predicated on speculation about a rival's behavior, or on the basis of an intuition or some other nonempirical technique. As the reader might expect, such cases arise most frequently at the higher levels of any enterprise, at the point where the organization becomes tangent to the world outside. It is here that the restricted realism of the scientific manager ill-serves him.

As for mechanistic man's predilection for objectivity, there are some potentially dysfunctional aspects here as well. Recall that rhetorical man is persuaded by such factors as emotion, sentiment, personality, friendship, and ideology, which tend to be viewed as extraneous by rational man. But, to repeat the old cliché, success in the real world is often more dependent on "who you know" than "what you know." Perhaps most important, however, are the distinct advantages in being able to intuit or "feel" the intentions of one's rivals or associates, or in being able to perform conceptual as opposed to data-based calculations. Now, because of the controlled objectivity of "scientific" man, such factors hardly affect him, and he is perhaps clumsy in manipulating or dealing with them. After all, one hardly becomes expert in treating factors that he *a priori* does not admit should exist. As a result, the scientific manager may appear to completely lack the diplomacy that is so critical at the higher levels of enterprise, or the broad strategic skills of the conceptualizer. The scientific staff member may be trotted out at some technical gathering or invited to a party to impress one's friends with his erudition, yet he may be very much distrusted to take charge of sensitive issues or negotiations believed to affect vital interests of the organization. These are usually left to those grand old rhetoricians the scientific administrators so deplore. Again, the objectivity of which the empiricist-realist is so proud may serve him very well in the development laboratory, on the plant floor, or in the budget office, but it may severely hamper his ability to "sense" the climate and conditions at the level where affairs are managed by manners, innuendos, and subtle turns of strategic judgment.

While the detriments associated with mechanistic man's predilection for realism and objectivity may have a behavioral base, the limitations stemming from his concentration on well-bounded problems, and his reductionism, and instrumentalism, have a technical basis as well as a behavioral grounding. His boundedness and reductionism set particularly serious limitations, for most of the problems which emerge at the very highest level of enterprise cannot be partitioned into parts without some loss of accuracy or relevance. Particularly, the closer one comes to the top of any organization hierarchy, the muddier the waters that have to be navigated. Here, social, political, economic, and technological factors all merge, often in the most complicated ways. But the skills of the scientific decision-maker or manager are usually associated primarily with his ability to produce neat, partitioned, and modular problem definitions, so that his technical instruments may be put to work. His tools demand this, for most do not have the power to resolve problems of great complexity. Our mathematical capabilities are limited in the number of variables that can be considered and in the number of different events that can be efficiently modeled or simulated. Moreover, as we have already suggested, many of the conditions or factors that operate at the highest level of enterprise do not lend themselves well to surrogation,* i.e., the translation into numerical or quantitative terms. Therefore, beyond a certain level of contextual or operational complexity, the instruments of the quantitatively oriented decision-maker or manager lose their resolution power, and therefore become irrelevant. In short, the limits of empiricist technology attach themselves to the scientific administrator or technical staff member, often eroding his "executive" potential *per se*. Therefore, more by way of hypothesis than assurance, we will have to consider the very serious indictment that "scientific" man has not acceded to the highest positions in industry or government mainly because the skills on which he depends—and which may exhaust his utility to any organization—are not capable of coping with the complexity of the problems found at higher levels. There, problems become successively less amenable to observation, measurement, and controlled manipulation.

Mechanistic man's penchant for instrumentalism aggravates this problem and further dilutes his immediate potential for rising to the top. Again, there are both behavioral and technical reasons we must consider. On the behavioral side, it is in the postulation of means to achieve assigned ends that the "scientific" manager finds himself most at home. Particularly, virtually all of his training consists of techniques designed to find a best alternative to achieve some objective. But for his instruments and methods to be useful, objectives must be well-defined, precise, and well-bounded. In the real world of commerce and government, however, high-order objectives are seldom well-defined, again because of the muddy waters in which top management must sail. Ill-defined or fuzzy objectives are a source of great frustration to scientific man. So, in the real world, he may always try to demand precision from his rhetorical superiors, even when the nature of the problem to be solved does not permit much precision. Therefore, mechanistic man is susceptible to indictment as an oversimplifier, as a person more interested in analytical expedience than ultimate success. There is compelling evidence to support this indictment. For example, most of

*See Section 3.3.

the econometric models that are built tend to ignore critical behavioral factors, largely because these cannot be neatly quantified. But, as every working executive knows, economic forecasts cannot be built from economic variables alone. Therefore, scientific forecasts tend always to be subjected to equivocation by rhetorical man's judgment. In the same way, the "optimal" systems constructed by staff engineers or operations researchers, while fully defensible on paper, may seldom work as expected when translated into the real world, again because many inconvenient variables are left out in the name of instrumental expediency. The long history of the failure of systems and artifices designed by supposedly rational people lends ample credence to rhetoricians' complaints that "scientific" man often promises more than he is capable of delivering, that he is more a mechanic than an architect when the operational chips are down.

As for the technical difficulties with the mechanist's predilection for instrumentalism, these are rather easily cited. They stem, basically, from his tool-orientation, an inescapable result of most of the educational programs open to him. Again, his technical education—following the long tradition of engineering in general—consists mainly of an introduction to some limited array of analytical instruments. For the most part, his practice with these instruments is with sample problems, each of which has been carefully circumscribed so that the particular instrument's role may be quickly seen and executed. In these problems, by and large, the objectives to be sought appear as if by miracle, and all the constraining and contextual factors have been carefully ordered so that the instrument may do its work directly and so that a single right answer may be obtained. But, virtually all such problems are unreflective of the qualifications, confoundations, and equivocations that attend real-world problems, as many of our "reconstructed" engineers are quick to point out.

The student may succeed at these artificially constrained quiz problems and still be useless to the real world, largely because real problems seldom emerge in the form that they had in the classroom or the textbook. But, as a rule, the education of the technical specialist does not involve much instruction in how to define problems. Rather, as suggested, nearly all of his educational experience is confined to learning how to solve predefined problems. In short, we have created a squadron of pilots who know how to fly their planes, but don't know anything about navigation, so they can't go anywhere on their own. The result is the often pathetic scene where the scientific decision-maker or manager tries to define problems in such a way that his tools can be used, even though such a recasting of the problem often results in its being deprived of both reality and relevance. This, perhaps more than any other factor, is the basis of the complaint that rhetorical man so often raises against his scientific colleagues, the complaint that they have a great facility for optimally solving the wrong problem.

All these limitations combine to produce the situation that we find so common in both industrial and governmental organizations these days. Scientific man is viewed as an instrument of rhetorical man. Particularly, he is given the role of providing the rhetorician with decision inputs, with the latter making the actual decisions. This situation, fraught with irony, is rather like using jet fuel to run a lawnmower. In addition, what is more ominous than ironic, many students of decision and management science are urged by their instructors to appreciate this situation. Like the prototypical instrumental scientist working on the atomic bomb or bacteriological warfare, students are taught that it is their place to merely provide value-free advice, with the responsibility for the use to which these inputs are eventually put resting elsewhere. This, of course, merely reflects the fact that so many of the educational programs in which scientific managers and decision-makers are taught are almost totally dependent upon the largess and fiscal support of government and industrial concerns. From the first, the management science student is initiated into a strategy of appeasement, containment of criticism, and instrumentalism, often in the most subtle ways. As a result, university business and public administration faculties often become merely operational satellites of the systems they are dependent upon. They become servants rather than critics of the establishment. It is perhaps no accident that very few journals of business administration make any criticism of industrial practices, but instead confine themselves to pandering new tools and techniques for the undirected, unconstrained use of industrial concerns. In the same way, many public administration faculties are presided over by ex-political hacks, with the curriculum biased toward recitations about the "realities" of life in public enterprise and short on analytical substance. Sadly, it seems that many professional management programs are determined not to turn out individuals who are any better prepared than the current practitioners, and those that do are prepared to apologize for it beforehand for fear of offending fiscal power.

There is thus some serious support for the accusation that students of scientific public and business administration are preconditioned to instrumental roles, roles where they will be well paid and free from responsibility for the ultimate effects of their efforts. So perhaps many individuals who would be well equipped to challenge the rhetoricians' dominance may be ill-disposed to do so. Thus, somewhat surprisingly, scientific man may have been put into the position of acting as a confederate of rhetorical man. When that happens, the community at large is the real loser, for rhetorical man has limitations that are perhaps as serious as those of his mechanistic counterpart.

Almost by default, as we have seen, responsibility for the major decisions of most complex organizations rests in the hands of individuals for whom management is an art rather than a science. The highest-order decision functions—goal-setting and strategic planning—are exercised mainly by individuals with only a qualitative educational background. In the domain of government and public enterprise, many of these individuals are products of a legal education, with the majority of their training consisting of sensitization to issues of semantics and to rather formalized, somewhat artificial rules of procedure. In the industrial sector, dominance is given to men and women with general business administration backgrounds, which may involve no real technical skills beyond simple accounting and basic arithmetic. The individual may have been exposed instead to sets of *principles* of management, with their practice consisting mainly of applying these principles to artificially defined case studies, and to the *principles* of other disciplines. His education in economics will probably be directed toward instilling an appreciation for the deduced optimality of democratic capitalism, relying on the reconstruction of neoclassical assertions. In sociology, he may receive some exposure to formal organization theory, which too often is merely a set of axiomatic assumptions about its prime theoretical referent, Weberian bureaucracy. If he studies any psychology at all, it is most likely that which is deemed useful to the person of practical affairs. In particular, he may be indoctrinated into the axiologies about how best to control employees, all subordinate to the human relations principle that "the happy worker is the productive worker." In short, his education may consist entirely of exposure to speculative constructs. Marshallian economics and Smith's axioms are artifices of logic, not descriptions of reality. Weberian bureaucracy is the theoretical referent for formal organization theory, not because of its inherent optimality, but because of Weber's fascination with Prussian administrative structure and because of later organization theorists' affection for this very tractable analytical artifice. Thus, the education of the student of rhetorical subjects is as circumscribed and artificial as is the education of his mechanist counterpart.

Now, just as the student of scientific management may have absorbed the principles and procedures of experimental science from his exposures, so will the student of rhetorical science become subtly sensitized to an entirely different set of procedures and analytical techniques. He may be introduced to the use of analogies, but may trust analogies too far. He may, for example, come to believe that theoretical capitalism is a description of the way the Western world works, not just an academic referent. Facts and evidence to the contrary may have no effect on the continuation of this belief, as a person of analogic sensitivity is sometimes capable of completely ignoring any contextual data. Thus, we have the anomaly of the businessman loudly proclaiming support of free enterprise, while actively engaged in trying to get government subsidies or to maintain some sort of protectionist structure in his industry. It has been suggested, perhaps more in seriousness than in jest, that modern capitalist is one who advocates competition for everyone except himself. At any rate, the rhetorician is always susceptible to these anomalies, for although he may have some idealistic structure as a referent, he may lack the logical discipline to apply its abstract dictates to concrete situations. He may be exposed to some creative subtlety of explanation and interpretive strategy. He may be able to develop imaginative and appealing scenarios, all built from essentially tacit, indirect evidence. He may look for hidden meanings, complex motives, and latent strategies; he may learn the invaluable art of prededuction. At the same time, he may become enamored of building deductive artifices for their own sake. In his enthusiasm to complete some logical crossword puzzle, he may be tempted to make elliptical rather than disciplined deductive inferences; he may transmogrify what should really be hypotheses into axioms, and insulate them from any attack or investigation. The realism of his structures may eventually become subordinate to their aesthetic appeal.

The rhetorician may also see how to take a theoretical construct and use it as the building block for enormously complex deductive edifices. But there may be some unsought consequences as well. He may see only one alternative deductive inference from some theoretical premise, when there are really several alternatives that could be formulated. Or his language may become imprecise, leading to ambiguities of interpretation and explanation. Eventually, he may come to the point where he uses ambiguities as a deliberate defense against criticism (and, as we will see later, as a defense against accountability as well). Finally, we may find that the different parts of his deductive structures are ill-connected, so that we find non sequiturs where we sought imperatives, or enthymemes where there should have been true syllogisms. In short, he may learn the rudiments of axiomatic reasoning, but may perhaps learn nothing of its perils. Some of his predictions and assurances may ultimately prove false, where once they seemed inescapable consequences of rigid logic.

Finally, the rhetorician may learn the use of normative referents, structures that suggest what *should* be rather than what necessarily is. In this way, he may learn to rise above circumstances, to transcend reality. But, unfortunately, he may also become heir to some liabilities. For example, he may confuse the normative—the idiosyncratic referents he himself evolves—as being the only and best course of action. When this happens, the rhetorician casts aside the mantle of rationality for the mantle of evangelism.[12] When this happens, his inferences often become distinctly procrustean, and he sees in situations only what he wants to see.

Thus, like that of the mechanist, the educational experience of the rhetorician is one of mixed blessings. While he learns conceptual sensitivity and deductive skills, he may also come to rely too much on introspection, artificial logic, and subjectivism. But what is more likely is that he will merely learn the substance of rhetorical fields and will get very little instruction in deductive methodology itself. Thus, for example, he may be familiar with the precepts of democratic capitalism, but get no practice in the techniques of proper analogy-building. He may read the social classics, but learn nothing about the technology of scenario-construction or the procedures of successive assumptive closure (which becomes a scientific exercise only when driven by logical probabilities, as we will later see). He may acquire a passing association with the implications of the grand-theory builders, but receive no instruction at all in proper, disciplined axiomatic reasoning. Finally, he may become sensitive to the apostolic assertions of normative thinkers, but may not be taught to avoid the perils of procrusteanism and projectionism inherent in most normative exercises.

Now, qualitative analysis can be "rational" when one is employing the instruments of disciplined deductive inference in appropriate contexts. For deductive inference is as much a proper procedure of science as is the inductive method, which exhausts the strict empiricist's repertoire. But, as we have suggested, very few graduates of rhetorical educational programs are likely to be facile in the scientific use of the instruments just mentioned: analogy-building, axiomatic reasoning, assumptive closure, and normative analysis. As a result, when they are conducting their goal-setting and strategic exercises, they will have recourse only to the casual and ill-disciplined rhetorical alternatives. In short, when many business executives or public administrators speak about logic, they are likely doing so without any firm idea about just what proper qualitative analysis entails. The results are all too familiar: predictions that don't come true, errors of judgment, dysfunctions and unsought consequences, proposed solutions that quickly become palliatives, and thus rampant suboptimality.

Now, with no real disciplinary skills to bring to the administrative functions of goal-setting and policymaking, the rhetorical manager necessarily takes recourse in the concepts of management as pure art and of qualifications as purely personal. What becomes important, in the absence of any specific technical skills or discipline, are one's charm, wit, tact, assumed loyalty, assiduity, dress, the right school, good connections, and so on. Promotion and selection in such a world will be based more on factors of pretention than on factors of performance. Thus, *getting* a job is often more important than doing it well. Organizational survival is to be had at any price, even that of effectiveness. In short, both government and industry become projections of the adolescent playing field and fraternity politics, and can be adequately comprehended only in the language of "gentlemen's games."

And it is in this world that mistakes are to be excused because the situation was simply too complex to comprehend, or because of bad luck. But the rhetorical manager brings complexity to virtually every situation, even those that are not inherently complex. This is because he lacks the skills—and often even the motivation—to reduce complex phenomena. For, to him, the world is a place where the luck of the draw, fast feet, and quick thinking bring success, and where failure is equally serendipitous and mysterious. The rhetorician's world is a wonderful place indeed, susceptible of being won by men and women of grace, subtlety, and tenacity. Only losers complain about the rules of the game being rigged, about things like nepotism, the "old boy" networks, discrimination, corruption, cover-ups, and collusion. Thus, the behavioral spiral of the rhetorician is the opposite of his mechanist counterpart. The latter will not tolerate mystery because it is inconsistent with his view of the world as essentially mechanical, manipulable, and knowable. Therefore, he is prone to remove mystery through analytical effort, using occasional oversimplification—which is derived from his sometimes too great enthusiasm to reduce unknowns to controllable knowns. The rhetorician, on the other hand, begins with the assumption that the world is too complex to analyze, and therefore does not bother with demanding, exhaustive research at all. Complexity, for him, is thus a self-fulfilling prophecy.

The truth of situations usually rests somewhere between these extremes. Reality will usually be a little more complicated than the die-hard mechanist would have us believe, but not the abject quandary that the rhetorician sees whenever he looks outward. Now, if the world were truly beyond comprehension, then the rhetorician's recourse to crude analytical instruments—intuition, personalistic speculation, casual deductive inference, and so on,—would be understandable, indeed rational. But in almost no case is mystery so deep, or complexity so complete, that no discipline can be applied. And this is the crux of the indictment against rhetorical man as a decision-maker. For rhetorical man consistently neglects opportunities to bring discipline and precision to his subjects, whereas mechanistic man is often too determined in this regard.

When we look at the way the rhetorical administrator might approach goal-setting or strategic analysis functions, we get a clearer defense of the assertions we have been making. Particularly, there will be a tendency to greet every exercise by introducing a priori constraints that serve to restrict the domain of inquiry. The reason for introducing preconceptions is usually a proper one. When we look far into an organization's future or far out into its environment, we see enormous complexity. The rational response is therefore to introduce tentative "order," usually by restraining one's vision into certain predefined areas, or by a priori eliminating certain alternatives or factors from active consideration. As we will see, however, there is a scientific way to do this, and a prescientific way. Rhetoricians usually opt for the latter. The a priori constraints they impose may be based largely on their own past experience (sometimes reinforced with certain unvalidated philosophical principles). This is the real origin of the conservativeness we note among most real-world organizations (i.e., the tendency to repeat certain patterns of behavior, irrespective of their inherent appropriateness to the contemporary context). Thus, successful strategies may tend to be iterated until they are no longer functional because the operational environment will have changed in ways unapparent to the rhetorical decision-maker; on the other hand, errors may tend to be repeated—or suboptimal strategies perpetuated—because of the reluctance to tamper with a going concern. To the rhetorical manager, his organization is always a bastion of security and utility existing in the face of a constant flow of hostile, perturbing outside events. Thus, both the environment and the future are to be distrusted and, if possible, ignored. For there is nothing there but uncertainty, and the rhetorical manager is not intellectually equipped to deal with uncertainty. So he tends to concentrate his attention on areas of immediate concern, making no effort to widen his vision. His philosophy of management and decision-making is thus something like this: successful administration means that one is able to maintain the status quo in the face of constantly changing external conditions. Under this conception, decision-making becomes a reactive function, and every effort may be made to minimize the number of decisions that have to be made in the first place.

Once again, the rhetorician tends to scan the future and the outside world not for opportunities, but for perils. Under the guise of reactive decision-making, top management becomes the first line of defense against organizational change, positive or otherwise. For they see themselves only as victims of events, not as potential authors of events. So, whereas the rhetorician's myopia stems from his lack of scientific skills, the mechanist's tendency to concentrate only on immediate situations stems from the limitations of his tools and on the behavioral referents he was taught to uphold. Both rhetorician and mechanist, for the most part, thus join in exercising limited vision and restricting the attention paid to further horizons. But they do so for different reasons.

The restricted concept of science and the technical limitations of the mechanist's demand that he always operate in near-time or near-space, whereas the rhetorician's excessive reliance on experience leads him inevitably into a reactive posture. Thus, it is not so much the scope of vision that differentiates rhetorical man from his scientific foil (for both tend to scan only near-term events), but the way in which each chooses to approach the problems they do recognize. In the "reactive" domain, the admired virtues are quickness and resilience (e.g., the ability to recover from errors is valued perhaps more highly than the ability to avoid them). The mechanist, on the other hand, is more concerned with the ultimate rectitude of decisions than with their timeliness, and may therefore be seen as something of an overcautious, reticent laggard by the quick-stepping, quick-to-fire rhetorical manager. Thus, both types of managers are reactive; one just tends to react a little quicker and with less discrimination than the other. And neither would criticize the concept of reactive management, for neither the strict rhetorician nor the mechanist has the general capability to take advantage of complexity—to exploit it—and they must therefore be content to contain or counter it. Thus, we find the real (if usually latent) goal of many organizations is really as simple unequivocal *survival*.[13]

In summary, the environment and future of the rhetorical decision-maker may often become comprehensible only in terms of his own experiences. Any element that cannot be made comprehensible in such terms is either to be distrusted, or ignored until it actually intrudes on the status quo. Here is the origin of *management by crisis* and also of the general resistance to change exhibited by organizations ruled by rhetoricians. Here is why the future is so seldom an improvement on the past, but rather so often a mere replication. And here, most fundamentally, is the course of most management's concentration on tactical decision-making, and its neglect of the goal-setting and strategic analysis functions. For when one chooses to neglect the future, one has no choice but to constantly react to a present that is a sequence of constant surprises—and tactics is the vehicle for such reaction. Finally, here is the reason why many organizations that so richly deserve to disband continue to exist.

1.4 TOWARD A RESOLUTION

Our two straw men have now been fleshed out a bit. As is to be expected, the mechanistic and rhetorical decision-makers differ in virtually every aspect of performance. To summarize these differences, consider Table 1.2. Now, obviously, these straw men of ours are a bit extreme. Few real-world decision-makers will be as restricted as the portraits we have drawn. Yet, and this is the important point, most decision-makers will tend toward one of these two polar positions, with the mid-range between them being populated very sparsely. So these distinctions are very important, if a bit artificial.

Again, the major source of information for the rhetorician will be opinion or, for decision situations that are unprecedented, casual observation. As a rule, whatever appreciation of a situation he gains will have been gained catch-as-catch-

Table 1.2. Differential characteristics of rhetorical and mechanistic decision-makers.

	Information Base	Source of Constraints	Analytical Base	Decision Premises	Decision Modality
Rhetorician	Casual Observation/ Opinion	Principle/ Indoctrination	Exegesis/ Intuition	Judgmental	Speculation
Mechanist	Algorithmic Observation/ Codification	Hypotheses/ Paradigms	Experimentation/ Inductive Inference	Calculative	Estimation

can, rather than according to the strict rules of procedure that characterize any proper scientific approach. He may observe a situation, but his observations will not be disciplined, nor will they result in the carefully codified, formulated observations of the mechanist. The reliance on opinion as fact merely reflects the rhetorician's lack of interest in—or facility with—the tools of data development and analysis, as well as his tolerance of ambiguity and uncertainty. For the mechanist, on the other hand, opinion is never a valid decision input. Rather, the information used by the strict empiricist must always be based on formal observation, and then be codified according to the rules of information analysis. For example, the mechanist will equip his observations with indexes of confidence based on the size of his sample (relative to the universe) and on the variability of the data themselves. Large samples with low variance generally receive higher indexes of confidence or expected accuracy than limited, highly protean samples. In short, all the information accepted by the "scientific" decision-maker will have been generated under the laws of observation and codifications that pertain to statistical or inductive inference.

Moving on, both the rhetorical and the mechanistic decision-maker will tend to employ generalizations of various kinds, which in practice act as constraints. These permit them to draw on the experience of others or to relate similarities of context so that each decision process need not necessarily be approached as an entirely unprecedented situation. These generalizations are also the primary sources of *a priori* decision constraints. The rhetorician is susceptible to constraints of principle and indoctrination. Among constraints of principle, for example, are those managerial adages we spoke of earlier (e.g., no subordinate should report to more than one supervisor). Principles may also take a moralistic or normative nature, restricting the means, for example, available to achieve an objective. Or principles may take a more direct role, perhaps in the form of dictating definite decision criteria. For instance, a business firm may operate under the principle of profit maximization, which will constrain the actions that managers may take and set the criteria for any evaluation of action alternatives. On the other hand, a firm may operate under the principle of maximum growth, so that considerations of profit are secondary to considerations of expansion. In a still broader sense, decision-makers of rhetorical background may be victims of indoctrination, which will restrict the range of evidence they will accept or perhaps predirect their analyses. For example, many business people were indoctrinated into the concept that labor and management compete irrevocably for scarce resources, so that wages, salaries, and motivation are all components of a zero-sum game. They are not, as a rule, open to alternative premises, and they often ignore evidence tending to contradict or dilute this treasured axiom. So far as internal relations problems are concerned, then, their indoctrination may automatically close off attention to any other perspectives.

Now, even though the mechanist makes much of his supposed value-free operations, he is also susceptible to certain *a priori* constraints. He may, for example, make use of hypotheses that restrict his decision premises or constrict his analyses. For instance, on the basis of past observation, he may have hypothesized that labor absenteeism reflects dissatisfaction with the attributes of the workplace (e.g., authoritarian managers, too few breaks, too little delegated decision authority). Therefore, if absenteeism emerges and the mechanist is asked to correct it, this hypothesis may enter to restrict his analysis to the evaluation of alternatives that alter the work context. Now, the presence of this hypothesis may mean that he will not consider other qualitative causes of absenteeism, such as weather, erosion of the work ethic, local agitators, or the aforementioned possibility of an inescapable zero-sum game played between management and labor. Thus, hypotheses may do for the mechanist what principles do for the rhetorician: they may constrain the research space into definite, predefined trajectories. Now, as long as the hypotheses are valid—or the rhetorician's principles operative—*a priori* constraints may result in decision efficiency, because some unproductive paths are automatically eliminated from consideration. But the danger is that any apriority may be misapplied, because of unwarranted confidence or the enthusiasm to save time or costs of analysis. In either case, decision error is virtually inescapable, with the magnitude of the error directly related to the apriority's degree of inappropriateness. Finally, whereas the rhetorical decision-maker is susceptible to generalizations in the form of indoctrination, the mechanist is sometimes swayed by paradigms.[14] A paradigm, in this case, is a complex collection of hypotheses that the decision-maker accepts as valid and does not investigate. The empiricist's scientific method is itself a paradigm, setting as its does the basic analytical envelope within which the scientific decision-maker operates, often at the expense of true rationality.

The matter of the different analytical bases employed by the two types of decision-maker may be disposed of rather quickly.* The rhetorician will, by default, usually be restricted either to simple exegesis or to reliance on intuition. Exegesis, in this instance, is the process by which abstractions are lent context-specific qualities (as, for example, when lawyers review a piece of legislation to see if it is constitutional). In the same way, an executive may employ exegesis in deciding whether a particular action or tactic is congruent with the policy constraints or "spirit" of the organization to which he belongs. This is a proper use of exegesis. Often, however, exegesis merely short-circuits proper analytical procedures, perhaps reflecting the rhetorician's fundamental disinterest in formal contextual analysis. In such a case, the executive may turn to his experiential base, his set of principles, or the products of his indoctrination and try to interpret the present situation solely in terms of these aprioristic predicates. Thus,

*We will deal with analytical methods in detail in Chapter 4.

there tends to be a conservative or iterative quality about the rhetorical executive's decisions. That is, they often fall into a definite pattern of repetition or similarity, which the realities of any specific decision context may belie. In short, the rhetorician is always reluctant to develop a new data base for specific situations, preferring instead to try to interpret the present situation in light of a historical experience, abstract principles, and so on. When this simply cannot be done at all, the rhetorician will most likely turn to his intuition, scanning a new situation rather than analyzing it, concentrating more on semantics than syntax. He must be willing to take grand risks, for the odds that intuition will be right in a truly complex situation are dim indeed.

Knowing this, the rhetorical managers have tended to elevate risk-taking into something of a virtue, founding what might be called the Wyatt Earp school of management ("shoot first, ask questions later"). The implication is that the fellow who is clever can always recover from an error and therefore need not be too concerned about making one. Beyond this, the rhetorician usually always overstates the real complexity of a situation and thereby overstates the contribution of luck. This overvaluation tends to lead to a reliance on trial-and-error tactics, for if a situation is completely beyond comprehension, then trial and error is indeed the *rational* analytical strategy. (For example, Lord Bertrand Russell once suggested that not even Isaac Newton could devise a better method for running a maze than trial and error.) So, in the gentlemen's game of rhetorical management, errors aren't something to worry about too much. The important thing is to accept your losses gracefully, like a good sport. "Errors are just the luck of the draw." "You can't win them all." These are the gentleman's alibis. The reader should recall, however, that the gentlemen's game is played only at the highest levels of industry and government, where promotion or continuance is largely independent of performance. This is a luxury that is effectively denied the middle-level manager or bureaucrat.

At any rate, the attitude of the mechanist manager toward the probability of error is completely the reverse of his rhetorical counterpart. He is, by predilection and training, a risk-avoider. While the rhetorician succeeds if he just copes, the mechanist fails if he is not optimal. Thus, he is sometimes criticized as being unwilling to make decisions, being too slow on the draw, as it were. In practice, we can distinguish between the risk-taker and the risk-averter by the level of confidence each requires before he will commit himself to an action. Of necessity, exegesis and intuition always leave a very high residual probability of error (a low level of confidence). But this may be tolerable to the game-playing rhetorician, especially if he is protected by the gentlemen's code, which considers errors a matter of ill luck rather than a product of analytical expedience or stupidity. The more rigorous and recriminatory world in which the "scientific" decision-maker dwells causes him to try to obtain very high levels of confidence before making a move. Therefore, he replaces expedient exegesis with experimentation, and employs measurement where the rhetorician employs raw intuition. The result is generally a longer delay between the demand for a decision and its enactment, and more resources committed to analysis or research. But the other result, it is hoped, is a lower incidence of error.

In overview then, we find that the decisions of the rhetorical manager are primarily judgmental in origin. When we search for the reasons for a particular action taken by a rhetorician, we will ultimately arrive back at opinion, by way of principles, exegesis, and intuition. And, if we challenge the rhetorical manager on his casual decision-making technology, he will take recourse in the excuse that, from his perspective, the problem was so complicated that no scientific discipline could have been applied. But again, the world is always a complicated place to those who lack the motivation and skill to simplify it. If then we had to come up with a single term to reflect the rhetorical decision-making process, it would probably best be *speculation*. Speculation, after all, is merely undisciplined judgment and casual opinion. And without question, it is the last resort for those who lack scientific preparation, and the first resort for those who are committed to analytical expedience in their decision-making. The latter, while perhaps having the qualifications to operate in a more disciplined fashion, do not do so. They may choose not to do so for various reasons; paramount among them is the fact that they may ultimately be unaccountable for the results of their decisions or actions, or otherwise insulated from any responsibility for the quality of their performances. As we will see later, both big business and big government have been very imaginative in obscuring decision-making responsibility, an exercise in which stockholders and voters have strongly participated.

As for the "scientific" decision-maker, virtually every move in his decision process is a matter of calculation. The statistically disciplined inputs, the reliance on inductive hypotheses (which are themselves equipped with a calculated probability of rectitude), and his constant recourse to experimentation and measurement lend his exercises great precision and formality. Where there are vagaries of opinion in the rhetorical process, there are codified, quantified data in the empirical process; where there are indoctrination and exegesis in the rhetorical context, there is usually context-specific, objective analysis in the empirical. Ultimately, whereas the decision premises and actions of the rhetorician are predicated on speculation, those of the mechanist "scientific" decision-maker are matters of estimation. Very simply, estimations differ from speculations because, for the former, we have an indication of their probable accuracy. This is because indexes of expected accuracy have been obtainable all through the process, from the basic data-collection process (with its codified observations) through the matter of the calculated effectiveness of action alternatives, and so forth. This, in essence, is what lends the mechanist process its scientific qualities.

While there is no guarantee that in any given instance an estimation will be more accurate than a speculation, we at least know how likely we are to be wrong. In the long run, as we will later see, this is perhaps the most valuable information that the decision-maker can possess.

As a final note on premises—although it is still too early in our inquiry to talk about them in detail—we can see immediately one of the most important sources of decision error in complex enterprise. The normal scenario we have constructed finds the mechanist acting as a source of inputs to his rhetorical superior. In this scenario, the scientific practitioner may have a line position at the lower levels of enterprise, or he may be a member of some executive's staff. In either case, his job usually revolves around providing decision premises to the superior, who is then responsible for actually selecting a course of action. Now, these premises may simply be a codified set of data (e.g., an estimate of the next year's sales generated by a statistical forecast, estimates of the promotional elasticity for some prospective advertising strategy). Or, the decision-maker may have asked the analyst to provide him with a series of structured, weighted alternatives (e.g., the several tactics available for solving a labor problem, the several different schemes for reducing the firm's debt-equity ratio, an analysis of several different methods for the production of regional energy, an analysis of the alternative methods available for delivering health-care services to the local population). In either case, the scientific analyst *qua* manager or staff member is pretty much responsible for all the predecision discipline, and the rhetorical superior or executive is the presumed beneficiary of these efforts. The propagandistic face put on this arrangement is that the rhetorical decision-maker has the advantage of scientific predicates for his decisions, without having to be adept himself at scientific analysis. (Of course, should the scientists make a mistake, the rhetorician may be quick to use this point to excuse himself from real responsibility.)

There are two potential problems here, and we seldom escape either of them. First, the superior, lacking any real technical competence, may be overconvinced of the utility of the scientific inputs of his subordinates, perhaps sharing their somewhat overoptimistic view of their instruments' resolution power. Not being in a position to evaluate the true "rationality" of the scientific inputs, he may accept and advance them without equivocation. But we already know that the mechanist's sensitivity to broad issues of context may be limited, and that they may in fact be ill-qualified to perform the analysis—and structure the action alternatives—for a high-order issue. Therefore, the unqualified acceptance of their inputs often sponsors errors, usually of oversimplification.

This was the source, for example, of the Ford Motor Company's Edsel debacle, where the statistical inputs were accepted as design criteria with none of the qualifications and modifications that a serious social scientist might have offered.* In this case, the social scientist might have suggested that a mere composite of interview preferences is not enough, because people often give interviewers information that they would not really act upon if given the opportunity. In short, when asked what kind of automobile they want—or would purchase—people may often overstate their requirements, perhaps simply to impress the interviewer. At any rate, the Ford executives accepted these statistical inputs as valid and exhaustive indexes of what people wanted in a car, and the Edsel was the cataclysmic result.

In another version of the scenario, the senior executive automatically devalues any scientific premises whatsoever, largely because he cannot comprehend the procedures by which they were generated. In this case, the scientific practitioners or staff members lend the organization a token discipline and precision, but have no real determination on the decisions of the enterprise. A good case in point is President Nixon's refusal to consider any of the data on marijuana that his select scientific committee offered him, and his predetermination to consider policies that many social scientists considered very detrimental.

The Edsel and the marijuana cases are extreme examples. One illustrates the danger of blind acceptance of the empiricist's decision premises; the other reflects the irrational, automatic disavowal of scientifically generated decision inputs. They give us the clue we need to suggest that many of the most serious errors of enterprise are spawned in the nexus between the scientist's misplaced reliance on the resolution power of his instruments (and their tendency to oversimplify complex situations), and the rhetorician's ignorance of any scientific potential whatsoever.

Later, we will have a great deal more to say about such procedural dysfunctions, and also about the details of rhetorical and mechanist decision processes as they are actually employed in government and business. But our inquiry is still in its formative stage, and many opportunities for clarification await us in further chapters. Nevertheless, we are at least now in a better position to appreciate (or tentatively evaluate) the assertion we made earlier—that many, if not most, decision-makers are fundamentally unqualified for the decision responsibilities they have inherited or elected, and that our educational programs are in large measure to blame.

Assumedly, the empiricist-mechanistic decision-maker, at least in comparison to his rhetorical counterpart, is to be preferred. His procedures appear so rigorous— and his demands for precision so satisfying—to those arguing for decision disci-

---

*It has been suggested that the judgmental (rhetorical) decision-makers rejected some market-research (scientific) findings that would have argued against manufacturing the Edsel. We cannot answer for this possibility here.

pline. Indeed, this is true, provided that we ignore issues of context. However, we cannot do this here, so we enter the qualification we gave earlier: the scientific decision-maker or management scientist is indeed well qualified and is the proper person to deal with *certain* type of problems, mainly those that appear at the lower levels of enterprise. He is not, in short, our man for all seasons or situations. Rather, his demand for codified, "hard" data only, and his instrument's inability to deal with qualitative or "fuzzy" inputs (and his own discomfort in the face of such factors) restrict his contributions to problems that are well bounded, amenable to surrogation, and accessible to analytic analysis (this latter process involves the empiricist technique of trying to comprehend a phenomenon by manipulating only one factor at a time, preferably in the context of what amounts to a controlled laboratory environment).[15] But as we will soon see—and as many readers already know—such problems appear far more frequently in the classroom than in the real world, and are rare indeed once we leave the plant floor, the inventory warehouse, or the accounting office.

Now, if the agents for management science, operations research, and the like have a place mainly at the lower levels of enterprise, where is the proper place for the rhetorician? In effect, he is where he belongs, dominating the value-significant, major strategic decisions of enterprise, where matters of judgment and principle are so essential. But when he is incapable of making *disciplined* decisions—when his qualitative skills are ill practiced—then he becomes the author of the truly dramatic and debilitating errors of our modern world.[16] He is the architect of the medicaid management system, the executor of the Bay Area Rapid Transit (BART) system in San Francisco, the director of Lockheed International, the manager of the abortive community action programs of the war on poverty, and the executives who gave us New York City's fiscal system and the precarious concept of social security. But if the scientific manager is not equipped to take his place, who is?

The obvious answer is that we might create two special classes of decision-maker, one equipped to deal with goal-setting problems, and the other skilled predominantly in strategic analysis. As our functional typology (Table 1.1) indicated, the goal-setter would be an expected master of heuristic analysis and skilled at dealing with normative factors. As we will later see, this would suggest that he have a strong grounding in the disciplines required to make sense of future and environmental contexts (e.g., economics, political science, sociology, social psychology). For his part, the strategic analyst would be expected to be skilled at conducting hypothetico-deductive analyses. Particularly, he would be trained in the various logics (e.g., Boolean analysis, predicate calculus) and also be equipped with a facility in qualitative analysis, including work with instruments such as the Delphi technique, consensus statistics, probability-based collective decision-making, "fuzzy set" theory, game theory, stochastic simulation, and scenario-building. At a later point, we will show just what all these various instruments can accomplish and explain some of their rudimentary mechanics.

But here we can see that it is certainly possible to isolate the requirements of the various decision categories outlined in the typology and to train individuals to be dedicated to just one of them. Were we to do this, however, some problems would have to be faced. First, the operatives in the several different sectors—goal-setting, strategic analysis, and operations analysis (tactics)—would be intellectual mysteries to each other. They would all be products of radically different perspectives and preparations and would be expected to interrelate only with some difficulty. Second, the Platonic system bias exists here. Particularly, individuals would be expected to remain in the category for which they were prepared; in effect, they would have to be made functionally immobile. This would demand a radical restructuring of many sociopsychological factors, from motivation to matters of human dignity, and perhaps demand widespread resocialization. If all other factors were ignored, this might very well be an acceptable alternative. But at least two factors confound this simple logic. For one thing, there is no assurance that modularity of tasks and preparations would lead to more efficient, effective organizational behavior. Rather, it might lead simply to institutionalized suboptimality. Moreover, enforced administrative specialization and insulation may often work against the realization of organizational synergy. System effectiveness and efficiency in many cases depend upon the shift from a bureaucratic, partitioned system to an "organic" structure. The first requirement for synergy in an organization is therefore some opportunity for interaction and complementation. Now, although modularity and specialization may not prevent complementation, they do artificially constrain interaction. In the military and in certain bureaucratic contexts, interaction is deliberately suppressed, usually in the name of discipline or system tractability. But when an organization elects to—or is forced to—operate in a complex, protean environment, discipline and tractability often work against real success.[17]

But the most important reason for avoiding legislated modularity of decision functions (and administrative classes) is that goals, strategies, and tactics are interdependent entities. In short, it is not enough to merely suggest that strategies are completely answerable to goals, and tactics completely answerable to strategies. This traditional hierarchization of decision functions may often breed the very irrationalities it was designed to deter. We should be able to see, rather, that goals must be set in the light of strategic capabilities and that, in many cases, tactical considerations might act to determine strategic functions. Thus, causality in the complex organization must be allowed to work both upward and downward.

Thus, we might deplore the practice of all the scientific talent concentrating on tactical problems (or on the even simpler deterministic issues that arise in an organization), which leaves the distinctly prescientific rhetoricians in command of higher-order issues. The alternative is simple, if somewhat difficult to effect. Particularly, it would consist of broadening our educational programs. Rhetorical skills should be complemented by an appreciation of the contributions of quantitative and experimental technologies and discipline; by the same token, the strict mechanist must be introduced to the sensitivities, qualitative skills, and deductive capabilities that are so essential for goal-setting and strategic operations. Only in this way can a true complementation exist among decision-makers at the various levels. And such complementation, as we will attempt to show, is the single most important step we can take on our way out of the administrative wilderness in which we have been wandering for so long.

In asking for complementary skills within a single individual, however, we must expect to face considerable problems. Initially, it has been the author's experience that many students tend to reflect the existing extremes of interest and capability. Those who perform extremely well in the deductive areas, such as pure mathematics, impact analysis, and logic, sometimes have considerable difficulty in dealing with practical problems. In fact, some of the most brilliant and promising academic mathematicians have performed very poorly in management science classes. In particular, individuals who have a great flair for comprehending the tortuous theses of modern algebra or the manipulation of topological spaces are seldom able to work out the simple word problems given in such texts as those on linear programming and inventory control. What is even more serious, on the other hand, is the genuine horror that social science students feel when they have to work in the area of applied mathematics (and, in some cases, even in the distinctly social-science-oriented statistical methodology classes). They keep wanting to go back to "people problems" and get away from the numbers; they see the scientific instruments as social threats rather than as potential therapies. As a result, scientific management instructors may see general management students only once—in the required survey course in scientific management. They do not return, and perhaps carry with them a deep-seated distrust of mathematicians and management scientists, so that it is improbable that they will make use of the potential that management science offers.

So, if we are to realize our aim of creating broadly skilled managers and decision-makers, we must revise our educational methods. As long as management scientists concentrate only on instruments, so that even advanced methodology courses look like freshman engineering offerings, they are going to obstruct the very end they hope to achieve—the emergence of a truly well-educated administrative practitioner. For neither the strict operations research person nor his casual rhetorical counterpart are "educated" in the sense that the domain of modern decision responsibilities demands. As things now stand, as soon as students enter a school of business (and perhaps public) administration, they are forced almost immediately to decide which "track" to follow. Will they join the ranks of the number-crunchers, or will they immerse themselves in the principles of management and spend most of the time trying to avoid a scientific management course altogether? And, in all likelihood, communication between the rhetorical and scientific students is likely to be as curtailed (and perhaps as acrimonious) as the communication between their faculty counterparts.

What is needed, then, is for the decision-maker to be as broad in analytical skills, as rich in his instrumental repertoire, as the range of administrative problems demands. It is just as pathetic and disturbing to see the rhetorician consistently neglecting opportunities for real rectitude as it is to see the mechanist so often embrace procedure and discipline to the point where it countermands the realities of a situation. So, just as the complex organization houses problems that range from the trivial to the effectively indeterminate, so must the proper decision-makers display skills that run the gamut from techniques of simple, mechanical optimization to qualitative analysis techniques of the most demanding and sophisticated order. Any gap in the continuum of skills will set the seed for irrationality, for there is no gap in the continuum of problems. As things now stand, our continuum of skills is sieve-like, so that many of the most debilitating problems—and indeed even some of the rather trivial ones—fall through the interstices and are then free to fester and swell. So we must close the gaps, and we will begin to show how this might be done once we are free of a last nagging issue.

This issue has been with us since the initiation of our work here: what is a proper definition of *rationality*? We once thought that it could be defined by simply citing the attributes of modern empirical science, but then we saw that empiricism is rational only within a limited range of contexts. But what we have since done may give us the answer we need, and the operational definition we seek. For what we know now is that the definition of rationality cannot be linked to any particular concept of the scientific method. Rather, because the scientific method is a continuum and not a single invariant procedure, the definition of rationality cannot be so fixed. But it must be invariant, or else it cannot be useful to us here, not when we have several different decision domains to consider and are arguing that the administrator should be at home in all. We are not, as it might appear, wrapped in a paradox. There is a simple way out. That way out is to generalize—or abstract—the criteria for rationality, and to do it so that it will operate at every level of enterprise and across the entire domain of decisions to be made. The definition of *rationality* that we will be working with in the remaining chapters is: *Rationality is a dependent variable of the decision-making process, and it reflects the extent to which the expected value of a decision error has been effectively minimized.** The relationship is a simple inverse:

*As we will see in Chapter 4, this is just about the only measure we have of the quality of a decision-making process *before* it has run its course, i.e., before we have allowed the organization to be committed to some course of action.

the lower the expected value of the error associated with a decision process, the higher is the demonstrated degree of rationality. The rational administrator, then, is one whose exercises consistently approach the effective minimum for the expected value of decision error.

Using this definition of rationality, we are able to compare the performances of decision-makers operating in fundamentally different domains. Each decision exercise will be assigned a rationality index measured with respect to the potential accuracy available (e.g., the "floor level" to which expected error might reasonably be expected to be reduced). Therefore, strategic and tactical decision-makers may be evaluated within the same framework, without running into the problem of trying to compare apples and oranges. This point will not really be clear until we have gone much further into our work. But what we do know is that the "floor level" of the expected value of a decision error will be related to the nature of the problems that are to be solved in the various decision domains. And so, we must now turn to an examination of the anatomy of organizational decision-making.

1.5 NOTES AND REFERENCES

1. Possibly the most popular administrative framework is that given by Robert N. Anthony in *Planning and Control Systems: A Framework for Analysis* (Boston: Harvard University Press, 1965). However, this structure responds rather completely to the traditional functional approach to management and is used primarily in those curriculums that are interested in management theory as a "distillation of experience." Therefore, its categorizations (e.g., strategic, management, and operations planning) are not quite strict enough for the purposes of the decision scientist *per se*. Particularly, we separate the goal-setting and strategic planning functions, whereas Anthony tends to collapse them. But there are other critical differences for those who wish to compare our typology with the more familiar one developed by Anthony.

2. For some computational algorithms dealing with promotional elasticities, see the appropriate selections in Patrick J. Robinson et al., *Promotional Decisions Using Mathematical Models* (Boston: Allyn & Bacon, Inc., 1967).

3. See, for example, Chapter III of Herbert Simon's *Administrative Behavior* (New York: Macmillan, 1957).

4. This, of course, is the bureaucracy as defined by Max Weber, who was perhaps a bit too enamored of the Prussian military to be an entirely objective analyst. At any rate, the fundamental implications of classical bureaucratic structure were defined in Weber's *The Theory of Social and Economic Organization*. Translated by Henderson and Parsons (New York: Free Press, 1947).

5. That an organization's structure and behavior should reflect environmental conditions has become something of an axiom of organization theory.

However, organizations must also be given credit for having some potential to structure their own environment. Thus, organizational structure and the resultant administrative demands tend to emerge within a "field" framework. At any rate, some of the common structural variations available are given in Chapter 4 of my *Systems: Analysis, Administration, and Architecture* (New York: Van Nostrand Reinhold Company, 1975).

6. The classic logic of this approach is that of Frederick Taylor himself, presented in *The Principles of Scientific Management* (New York: Harper, 1923).

7. For a thorough, if rhetorical, treatment of these problems, see the initial chapters of Newman and Logan, *Strategy, Policy and Central Management* (Cincinnati: South-western Publishing Company, 1971).

8. For a defense of such formulations, see Hood and Koopman's *Studies in Econometric Method* (New Haven: Yale University Press, 1953).

9. Although there are many excellent books on statistical methods, I would recommend that those readers unfamiliar with some of our terminology with regard to simple statistical inference turn to William Hays, *Statistics* (New York: Holt, Rinehart and Winston, Inc., 1963). The use of standard deviation is explained in Chapter 6.

10. The logic for a multimodal health-care delivery system is outlined in my *Managing Social Service Systems* (New York: Petrocelli Books, Inc., 1977).

11. An excellent discussion of the dominance of instrumentalistic science is given in Walter A. Weisskopf's *Alienation and Economics* (New York: E. P. Dutton & Co., Inc., 1971).

12. I tried to describe the process by which the scientist becomes evangelist in my *A General Systems Philosophy for the Social and Behavioral Sciences* (New York: George Braziller, Inc., 1973).

13. The concept of the organization as slave of the environment leads inevitably to a pseudo-biological adulation of adaptivity as the highest achievement of the organization, and thus to the normation of reactive management. Such logics are of course troublesome, but popular. Especially popular was the conceptual defense of organizational adaptivity given by Shirley Terreberry in "The Evolution of Organizational Environments," *Administrative Sciences Quarterly*, 12 (1968), pp. 590–613. Our point here is that pure adaptivity may be the least sophisticated strategy that an organization can apply, not the most favorable.

14. For the classic treatment of the role of scientific paradigms, see Thomas Kuhn's *The Structure of Scientific Revolutions* (Chicago: University of Chicago Press, 1962).

15. Compare Gardner Murphy, "The Inside and Outside of Creativity," *Fields within Fields . . . Within Fields* 2 (1969).

16. One of the most troublesome and ludicrous examples of the degradations of rhetorical decision-making occurs when an issue is brought into the courts for resolution. There, some judge—who likely has no technical qualifications whatsoever—is asked to make often critical and sweeping decisions. Two examples of this come immediately to mind. First is the disaster of the

Grand Teton Dam; the adverse role played by the court system is described well in Dorothy Gallagher's "The Collapse of the Great Teton Dam," in *The New York Times Magazine* (September 19, 1976). The other fiasco took place in the United States District Court for the Middle District of Alabama (Civil Action No. 3195-N), where a federal judge took it upon himself to determine the administrative structure of mental health facilities, and thus virtually ensured the diseconomy of such processes.

17. That there are organizational forms other than bureaucracy has been brought out by many serious social scholars. See, for example, Warren Bennis, "Beyond Bureaucracy," *Transactions* (July-August 1965) and the classic article by Emery and Trist, "The Causal Texture of the Environment," *Human Relations* **18** (1965).

2
The Structure
of Decision
Responsibilities

2.0 INTRODUCTION

In the first chapter we defined the different decision functions to be performed within the context of a complex organization, and the different categories of problems that decision-makers are called upon to face. Here we want to be more explicit about the way in which decision-makers perform their tasks, and about the significance of the various decision domains to the organization itself.

Thus, we will take a close look at the major responsibilities of goal-setting, strategic analysis, tactical analysis, and deterministic decision-making. We will also search the interfaces of the several different decision domains, looking at the interrelationships among goals, strategies, and tactics.

The lesson we should learn is that it takes a great deal of intelligence, discipline, and ingenuity to properly administer a complex organization. We also hope to show that the isolation of decision responsibilities from analytical capabilities is a cause for serious concern, and that the traditional distinction between staff (scientific decision-makers) and line functionaries (usually rhetorical in training) is at the root of much of the trouble.

Thus, we are now going to add another set of components to our emerging taxonomy of decision functions—the focuses of organizational significance, which are listed in Table 2.1. We will then try to elaborate and defend the several sets of associations in this taxonomy.

2.1 THE DECISION CONTEXTS

We know from the previous chapter that there are essentially four different decision functions with which we need be concerned (goal-setting, strategic analysis,

Table 2.1. Dimensions of organizational significance.

Decision Function	Functionary	Associated Problem Category	Organizational Significance
Goal-setting	Director/officer	Indeterminate	Integrity (viability and normativity)
Strategic programming	Executive	Severely stochastic	Effectiveness
Tactical programming	Manager	Moderately stochastic	Efficiency
Operations programming	Supervisor	Deterministic	Mechanisticity

tactical analysis, and instrumental analysis), and also four different problem categories that set the demands of the various decision domains: indeterminate, severely stochastic, moderately stochastic, and deterministic. We also suggested that indeterminate decisions would tend to dominate at the higher levels of organization, with deterministic problems appearing with greatest frequency at the lower levels, and so on. In effect, we have had some things to say about the first two columns of our major typology, Table 1.1. We will now elaborate on the second and third columns of that construct, and in the process try to further defend many of the assertions we made in the first chapter.

One point should be offered before we begin. It is a common ploy of organizations to have line responsibilities in the hands of essentially rhetorical functionaries, while its "scientific" talent is arrayed as staff to the line functionaries—in effect, subordinate to them. In the pages that follow, however, we will not even try to distinguish between line and staff functions. For the analytical aspects of decision-making cannot be delegated to others without ill effects. Therefore, scientific and functional authorities should reside within every decision-maker. In short, as we will view it here, the analyst and decision-maker is the same person at all levels of operation. Yet the analytical demands and decision implications differ distinctly from level to level, as we will now try to show.

2.1.1 Directors and System Integrity

Initially, we can see that Table 2.1 assigns an organization's directors and senior officers the responsibility for basic system integrity with the correlative assertion that many directorial-level decisions will involve effectively indeterminate problems. But the role of the director in modern organizations, whether industrial, commercial, or governmental, is rather ill-defined. So, before we attempt to define what is meant by system integrity and to set forth the implications of directorial decisions, we will spend a few words trying to identify directors *per se*.

A first element of confusion is that directors tend to emerge under different labels and in different organizational contexts. The term *director* is most specifically used to define an elected agent of a firm's stockholders, who is essentially their direct line to the operating management of a corporation with distributed shares. But even closed, private corporations have boards of directors, as do public enterprises. Universities, for example, have their boards of trustees and their governors, as do many hospitals, theater groups, and community systems (e.g., the board of education overseeing a local school system). Even distinctly governmental units have their boards of advisers or directors. These are often called commissioners, especially in the domain of regulatory agencies. In another level of government, there are the congressional committees that supposedly oversee the functions of certain executive agencies, such as the United States Postal Service or the Central Intelligence Agency.

Now again, the board is usually composed of a collection of agents from outside the organization. But, in many cases, the chief operating officers of the company or government agency are also members of the board, and thus they have directorial as well as line functions. In theory, the board of directors (or trustees, governors, commissioners, etc.) represents the point of highest authority within an organization. We can see immediately that it is the primary vehicle by which an organization interfaces with the world outside. In fact, the composition of boards is often deliberately designed to effect specific interactions. For example, a corporation might have a politician on its board or a representative of labor and consumer interests. A charitable organization might have a famous actor, athlete, or statesman to lend it popular legitimacy. A government agency might, in its right, try to give representation to elements of the community that the agency serves; this often extends to the point where regulatory agencies have directors who represent the industries to be regulated. In other cases, a social agency might seek representation from community leaders, the academic community, or others who have an ostensible interest in the proceedings of the organization.

Thus, the board of directors represents the theoretically highest point of authority for the organization. In this sense, we may suggest that the directors are responsible for the decisions that establish (or diminish) the basic integrity of the organization. The way they do this depends on the origin of the board's authority. Particularly, some board prerogatives are a matter of legislation. For example, an industrial or commercial corporation is required by law to have a board of directors to represent stockholder interests and to validate—if not effect—the more critical decisions of the firm. In the same way, community and state constitutions may demand that certain public agencies or enterprises have a board, and in some cases may set forth not only the board's ostensible decision prerogatives, but also its composition. For example, the hospital charter may demand that some percentage of the directors be locally practicing, locally licensed, medical doctors; the charter for a state university may demand that at least one member of the board be an attorney licensed to practice in the state. Thus, the functions and composition of the board may in part be determined external to the organization, and not available for manipulation. On the other hand, some organizations will have a board of directors not because of legislative requirements, but by convention. In such cases (as with a privately held corporation, an unlicensed charity, etc.), the board's prerogatives and composition are entirely within the scope of authority of operating management or the actual owners of enterprise (or their designated agents, as in the case of the executor of an estate or someone holding a legal proxy for the owners). The implication for members of the latter type of board is that they serve at the sufferance of operational management or ownership, and have no enforceable authority over organizational decisions unless specified in a private contract.

Thus, we must be primarily concerned with those directors that serve with legislative protection, and are members of boards with certain specified decision prerogatives. We will usually find that these prescribed responsibilities demand that the directors not only approve or veto certain actions initiated by operating management, but that they initiate certain actions themselves.

In general, these prescribed actions are often merely procedural. For example, the board may be required to initiate the search for an operating officer and to effect the actual appointment. In this sense, the board of directors may be the only authority allowed to contract for the employment of an organization's president or executive vice-president. In other cases, the chairman of the board of directors may be the chief operating authority of the company or agency, with the president serving in a subordinate role. The variations on the directorial theme are legion, as are the *de facto* roles they play (irrespective of any legislative requirements).

Getting back to the main theme, the integrity of an organization is in the hands of the formally constituted directors in one or both of two ways. First, because they have veto authority over commitments of operating management, the directors become the organizational court of last resort. In this, their authority is theoretically quite clear, and derives from the rhetorical principle of management that "one may delegate authority, but not responsibility." Therefore, the directors may allow operating management to make the decisions, but their veto authority (or the requirement for their accession to managerial decisions) places the ultimate responsibility on them. Now, the second aspect of the director's responsibility for the basic integrity of an organization stems from the basic structure of the board; in short, it evolves from the principle that "function follows structure." This is a more subtle reading of the situation, but an important one. As we suggested earlier, an organization's integrity concerns its place in the broader environment. But integrity has two dimensions.

First, there is the functional *viability* of the organization. Now, viability may be interpreted quite widely (and for our purposes here, a little ambiguity is tolerable), but essentially what we are talking about is the extent to which the organization is valued by the world outside. For an industrial concern, this means: (a) the utility of its products to consumers, and (b) the utility of its rate of return on investment to stockholders or other investors, either in terms of dividends or capital gains. In other words, in the industrial and commercial arena, viability refers to market and fiscal competitivity of the firm. In the domain of governmental or public enterprise, viability means something a little different. In this case, we are primarily concerned with the perceived utility of the functions that the agency or enterprise performs—in other words, how the broader community values the services, goods, and so on that the institution offers. In short, viability may be very much tied to efficiency in the industrial and commercial sector, whereas it is tied more to perceived effectiveness in the public domain. As an ancillary aspect of organizational viability—operable in both the industrial and public arenas—we suggest that the board, as the source of highest responsibility and authority, also take responsibility for the fundamental coherence of the organization. That is, the extent to which, when viewed from outside, the organization is seen to be differentiated from other entities in the environment— the extent to which it has a definite boundary and substance.

If viability is one aspect of system integrity, the other is the organization's *normativity*. That is, the directors are ultimately responsible for seeing that the organization's behavior aligns with the moral or axiological dictates of the broader community, or with any legislative restrictions on means that can be employed to achieve organizational objectives or to advance its own mission. Like viability, normativity has many meanings, the proper use of which depends on the particular context in which the organization operates. For an industrial concern, it may mean that the organization does not contradict the prevailing socioeconomic ethic in its operations, e.g., that it does not use slave labor, produce dangerous products, or engage in activities that might act to the detriment of the community (such as air pollution or political subornation). In other cases, the directors may have a distinctly fiduciary responsibility to the stockholders or other investors (e.g., bondholders, noteholders). This responsibility may be strictly interpreted or defined very broadly. For example, some directors or boards may be mandated merely to prevent such things as managerial abuses of funds, excessively liberal executive expense accounts, or private borrowing against pensions or sinking funds. Others, broader in interpretation, may believe that they are there to protect the rate of return of the stockholders and investors, even to the point of refusing management the right to retain earnings for reinvestment; that is, the directors may want earnings put into another more promising investment or distributed as dividends so that stockholders may decide the best investment for themselves. In such instances, the directors make the firm comply with the normative dictates of theoretical capitalism. And, of course, the directors are responsibile for seeing that the firm abides by any standing laws or regulations, a responsibility that is usually written into the charter of those boards having a legislative base.

The boards of directors (or commissioners, trustees, or governors) of such public enterprises as regulatory agencies, union trust funds, universities, hospitals, museums, and school systems share many of the responsibilities of their industrial and commercial counterparts. But rather than being accountable to a set of stockholders or investors, the director of a public enterprise is responsible directly to an unrestricted, at-large community. Again, their control over the normativity of the organization may take many guises. Some directors may feel responsible for the efficiency with which public funds are used, just as the private director was concerned about the rate of return on shareholder's investments. Others may have only *post facto* responsibility for the legality of means, such as the congressional committees charged with overseeing the military or intelligence communites. In other cases, again like certain of their industrial and commercial counterparts, directors of public enterprises may guard against abuses by operating management, elected officials, or other public functionaries (e.g., members of civilian review boards or trustees of a foundation).

The organizational principle that "structure follows function" lends an organization's directors the authorities that we have just outlined. Particularly, the structure of experience and perspective should be more diverse within the group of directors than within any group of operating personnel *per se*. Thus, the directors—given a broadly diverse composition—are theoretically best suited to handle matters of basic system integrity. Because directors are drawn from the outside world, they become its interpreters and therefore the primary link between present and future. Also, the diversity of background and perspective that should be present in a proper board supplies the essential ingredients for the resolution (often syncretic) of normative disputes—matters of morality, convention, or philosophical congruence. Moreover, because the issues of the organization's place in the outside world involve variables from many different sectors—social, political, economic, and humanistic—the director's breadth of perspective and depths of external experience presumably make their inputs and advice essential for matters of mission analysis and definition. In short, the board, acting in concert, would probably need *less additional information* to deal with issues of mission and goals than any other administrative body that might be organized within the normal organization.

There is another, even more pressing reason why the fundamental integrity of the organization should rest with the board: their presumed objectivity. In the broadest theoretical interpretation, not only does a board of directors serve the organization, but it also serves to protect the integrity of the basic socioeconomic or sociopolitical engines under which any society labors. Thus, the directors of an industrial or commercial organization must be viewed as agents of capitalist economics; the directors of public enterprise, in turn, become the agents of political democracy. Their loyalty is presumably Janus-faced, with one eye on the interests of the organization, and the other on the basic philosophical referents of the larger society. This contrasts with the presumably unilateral interests of other organization members, including those organizational officers who might happen to be board members.

This aspect of the directors' role is almost never made explicit, yet it is perhaps the key function they can perform. As the agent of theoretical capitalism, the director serves as the front-line defense for the welfare of the economic system as a whole. Specifically, his responsibility to the capitalist economy is to see that the organization he directs represents an effectively *zero-opportunity-cost* investment for shareholders. In short, if there is some other investment for stockholder funds that promises to yield a higher rate of return, then the funds the director manages should be moved to that investment. Thus, the informed, alert director is the central actor on the capitalist stage; to the extent that he is unwilling to make, or is incapable of making, opportunity-cost calculations, the welfare of the economy as a whole is imperiled. On the public dimension, as the agent for the citizen taxpayer, the director has a similar responsibility—to see that there is no other public function to which funds might be applied that would provide a higher aggregate *cost-benefit* ratio.* Unless the director of public organizations can make such calculations, then the health of the democratic system, at least in its fiscal and operational respects, is also in peril. Thus, the ultimate demand for directorial rationality extends all the way from the boardroom of an individual company, to the local school board, to the regulatory agency or government bureau, into the halls of congress itself.

We now have some idea of what the director of an organization should do. He acts as an agent for both the organization that has elected him and the external community he represents. (This community must ultimately be defined in terms of the basic units of society, the capitalist economy or the democratic politic.) But, as the reader might expect, many directors are poor agents indeed. For these theoretical implications of directorial responsibility are not always carried over into actual practice. One reason is that the normative aspects of the directorial function are not widely broadcast, for rhetorical management professors have been largely content to merely answer for what directors actually do and

---

*In the next chapter, we will see that cost-benefit calculations can be made, using rather innovative techniques, for organizations whose properties would appear to defy opportunity-cost calculations. This is especially important for the type of "service" organizations that predominate in the public sector.

avoid the issue of what they *should* be doing. Most of the available literature, with a few notable exceptions,[1] has confined itself to field interviews of "top" management and directors. Of course, the field interview is the lowest form of scholarship.* All that is gained is a sort of selective diary of directorial behavior. In many cases, these interview-based researches simply pander to the interviewees' own ideas of themselves and their functions; there may be no critical analysis at all by the author. In short, such exercises are mere reportage, and as close as academia comes to emulating the techniques of a gossip columnist. The serious scholar will react to these recitations of what is being done by asking, "Compared to what?" In other words, if there is no normative basis by which to judge an administrator's performance, then a mere recitation of what is being done cannot serve adequately as a source of scholarly information, nor as the basis for advancing functional education. But these field studies do tell us one thing: very rarely do we find a director performing the functions that theory would assign him.

Indeed, rather than acting as the alert, Janus-faced representatives of both organizational and societal interests, most directors draw their functional guidance from three disputable and essentially rhetorical "principles" of general management theory. To a great extent, top operating management also may adhere to these principles rather than to any normative theoretical bases for administrative behavior.

The first of these principles which tends to restrict directorial behavior, is one we have already mentioned: *one may delegate authority, but not responsibility*. Under this principle, a director may serve no function other than to provide a presence; he carries responsibility, but no authority. This situation is most typical of organizations that use the board of directors, not as decision-makers, but merely as sources of legitimacy. Many voluntary and social organizations are of this type, where the board is comprised of people whose reputations lend some semblance of substance, but who are neither required nor expected to take an active hand in administration. Of course, if there is ever any real question of responsibility for an error or impropriety, such directors are quick to reject their theoretical ultimate responsibility, and plead ignorance of the organization's operations.

The second principle of management, which allows directors the luxury of a position without real functional responsibilities, is: *management is a distillation of experience*. Under this precept, the director really becomes little more than a

---

*At least within the management sciences. Cultural anthropologists and other social scientists use field interviews to develop data bases, from which hypotheses *qua* generalizations are induced. We would have few objections were cultural anthropologists to conduct field interviews of organizational "lore," but we do not find management theorists' reportage very interesting as an academic exercise.

quasi-canonized *consultant*. He is neither required nor expected to initiate any decisions; neither may he be said to be anything but theoretically responsible for the organization's integrity. He may plead legitimate ignorance of anything except the few projects in which he has been asked—or has elected—to participate. He normally expects to receive a retainer (a director's fee) for his presence, and, to the extent that this is nominal, so may be his participation. In short, he is there to make his experience available when he is called upon and to perhaps bring initiative to the organization. In other cases, he may represent some outside interest and in fact serve as *its* consultant. For example, the director may be a banker, who is on the board to protect the interests of a lending institution that holds the firm's stocks or bonds. The director acting as casual consultant is encountered frequently in government enterprise as well as in the corporate world. Indeed, the boards of many government bureaus, agencies, and offices are filled with retired business executives, ex-political hacks, and others for whom a directorship represents a sort of emeritus position, to be enjoyed but not really exercised. If their advice is made available at all, it may be with great reluctance and only infrequently.

The third disputable principle of management from which directors take their clue is: *management is getting things done through people*. Thus, the director may operate merely as a source of external influence, and not as an adviser or decision-maker. He may be chosen for his political or social contacts, not for any skills or functional contributions. He may be a local politician or an influence-peddling lawyer; he may be the underemployed scion of a wealthy family, or a relative of an influential businessman or public functionary; he may have a suspected influence among certain ethnic or religious groups. Directors of this genre thus become comprehensible as *lobbyists*. A disturbing variation on this theme is the "interlocking" directorates, which often operate as an unofficial network to evade antitrust restrictions or to defy *de facto* other aspects of proper capitalist behavior. In this sense, the director may act as the lobbyist for an emergent cartel and may deliberately disserve the public interest. Many such directors are "professional," deriving all their income from being seated on the boards of many different corporations or public bodies. And, they have the advantage of not having to register as lobbyists.

Thus, although there is a most demanding set of theoretical functions for directors to perform, many directors are of no real administrative significance. Rather than exercising control over the viability and normativity of an organization, they are there to lend legitimacy, or they function as consultants or lobbyists only. In either case, they deny the theoretical dictate that finds them as the ultimate source of authority and responsibility. For whatever limited services they perform, they may be given a token fee, obtain some social status, or simply find a way to fill up idle time and give them a feeling of importance. But because they do not, as a rule, fill the administrative functions that are really theirs alone, society at large suffers. Most instances of corporate or governmental impropriety—where norms of either behavior or process are contravened—may be laid at the doorstep of the dilatory director. Moreover, many inefficient corporations or government operations—representing positive opportunity-cost entities or entities with unfavorable cost-benefit ratios—exist because of their directors' unwarranted tolerance or parochialism. But the most telling, troublesome aspect of the directors' dismissal of their administrative functions is that responsibility for an organization's integrity often passes into the hands of its operating executives. And this, as we will see, is not where it belongs.

2.1.2 The Strategic Decision Domain

We spent a relatively great amount of time on directorial decision-making because it is an area often ignored in decision and management literature. Moreover, being the superior decision domain, directorial functions serve to constrain (or make subordinate) decisions available at all other levels of enterprise. This successive closure of decision latitude is a critical feature of the complex organization, and perhaps its single most important structural aspect for the decision theorist.

We have already suggested, somewhat obliquely, exactly what this closure implies. Here we may be more explicit. Initially, a decision context may be defined in terms of the number of alternatives available, and the analytical tractability of the alternatives. These are really the variables that gave rise to our definitions of the problem categories in Figure 1.4. Now, for goal-setting decisions, as we have explained, there is virtually no constraint on the number of alternatives available. Because goals are future oriented—and because the future is the place where all constraints potentially disappear—the alternative goals available to an organization are virtually unlimited.

Moreover, because goals are concerned with defining the organization's place in the world outside, the goal alternatives may be very complex in their implications and in the number of factors to be considered in their formulation. That is, as we move out into the environment, and into the far future, both the number of goal alternatives and their inherent complexity expectedly begin to increase. For the future environment will, in most cases, be an effectively indeterminate "system" from the standpoint of the current generation of goal-setters.

We may now begin to think of the goal-setting function in different terms. Particularly, any proper goal formulation will set out some *destination* the organization wants to arrive at by some point-in-time. A destination is a dimensioned variable, and may be virtually anything—a particular market share, profit level, level of effectiveness, asset level, and so forth. Therefore, we look at goals in simple set terms,[2] with each goal being definable as a point on a goal "map" such as Figure 2.1.

Now, the area bounded by the rectangular perimeter represents what is called the *universe* of destinations (goals) available to the organization. That is, it holds all possible destinations the organization might choose to occupy. Thus, our universe set is a collection of simple Cartesian coordinates, a space-time grid, as it were. Now, were we to allow all *a priori* constraints to collapse, then any organization would theoretically be able to pick any set of coordinates from the entire universal set. The goal-setting problem, in this formulation, is thus to elect some particular pair of coordinates (s_i, t_j) representing the goal target existing at the conjunction of the ith spatial and j^{th} time units.

In actual practice, there may be *a priori* constraints at work that reduce the range of alternatives considered. These *a priori* constraints will generally take any of three forms (all or any one of which may be operative in any given directorial context):

(a) There may be *axiological* constraints at work, giving substance to any ideological, religious, and moralistic or ethical precepts the directors might hold. Such constraints might obviate certain missions for the organization, such as serving in the slave trade, distributing narcotics, running gambling operations, or manufacturing weapons.

(b) *Axiomatic* constraints may also be operative, having been derived from logical, philosophical, or theoretical apriorities. For example, a community organization whose directors believe in the value of individual self-reliance may bar the organization from participation in any type of welfare missions, or corporate directors committed to free enterprise may

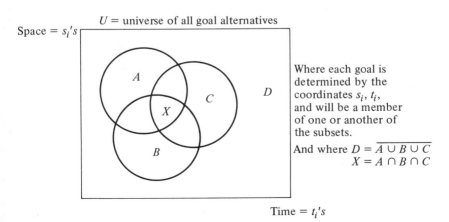

U = universe of all goal alternatives

Space = $s_i's$

Where each goal is determined by the coordinates s_i, t_i, and will be a member of one or another of the subsets.

And where $D = \overline{A \cup B \cup C}$
$X = A \cap B \cap C$

Time = $t_i's$

Figure 2.1. The goal map as a set formulation.

direct the organization away from any missions that might require government subsidy.

(c) Finally, there are *inertial* constraints. These would simply reflect the limitations of the directors' experience or the tendency of historical organizational properties to be retained. In this sense, inertial constraints reflect boundaries on the vision of the directors; they might, therefore, restrict them to considering goals that are simple evolutionary variations on current and past themes, and lead them to ignore radical or revolutionary alternatives.

Thus, from the entire universal set of goals theoretically available to the organization, there will emerge some feasible goal space that is confined by whatever of these three types of *a priori* constraints are operating. In Figure 2.1, the domain of axiologically acceptable goals is given as A. The area of axiomatically permissible goals is given as B. Finally, those goals that inertial constraints do not prohibit is represented by C.

Thus, the feasible search space from which possible organizational goals will be selected is the area X. We can see that X contains only those goals not proscribed by either axiological, axiomatic, or inertial apriorities. In short, X is the joint union of the several *a priori* subsets, calculated as $X = A \cap B \cap C$. The alternatives in D—the complement of $A \cup B \cup C$—are goals that are not permissible on any grounds, goals that would be outside the visionary range of the directors because of inertial constraints, and that would be nonnormative and contradictory to philosophical or theoretical principles. Thus, the *a priori* predictions of the directors eventually reduce the universe of possibilities to some permissible function, (X/U). The value of this fraction indicates the strength of the apriorities operating among the directors, or less charitably, it reflects their degree of preconceptual closure (their prejudices, biases, or lack of imagination). Nevertheless, we expect that, were other members of the organization responsible for goal-setting, the ratio of X to U would be even smaller, reflecting the expectedly greater parochialism of executives, managers, and the like. Thus, it is the broad-based composition of the board—the presence of different backgrounds, interests, and perspectives operating in concert—that gives the directors the expected advantage of considering more goal alternatives than would a committee with less diversity, such as one drawn exclusively from a firm's operating executives, who might be expected to be quite homogenous in vision, values, and philosophy.

We should, however, be aware of a significant qualification. Although the successive closure of the goal search space is necessary if an organization is to have any actionable direction or purposiveness, there are rational and irrational ways to effect the closure. The least satisfactory process is to partition the search space using only experiential or axiological (i.e., affective) predicates. Such a closure is accomplished primarily through the use of unvalidated opinion or preselection, and would hardly represent a proper scientific procedure. Later, we will see that a disciplined procedure is available for partitioning the goal space—the heuristic analytical modality—which sets the entire decision-making process into a formalized "learning" process. For the moment, it is enough to suggest that the process by which some $(X \subseteq U)$ is generated is the critical factor determining the *quality* of the goal-setter's performance. That is, we must be able to determine whether a particular X is the objectively best set a group of goal-setters could have found, a problem we reserve for the next chapter.

The residual responsibility of the directors is to select a specific goal (or destination) from the alternatives included in the set X. Again, this selection process may be performed either scientifically or casually. But what concerns us here is the nature of the definition of the goal that is finally selected. This is a subtle but critical point. For the precision of the definition of the organizational destination may vary widely, and so then will its implications for the strategic analysts who must seek to obtain it. In general, we must consider that there are two possible generic types of goal definitions. First is what we will call the *point* definition. This type of definition, in the time-space formulation we are using, will yield a very specific set of coordinates. In fact, it will give us a target in terms of a specific element of the set X, which is $(x_i, j \in X)$. A point goal may be to capture a 50 percent share of the widget market by the end of fiscal year 1980. Note that the destination is effectively deterministic; there is one single point on the time-space grid that will satisfy the conditions of the goal. There is no ambiguity, and there is no element of judgment required to determine whether the goal has been reached in the specified time frame. In short, the goal is either achieved, or not. We must also consider the *neighborhood* goal. This envisions a contiguous collection of points on the space-time grid, rather than any specific point. That is, within a neighborhood, there may be many specific point goals, any one of which would result in the director's goal having been obtained. Our destination here is thus a region rather than a point *per se*. We can easily transform the preceding point goal into a neighborhood goal. Instead of asking for a 50 percent share of the widget market by end of fiscal year 1980, the directors might ask that the organization merely have the largest share of the market. Thus, there might be many alternative market shares that fit the bill— all those in fact that are larger than any competitor's market share. Thus, the specific market share that would realize this goal is now a variable, contingent on the value obtained by other firms in the widget industry. The time coordinate may also be manipulated to result in a neighborhood goal. For example, instead of setting the end of 1980 as the requisite time coordinate, the directors might specify that the 50 percent market share be achieved sometime within the decade.

The neighborhood goal may also be defined so that both the space and time coordinates are variables; e.g., the organization should have the greatest share of the widget market sometime during the 1980s. Here, then, many possible pairs of space-time coordinates exist that, if arrived at, would satisfy the directors' goal. Finally, the neighborhood formulation is as legitimate as the point formulation, for the criteria for its achievements are clear and unambiguous.

The point and neighborhood goal formulations are really the only legitimate forms that directors should advance. Contrasted with those are the *rhetorical* goals; in administrative practice, these may often appear more frequently than their legitimate counterparts. Rhetorical goals come in essentially two forms. First is the *infeasible* goal, one which the directors have established but which is incapable of being achieved. For example, suppose that a government executive has formulated the following goal: to achieve a national unemployment rate that is less than 3 percent, in company with an inflation rate that does not exceed 3.5 percent, by Election Day, 1980. Like all rhetorical goals, this sounds good, but when mapped might result in a situation such as illustrated in Figure 2.2.

In actual practice, we would probably have to use some sort of topological construct (or at least a three-dimensional "map"), as time is an implicit factor of the goal set. But in this formulation, consider the set A to contain all values for inflation that are lower than 3.5 percent, while assuming the set B to contain all values for unemployment less than 3 percent. Now, we can see that the goal is effectively incapable of being achieved, for *the intersection between these two sets is empty* ... $A \cap B = 0$. The implication is that the two variables, inflation and unemployment, are inversely related. That is, unemployment can only be reduced at the expense of increases in inflation, and vice versa. This, of course, merely reflects the theoretical implications of the Phillip's curve, which suggests that we cannot expect unemployment and inflation to move together (although

Inflation Levels

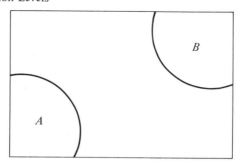

Unemployment Levels

Figure 2.2. Contradictory goal set.

recent events suggest that they can indeed move upward together, as in the United States there is currently both relatively high inflation and unemployment). The point is, however, that rhetorical goals may often prescribe contradictory conditions, and therefore set the organization on the path to a destination that does not exist.

The second type of rhetorical goal is what might be called the *unactionable* formulation. Such goals, which are common, demonstrate what happens when a director fails to do a proper job. As an example, take the case of the widget manufacturer and translate the proper point and neighborhood goals into the following rhetorical formulation: *the goal of this organization is to give the consumer the best possible widget at the lowest possible price.* As is usually the case with rhetorical goals, this sounds good, but it gives no real qualitative direction to those executives who will be responsible for trying to achieve the goal. For, as stated, virtually all possible price-quality combinations could be used to satisfy the goal, depending on the qualifications advanced. So someone must introduce some constraining assumptions (of a normative nature) before work to achieve the goal can begin—we will have to give either quality or price a preferential position. In short, unactionable goals raise value issues that must be resolved before work can begin. And it is the operating executives—or the strategic analysts—who must try to resolve these issues, even though normative analyses are not really their proper province.

Particularly, the strategists would have to try to second-guess the director's value preferences. Would the directors be happy if we made price the superior factor and produced low-cost junk? If we set such a high-quality criterion that the "lowest possible price" was still exorbitant? Clearly, the executives must now try to do the director's job, for some normative preferences (for quality or price) have to be specified. As the reader may see, quality products and cheap products may be members of *qualitatively different sets*. Certainly, the directors will have *a priori* constraints that would tend to restrict the extremes of these two sets from serious consideration, but they left them unexplicated. They would probably not want the firm to produce a widget of such great quality that only a very few buyers would be able to afford it, nor would they want it to produce extremely cheap widgets that failed the first time they were used. But from the standpoint of the executives asked to reach this goal, all possible combinations could be set to fall within the latitude provided by the goal statement, and each alternative could be defended rhetorically.

To continue with this illustration, suppose we were now to convert the unactionable rhetorical goal into a proper formulation such as: *the organization is to undertake to produce widgets that will yield the maximum profit contribution during the following fiscal interval.* The organization's goal is now explicit, unqualified, and measurable. The operating executives have thus been

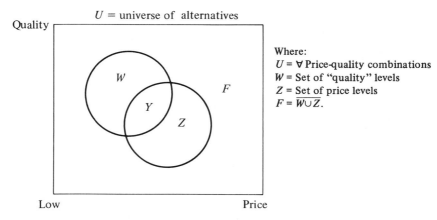

Figure 2.3. Goal set for a trade-off problem.

excused from the responsibility of making value judgments. They may now evaluate the various price-quality alternatives, not in terms of the imagined preferences of the directors (or by imputing values to them), but on the basis of an absolute criterion such as profit maximization.*

We can employ our simple set formulations to further clarify the difference between actionable and unactionable goal formulations. Consider Figure 2.3. We have altered the coordinates in the figure to read "quality and price" instead of "time and space." In this case, then, the universal set represents all possible combinations of price and quality. Now, under the rhetorical goal, every point in U would be defensible as a solution (e.g., every point in U is a feasible destination for the organization, given the ambiguity of the rhetorical goal statement).

However, when we change the goal to one of finding a combination of price and quality that will maximize profits, two things happen. First, the extremes of quality or price become improbable as feasible solution points; some extreme combinations (e.g., those in F) will have been effectively eliminated. Therefore, the sets W and Z now contain only moderate positions; extremely high and low qualities may be ignored, as are the extremely high and low prices. Now, as so often happens with tradeoff problems, the optimal solution (i.e., the point of maximum profit) will most likely be found in the neighborhood of the intersection between the two qualitatively different sets . . . in $Y = W \cap Z$. This suggests that the executives should *start* their search for the optimum combina-

---

*Of course, the criterion of profit maximization—or any absolute criterion—is "operational" only to the extent that decision-makers or analysts are willing and able to effect it. In many cases, we will have to be content with more loosely structured criteria, such as "effective optimality," which at least poses optimality (rather than sufficiency) as a target, even if it does not presume its attainment.

tion in Y. If the point of optimal price-quality trade-off were not found there, then the search space would be expanded.* Potentially, every point in W and Z is available for inspection. But at least the executives will know when they have obtained the directors' goal, for the criterion of profit maximization is unambiguous and amenable to precise measurement. Thus, the executives may go directly to work in the face of disciplined goal formulations, without having to try to second-guess the directors' value preferences. Hence, the "actionability" of proper point and neighborhood goals.

We can extend the relationship between goal-setting and strategic analysis into another context, where two principles of action or constraints are in apparent conflict. This conflict may threaten to close the goal space altogether and deny the organization any strategic option. But certain techniques of strategic (qualitative) analysis may be exercised, which can sometimes solve such problems. For example, suppose we are a firm in the energy industry that has developed a set of nuclear products. We may be faced with two conflicting *a priori* predicates:

(a) On the one hand, the principles of economics would demand that we give substance to the concepts of comparative advantage and the laws of microeconomics. Particularly, we should seek to expand our market as greatly as possible, within the production range where marginal costs do not exceed marginal revenues.

(b) But, it is also clear that exporting nuclear technology is perilous, because by-products of nuclear energy production may be used to develop military weapons, an undesirable consequence.

Now, neither of these *a priori* predicates may be neglected. Therefore, we have to develop a goal map—a set formulation—which might have the properties shown in Figure 2.4.

This goal map—comprising successively more confined subsets—may be thought to represent a situation where we are going to try to fix a best compromise between the two conflicting constraint sets, the first set representing an economic *prescription*, the second comprising a common-sense *proscription*. We may now think of a goal formulated as follows: *to maximize profits from sales of nuclear technologies, subject to the constraint that a situation of reasonable risk is not exceeded*. With this goal, the strategic analysts can go to work defining certain qualitative classes (or subsets), which will permit the goal to be realized. The qualitative classes they develop might be the following:

U = universal set of all nations

*The preferred formulation would be to develop a three-dimensional search space, using price, quality, and profits as coordinates; in this case, we would search over a *surface* for the optimal combinations. That is, in a trade-off formulation, there may be more than one optimal solution when we neglect preference operators (e.g., a preference operator might give priority here to either price or quality for strategic reasons).

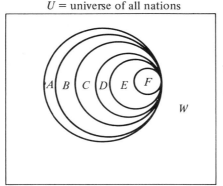

U = universe of all nations

Where: $F \subseteq E \subseteq D \subseteq C$, etc.

And: $W = \overline{A}$,
$U = W \cup A$.

Figure 2.4. The subset goal map.

A = subset of all nations exhibiting some level of effective demand for nuclear technology

B = subset of all nations who have *not refused* to sign a pact prohibiting the transformation of domestic nuclear technology into military technology

C = subset of all nations who *have signed* a guarantee against such a transformation

D = subset of all nations who have a history of friendly relations with the United States or its allies

E = subset of all nations who have existing treaty obligations to the United States

F = subset of all nations who already have a nuclear military capability.

Essentially, we have defined five different classes of nuclear consumer (subsets B through F). The implication is that each successive subset represents a situation of effectively lower risk. But we are operating within the range of qualitative analysis, as the problem at hand is actually severely stochastic.

We can see immediately why this is so. Suppose that our goal was merely to maximize sales (without the constraint of reasonable risk). In this case, the only relevant subset would be A—the nations that merely exhibit an effective demand for our nuclear exports. Now, given the lack of discrimination inherent in A, any sale could be expected to have one of three qualitatively different outcomes:

(x) The exports could be used only as intended, for the generation of peaceful nuclear services.

(y) The exports could be transformed into a military potential (e.g., the atomic by-products used to develop nuclear weapons).

(z) The nuclear exports could be reexported by the immediate purchaser to some third-party nations, where either x or y could occur.

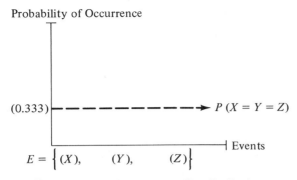

Figure 2.5. Initial event probability distribution.

Now, were only set A available to us, then we might initially suggest that the probability distribution for these three events might look like that shown in Figure 2.5. This figure implies that, with no differentiating *a priori* information available, each of the three alternatives (qualitatively different events) may be assumed to have a more or less equal probability of occurrence; hence, the perfectly horizontal probability curve at 0.333.*

Now the purpose of developing the various subsets (B through F) is that each successive subset presumably represents a situation where the probabilities more and more favor event x as opposed to events y or z. Thus, the qualitative discipline brought to this problem by the strategic analysts (resulting in the partitioned space shown as Figure 2.4) would promote a transformation of the probability distribution's configuration as shown in Figure 2.6.

Obviously, Figure 2.6b represents a case of considerably less risk than does Figure 2.6a. In the former, the probability of event x rises considerably relative to the probabilities of the two less favorable qualitative alternatives. Thus, in our original problem, the sales executives (or strategic decision-makers) might now elect to set some qualitative limit beyond which risk will not be tolerated. For example, they may proscribe exports to any nation that is not a member of at least subset C. Thus, we have set a qualitative value for the goal constraint of "reasonable risk" and have thus performed the strategic analysis portion of the nuclear export problem. For each subset may now be thought to take on some qualitative (i.e., "fuzzy") value. For example, we might let A be the category of *extreme* risk, ultimating at subset F, which might be classified as *negligible* risk. At any rate, the problem can now be passed to the level of tactical analysis, and we will later see what would be involved in such a transfer.

There is a final generic situation with which we will be concerned, one that

---

*Actually, we have three discrete events, so we would use a frequency distribution here; but, for explanatory purposes, we have imposed a continuous distribution.

Probability of Occurrence

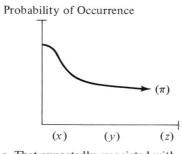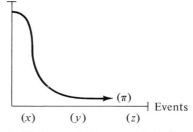

a. That expectedly associated with subset B.

b. That expectedly associated with subset E.

Figure 2.6. Discriminate event probability distribution.

will allow us to make the relationships among goal-setting, strategic decision-making, and tactical decision-making quite specific indeed. This is the case where an organization may be required to balance out two effectively opposite interests. Consider a local school board, which must simultaneously represent the interests of both students and taxpayers, interests that may dictate opposite strategies. If the board sides excessively with the taxpayers' interests, it may act to minimize expenditures per student in an effort to reduce the tax burden; if the board considers the students' interests as paramount, it may act to maximize expenditures per student, irrespective of tax-rate implications. Now, this situation gives rise to a special set formulation, as given in Figure 2.7.

The universal set represents all possible trade-off solutions. Those that would be most probable, were student interests to take complete precedence, would be found in the upper right-hand area of the map. Were taxpayer welfare to be maximized (presumably by minimizing the tax burden), resolutions in the lower

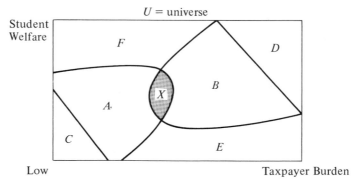

Figure 2.7. Strategic map formulation.

left-hand area would become most probable. However, there may be constraints that serve in practice to make solutions in either of these extreme ranges immediately infeasible. For example, solutions in C may be proscribed by law or other conventions. There may be some statewide *per capita* expenditure level below which local school districts cannot fall. By the same token, solutions in D may be proscribed because the resultant tax burden would be so high that it would be expected to result in a taxpayer revolt (e.g., rejection of bond issues). Or, certain types of strategic constraints might be postulated to remove these extreme positions from consideration. The solutions in C may be disregarded because the resultant quality of education would be so low that it would ultimately disserve the community. Solutions in D may be deleted because they would so drain the resources of the community that future employment opportunities for graduates would be imperiled, the ability of parents to provide proper homes would be jeopardized, and so on. Therefore, the domain of feasible solutions is reduced, and the actual trade-off between effect and cost should be sought in the region defined by $U - D \cup C$. Within this still broad region, the optimal trade-off will most likely be found in the neighborhood of the center of the map, particularly in the area X (where $X = A \cap B$). Again, the search for an actual operating solution (presumably to be undertaken by operating executives of the system rather than the board members *per se*) would best begin in this region. If the optimal point is not found there, then the search should be expanded into areas A and B. Moreover, the search pattern should probably follow the fan-shaped curves we have drawn there, as this would be the topological trajectory of the expected greatest sensitivity—with the expected optimality of a solution being positively related to its proximity to begin X. In short, we have symmetrically partitioned the universe of solutions into several spaces, each carrying different qualitative implications:

- Spaces C and D are *infeasible*.
- Spaces F and E are *improbable*.
- Spaces A and B are *probable*.
- Space X is the region of highest *a priori* probability (and is therefore our first target area for strategic analysis).

Now, this example serves as good indication of what we have meant by *strategic analysis*. Note that the net effect of the partitioning of the goal map was to produce several distinct qualitative sets. Now, let us suppose that no funds were available to pursue the issue any further than we have taken it. This would mean that the executives of the school system (perhaps including the superintendent) would be rational if they accepted virtually any point in X as the per-student-expenditure level for the coming fiscal year. Note that the school board merely passed on a goal, a demand that some optimal trade-off be found between student welfare and taxpayer burdens. The strategic analysts then defined the several different qualitative spaces on the universe of alternatives (infeasible, improbable, etc.) Thus, were they required to stop the analysis process here—before it passed the tactical analysts—then any point in the set assigned the quality of "highest *a priori* probability" would be more likely to be favorable with respect to the goal than any point in any other subset. In short, strategic analysts would make their decision based on qualitative information and would select among alternatives partitioned into qualitatively different sets. Thus, once again, we see the correlation between strategic decision-making and severely stochastic problems.

Now, the optimal point may or may not actually reside in X. Note that the strategic decision-makers merely considered X to be the most *probable* location for the optimal trade-off point. But it might exist elsewhere, and therefore there is a probability that the strategic decision-makers would suffer a serious error were they to decide on an expenditure level simply on the basis of their qualitative analysis.

This probability of error would result from the type of strategic analysis that might have gone into the goal-set partitioning they accomplished. Without going into great detail, their partitioning could have been accomplished by any of three means. First, they might have used simple contextual cause-effect analysis, trying to "read" the effects that would result from any particular student-expenditure level they fixed. This is usually the most expedient from of strategic analysis, and probably the most popular, but it subverts the goal the directors (or, in this case, the board of education) set. For the "strategic" aspect of this casual analytical process involves determining what would be the likely recriminations or outcomes from one or another choice to the decision-maker himself. Were taxpayer interests significantly more powerful than student interests, then region A would have been expected to be the primary choice. On the other hand, if student and parent interests were vocal and powerful, then the strategic decision may have been to pick a point in B. Thus, we presume that the final strategic decision-makers had three qualitatively different alternatives from which to select:

(a) Set a high expenditure (in B) and run the risk of irritating taxpayers.
(b) Set an expenditure level in A, and risk incurring the wrath of parents, teachers, students, etc.
(c) Set an expenditure level in X, and thus be able to play off the anger of one side against the other.

In settling on X, our particular strategic decision-makers selected the alternative that promised them the least grief. Thus, the probable rectitude of their decision in terms of the original goal formulation (maximize cost-effectiveness of the educational system) was less important than the possible repercussions to themselves. In short, this is a case where the strategic decision-maker becomes the key unit of analysis in the decision-making process. As such, there may be only a slight probability that the strategy actually evolved would meet the goal of optimality. As we will see in the next chapter, this type of decision process is very common when no mechanism for accountability is in force.

A second highly generalized approach to strategic analysis falls within the realm of directed logic. There are many different logics one might use, some highly specialized (e.g., Boolean logic or any of the formal praxeological forms). But, to generalize, the directed logic is the exercise of axiomatic reasoning, a deductive form. This may involve using some ideological referent as a source of principles or suggestions, or may simply mean that the individuals in question are adopting particular theoretical premises borrowed from some science. Or, it may simply mean that the strategic decision-makers are working within the framework of common logic. In the present case, they might evolve (or borrow) an axiom such as the following: when two antithetical positions are to be resolved toward an optimal tradeoff, then the most probable point may be expected to rest somewhere in the neighborhood of the perfect compromise, i.e., at the point where each of the competing interests is half-served. In our example, assuming that the two axes of our goal map (Figure 2.4) were more or less symmetrical, then that point would be expected to appear somewhere near the middle of the figure (somewhere in X). In this case, the strategic decision-makers used a logical principle to direct their decision. Of course, like many pseudo-axiomatic formulations, there is some probability that it is wrong. But the focus here was directly toward the goal itself—toward the optimal solution. A a general rule then, one option open to strategic decision-makers is to search the literature or their own logic for theoretical or philosophical principles that might be applied to the situation at hand. In short, they are operating deductively, trying to find some way of reasoning from a generalization to a particular case.

The third alternative procedure open to the strategic analyst is a special form of generalization. While theoretical and philosophical principles may have no grounding in the real world, there are certain generalizations that have distinctly empirical roots. These, for example, would be laws or rules that have been evolved from observation of real-world phenomena—results of observation, experimentation, and measurement. The question is not whether such generalizations are valid (as is always the question with any purely logical or theoretical construct), but whether the situation at hand is one in which the generalizations may apply. This is obviously a critical point, for the generalizations we are talking about are ultimately inductive formulations. What this means is that some scientists observed a set of phenomena and noted their characteristics. Later, when a sufficient number of such specific phenomena had been observed, and where significant similarities were noted, they have the basis for inducing a scientific classification. What gives a classification its significance for us are certain rules or laws of behavior that can be arrived at, which will summarize characteristics of the case as a whole. But the point is that these laws or rules were induced; that is, they were arrived at by leaping from the particular to the general. Moreover, there is usually some numerical probability of accuracy that can be assigned induced generalizations, perhaps based on the size of sample or on the variance of the characteristics observed. The problem for one now attempting to use such generalizations or rules is to decide if the context in which he is working is sufficiently similar to the context in which the original observations were made; in effect, does the subject at hand belong to the classification for which the rule or law was developed?

Later, we will have more to say about inductive and deductive analytical processes. Here, however, we can give an indication of how an inductive discipline might have been brought to the problem at hand. Particularly, measurements of the growth and decline of many populations—based on observations taken on those populations—have shown a very specific type of relationship with respect to nutritional input. In effect, from generations of empirical observations, scientists were able to induce what might be called the generic production function, a formulation appropriate to a large range of problems where we are concerned about input-output relationships. Figure 2.8 illustrates what the generic production looks like when graphed.

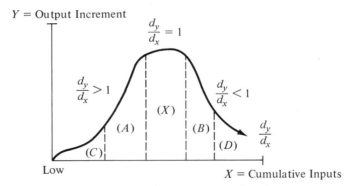

Figure 2.8. The generic production function.

An example that I have often used to explain the implications of the generic production function follows. Suppose that we are trying to operate a very large aquarium, where we are breeding a certain species of fish. Suppose we now take some quantum of food—an initially small amount—and sprinkle it on the water. Now, to the extent that the surface of the aquarium is large, and the population of fish small, it is possible to conceive of a situation where the fish would be un-

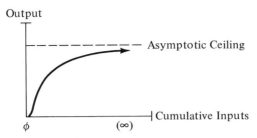

Figure 2.9. Natural growth curve.

likely to find the food; that is, the probability of an intersection between a fish and a particle of food becomes improbable due to the scarcity of the latter. This, in a sense, is the interpretation of space *A*: we have not yet injected sufficient food to cause any change in the growth of the fish. Now, as we add more food (i.e., enter the domain of *A*) we have passed the critical threshold and the fish begin to grow at an accelerated rate relative to the input of food. Eventually, when even more food has been added, the growth of the fish becomes proportional to the food input; their change in weight, for example, is roughly equal to the weight of the nutrients supplied. Beyond this point, we reach the domain of diminishing marginal returns, the point where there is more food available than the fish can eat. Thus, relative to the cumulative food stock, we are getting proportionally less effectiveness, as some of the food is wasted. In short, the generic production function is a derivative of the natural growth curve, which eventually reaches an asymptote despite the increase in the cumulative investment of resources (input), as in Figure 2.9.

The curve presumes to reflect the behavior of some outputs (Y) given an input (X). In the growth curve configuration, there are basically four qualitatively distinct areas:

C = area where the initial response of Y to X is slow because some threshold value has to be reached before output will begin to be affected.

A = area where output (Y) accelerates with incremental input, e.g., $dx/dy > 1$.

X = area where output (Y) begins to become proportional with respect to input, and eventually reaches the point where each increment of X results in an equal increment of output, e.g., $dx/dy = 1$.

D = area where diminishing marginal returns set in, so that each incremental unit of input (X) results in an incremental output that is less than the previous increment, e.g., $dx/dy < 1$. [B] is the area where this reduction in marginal productivity begins to accelerate, and is therefore a transitional interval.

As suggested, this formulation is widely known, and might have been applied to the strategic analysis exercise at hand. For example, X could be equal to expenditures on education, while Y = educational effectiveness. Thus, we might find area D in our goal map (Figure 2.4) corresponding to area D in Figure 2.9, which is the area of diminishing marginal returns. Possible alternatives in this area could then be eliminated on the probability that they represent instances where expenditures will result in lower than optimal marginal effectiveness.

By the same token, area A on our goal map would correspond with area A on our growth curve, indicating that increased input (student expenditures) will result in proportionally greater increases in education (student welfare). Therefore, points in A would be suboptimal, for increased expenditures would be expected to be marginally more productive. Therefore, any point in A would represent a case of underexpenditure, just as points in D would be instances of overexpenditure. As for area C, points here would be eliminated because we are still in the preacceleration stage; we still have not reached the point of "critical mass." Therefore, to stop at any point in C would be a waste of resources.

What is left for consideration then is the area X on both the growth curve and the goal map. The interpretation of the growth curve is that X would be the area where expenditures should remain. Increasing them would take us into the area of diminishing returns; leaving them in A or C would mean that we have ignored an opportunity to increase the effectiveness of our resources. In short, the point of optimal cost-benefit would rest somewhere in X, particularly in the neighborhood of the point where $dx/dy = 1$. For those familiar with economics, this is the point where marginal revenue equals marginal cost, and hence defines the optimal scale of plant, production, or process.[3] Were our strategic decision-makers familiar with either the natural growth curve or the principles of microeconomics, then their decision to mark X as the preferred area would be an example of the use to which inductive generalizations (laws, principles) may be put. And they would in this sense directly attempt to achieve the goal set by the board of education.

We may now continue with this example, taking it into the domain of tactical analysis. In the process, we hope to see even more clearly the point at which executive responsibility and strategic decision-making become transformed into proper tactical functions.

2.1.3 The Tactical Decision Domain

In transferring from the strategic to the tactical problem-solving domain, two things will normally occur:

(a) The problem formulation will be removed from severe stochasticity and become an exercise in moderate stochasticity.

(b) The subjective (logical, judgmental) data associated with essentially deductive strategic exercises will be replaced by objective (empirical) data.

The second of these events will not fully concern us until the next chapter, but the first is a proper subject for immediate discussion. We may use two examples from our previous section to guide our inquiry—the nuclear export case and the school-board problem.

Let us continue first with the school-board problem. Coming out of the strategic analysis process, we were left with a partitioned space of expenditure alternatives, with the suggestion that the search for an optimum point should begin in space X. Now, it is the job of the tactical analysts to zero in on that optimum and to decide its implementation. In short, just as at the strategic level, there are *both* analytical and decision implications. However, the feasible space over which the tacticians must search has been well-bounded by the strategic decision-makers. The delineation of space X as most favorable and the implication that spaces A and B would be next in order represent what some writers may refer to as *policy constraints*.[4] In effect, the problem has been reduced to a moderately stochastic one for, in the normal course of events, all the alternatives to be evaluated by the tacticians will be members of a single qualitative set, set X. If the solution is not found there, then the search will shift to another well-bounded set such as A or B.

In practice, the tactical analysts will now be responsible for finding that particular point in X that satisfies the requirement that it be the optimal cost-effectiveness solution. This is the point where, following the logic of Figure 2.8, the value of dy/dx (the relationship between dollar input and educational benefits) approaches unity. When this occurs, the tactical analysts will know they are in the neighborhood of the optimal solution. In most cases, a neighborhood solution is reasonable, for seldom would the analyst expect to find a point that emerged as the optimum with no probability of error. Thus, the school-board issue cannot be treated as deterministic, but will likely remain as moderately stochastic, where any solution holds some probability of being suboptimal. Obviously, the tactical analysts will try to minimize this probability (consistent with the time, talent, and analytical resources available).

In short, similar to the example in Figure 2.4, we will probably emerge from the tactical analysis with a configuration such as that in Figure 2.10. In this case, $\bar{p}$ will be the best statistical estimate of the true optimum, which of course may remain forever beyond our knowledge. And the assuredness with which we advance $\bar{p}$ as a decision premise (to be enacted as the actual expenditure level) will depend largely on the configuration of the resultant probability distribution, a point we will defend in great detail in Chapter 4. Were the tactical analysts to present $\bar{p}$ as just a single value, without an index of probability, then the problem would have been solved as a deterministic one, implying that none

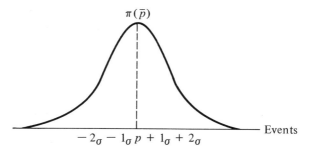

Figure 2.10. Range output from a moderately stochastic analysis process.

of the calculations of the tactical analysts could contain an error. Obviously, where we must deal with complex cost and benefit variables, such faith in one's rectitude would be sorely misplaced. Thus, the moderately stochastic formulation is the preferable alternative, and involves the pursuit of an *approximate* rather than a point solution.

Two substantive problems immediately face the tactical decision-makers *qua* analysts. Initially, they must select a particular search algorithm. Second, they must decide issues of evidence. There are, of course, many different search patterns that might be followed in trying to find an effective optimum in some bounded space. There are some deterministic techniques where the optimum point is found analytically (as with linear programming formulations). But the very special requirements for most analytic methods restrict them to treating inherently deterministic problems; thus, analytical solutions are seldom available to us above the operation levels of organizations.* Rather, we must wander through the feasible search space and hope that, through some disciplined route of travel, we eventually strike the neighborhood of the optimum.

In the case at hand, two simple search algorithms immediately present themselves as candidates. In this regard, let us reproduce the relevant portions of Figure 2.7 and superimpose a search pattern.[5] Figure 2.11 illustrates a case where we expect the optimum point to be found most efficiently by moving gradually outward from X along *hyperbolic* trajectories. The exact logic for this search pattern involves knowledge of a particular type of configuration (the hyperbolic paraboloid) and its properties as a type of quadratic.[6] For our purposes, we suggest that we might use the hyperbolic form because we expect that if the optimum is not found in X, then it will more likely be found in A or B than in either E or F. To clarify this point, consider Figure 2.12 where we employ a different kind of partitioning logic. Here, the sets themselves have been

*See Section 4.1.

$$W \subseteq U (= U - C \cup D)$$

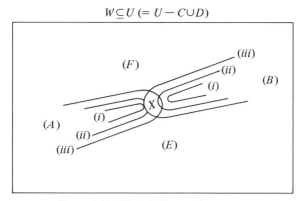

Figure 2.11. Hyperbolic search pattern.

defined in terms of circular rather than hyperbolic configuration; the search pattern is also circular. However, this pattern is expected to be less productive than the hyperbolic, for our analysis of the generic trade-off problem would suggest that the optimal solution would lie somewhere close to the main diagonal of the search space, as shown in Figure 2.13. From this figure we can see that the hyperbolic search pattern causes us to spend more time in the vicinity of the major diagonal (the expectedly most sensitive area) than does the centripetal pattern, which for each iteration takes us out into the neighborhoods of E and F where the optimal point is not at all likely to reside. Thus, the hyperbolic pattern is likely to be more favorable than the circular, because it should lead us to strike the optimum neighborhood more quickly (i.e., with fewer iterations of the search process). Of course, certain arguments may be raised about these

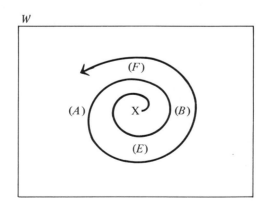

Figure 2.12. Centripetal search pattern.

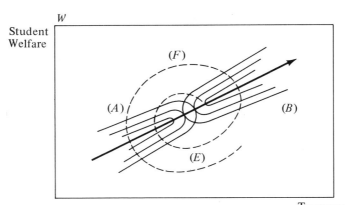

Figure 2.13. Pattern comparison.

assumptions, but we hope that we have indicated something of the nature of the search-pattern selection that tactical analysts go through.

As for evidence, there is not too much we can say at this point in our study. We do know that the tactical analysts, following their expectedly empirical preferences, will try to employ "hard facts" wherever possible. And we can see immediately the issue that faces them, distinguishing their efforts from those of the strategic analysts. For the strategic analysts made an assumption about the *direction of influence* between two critical variables of this problem. Their *a priori* assumption was that the level of student welfare could be positively related to the level of expenditures. Now, it is not the tactician's place to question this assumption, because it is a judgment that the executive level passes on as a constraint to the managerial level. Rather, the tactician calculates the *magnitude* of the relations between student welfare and expenditure levels. Whereas the strategic analysts worked with conceptual constructs (qualitative variables), the tactical analysts will now work with numbers, i.e., quantities.

In particular, they are going to try to measure the incremental increase in expenditure, until they have found the point where the marginal effectiveness of the next incremental increase begins to decline. In short, they will evaluate dy/dx for each value of x contained in space X. The evidence requirements would thus find them going into the real world to try to measure, for instance, the real effect of having better textbooks or laboratory equipment, or more salubrious (and presumably more expensive) classrooms. Such data would then lead to the numerical values for the various dy/dx alternatives, and the data driving the calculations are empirical—derived from observation, measurement, and manipulation. This is consistent with the moderately stochastic framework within which the tactical analyst/decision-maker works.

In summary, the probability of error associated with any expenditure level selected under the tactical decision-making process should be lower than that which would have been realized had the decision been made at the strategic level. Recall that if the strategic decision-makers were required to pick an expenditure level, their logic would have led them to any point in X. But, even granting that X does contain the optimum, we know that not every point in X will be as good as every other, for the space X (although well-bounded) would still contain a relatively large population of points, all but one of which would be suboptimal to some degree.* Therefore, by taking the problem down to the level where we are establishing the magnitude of cost-effect relationships, we can expect to arrive at a solution that is closer to the true optimum than were we to simply throw a dart at X and select whatever point we hit. Of course, it is always possible that, for any given situation, the dart might hit the true optimum. But the odds of this are extremely limited, proportional in fact to the number of points in X. Moreover, if such a decision were made periodically, the dart-throwing exercise could not really be expected to work again. Therefore, over the long run—involving any iterations of the expenditure decision— the aggregate probability of accuracy distinctly favors the disciplined tactical approach, and would argue against making the decision with only qualitative information at our disposal—at the strategic level. Thus, although there is still a probability that the tacticians will arrive at a suboptimal solution, their "neighborhood" will be much narrower and more promising than the broader neighborhood (the entire space X) that was available to the strategic decision-makers.

This same concept will repeat itself when we briefly examine the second of cases with which we have been working, the nuclear export problem. At the strategic level, we partitioned all possible purchasers for our technologies into several different subsets, each with a different qualitative risk index (extremely risky, negligibly risky, etc.). Presumably, the strategic decision-makers would have set some qualitative level above which risk cannot be tolerated, by specifying the particular subsets that could be considered as possible purchasers (for example, nations falling into subsets C through F). Thus, the strategic decision-makers have set the broad qualitative constraints within which actual sales decisions must be made, decisions that will be made by tacticians.

For, assuming that a nation proposing a purchase falls within one of the tolerable risk categories, then it is the task of the tactical decision-maker to decide under what conditions to consummate the sale. The information that would be required for this decision would be the amount of contribution to profit (marginal revenue) the export would be expected to provide, relative to the computed risk. Once again, we see that the tactical decision-maker's problems tend to be reduced to numerical form and to moderately stochastic formulation.

*To hedge a bit, we can suggest that there will be one neighborhood, perhaps quite narrowly defined, that will be demonstrably superior to all others.

To make this clearer, let us outline some very simple logic for our tactical decision domain with respect to the case at hand. Initially, we might set out the format for an export request as follows:

$$A = f(X, Y, Z)$$

where X = subset category to which the nation belongs, Y = the schedule of equipment to be purchased, and Z = the price schedule the prospective purchaser proposes.

At this point, we are able to diagram a simple process, such as that in Figure 2.14. In the first decision blocks, it is determined whether the particular nation in question X qualifies for the particular nuclear equipment requested (Y). Is Y, given X, a tolerable risk situation? The point is that some types of nuclear technology or exports will be inherently safer than others, and thus there may be

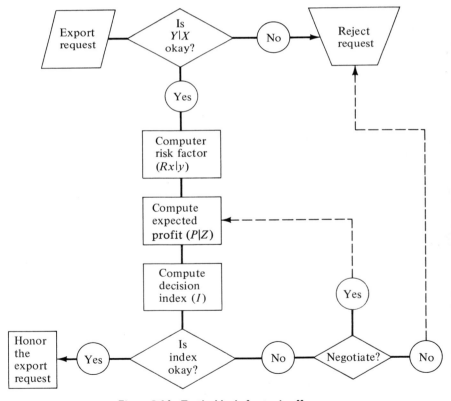

Figure 2.14. Tactical logic for trade-off case.

different qualitative risk categories for different classes of export. Just for the sake of argument, let us suggest that any nation seeking to purchase the particular schedule of equipment (Y) asked for in this example must belong at least to risk category D (which would mean, in terms of the original example, that the nation would have had to have actually signed the nonproliferation pact and have had a history of friendly relations with the United States and its allies). Now, if nation X is not a member of D, E, or F, then the request is automatically refused—it would fall outside the tolerance limits set by the strategic decision-makers. If, on the other hand, the requesting nation does belong to one or another of the acceptable sets, then it has passed the first test, and we would go on.

The next point in the tactical process asks the tactical decision-maker to compute a risk factor for the nation in question, given its schedule of proposed purchases. That is, even with qualitative categories (defined by the subsets), some nations are better risks than others for certain nuclear exports. Next, the expected profit (marginal revenue) is computed, which would be associated with this particular export request, using Z as the basis. In short, we are now concerned with looking at the profit contribution (P), which would result from filling the export request.

This brings us to the key decision point in the process: whether to accept a particular request, given that the nation qualifies under our strategic constraints. This would involve computing an overall index (I) for the case at hand, which would *measure* the terms of the trade-off between profitability (P) and risk (R). The demands on the tactical decision-makers in this case directly reflect the normative requirements set in the original goal formulation: to maximize profits subject to risk factors. If we took the simplest possible approach to creating and using such an index, we might come up with something like that shown in Figure 2.15. The figure implies that acceptance of a proposition will be based on a joint

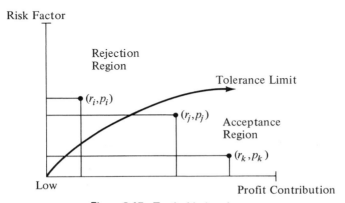

Figure 2.15. Tactical index chart.

valuation of risk and profit, with the demand that relatively higher risks return relatively higher profits. On the other hand, sales carrying little risk might be accepted at a lower profit level (profit here is determined as a percent of sales or as the marginal contribution to aggregate revenue). The use of the chart is simple. For any given risk factor, the associated profit contribution would have to fall to the right of the tolerance curve, in the region of acceptance. If the profit contribution for a proposed sale, relative to risk, falls to the left of the tolerance curve, then it is rejected. If a situation occurs where the firm is supply-bound (that is, where there are insufficient inventories to meet all demands), then those alternatives that involve points furthest to the right of the tolerance curve would be serviced first. In our example, then, the situation described by point (r_j, p_j) calls for rejection. The situations described by points (r_i, p_i) and (r_k, p_k) would both be acceptable; however, if only one order could be accepted because of supply constraints, then (r_k, p_k) would be given priority because it returns the most profit for a given degree of risk. Finally, where a proposed deal fell into the rejection region, we might want to bargain with the prospective purchaser to raise the price—and the profit contribution—to make the situation acceptable. If not, then we properly reject the export request.

In short, we have the rough equivalent of a "search" procedure of the type we employed for our school-board problem, but that is more suited to the type of decision situations that might arise in a commercial context (whereas the former case was quite reminiscent of the type of situations faced by many public enterprises). We also have essentially the same evidentiary implications here as we had with the school-board problem. Once again, our tactical decision-makers have been passed strategic (qualitative) constraints from their organizational superiors, which allow the tacticians to be concerned with matters of observation, measurement, and manipulation of quantities. Particularly, they would search for any data that would help support the calculation of specific risk indexes; e.g., historical data about the nation in question, or factual data about the military potential of the scheduled purchases (the set Y). They would also try to collect hard data in order to calculate the expected profit contribution from a sale, presumably by looking at their own production costs and perhaps elaborating these with cost data available from other competitors in the field. Thus, the calculation of the two tactical decision factors—the risk factors and the expected profit levels—is a matter for empirical analysis, consistent with the tacticians' presumed facility in mathematical and statistical operations.

Finally, the tactical problem is moderately stochastic compared to the severely stochastic problem that existed at the strategic level. Particularly, our control chart (Figure 2.15, which shows the feasible combinations of risk and profit) now means that all alternatives considered by the tacticians belong to the same qualitative set—they are all values for the risk-profit index (I). And just as with the school-board problem, the index value assigned any specific export request regarding risk and expected profit is expected to entail some probability of error. So, as is consistent with operations in the face of moderate stochasticity, we emerge with solutions that are approximations, or with decision premises that take the form of "range" estimates (as with Figure 2.10). Once again, we can expect that the probability of making an error on a sale is less when we have gone through the tactical analysis process than if we had stopped at the strategic level. For, with only the qualitative risk intervals to guide us, we may have consummated some deals where the risk was expectedly tolerable, but where the profitability was inadequate. This would have violated one of the conditions set by our original goal, which demanded that we avoid unreasonable risk, but nevertheless maximize profits.

2.1.4 The Deterministic Domain

Before we leave this section, we must, of course, consider the deterministic decisions. Such decisions are the subjects of least significance in this volume. In the first place, the analytical demands on the deterministic decision-maker are the simplest and most straightforward. Most deterministic decisions can be solved either through rather mechanical trial and error or through the application of what are essentially analytic instruments (e.g., tools of basic engineering, finite mathematics, or linear programming). In short, when these analytic instruments are given proper input, the problem is solved completely.[7] In goal-setting, or in strategic or tactical analysis, however, we are always left with some doubt about optimality (or sometimes even the propriety) of our solution. Therefore, these latter cases represent the areas where rationality is most consistently and seriously challenged.

In addition, the instruments (tools and procedural algorithms) for solving deterministic problems are widely known and distributed. Indeed, books purporting to train deterministic decision-makers are virtually uncountable. On the other hand, specific treatments of the goal-setting and strategic and tactical decision domains are scarce. For goal-setting and strategic analysis operations, there are few instruments available, and very little information about the contextual requirements for their use. Therefore, the three-higher-order decision domains must occupy our attention here.

There is a third and perhaps most telling reason why we will be giving deterministic decisions little space in these pages. This has to do with two assertions we made earlier. The first is that, if a decision error must be made, the deterministic domain is the place to make it. In short, the "costs" of errors made in the face of deterministic decisions are lowest of all categories, for deterministic decisions emerge with frequency only at the lower levels of the normal organization.

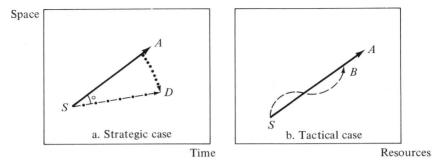

Figure 2.16. Trajectory formulations.

The second point is that the probability of making errors of any significant magnitude is lowest at the deterministic level. For deterministic problems are not only the most inherently simple issues one might have to face; they are also the problems for which we have the best developed, most mature set of solution instruments. But perhaps we can convert these arguments to a somewhat different form. It is possible to complement the simple set logic we have been using by turning to a trajectory formulation, as seen in Figure 2.16. This trajectory formulation allows us to make some allegorical comments about the organizational significance of the strategic and tactical decision domains. Recall that the major typology, Table 1.1, set out the following correlations:

Function		**Significance**
Goal-setting	$\longrightarrow$	Integrity
Strategic analysis	$\longrightarrow$	Effectiveness
Tactical analysis	$\longrightarrow$	Efficiency
Instrumental analysis	$\longrightarrow$	Mechanisticity

We already have had an opportunity to work on the concept of organizational integrity (a function of viability and normativity). We may now make some essential if preliminary remarks about effectiveness and efficiency.

In Figure 2.16a, let us consider that D is the organizational goal passed down from the directorial level. We are back to our original space-time map, and this goal may be thought of as a desired destination (location) that the organization will occupy at some point in time. Now this destination, following our earlier discussion, may be thought of as a "neighborhood" formulation (in which D represents a topological space) or it may be a "point" formulation (in which it is a unique location on the map). We also know that this goal now becomes the objective to be achieved by the operating officers of the organization (the executives, *per se*).

Effectiveness may now be taken to mean whether this goal was actually achieved. But effectiveness cannot be taken merely as a binary condition (yes or no) but also as a variable; that is, the degree to which the goal was achieved. In Figure 2.16, then, let us assume that S represents the starting state for the organization and that D is the desired destination. There exists some optimal trajectory from point S to D, which is the dotted vector SD. The implication is that if the strategic analysis and decision exercises were perfectly performed, then the organization would follow this trajectory. But to the extent that the strategic analysis contains errors or invokes suboptimalities, then we will expect departures from the optimal strategic trajectory. These departures may be measured in terms of an *angle of deflection*. Now, if SA is the actual trajectory the strategic decision-makers have led us on, then there is a strategic error that can be measured by the angle indicated. The overall result is that the organization proves ineffective to some degree, particularly to the degree measured by a vector AD. This difference vector gives us a diagrammatic representation of the extent to which the strategic decision-making exercises were ill-performed.

Turning now to Figure 2.16b, we may interpret the complications of tactical analysis in the same trajectory framework. But here we look for different things. Notice, first of all, that the only trajectory on this map is SA; this is because the strategic trajectory is predetermined by the organization executives, and hence becomes the referent for their subordinates, the tactical decision-makers. In short, to reapply a term used earlier in a different context, it is the strategic decision-makers who determine the basic *direction* in which the organization will travel. Here, as in the other figure, there exists some optimal trajectory, indicated by the undotted line. It is implied that this vector represents the *optimally efficient* path between S and A (the objective destination set by the strategists and passed down to the tacticians). To stretch our trajectory allegory, suppose that we have a spaceship, a destination (A), and a certain fuel reserve. Now, if no fuel is wasted in pursuing unproductive paths, then we should have just enough reserve to meet our target. However, to the extent that we waste fuel, then we will run out of reserves before we reach our goal.

What Figure 2.16b shows is a variation of this theme. Note that the X-axis of the map now reads "resources" instead of "time." The point is that the actual managers of an organization are given an objective, and may also be allotted certain resources with which to achieve it. Hence, the fuel-reserve analogy is appropriate, because if these resources are not properly husbanded, or if tactical errors are made, then inefficiency will result, which will leave us short of our objectives, say at point B instead of A. Thus, the degree of inefficiency may be measured by a difference vector AB. And the diagrammatic indication of inefficiency is measured by the *amplitude of oscillations* from the optimal trajectory (whereas strategic error—ineffectiveness—was measured by an angle of deflection from the optimal path). The picture this should convey is of an organization that knows where it wants to go and how to get there, but is being driven by poor pilots. They simply could not stay on a true course, but constantly veered off and then had to make course corrections. In the process, they used up a portion of the resource reserve that would otherwise have been sufficient to take us all the way to A.

We will say more about measuring effectiveness and efficiency in another section, and will make much more thorough use of trajectory formulation. In particular, we will see that the overall performance for an organization's administrators will be in part accessible to us by joining the error magnitude, DA and AB. But getting back to our main point, we can see that if the strategic and tactical functions are well-performed, then the damage that deterministic decision-makers can do is definitely limited. In the first place, their errors cannot take us too far off the settled course, simply because they each control only limited resource stocks. Second, with supervisory (or deterministic decision functions), errors tend to become apparent rather quickly and may therefore usually be corrected quickly. Strategic and tactical errors, on the other hand, tend to have ramifications that are broader and more obtuse on any space-time map; often, they are not recognized until they have considerable momentum, which often makes them quite difficult to correct.

Getting back to a point we raised early in this volume, we expect to find decision latitude diminishing as we move from higher to lower decision domains within any organization. At the same time, the expected value of decision errors also decreases. This is essentially what we meant when we suggested that the deterministic decision-maker operates within an *envelope of certainty* gradually passed down from above, as shown in Figure 2.17. Perhaps a final look at our

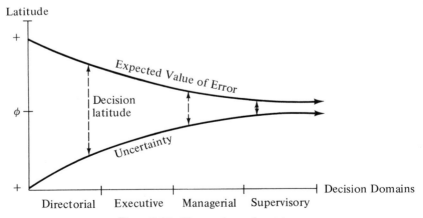

Figure 2.17. The envelope of certainty.

two situational examples—the school-board and nuclear export problems—will clarify the implications of the preceding figure. By the time the school-board problem had passed through the tactical decision-making stage, an aggregate level of expenditures had been agreed on. This means that the task of actually implementing the tactical decision is essentially deterministic. We would anticipate that the supervisory level would determine which schools get what share of the aggregate budget. Now, this task is likely to be deterministic because some "formula" (algorithm) will probably exist to direct the distributions. For example, a specific school might be allotted a budget based on the average school enrollment plus some overhead percentage. Thus, the deterministic decision-maker collects evidence of school enrollment, makes the calculations, and sends out the installment checks. One critical property of deterministic administrative functions thus becomes clear: deterministic administrative functions are identified by the fact that they can usually be performed, in entirety, by a computer, with the programming algorithms being supplied to direct the operation. In this way, deterministic functions lend an organization a degree of *mechanisticity*.

If we were to look at the nuclear export example, we might get a similar picture. Particularly, the tactical analyst/decision-maker developed the index chart presented earlier in Figure 2.14, which formalized the relationship between risk and profit factors and envisioned two possible outcomes for any export request: rejection or acceptance. Now, in this example, the supervisory functions may simply be to evaluate export requests within the tactical constraints provided by their managerial superiors. No real element of judgment need enter into their functional activities, for they have no decision latitude. If a particular index falls into the acceptable region, indicating a favorable risk-profit situation, they are to accept the order and fill it; if the index value falls into the rejection region (to the left of the tolerance curve in Figure 2.15), then the order is denied. A computer could have been used to perform this function. And I suspect that if certain social and economic considerations do not appear to constrain the process, more and more deterministic administrative functions will indeed be performed by "mechanical" supervisors.

Of course, supervisors also have other, ancillary responsibilities that might be important in another context of inquiry. For example, supervisors presumably have some personnel reporting to them, so their behavioral characteristics (socio-psychological dimensions) might be important to those human-relations theorists who consider management as the "art of getting things done through people." Or, from the traditional functional management standpoint, supervisors may be little differentiated from other functionaries in the firm—they have objectives to fulfill and functions for which they are responsible. However, from the standpoint of the decision scientist, the supervisory level is one that does not interest us as much as do the higher-order decision domains.

2.2 THE DECISION CONFIGURATION

Before leaving this chapter, we should perhaps try to broaden our perspective a bit, taking a look at a more generalized model of the relationships among the several decision domains. Particularly, we can be concerned about three broad parameters of decision structure: concatenation, periodicity, and spread. The former is a function of the latter two, as Figure 2.18 indicates. The key entries in this figure are the F's. These imply a relationship among the various decision levels in a complex organization and have two subcomponents:

$$F_i = f_i, g_i$$

where f_i = the concatenative coefficient, and g_i = the maturity index.

The f_i's suggest that higher-level decisions will tend to give rise to a greater number of lower-level decisions. Thus, the concatenative index measures the magnitude of the decision explosion that takes place as we move downward in an organization. For example, f_1 would reflect the number of strategic decisions evolving from some goal formulation; f_2 would measure the number of tactical decisions that follow strategic decisions; and f_3 gives a magnitude to the number of deterministic decisions required to implement any set of tactical decisions. The values that emerge for these f_i's are thus a measure of the degree of *decision spread* within an organization—a measure of the "leverage" that one decision level exerts on the immediately subordinate level.

In the normal organization, we expect that $f_1 < f_2 < f_3$. This property, in effect, is what lends an organization its operating stability (and also reflects our earlier assertion that the normal organization will tend to have more deter-

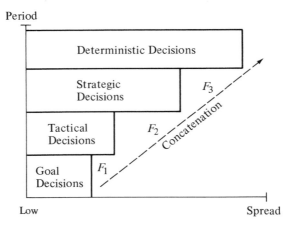

Figure 2.18. The decision configuration.

ministic decision-makers than tacticians, more tacticians than strategists, and so on). The degree of spread also reflects the concentration of decision responsibility within an organization, and is an indirect measure of the functional efficiency of the decision-makers themselves. To this extent, the f_i's are a surrogate for the rhetorical management concept of the "span of management." In still another interpretation, the ratios reflect the "rationality" of the organization's administrative structure itself. What we want to see is a strong morphological correlation between the decision configuration and the organizational configuration; we do not want to find tactical decision-makers (i.e., managers) forced to deal with strategic issues, or strategic analysts (executives) dealing with normative problems. In short, the distribution of decision functions should correlate with the distribution of decision-makers. Thus, decision spread may indicate the extent to which particular decisions fall to those ostensibly best prepared to deal with them, and hence reflect the "quality" of the administrative structure.

The maturity indexes (the g_i's) merely give moment to the assertion that different types of decisions will have different *horizons*, and will therefore tend to be reviewed or renewed at different intervals, or both. In the normal organization, we would expect to find a situation where $g_3 > g_2 > g_1$ (where the g_i's measure the *differences* between the times to maturity of the various decision categories). This model has distinct implications for the subjects of the next two chapters: decision accountability and decision reliability. Accountability is basically concerned with the ability to audit the results of a decision. We now know that goal-setting decisions will take longer to mature (to have all their consequences become evident) than strategic decisions and that these in turn will have a more distant horizon than tactical decisions. This, of course, suggests that any organizational accountability process will have different frequencies associated with the different decision levels. Simply, we would expect to be able to audit goal-setters least frequently, deterministic decision-makers most frequently, and so forth.

From what we now know, there will be an expected accountability concentration index that, in a normal organization, should look something like Figure 2.19.

But if spread (f) and horizon (g) are dimensions of the process, there is at least one more that must concern us, precision (p). Precision concerns the extent to which we can expect our accountability exercises to be accurate, to adequately exhaust the actuality of a decision-making function. In particular, when we make an individual, an organization, or any unit with decision responsibilities accountable for its own performance, we must always be concerned with the degree to which our evaluation will return a true picture. As is to be expected, the normal organization should yield a precision index such as that illustrated in Figure 2.20. The graph suggests that we expect precision to decrease as we move upward in an organization. In short, we suggest that the probable accuracy of

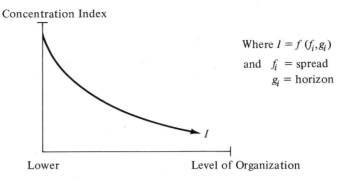

Figure 2.19. Accountability concentration index.

any accountability exercise we impose will be least at the goal-setting level and greatest at the level of deterministic decisions.

The dotted portion of Figure 2.20 leads to a refinement of this concept. Particularly, it proposes that the expected accuracy of accountability exercises is not continuous, but rather a discrete function tied to the different levels of the organization (and therefore to the different decision domains). The reason for this formulation is simple and stems from a proposition we advanced earlier: the decision functions and their attributes ultimately reflect the properties of the types of problems that dominate at different levels. Therefore, in a subordinate formulation, we find that

$$p_i = f(c_i)$$

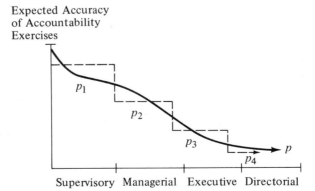

Figure 2.20. The precision index.

where

c_1 = deterministic problem category
c_2 = moderately stochastic problem category
c_3 = severely stochastic problem category
c_4 = indeterminate problem category.

Thus, to the extent that supervisors deal mainly with deterministic problems, we may be relatively more confident about assessments of their performance than about assessments of the tactical decision-makers, and so forth. These assertions may be made more explicit if we partition the variable c_i, as follows:

$$c_i = f(v, r, t, x_i)$$

where

v = number of state variables (determinants) involved in a problem
r = number of different relational states that might exist among the state-variables
t = decision horizon
x_i = index of analytical tractability.

We will not make full use of this model until later, but we can here give a rough idea of the several different dimensions of the variable x_i:

x_1 = the extent to which the problem's properties are empirically accessible (i.e., observable)
x_2 = the extent to which the problem's properties are amenable to measurement (either directly or via surrogation)
x_3 = the extent to which the problem as a whole is susceptible to controlled manipulation.

From our earlier work, we should know that the problems that are presented to the highest-level decision-makers—the goal-setters—will score poorly on all the preceding dimensions. Initially, because the goal-setters look far out into the environment, the number of different factors they must consider (the set of state-variables or determinants with which they must be concerned) will be very high. Moreover, as the domain of interest increases, the complexity of the relationships between these state-variables also grows (the behavioral latitude of the state-variables increases). The time factor (t) amplifies this potential complexity, for the decision horizon of the goal-setter is more distant than that of any other decision-makers. As a general rule, we may suggest that, for any given level of structural and dynamic complexity associated with a process or entity that one is trying to comprehend or predict, the probable accuracy of the descriptive or predictive models will decrease as the time horizon lengthens. In general, we do the best job when attempting to understand or predict short-run behavior. Finally, there is the matter of tractability. Indeterminate problems will score low on all three subdimensions. First, they are likely to involve state-variables that are empirically inaccessible as they cannot be fully observed. Second, the probability that some state-variables and relationships may not be measurable increases. Simply, we may be forced to treat some aspects of the far future and wide environment in very gross terms, being denied quantitative discipline. For example, relationships may have to be dealt with only in terms of assertions about probable directions of influence (as with comparative-static analysis of economic processes), and the descriptive models of entities or phenomena existing far out in the environment may contain many lacunae, and be specified only most crudely (e.g., we may use simple ideal-type constructs rather than fully developed, mathematical models). Finally, the entities that concern the goal-setter may not even be tangible at the point where goal-oriented decisions must be made; they may be mere fictions or simply hypothetical factors. Many of the processes or entities considered by goal-setters may thus not be at all amenable to actual manipulation. Therefore, we are denied the opportunity to "experiment" with our subjects, and must be content with judgmental rather than objective information.

The envelope of certainty that descended on deterministic decision-makers (the organization's supervisory personnel, for the most part) leads us to opposite conclusions. Initially, their highly constrained, narrowly derived decision environment is capable of housing only a few state-variables. The boundedness or localization of phenomena dealt with by deterministic decision-makers also limits the nature of the relationships that might emerge between the state-variables. In fact, it is a characteristic of deterministic problems that each state-variable may be capable of interacting with any other in only a single way. The near time horizon limits the possibility for new state-variables to emerge and sets constraints on the extent to which new relationships might be formed. Finally, as suggested earlier, deterministic entities or processes will tend to most completely meet the criteria for analytical tractability (the x_i's). The interpretations for the moderately stochastic problems that dominate the tactical decision-making level, and the severely stochastic problems with which strategic decision-makers are mainly concerned, are variants on these two extreme positions; the latter tends to approach the properties of the indeterminate problem while the former tends toward the properties for deterministic entities.

In overview, the decision configuration of any organization may be described when we give actual values (point values, interval values, or qualitative labels) to the factors involved in the following formulation:

$$F = f(f_i, g_i, p_i \, [e_i \, \{v, r, t, x_i\}])$$

When we inquire into these various factors, we find that two very disturbing events occur. First, as we move upward in any complex organization, the amenability of decisions to accountability tends to decrease. Second, as we move upward in any complex organization, the expected accuracy of decision exercises decreases. Thus, the distribution of decision error and the immunity from precise accountability tend to move together. The net effect is that the *expected quality* of decision-making also decreases as we move from lower to higher levels within the normal organization. But we must mention here that we are using quality in an absolute sense. This means that decision-making exercises would not be adjusted for the inherent difficulty of the problem at hand, which, clearly, should be done. Therefore, we will spend some time discussing the *relativistic* aspects of decision quality.

2.3 RELATIVISTIC DECISION CRITERIA

Whenever we are interested in the quality of a decision-making unit (either an individual decision-maker or some organized collectivity of decision-makers), we must investigate the following dimensions:

   (a) The *frequency* of error, which is the number of times errors have been committed, relative to the number of decision exercises in which the unit engaged.

   (b) The *severity* of error, which measures the degree to which the expectations were in error.

   (c) The *duration* of error, which is how long a decision error was allowed to run its course unchecked.

The ultimate cost of any single decision error will be a product of the severity of the error and the duration factor. The aggregate "cost" to the organization associated with any decision-making unit will be the product of these two factors for all incidences of decision error:

$$C_i = \sum_{j=1}^{m} (c_j), \quad \text{for all } j$$

$$c_j = f(s,d)_j$$

where

   i = a specific decision unit
   j = a specific decision exercise for which that unit was responsible
   s = the severity factor for the jth decision error
   d = duration factor for j^{th} decision error, and
   m = frequency of error.

The frequency factor m is really an absolute. We may easily translate it into the relative factor we want by calculating m/N, where N indicates the aggregate number of decisions that a functionary (or decision unit) had to make during the interval in question.

As for the matter of severity and duration, we might want to turn again to the trajectory formulation. Hence, Figure 2.21. Angle a is a measure of the severity of a decision error, whereas the two trajectories represent the durational factor. This is a relatively complicated construct, best approached through the development of a simple example. Let us suppose that we are a manufacturing company that must decide on how much product to produce for the coming period. We must, in short, estimate demand for our product. Let us further suppose that we use the most common forecasting technique, correlation-regression analysis, and emerge with a situation such as that shown in Figure 2.22. Figure 2.22 shows the relationship between historical demand levels (p_t) and the values for the gross national product that pertained at the time (GNP$_t$). That is, we have evaluated GNP as a factor by which demand may be predicted. The relationship was calculated as a regression function, $p_t(r)$GNP$_t$, which sets out demand as the dependent variable and attempts to capture the magnitude of the historical relationship between the factors.[8] We have then set out points on the map that represent historical values for the demand and GNP coordinates, and have fitted the regression function as a simple straight line (in practice, it would be the least-squares curve). Now, knowing something about the relationship

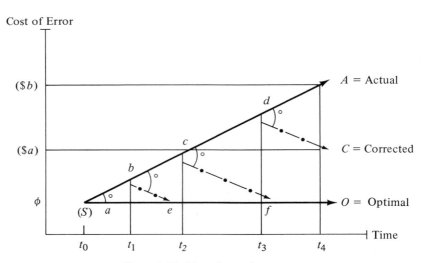

Figure 2.21. Map of error factors.

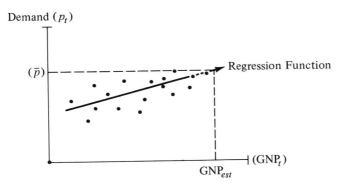

Figure 2.22. Extrapolative function.

between demand and GNP, we can make a statistical prediction about demand based on projection of GNP. As a rule, government statisticians (as well as a legion of private forecasters) either donate or sell GNP estimates to industry. In the very simple example of Figure 2.22, the GNP projection is made by extrapolating the regression function (shown as the dotted portion of the *least-squares* line). This yields a value for GNP_{est}, which leads back to a specific demand estimate, $\bar{p}$.

As a rule, we will set this GNP_{est} value in the framework of a probability distribution, the morphology of the distribution being determined by the correlation factor, c. The particular value used for c will be a function of the variance in demand that is not accounted for by GNP acting as a regression variable—the unexplained variance. Graphically, this variance is expressed by the extent to which historical coordinates depart from the regression line, that is, their spread around the least-squares curve. When the spread is very large, we impose a generally unfavorable (squat) distribution of the regression function at the point of projection, indicating that we are less confident about the accuracy of the p_{est}. On the other hand, when c is very large, accompanying a significant clustering of historical points about the regression curve, we are more confident that the p_{est} $(\bar{p})$ will be accurate (that is, c is inversely related to historical variance). In this respect, consider Figure 2.23. In the left-hand diagram, the inverse relationship is shown between the correlation coefficient (c) and variance, with the consequence that the expected departure of the demand estimate $(\bar{p})$ from the true demand parameter (p) is reduced as the correlation coefficient increases. The value for $(p - \bar{p})$ that pertains with respect to any c may be taken as the *expected error of estimate* and thus used as the guiding factor in the determination of how confident we are that our demand estimator is accurate. The components of Figure

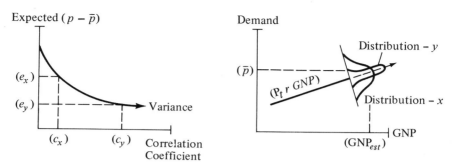

Figure 2.23. Relationship between correlation coefficients and expected error of estimate.

2.23a now translate themselves directly into Figure 2.23b, where we can see the morphology of the probability distributions imposed on the extrapolations of GNP and demand. The higher value for $(p - \bar{p})$ yields an expected error of estimate e_x (associated with the lower correlation coefficient value, c_x), which in turn dictates a situation of less certainty. This situation in turn gives rise to the fatter probability distribution, distribution x. On the other hand, when historical variance has been low (e.g., when the relationship between demand and GNP has been "better behaved"), then the expected departure of p from $\bar{p}$ decreases, yielding the much more peaked and favorable distribution-y. The greater "favorability" of the distribution-y stems from the fact that some of the more extreme values of $(p - \bar{p})$ have been eliminated (e.g., assigned no significant probability of occurrence).

In the error model, Figure 2.21, the angle of deflection, a, might now be considered to be the deviation between the expected demand level $(\bar{p})$, and the true demand that emerges during the period in question, p. That is, $a = f(p - \bar{p})$. Now we may try to interpret the trajectories. For the problem at hand, they become intelligible as production schedules. The optimal trajectory would be that particular production schedule that would see us producing exactly the amount of product that is actually demanded during the interval. That is, at the end of the period in question (at t_4), we would have produced exactly p units. But, when we produce according to the demand estimate, $\bar{p}$, we follow the actual trajectory, and will therefore overproduce relative to real demand, with the degree of overproduction related to the severity of the error of estimate (measured, again, by $a = f(p - \bar{p})$, reflecting the extent to which we overestimated demand). Thus, if we follow the actual trajectory throughout the entire period, we will produce $\bar{p}$ units. The difference between $\bar{p}$ and the actual demand, p, is the value for the cost of decision error, $\$b$. This cost simply reflects the cost of goods that were produced but not sold—the material, labor, administrative overhead, and so forth, associated with the units of overproduction ($u_i = [\bar{p} - p]$, after we have adjusted for any salvage value, differential carrying costs, and so on).

There are two conditions under which we might have to bear the full burden of loss, $b. The first and most obvious is where we simply do not recognize that an error has been made, and thus continue to produce along the actual trajectory through the full interval, $t_0 \rightarrow t_4$. This, in essence, restates what we just suggested. The other way we might realize the full loss is when we have had to commit beforehand to capital equipment, labor, and so on, on the basis of estimated demand, $\bar{p}$. That is, we have an ironclad contract to employ a certain labor population at a certain rate throughout the entire period, and have purchased capital equipment that cannot be returned, nor employed for any other purpose within the organization (that is, it is dedicated), nor resold without incurring considerable loss. In such a case, the original severity of error (La) is the only *variable* in the error process; duration becomes, for all purposes, a constant and is therefore beyond our control.

Now, when we relax the assumption of irrevocable commitments to a certain predetermined production schedule (to the actual trajectory), we may consider the implications of duration a controllable factor (an endogenous variable of the error process). For, when duration is a variable, we can introduce *rectification trajectories*, which will reduce the overall loss associated with the decision error. Under some conditions, the relationship between duration and loss will be very elastic. That is, early recognition and correction of our error of estimate can result in a strong reduction in ultimate loss. This would be especially true if the product were one that, for instance, was not perishable or had a long shelf life. Under such conditions, we can adjust the production schedule downward upon realizing that the inventory level is secularly increasing and thus that we are overproducing. Now, when we recognize our error early enough, we may avoid a loss altogether. This is the implication of the rectification trajectory ($b \rightarrow e$), culminating at time t_2 with the error of estimate having been recognized at t_1. The rectification strategy is to reduce the remaining production schedule by the amount of product now held in inventory, or to assume some $\bar{p}_m$ that is modified downward relative to the original $\bar{p}$. In simple symbolic terms, m is a modifier determined as:

$$m = f\left(\pi\ [\bar{p} = p]\ |\ P_{a_{[t_0 \rightarrow t_1]}}\right)$$

Particularly, we have actual demand figures for the period $t_0 \rightarrow t_1$. Given this new information, we now ask if $\bar{p}$ is still the best estimator for actual demand

(p). The factor m will then be used to inflate or deflate the *a priori* estimator $\overline{p}$ on the basis of the probability just calculated. If the actual information indicates that $\overline{p}$ is unlikely to be the true estimate because actual demand is too low relative to what we would expect were $\overline{p} = p$, then we would use m to deflate our demand estimator (e.g., $\overline{p}_m < \overline{p}$ by a factor of m). Thus, the remaining production schedule (from $t_2 \rightarrow t_4$) would be reduced accordingly, and a level of resources, labor, and so on, would be committed to other projects or released. Through several modification processes of this sort, provided that we initiate them at the proper time, we might eventually emerge with a very low loss level, even though the original severity of error was quite high.

Were we to assume, however, that the product was perishable, then we must expect to incur some cost associated with overproduction, irrespective of how quickly we identify the error of estimate and introduce a rectification trajectory. In this case, the importance of duration becomes even clearer. Particularly, the correction trajectory ($b \rightarrow e$) taken at ($t_1 \rightarrow t_2$) may be expected to result in a lower level of loss than a later correction trajectory, say ($c \rightarrow f$). In fact, given that the angle of rectification is the same for both trajectories ($\angle b = \angle c$), the differential loss may be considered proportional to the *length* of the trajectories. Thus, the earlier we recognize and move to correct an error—the shorter the duration allowed an error—the lower will be the expected loss.

We may, finally, make this clear from another aspect of the trajectory diagram. Consider what happens when we don't recognize our error until time t_3. In this case, it is simply too late to avoid a significant loss, even when the product is *not* perishable. That is, following the constant angle of correction (which might reflect constraints on the correction process such as the notice that must be given to employees we intend to lay off and the notice that we must give to a company we are renting equipment from before billing will be stopped), the best we can arrive at is loss level $\$a$. This is less than $\$b$ but still greater than the zero-loss levels (or approximately so) that would have been associated with those cases where we noticed our error and corrected it earlier, thus considerably shortening duration. In summary, wherever duration enters the cost calculus as a variable, we can expect a situation such as that in Figure 2.24. Figure 2.24 shows that we are essentially *indifferent* between a large error with a short duration and a smaller error with a longer duration (e.g., the curves $s_1 \rightarrow d_0$ and $s_0 \rightarrow d_1$ yield the same cost of error). As both duration and severity increase, the cost of error also increases, to the point where we have cost (c_j) associated with the trajectory ($s_1 \rightarrow d_1$). In summary, we want a decision-maker (or decision-making collectivity) to avoid errors in the first place, to realize a significantly small m/N. For any m_j (decision error) that does occur, we then want the decision-maker to keep the cost of error (c_j) as low as possible. He does this in one of three ways:

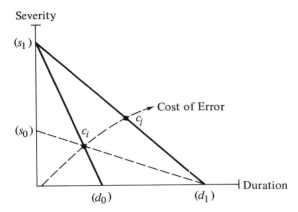

Figure 2.24. Functional relationship between severity of error and duration.

(1) by exercising good judgment and proper analytical methods so that the severity of error $(s_j|m_j)$ is small (2) given any (s_j), by being alert to the possibility of error so that the duration factor (d_j) is as small as possible, or, as is most preferable, (3) being both cautious and alert, so that $\Sigma^m c_j$ is effectively minimized for any set of decision problems (N).

Thus, we would tend to measure the *quality* of a decision-maker (or of a decision-making unit, such as a marketing department) by the aggregate cost of error (or loss) associated with the decisions made during some period, that is, as a product of the frequency of errors, severity, and duration. But let us introduce a qualifying assumption: let us assume that all decision-makers in all four decision domains of an organization are equally competent. In this case, using the absolute cost function $(C_i = \Sigma^m c_j)$ to measure their performance might be something of a disservice to the higher-level decision-makers (e.g., the goal-setters or strategic programmers). The reason is clear: the problems with which the higher-level goal-setters or strategic programmers must work are inherently less tractable than those at the lower-levels of the organization, which are dealt with by the tactical and deterministic (supervisory) functionaries. Therefore, any attempt to measure the quality of decision-making performance must consider the category of problems appearing at that level. In short, the error indicators $(C_i$'s) must be considered *relative* to the nature of the problems the decision-maker or unit faced. Fortunately, some of the work we just did can help us clarify this point.

Our little sample problem attempted to use the past to discipline our predictions about the future. In effect, the correlation coefficient that we developed gave us some idea about the validity of that procedure, in the following framework of relationships:

$$\text{Expected cost of error} = f(c)$$

$$c = f(v)$$

where c = the correlation coefficient, and v = variance. Therefore,

$$\text{Expected cost of error} = f(v)$$

That is, the expected cost of error associated with the attempt to predict the future using historical information is a direct function of the variance inherent in the information base we develop. The conclusion we may reach, and a critical one within the confines of the decision sciences, is that *the relevance of any historical information base generally declines as the variance associated with that base increases*. This is critical because we have suggested that virtually every decision problem involves making predictions of some kind. But what this suggests is that as variance increases, *the rationality of using historical information as a predicate for our predictions decreases*.

The critical question now is *what are the determinants of the variance that is expected to be associated with any historical (empirical) information base we might develop*? The answer is simple: the variance of any historical data base—developed by observing the subject of process of interest—will be some function of the properties of the subject or process itself.[9] The two properties that most concern us are:

(a) The *structural complexity* of the subject or process, which is a function of the number of different components of which it is comprised and the heterogeneity of their attributes.
(b) The *acceleration factor*, which reflects the dynamic potential of the subject or process with which we are dealing, i.e., the potential for change.

As a general rule, the greater the structural complexity of the subject or process at hand—and the greater the acceleration factor—the higher will be the variance associated with that process or subject's historical behavior, and therefore the less reliable any projections about its future behavior based on its historical behavior. Thus, as acceleration and structural complexity increase, the expected cost of error associated with our historically predicated, statistically driven projections will also tend to increase.

We have already suggested that the relevance of an information base as a source of statistical projections declines as variance declines. But we should also consider another factor, which can be just as important as variance: the *time* elapsed between the generation of a data base—the point in time or interval over which the empirical observations were made—the the point in time toward which we are projecting (the decision horizon). As the elapsed time factor increases, the predictive relevance of any historical information base will decrease, given any level of structural complexity and acceleration associated with the problem (process, subject, and so on) at hand. And, as the relevance of the historical information base begins to decrease because of either an increase in one of the variance determinants or elapsed time, the cost of error associated with empirically predicated predictions increases. Thus, consider Figure 2.25. For illustrative purposes, we are going to countermand a mathematical principle and let our three dimensions define a plane in space (rather than a point). The vector running from the origin of the iconograph to the midpoint on each of the four planes defines the several different levels of predictive error we expect to be associated with the conditions defining the planes. At e_1, the lowest error level, we find acceleration, elapsed time, and structural complexity all uniformly low; for the condition (a_1, c_1, t_1), we may thus suggest that the relevance of the historical data base is significantly high, and we may be quite confident of any pre-

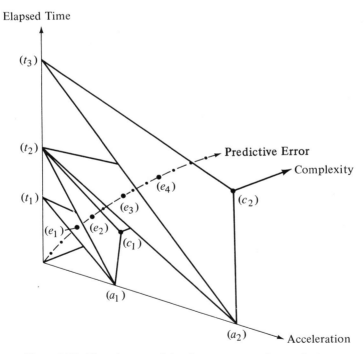

Figure 2.25. The relevance of data bases as sources for prediction.

dictions we might make using its components as the basis for our projections. In short, the condition (a_1, c_1) indicates that the process or subject we are working with is well-behaved, and t_1 means that we are working with information that is current relative to the decision horizon.

The other planar alternatives suggest different situations, all of them less favorable. Error level e_2 is found by keeping acceleration and complexity constant, but raising the elapsed time factor to t_2. Here, the system is still fundamentally well-behaved in its own right, but the *degree of projection* is increased. As a result, the ultimate predictions will rely proportionally more on the statistical instrument manipulations and less on the original data components. In this case, the possible error of estimate (projective error) will increase. We finally arrive at the worst of all worlds as far as projection is concerned, the case where the system, process, or subject with which we are concerned is inherently ill-behaved (given a_2 and c_2 as the coordinates for variance), and where the decision horizon is very extended (or the information base is very old). In this case, the error of projections is significant, possibly significant enough to warrant abandoning the attempt to predict the subject's future on the basis of its historical behavior. When we must abandon the strategy of predicting problem conditions on the basis of historical information—and hence are denied access to the instruments of statistical projection or, more generally, inductive analysis—what recourse do we have? The answer is that we must attempt to bring discipline to the problem using another set of techniques—deductive analysis. Although we will say more about this later on, we suggest for now we will have to displace observation and measurement (statistically disciplined information) with *judgment*. And, as we will later show, the use of judgment as a source of decision discipline is inherently more perilous than projective discipline.

Finally, we can reconsider the several different problem types associated with the different decision domains. Given the way in which we have defined the problem types, we can see that indeterminate problems may be defined as having extremely high potential for variance; in fact, their future properties are likely to be completely different than their historical properties, or they may be unprecedented so that they have no history. Deterministic problems, on the other hand, are those whose future is potentially predictable in all its aspects. In short, when we introduce our problem types, we may develop a construct such as Figure 2.26. In short, the various decision domains identified earlier are characterized by very different error conditions. In fact, there will be some *floor* error level below which we legitimately cannot expect to go, irrespective of how clever, assiduous, and talented we are as decision-makers. In short, long-range programming exercises, mission definitions, and goal decisions must also be expected to have a greater expected cost of error than decisions on where to put what lathe on the plant floor or how many barrels of oil to order to operate a plant generator for a month.

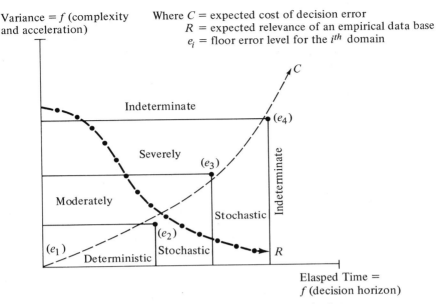

Variance = f (complexity and acceleration)

Where C = expected cost of decision error
R = expected relevance of an empirical data base
e_i = floor error level for the ith domain

Figure 2.26. Origin of relativistic decision criteria.

In summary, any accountability process aimed at evaluating the quality of an organization's decision-makers (or decision-making units) will have to consider that higher-level decision-makers will face problems that are going to incur more errors (a higher m/N), more severe errors (higher s_i's), and probably errors that are more difficult to identify and correct, and therefore likely to be index with a higher duration factor (d_i). In short, when we evaluate the performance of a decision-making unit, we would modify the absolute criterion with which we began this section. Specifically, we would want the following formulation:

$$C_i = f\left([m/N, s_j, d_j]\,; e_i\right)$$

This suggests that we ultimately want to be able to evaluate decision performances, not in absolute terms, but as adjusted for the expected cost of errors associated with the various decision domains. As we can see from Figure 2.26, $e_1 = 0 < e_2 < e_3 < e_4$. Inasmuch as e_1 refers to deterministic decisions, we must expect that the rational decision-maker will be able to solve such problems with no significant error at all; that is, he would be measured by taking the actual C_i relative to zero. On the other hand, the *inherent error potential* for the other decision domains increases at an increasing rate, and therefore would act to dilute the weight attached to any specific C_i that a decision-maker might emerge with over some period. Thus, the performance measure now becomes a contingent index, $C_i | e_i$ (aggregate cost *given* the floor condition).

It will be many pages before we can suggest how such an accountability criterion can be made operational. But the relativity of the accountability logic we use here should be clear before we attend to accountability itself. Thus, the next chapter should be considered with respect to what we have said here.

2.4 NOTES AND REFERENCES

1. Among these would be the classic study by Berle and Means, *The Modern Corporation and Private Property*, and the report by Robert Larner, "Ownership and Control in the 200 Largest Nonfinancial Corporations, 1929 and 1963," *American Economic Review* 56 no. 4 (September, 1966). Along with this, there are the sometimes excellent criticisms by John Kenneth Galbraith, especially in his *Economics and the Public Purpose* (Boston: Houghton Mifflin Company, 1973).

2. A good, quick introduction to the simple set concepts we will be using is Chapter 5 in Seymour Lipschutz, *Finite Mathematics* (a volume in the Schaum Outline Series. (New York: McGraw-Hill, 1966).

3. For a rather neat explanation of this and other essential microeconomic formulations, see Josef Hadar's *Elementary Theory of Microeconomic Behavior* (Reading, Massachusetts: Addison-Wesley Publishing Co., Inc., 1974).

4. I try to avoid using the term *policy*. To me, it has always been involved with the concept of developing certain normative constraints on the behavior of an organization's employees. But, in the case at hand, one could suggest that the specificiation of space X reflected the executives' policy of minimizing the risk of recrimination to themselves. But were space X defined by the logical or inductive methods earlier outlined (rather than the self-centered process), then we could hardly suggest that the partitioning process was a matter of policy, or that space X represented a policy constraint. Thus, the more general term for the partitioning of action spaces is "strategic constraint," and we will use it in preference to policy constraint.

5. Many of the more popular search algorithms are discussed by Douglas Wilde in his *Optimum Seeking Methods* (Englewood Cliffs, New Jersey: Prentice-Hall, Inc. 1964).

6. For a nice treatment of quadratic polynomials, see the section in Williamson et al., *Calculus of Vector Functions* (Englewood Cliffs, New Jersey: Prentice-Hall, Inc., 1972), pp. 361ff.

7. A fine reference for those interested in the scope and ingenuity of analytical algorithms for inherently deterministic problems is Beveridge and Schechter's *Optimization: Theory and Practice* (New York: McGraw-Hill, 1970).

8. For an excellent discussion of the technology of correlation-regression analysis (within the confines of economic time-series decomposition), see Croxton and Crowden's *Applied General Statistics*, especially Chapter 22 (New York: Prentice-Hall, 1955). For the general purposes of economic forecasting, I have had better luck with spectral analytic techniques rather than the more

popular time-series decomposition methods that do not deal well with periodic inputs. For a note on how power spectral coefficients may be used to displace standard regression coefficients, see the write-up on time-series analysis in *Biomedical Computer Programs*, ed. Dixon (Berkeley: University of California Press, 1970).

9. For more on this, see my "Honing Occam's Razor," in *Developments in the Methodology of Social Science*, ed. Leinfeller (Dordrecht, Holland: D. Reidel Publishing Company, Inc., 1975).

3

Decision Performance and Propriety

3.0 INTRODUCTION

Our major interest in this chapter will be the technology available for controlling the performance and propriety of decision-makers. Performance audits are directed toward an analysis of the *results* associated with decision actions. Decision propriety, on the other hand, is concerned with the *behavior* of the decision-makers, the extent to which they operate within the bounds of normativity.

The three major decision domains—goal-setting, strategy, and tactics—will each impose different conditions on the accountability process. As expected, the performance and propriety of goal-setters (organizational directors or chief officers) are the most elusive targets. The strategic decision-makers' performances are also sometimes very difficult to measure in an objective way. In some extreme situations, even tactical decision-makers may elude traditional accountability criteria. Yet, from the perspective we will be developing, virtually any decision becomes susceptible to accountability, even though the precision and exhaustiveness of the audit may leave something lacking.

Finally, we will have an opportunity to say more about the procedures of rational decision-making, considerably amplifying our arguments of the first two chapters.

3.1 THE FOCUSES OF ACCOUNTABILITY

The mechanisms by which decision-makers may be made accountable for the results of their decisions—their commitments—must be at the focus of any inquiry into the potential of decision science. But accountability is a much-disputed and perhaps very immature subject, and we will refer to some of the discussions we have had already to help us here. Particularly, we can use our standing decision taxonomy to suggest something about the different focuses of accountability associated with the several different decision functions. Consider Table 3.1:

Table 3.1. Accountability dimensions.

Decision Domain	Associated Problem Category	Organizational Significance	Focus of Accountability
Directorial (officerial)	Indeterminate	Integrity	Propriety
Executive	Severely stochastic	Effectiveness	Utility
Managerial	Moderately stochastic	Efficiency	Return
Supervisory	Deterministic	Mechanisticity	Productivity

As a general rule, we may expect (often without legitimate reason) that these accountability focuses are cumulative, e.g., the higher-order decision-makers are not only responsible for their own performance, but for that of the decision-makers at the lower levels. We will, moreover, concentrate primarily on the first three accountability focuses, as *productivity* is always calculable as a neatly localized and precise input-output ratio—on whatever dimensions apply. Again, operations at the deterministic level are of little concern to us here, although many volumes exist that deal with the way that cost-accounting systems (and finite-state process control techniques) may be applied to the measurement of productivity in the normal line functions of enterprise. Therefore, we must concentrate on those cases where direct productivity measurements are unavailable because of the nature of the process we are trying to control.

Moreover, before we begin to discuss the several focuses of accountability, we must examine three dimensions of accountability processes that operate across all decision domains:

(a) *Access:* reflects the extent to which those conducting accountability exercises may be possessed of complete and relevant information on a decision-maker's performance.

(b) *Motivation*: reflects the fundamental willingness of those responsible for performing accountability exercises to conduct them with integrity, assiduity, and completeness.

(c) *Capability*: will reflect the technological adequacy of those responsible for conducting accountability exercises.

For various reasons, we expect that all three of these attributes will tend to appear with successively greater strength as we move downward through the organization. In short, access, motivation, and capability will usually reach a simultaneous maximum at the supervisory levels, where we are concerned with evaluating the performance of instrumental decision-makers (facing deterministic problems). The point of minimal realization of access, motivation, and capability is expected to appear at the point where we are attempting to evaluate the performance of the highest-order decision-makers, the goal-setters. We now turn to a brief defense of these propositions, dealing first with the issue of directorial propriety.

3.1.1 Propriety and Performance

We really have very little mature technology to draw on when it comes to evaluating the performance of goal-setters. But before we lament this fact, we should also mention that goal-setting exercises are encountered only infrequently anyway. In too many cases, goal-setting is performed only at the initiation of an organization and then never repeated. Because of the inherent difficulty of goal and mission analysis, we would expect some reluctance, although organizational directors never seem to miss an opportunity to establish crude rhetorical goals or to produce goal formulations without any proper analytical effort. As a result, the vast majority of organizations tend to operate under goals that either are obsolete or products of dramatic irrationality. Thus, we find many organizational directors *per se* either taking no hand at all in organizational administration or involved only with the strategic decision-making functions (which are usually better left to operating executives).

One reason for this is that many administrators view management as a reactive rather than reflective exercise. Indeed, it is fair to suggest that there is a *de facto* variant of Gresham's law at work in most modern enterprises: considerations of near future and immediate environment will tend to drive out considerations of the far future and the wider environment. Thus, most organizations tend to have futures that are mere extrapolations of the past, or to give themselves over to management by crisis.

This "law" tends to become more true the less frequent the goal-setting exercises. For it is these, after all, which introduce qualitatively unprecedented, innovative aspects into an organization's structure or dynamics. In practice, we find that these new qualitative considerations enter most often in the face of dramatic perturbations and are dictated rather than authored. For example, goal-reassessments are generally performed by new management taking over from unsuccessful administrations. Or, we expect goal-redefinition when a national leader dies or a top corporate executive is removed or retired. But we do not generally find the goal-setting process kicked in at normal changes of administration. The federal elections in the United States, for the most part, only involve promises of strategic changes. In cases where an executive is retired without prejudice, we often find the new executive pledging to continue the policies of the old, with the implication that major goal-setting will not take place at all.

At any rate, the point is that goal-setting, as we have described it, is usually the most infrequently conducted of the various decision exercises. Traditional management theory logic would suggest that this is the preferred situation. For rapid, frequent, and protean revisions of basic goals might lend the organization hysterical quality, or at best serve to frustrate the lower-level decision functions. But as we will later show, as with so many rhetorical management principles, this sometimes tends to be overapplied, leading to the situation where goal-setting exercises are spaced too far apart (or, as we just suggested, performed once and never again).

But, when they are performed, no matter how seldom, their target is system integrity, with its two subdimensions, viability and normativity. Recall that viability concerns the perceived or demonstrated utility of the organization, and its attractiveness as a destination for capital investment (through either bonds, stocks, or notes). In the public domain, viability usually suggests something about the perceived value of the goods or services offered by the organization to the community (or some constituency of the community—a client subset), and the organization's attractiveness as an agency for public support via tax dollars or charitable contributions. Thus, the concept of viability applies in much the same way—at least in the abstract—to both industrial-commercial and public enterprises.

The other dimension of organizational integrity, the normativity of operations, also operates in both the industrial-commercial and public sectors. Again, normativity essentially concerns the behavioral constraints on the organization, the restraints on means by which organizational ends (goals) may be pursued. In all, there are strong parallels between directorial responsibilities in the two major sectors of society. The overall implication is that the industrial-commercial director is responsible for the organization *vis-à-vis* the capitalist economy as a whole, and that the directors of public enterprise are the first line of defense for the health of the democratic politic. In theory, then, in both sectors, the directors are agents of ultimate *accountability*.

We also saw that our theoretical expectations are not always fulfilled. The principle under which directorial responsibilities are defined ("one may delegate authority, but not responsibility") may be frustrated in several ways. First, the directors may not have *access* to the information necessary to implement accountability. For example, in the senate and congressional investigations of the intelligence community in the United States, the Central Intelligence Agency consistently withheld information that was vital for accountability. In the name of "national security," members of the Congress and Senate were denied access to the data required to make a complete accountability calculation.[1] In much the same way, certain government agencies operate under the shield of "executive privilege," and are thus able to frustrate the accountability process at its very initiation. While exclusion of information is quite common in government (although quite contrary to the spirit of theoretical democracy), there are also instances where industrial or commercial organizations deny access to their directors. For example, under certain accounting conventions, expenditures for illegal activities (e.g., bribes to purchasing officers, subornation of public officials, contributions to political campaigns, maintenance of excessive executive expense accounts, payments for industrial espionage) are hidden in the year-end statement. In short, the directorial review function may be easily frustrated by aggregating income or expense accounts, or by delivering accounting summaries that are doctored to meet directorial expectations.

The second major detriment to accountability involves the behavioral referents of the directors themselves. We saw earlier, for example, that at least three different concepts of directorial responsibilities are operable in the real world, all of which will dilute accountability. When the directors see themselves in the role of casual consultants, lobbyists, or agents for legitimacy,* then accountability functions are simply not part of their operational repertoire. In short, under such conditions, the directors lack the *motivation* to conduct accountability exercises.

Finally, even if access to relevant information exists and the directors are well-motivated, accountability may still be frustrated. This would occur when the directors simply do not have the *capability* to perform accountability calculations. Thus, while some faults of public and private enterprise may be laid at the door of venal, duplicitous, or corrupt functionaries, many others result from intellectual ill-preparedness. In short, everyone involved may be willing to perform accountability exercises, but simply may not be able to do so because they lack the technical and intellectual prerequisites.

Now we will examine the selection of *propriety* as the focus of accountability for directorial functions. Our reasons are practical, if somewhat tortuous. Initially, recall that the fundamental function of the directors of an organization is goal-setting. From what we earlier suggested, directors would be expected to be responsible for setting the "optimal" goal for an organization, i.e., the best possible destination from among all alternatives. But also recall that the universal set of alternatives for the goal-setting process is enormous. As such, goal-setting often involves the development of a best solution to an indeterminate problem. As also mentioned, the technology for solving indeterminate problems is immature, ill-developed, and highly complex. Now, most boards are not likely to contain individuals skilled in such techniques (or even familiar with the heuristic analyses that represent the "scientific" approach to goal-setting). Therefore, we cannot expect them to answer frequently or satisfactorily for the rationality of the goals they establish. That is, most boards of directors will not be able to

*See Section 2.1.1.

answer for the optimality of their goals and probably will not even be able to reconstruct their search and selection processes. And if it is unlikely that such sophisticated analytical abilities will exist among board members, it is perhaps even less likely that they will exist among the constituencies to whom the boards are accountable, e.g., stockholder groups, community interests. Therefore, under normal circumstances, directors are effectively immune from challenge as to the performance of their major function, goal-setting.

We can see the kinds of questions that are being asked of organizational directors, but not answered properly (if at all). As a rule, they would all fall into the "guns or butter" category. For example, whether resources used to support space research would be better spent in the social sector is a recurrent and widely broadcast query. Similar questions are asked about military budgets, about funds that subsidize various technological sectors (such as the aircraft industry, energy, and transportation), and about public resources that support education, medical care, and other functions of the public sector. Those who expect only vague or rhetorical answers to such questions are seldom disappointed (and sometimes even their most pessimistic expectations are dramatically exceeded). For the unfortunate but striking fact is that no one seems to know whether a dollar spent on social welfare is worth more than a dollar spent on national defense or whether a billion dollars spent on space exploration is worth more than the same amount invested in mass transportation activities. No one knows how much a government should cost for the level of services it offers its citizens; no one knows whether the raft of regulatory agencies that Washington, D.C., and the various states and municipalities support save the consumers money or actually decrease the worth of their income. No one knows how much the U.S. Department of State is worth. And no one knows whether New York City's new subway cars are a better investment than if the same amount were spent on hiring more fire fighters—or whether more fire fighters are really more valuable than more police or more social workers. In a particular community, is it worth more to educate a student in medieval French literature or in engineering? How much should be spent on a methadone program for controlling heroin addicts? Is a new elementary school worth more to a township than paving a new surface on the main street?

Questions on a similar scale—and at a similar level of urgency—are asked in the industrial and commercial sectors. For example, are dollars invested (or captured) by conglomerates expected to be less productive than dollars invested in smaller dedicated enterprises? What is the real effect of protective mechanisms such as subsidies and tariffs on the health of the economy as a whole? Is a dollar invested in the oil industry more productive than a dollar invested in solar energy or the arms industry or the private housing market? Is a firm's investment in an additional staff accountant worth more than another lathe machine or another public relations officer? Are investments in high capital-labor–ratio enterprises ultimately more or less productive than funds flowing to enterprises with more primitive (and more labor-intensive) processes? Just what are the terms of the real trade-off between domestic industrial health and competivity in foreign markets? Are big corporations more efficient users of productive resources than smaller corporations, or is "bigness" a *prima facie* case for inefficiency because optimal scale-of-plant has likely been exceeded? Should manufacturers be forced to *internalize* social costs that they impose on the population as a whole (e.g., should they be forced to make reparations for air or water pollution through the normal pricing mechanism)?* And at an even broader level, questions are being asked about the fundamental efficacy of capitalist enterprise itself, presumably in relation to socialist alternatives. This, of course, also raises the issue of whether industrial and commercial enterprise exist for the stock-holder, the consumer, the citizen, the world, or perhaps for all peoples, and, if so, with what priorities?

Again, although questions of such broad implications are often asked, they are seldom answered (and we are not sure that most of those asking the questions seriously expect an answer). The usual situation, of course, is that issues of value-significance (i.e., involving goals) tend to be resolved at the political level. Some analysts take great comfort in this, suggesting that political solutions tend to be the societal counterpart to the "market mechanism" that presumably guides economic production. In fact, both socialists and democratic apologists make this claim for their respective systems. It is a flaccid claim at best. For, in the complex world of goal-setting, political solutions will have very little proba-bility of being optimal. Rather, the probability of optimality may be expressly traded off against the probability of being absolutely wrong (a feature common to most committee-based decision processes). As we will later see, political solu-tions usually are reactive, and secondarily they may be driven almost entirely by *a priori* (especially axiological) predicates. As such, they effectively deny any scientific input and hence tend to be taken almost entirely in the realm of rhetoric.

We assure the reader that we will shortly suggest how the "guns and butter" decisions may be subjected to scientific scrutiny, and made at least partially susceptible to accountability. For the moment, however, the broadest, most significant decisions of both public and private enterprise will tend to be immune to such discipline, largely because neither goal-setters nor the outside stockholder or citizen interests tend to be well-versed in the technology of goal-setting. Thus, propriety comes to the fore by default.

---

*Presumably, this would be done by making manufacturers impose a surcharge on their products, reflecting the costs for correcting ecological defects to the community in which the manufacturer is located, or the cost to communities in which the products are sold for disposing of nondegradable packaging, and so forth.

Given the lack of analytical sophistication inherent in many boards, the directors themselves may only be effective in setting procedural constraints on the executives. That is, they themselves may restrict their operations to the normative domain, being unequipped (or unwilling) to perform the effortful and demanding goal-definition and mission-analysis tasks. Thus, again almost by default, outside interests are forced to assess directors, not on the basis of objective performance criteria, but on the basis of actual or expected propriety. In short, we focus on the directors' demonstrated or assumed ability to see that the organization behaves itself. In the broadest sense, this is important if not ideal, for contravention of norms may have the same effect as errors in the goal-setting process—both result in a real or potential loss to the constituency the board is supposed to represent.

Actual impropriety may (when an organization is caught) yield hard, incontrovertible evidence for outside interests to weigh. For example, if a firm were convicted of breaking pollution laws, then there is hard evidence that the board failed to perform on the normative dimension. In some cases, contradictions of tacit or explicit laws, principles, or norms condoned or tolerated by the board can be a disservice to stockholders or other interested parties. Often, these refutations of stockholder interests are direct and immediately visible; for example, with the dilution of equity in an investment or pension fund that accompanies loans made on criteria that subordinate matters of profitability, safety, and so forth. In other cases, the effects of improprieties may be indirect, thereby escaping stockholder attention until they have run a long course. For example, marketing irregularities on the part of capital goods exporters may eventually result in a loss of market. Or, as environmental constraints become more strict and penalties more representative of real damages, contradictions of pollution laws may seriously erode a company's asset base and, with it, stockholder equity. Although, to the extent that penalties remain below the cost of compliance with social conventions or environmental laws, etc., then stockholders may consider themselves well-served in the short run, or in a bounded locality. But, in the long run, improprieties have a way of returning to haunt us. Most often they result in a dilution of the quality of life available to all citizens of a society, including stockholders. And on the fiscal side, they might cause a rise in the tax base, which wipes out any incremental gains that stockholders might have made from their firm's expediencies. In the public sector, improprieties usually directly reduce the level of service available to community or citizen interests. For example, the fiscal irregularities in New York have resulted in a reduction of services to the extent that the debt-servicing burden is greater than it would have been with proper management, thereby channeling off resources that could have been put to productive use.

Actual improprieties are always after the fact. Nevertheless, the rational stockholder or citizen will try to protect himself against *potential* improprieties by searching for clues as to latent interests that might conflict with his own or that might lead to contraventions of economic or political principles. Perhaps the best way to assess probable impropriety is to examine the composition of the board of directors, taking a look at who sits on the board, who acts as a trustee, and so on. To give an idea of the kind of information to be gained here, let us look at a very popular, often mentioned example, the directorates of America's oil companies. When we look at their boards of directors, we find many representatives of "block" investors, e.g., insurance companies, large banks, pension funds, investment funds. Even though the Clayton Act forbids directors to sit on boards of competing firms, the phenomenon of "interlocking" director-ates subverts the spirit of the act, even if it contravenes no law *per se*. Interlocking provides a mechanism whereby directors of competing companies can come to-gether and thus exert a common control on supposedly nonallied oil companies. For example, suppose that Mr. X is on the boards of oil company A and insurance company D; further suppose that Ms. Y sits on the boards of insurance company D and oil company B. Thus, the insurance company's board provides a *node* at which the two oil companies can exchange information or coordinate their activ-ities. Thus, the interlocking directorate provides a vehicle for collusion, one which obscures the act so that prosecution would be difficult.

But interlocking provides a mechanism for another activity, one just as unpal-atable. Consider that a block investor may own shares in several different oil companies. This block investor, such as an insurance company, bank, or fund, measures its success on the basis of an aggregate rate of return on an investment; that is, the returns from the several oil companies will be figured on the aggregate total. Under such a situation, it may be distinctly to their advantage to *prevent competition*. For competition, in an oligopolistic industry, usually means one thing—a price war. For oligopolistic industries tend to be characterized by situa-tions where there are distinct limits on product differentiation (e.g., one com-pany's oil is pretty much like another's; the automobiles of the different manu-facturers—in the different price categories—are very similar; one airline's service on a route is virtually indistinguishable from another's; one firm's rolled steel is pretty much like another's). Therefore, about the only dimension in which they can compete is price. And when they try to compete in price, the "kinked" demand curve kicks in. In other words, if any single firm raises its price, its de-mand will fall off; therefore, no firm will raise its price unless it has a preagree-ment that all others in the industry will follow suit. If it chooses to reduce its prices, then all its competitors must reduce their prices. This simply means lower prices—and hence reduced profit—for all the firms. Therefore, head-to-head competition is anathema to all firms in an oligopolistic industry. And in this abrogation of the norm of competition, they may have the support of the block investors. For competition might cause the elimination of certain firms and the concentration of power in the most efficient firms only. This might reduce the block investor's aggregate return on investment, for the increase in the earnings per share of the efficient, surviving firms may not offset the total loss of value of their equity in the firms that failed. Therefore, the block investor may argue for the protection of all firms against any single firm aiming for optimal efficiency. As a case in point, when the federal government recently suggested the deregulation of commercial airlines in the hope of introducing more competition, it was the large banks that were most vocal in opposing deregulation.

Therefore, when the individual stockholders find directors on their board who are also directors (or perhaps employees) of block investors, they might assume that their own interests will be ill-served. For the interests of the individuals owning stock in any single firm, and the interest of the block investor, are often contradictory. The individual investors want to maximize their returns, which means that their firm should aim for optimal efficiency and neglect no opportunity for competition. But when directors are more responsive to block interests than to individual investors, then anticompetititve practices are more likely to be in force, so that there is a *de facto* ceiling on the return that any investors can expect. They may also expect that dividend or retention policies might favor the block investor, or that directors' salaries may be set to reduce the salary expenses of the block investors themselves (e.g., the fee paid to Mr. X by oil company *A* may be charged against his regular wages as an officer of the insurance company or bank). Thus, the stockholders may expect that a board of directors who are interlocked with other investment interests may act with impropriety. Thus, they may expect that the goals set for the firm—or the procedures tolerated—will not be those that would be dictated under the principles of pure capitalist competition.

Issues of board composition also occur in the public sector. For example, a regulatory commission that is directed by a board with strong industry representation may be presumed to have a probability of acting improperly; that is, favoring the interests of the industry itself over the public should a conflict emerge. To obscure such situations, many commissions or regulatory agencies are staffed by what we might call the "peripatetic" director or commissioner. He leaves a job in an industry to take a job as commissioner; however, while acting as a commissioner, he knows that his future will consist of returning to the industry he left (often with the promise of promotion). Therefore, he may use his government post to foster contacts in the industry he is supposed to be regulating. Or, at best, he may be reluctant to further the public interest at the direct expense of industry interests. Therefore, citizens may expect to have their interests subordinated when a commission is staffed with temporary government servants, or when industry and government become "interlocked" by people constantly moving back and forth between the two sectors.

In summary, even when impropriety has not been detected (as opposed to, for example, the firm actually convicted for pollution), the stockholders or citizens may seek to preassess the probable propriety of the directors by looking at the composition of the board. Even though they may lack the technical facility to assess the performance of the directors in their role as goal-setters, they should be able to assess the probability that the goals the directors set will be in the interests of the constituency they represent. Where the board is an interlocked one—staffed with peripatetics or serving as the home of the director *qua* lobbyist, etc.—then the constituency should have cause for concern and should exercise this concern through the election process.[2]

Access, motivation, and capability all tend to neglect the performance dimension of directorial responsibilities and focus on the normative dimension—the matters of propriety. The leading factor here is probably capability; if one does not conceive that he can force an accounting for the rectitude of a decision—in this case, for the "optimality" of organizational goals—then his motivation will certainly dwindle. Lack of access follows, for he would not know what information to ask for, even if management were willing to make it available.

To some readers, this argument about the inaccessibility of goal-oriented accountability criteria might seem something of a straw man. They might suggest that we have the best possible indication of the *performance* of an organization merely by looking at its rate of return on investment, aggregate profit, share of markets, and so on. However, there is a problem with this assertion. Particularly, rate of return, share of market, etc., are all reflective measures. That is, they compare the organization's performance only to that of other organizations and may yield no information about the extent to which the organization exhausted the potential of a situation, about what *could* have been done. Indeed, perhaps none of the organizations used for comparison purposes are really aiming to be optimally efficient. Given the expected lack of sophisticated analytical skills among most top managements, this is very likely to be the case. So, using contextually reflective performance criteria may be like trying to ascertain a winner from a group of runners who are all pacing themselves to the same easy lead. Nobody is required to put forth any extreme effort, for they know the finishing results will be too close to really embarrass anyone. In such a situation, nobody loses except the spectator.

Comparative performance measures are also diluted because so many industrial and commercial organizations consistently try to abrogate the relationship between growth and efficiency. In short, share of market or relative size may be no real indicator of inherent efficiency or optimality. Under strict economic criteria, any firm that grows beyond the optimal scale of plant would be at a competitive disadvantage, for its *pro rata* production costs would begin to increase relative to those of firms at a more efficient size. As might be expected, however, the calculation of optimal scale of plant requires considerable analytical sophistication (e.g., it would involve a "model" of the enterprise in some detail). So, for the most part, this condition is neglected. Growth thus becomes a great deal more expedient, and hence popular, as a goal than does an absolute (nonreflective) objective such as optimal efficiency or maximum profitability. But how might firms grow beyond their optimal scale of plant and still remain viable? First, they can use retained earnings, which is perhaps the most significant single source of investment capital for most larger firms. Retained earnings are automatically reinvested in the original organization, without consideration that they might yield a higher return (be invested more "rationally") in some other enterprise—as they indeed might be were they returned to stockholders. Second, certain common improprieties may also act to make growth independent of efficiency. One that we have already noted was the action of block investors to prevent the inefficient firms in an industry from going out of business, as this might be against the investor's interests (even though it would probably benefit the economy as a whole). But large organizations have techniques of their own: cartel-building, collusion, preemption of potential competitors, artificial partitioning of markets, price-fixing, provision of cost-plus government contracts, and, of course, the interlocking directorate.

The techniques that dissolve the normative relationship between growth and efficiency also abrogate another relationship, that between profit and risk. Normatively, greater profit presumes greater risk. But, through collusion (and so forth) risk can be reduced and profit maintained. It can also be reduced by government subsidies, by the widespread practice of merely aping one's competitors, by substituting advertising for real product development or differentiation, and so on. Risk can also be reduced to the extent that the firm can insulate itself from exogenous factors—from environmentalist pressure, perturbations in the fiscal structure, open (unmediated) confrontation with labor, acts of foreign governments, and organized consumer groups acting as a lobby. In short, risk and profit may be disjoined to the extent that industry and government collude. Thus, the indispensable tools in the arsenal of any large organization are subornation of enforcement or regulatory agencies, bribery of political influences, and manipulation of the legal system in favor of disassociation of corporate officers from results of corporate actions. It is probably not true, as many of the more enthusiastic critics of big business suggest, that the corporation has become a sovereign in its own right. Closer to the truth, perhaps, is that the corporation has become the mistress of the ministers.

The whole point, again, is that a firm may be enjoying a superior rate of return on investment—or have the largest comparative share of the market—and still be inefficient and therefore a liability to the economic system as a whole. To the rhetorical manager, there may be some source of comfort and pride in being first among equals; but from our standpoint, this pride should be diluted by the knowledge that one's equals are possibly mediocrities. This, essentially, is the problem with the entire concept of *management by objectives*. For those who most often advocate this concept are our rhetorical friends; the goals (or objectives) they offer are likely to sound good, but perhaps be unrelated to any optimality considerations. If the fundamental goals set for the organization at the directorial/officerial level are merely reflective (e.g., be the largest manufacturer of widgets; earn an aggregate rate of return on investment at least equal to the real increase in GNP; have the largest share of the widget market; have the highest price-earning ratio in the industry) rather than absolute (e.g., maximize profit; optimize the aggregate cost-effectiveness ratio for the organization), then all subsequent or lower-level organizational objectives are likely to be merely reflective. Particularly, executives, managers, or supervisors will *bargain* with their superiors as to the appropriate index of performance. Ostensibly, the superiors and subordinates—in the objective-setting process—would have very large domains over which they might wander. But, in most cases, bargaining takes place over a very narrow space. Objectives tend to be historically reflective (e.g., earn a rate of return that is 5 percent higher than last year; improve departmental productivity by 10 percent over last period). And the actual performance audit of lower-level functionaries may often be entirely independent of these objectives. For example, in practice, a profit center may fail to meet its goals, but still be applauded if its rate of return is favorable with respect to other organizational units. Thus, even bargained objectives may be abandoned in actual accountability exercises.

The reason why this occurs so often is an interesting one. The individual being audited might suggest that circumstances have changed since the original goal was set, and that he is thereby absolved from its implications. Thus, reflective goals or objectives are not only easier to set than absolute goals or objectives, but they offer a great latitude when performance is actually measured. For, to set an absolute goal—involving some optimality criterion—one would have to build a "model" that would project the maximum feasible performance level that could be reached by an organizational unit, given some level of resources. Moreover, under rational management critieria, this absolute goal could not be held invariant over any significant interval because the conditions affecting the optimum would be constantly changing. In short, in many real-world situations, yesterday's optimum is today's suboptimum, and vice versa. This consideration would cast serious doubt on existing budgeting and management-planning activities, and with good reason (as we will see in the next chapter), predicated as they are on periodic as opposed to real-time review.

In addition, reflective goals might be popular for reasons other than their analytical expediency. It is easy to see that they would fit very nicely with the rhetorician's concept of management as an essentially *reactive* process and with the concept of unconditional *survival* as the *sine qua non* of organizational success. Moreover, reflective goals and objectives coincide nicely with the appreciation of business or commerce as a "gentleman's sport," where one competes not against oneself, or against some idealized performance criteria, but only against one's peers. It is entirely understandable, then, that absolute goals would be considered by many decision-makers to be the province of the long-distance runner or the academic. Together, all these reasons give us what we believe to be a fair portrait of modern enterprise: much greater emphasis on action than analysis; greater attention paid to a decision-maker's social (and sometimes imputed psychological) attributes than to his technical capabilities; organizational futures that are largely just replays of organization history; constant confoundation of the principles of economics, characterized by frequent collusion between government bureaucrats (and elected officials) and business executives, and among ostensible competitors themselves; ingenious attempts to separate risk from profit, growth from efficiency, and survival from real success; tacit acceptance of the future and the environment as residences of perils than as arenas of opportunity; and, finally, a determination to avoid decision-making at all, if possible. Somewhere within this mix of unpalatable properties rests the cause for the high frequency of administrative error and the enormous waste of resources and energy with which we are all familiar. And, perhaps most importantly, these properties give us a clue to why decision-makers are so seldom willing to apologize for their errors, or to act to correct them. For in the reflective, reactive world of modern administration, appearances are emphasized more than facts. It is thus deemed more important to be able to camouflage or recover from an error than to avoid one in the first place.

As a final note, we must suggest that the public administrator or government functionary labors under a somewhat different set of conditions than his industrial or commercial counterpart. In particular, even reflective goals are difficult to come by in the domain of public enterprise, so the public administrator often has even greater immunity from performance accountability. In this respect, consider the following:

(a) There is the problem that the outputs (products) around which most public enterprise centers simply do not lend themselves to precise, objective, and quantitative formulation. In many cases, the public system has no clear-cut definition of the product it produces (e.g., is the output of a university the number of graduates it produces, the quality of the graduates, or a complex combination of the two; or should output be thought of in terms of positive impact on the surrounding community? What about the proper output target for a community hospital or a local welfare agency?). In short, the lack of definability of numericalized outputs prevents many public enterprises from adopting, in any meaningful way, the kind of cost-effectiveness calculus that is available to firms producing a highly structured, easily defined, "countable" output.

(b) While a majority of decisions undertaken within the private sector may legitimately involve alternatives with clearly specified outcomes (being matters mainly of precisely defined or evenly numericalized quantities), many decisions that must be made by public administrators, operating even at the lower levels, involve "value" issues or have distinct policy or broad sociopolitical implications. Most managers within the private sector—except for those operating at the highest levels—are shielded from such considerations by the certainty umbrella under which they operate. Thus, they may behave as if the system or phenomena with which they deal are effectively deterministic, whereas virtually all problems emerging within the confines of public enterprise may involve elements of uncertainty that are largely "external" to the normal business decision-maker.

(c) Because public enterprise so often deals with issues involving the public welfare, the common good, the dignity of human beings, or other such elusive criteria, the public manager must treat the consumer of his product as a "client" *per se*, with all the ambiguity and ethical responsibility that entails. On the other hand, the business manager is largely freed from any fiduciary responsibility toward the consumer (and in many cases, the link between the operating manager and the consumer may be a long and indirect one). In short, the business decision-maker more or less legitimately can consider only the welfare of his own firm, whereas the public manager (for admittedly political as well as philosophical reasons) must have a bifold calculus, which involves client as well as system welfare.*

(d) The performance of the decision-maker in the private sector is most often audited on objective bases, with the specific criteria generally known to the manager beforehand (and often a result of a bargaining process between the manager and his superior). In such a context, the decision-maker can approach his function in terms of its probable impact on his overall performance audit (e.g., as a profit center). But in the public sector, the manager (at virtually all levels) often has his performance—and therefore his career and personal welfare—judged on the basis of subjective criteria, some of which may not even be known to him beforehand or which are only tacit rather than explicit. In fact, many real performance criteria in

*To some extent, business organizations have become more susceptible to exogenous factors (e.g., environmental constraints, inquiries into marketing or political functions, class-action consumer suits). It is interesting to note, however, that these considerations may never be incorporated into the calculus of the line manager, but rather may be dealt with as a public relations problem. Hence, they pass from the realm of responsibility to the realm of appearances in which public relations people travel.

the public sector run contrary to policy statements and therefore cannot even be articulated after the fact (e.g., as with the auditor of the United States Navy who found significant cost overruns—which was his job—but who was fired for reporting them). Thus, the path the public administrator follows is tortuous and perilous; often by doing the job formally assigned him, he can run afoul of "latent" criteria or of the irrational components so prevalent among bureaucracies. Small wonder, then, that there is the tendency among many officers of public enterprise to make as few decisions as possible. For, in the ill-structured, subjective, *ad hoc* public arena, a positive action may often correctly be perceived as carrying more potential for unpleasant surprises than for adulation or reward. And in this predilection, the officer of public enterprise joins a majority of his counterparts in private industry.

The defense offered by the public administrator may thus be summarized as follows: the basic unamenability of public enterprise to objective accountability criteria means that the public administrator can be *legitimately* freed from the objective (if reflective) criteria under which the performance of his commercial counterpart is assessed. And if he is legitimately freed from objective performance criteria, on what basis can his performance really be audited? The answer many public administrators would have us accept might be phrased like this: "Well, if there are no objective criteria by which my performance can be legitimately judged, then my performance really cannot be judged at all—especially not by any outside agency!"

In this way, we arrive at the situation that so amazes and frustrates those of us who sit outside the public sector. The individual public administrator is hired, fired, promoted, or demoted largely on the basis of criteria that remain inaccessible and undefined outside the particular system involved. (Perhaps, as suggested earlier, often the real criteria are contradictory in the face of the manifest policies of the system, or perhaps embarrassing in that they involve personality or political rather than substantive issues.) The ostensibly valued attributes—assiduity, uncorruptibility, tenacity, professional rather than personal loyalty, placing community interest ahead of agency interests—all have a perilous existence within the realm of practical enterprise. The net result is that the well-connected, charming, or cautious incompetent can hold his position in the public sector with virtual impunity. Every effort is made to conceal errors from outside agencies; bureaucracies of all kinds—hospitals, universities, military departments, government agencies—become secretive and determinedly adept at "washing their own dirty linen." But most critical of all, the functionary in public enterprise earns respect, loyalty, and a sort of unearned "tenure" simply by occupying his position, irrespective of whether he is any good at his job. We are asked to adulate the man not because of any personal qualities or demonstrable successes, but simply because of the office he holds. Thus, agency heads and other executives in the public sector often employ the rather patent affectation of the royal "we," indicating that they perhaps are unsure of the point at which they begin and their office leaves off. But most significantly, and perhaps saddest of all, their self-avowed isolation from objective performance criteria allows them the luxury of treating their office more as a "social" than a functional position, much in the fashion of the largely insular and generally functionless members of the older order of European aristocracy. Their right to occupy their position is beyond real question, and any issue raised about quality of performance is largely irrelevant or simply put down to the carping of the envious or the neurotically disrespectful. This fantastic perspective is often deliberately reinforced by the hypocritical behavior of others, notably the wild applause that greets a president whenever he addresses Congress, even though a majority of those clapping are on record as opposing the man.

In summary, then, certain behavioral or psychological aberrations evolve from the supposed impossibility of adequate accountability in the public sector. And it is this purported (and widely accepted) impossibility of adequate accountability that leads to certain clearly arrogant behavior, which, although insulting and frustrating, is mainly tolerated. For example, a state university president can, in the name of "academic freedom," ask a state legislature for a budget and at the same time suggest that how it is spent is none of their business. Somewhat the same arrogance is justified by government officials in the name of "national security," by public physicians in the name of "professional prerogative," or by politicians in the name of "the public interest." Of course, this penchant for secrecy is an old an honored one. Indeed, today's public official often seems to be little more than the living inheritor of the arrogance, mysteriousness, and ill-concealed disregard for his constituents that the ancient Druids honed to such a fine edge.

The strategy heard most often to correct this situation is this: public enterprise should be run more like a business. This is a fatuous suggestion, for many business organizations share the same analytical debilities as the public enterprises they criticize so freely.

3.2 CONGRUENCE AND UTILITY

In this section, we will be concerned about *effectiveness* with regard to strategic decisions. In a static world (and we will later enter some dynamic qualifications), effectiveness is measured by noting the extent to which the strategic decision-makers have achieved the goal passed down by the goal-setters or mission analysts (the directors or officers of the organization). Efficiency, on the other hand, measures the cost of resources expended to achieve an objective set by the strategic analysts. To refresh ourselves on these implications, consider Figure 3.1.

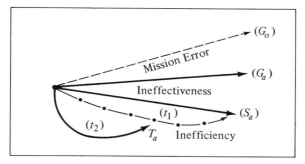

Figure 3.1. Trajectory reformulations.

Again we have a simple trajectory map, much like that given in Figure 2.15. Now, let us suppose that G_o is the theoretically optimal destination the mission analysts (directors) could have established for the organization. However, for various reasons (mainly those given in the preceding section), a suboptimal goal, G_a, is selected. This point, G_a, now becomes the target for the strategic analysts, and they must select a trajectory to take the organization there (assumedly within some time or resource constraints, or both). Now, the difference between points G_o and G_a represents the *opportunity loss* that may be charged to the goal-setters. That is, what the organization would have gained at G_o, relative to gains available at G_a, is lost to the organization because of an error in the goal-setting process. Now, the vector CG_a (where C merely represents the current or existing "state" of the organization) represents an optimally effective trajectory for the strategic analysts to follow in their pursuit of point G_a. That is, this is the most direct route and is "effective" because it eventually arrives at the actual goal point. Of course, leaving aside resource or time constraints, there are innumerable strategic trajectories we might follow that will be effective. For our purposes, however, let us suggest that the strategic analysts pursue the trajectory CS_a. Now, S_a represents the actual destination arrived at as the result of a strategic decision, and hence is in error by the amount $(G_a - S_a)$. This amount will represent the *degree of ineffectiveness* that attaches itself to the strategic analysts. Now, for the tactical decision-makers, S_a becomes the objective to be sought, and they are unlikely to be aware that it is ineffectual with respect to G_a. There is some optimal tractical trajectory available to them, particularly CS_a. To repeat an earlier argument, this is the path that will take them to the strategic objective with the least waste of time or resources. Let us suppose, finally, that the tacticians were inefficient to an extent, and hence wasted time, resources, or both. For the given level of resources then, the tactical decision-makers took the organization only to point T_a. They may eventually arrive at S_a, but will do so only at the expense of greater resource or time expenditures, or both. Thus, we would measure the *level of inefficiency* by the distance $(S_a - T_a)$, which is the loss to the organization that results from tactical errors.

Now, for the illustration at hand, we have a total error, given by the distance $(G_o - T_a)$, which is the *aggregate cost of decision error* at all levels. We have simply partitioned it so that the various origins of error are identifiable. Now, from the standpoint of theoretical economics, the organization would be an *optimal* entity (and would behave with perfect rationality) were it to have followed the trajectory CG_o. The direct implication of this statement is that the point G_o, arrived at via the trajectory CG_o, would have maximum use of resources or time expended, or both, and thus would have resulted in the achievement of the *optimal cost-benefit ratio*. Now, all the other points and trajectories are suboptimal, as we have seen. Particularly, point G_a represents a case where the benefit level is expectedly less than that associated with G_o. That is, for some given level of expenditures of resources and/or time, G_a would have been superior to S_a, but inferior to G_o. Now it is the tactical trajectories, t_1 and t_2, that concern us. Note that t_1 takes us to point S_a, but does so only at a greater level of expenditure than the apparently optimal trajectory, CS_a. Therefore, although the same level of benefits is arrived at by these two trajectories, t_1 has a cost-benefit ratio that is inferior to that associated with CS_a. Trajectory t_2 (CT_a) fails on the benefit dimension, and therefore yields the most unfavorable cost-benefit ratio.

Although this discussion has been concerned with the *concatenation* of decision error, it also allows us to reillustrate a couple of important points from earlier sections. First, had the strategic decision-makers effected the trajectory CG_a, their performance would have been optimal from the standpoint of those to whom they are accountable, the goal-setters. In short, their strategic decisions would have taken the organization to where the goal-setters wanted it to go. At that point, then, the only error component would have been $(G_o - G_a)$, attributable to the directors (goal-setters). Now, had the tactical decision-makers also followed CG_a without variation or departure, then they would have performed optimally from the standpoint of those to whom they are accountable, the strategic decision-makers. Again, the only error would have been the suboptimal goal itself. In this case, *the organization is heading with optimal efficiency and rapidity in a wrong direction*. Thus, the strategic and tactical analysts and decision-makers are the inadvertent inheritors of the goal-setter's error, but have not amplified it on their own.

However, for the remaining trajectories, the original goal-setting error is enlarged. Trajectory S_a takes us even further from an optimal destination than did CG_a. But if the tactical analysts were able to remain on the optimal trajectory CS_a, they would still have performed optimally from the standpoint of their strategic superiors. They, in effect, would be immune from error, even though they contributed to it through no fault of their own. But trajectories t_1 and t_2 concatenate error still further, the former on the cost dimension, the latter on both cost and benefit dimensions.

At any rate, with these considerations in mind, we may briefly explore strategic and tactical accountability within the framework given in Figure 3.2. We can see that strategic and tactical decisions each have their own accountability trajectory. In either case, we can see that accountability is a Janus-faced process. The audit face looks toward the past and reviews what has actually been done (the results of decisions). The projective dimension looks toward the future, asking about various proposed actions and trying to investigate the decision-making functions as origins of action. Of the two faces, the audit emphasis is simpler and direct, so we will begin our discussion there, saving the matter of projective discipline for the next chapter.

Initially, the effectiveness of strategic decisions will be subject to audit in terms of both congruence and utility. Congruence, as employed within the accountability process, invokes our concern over propriety, but does so a little differently than in the examination of goal-setter's behavior. We must first recall that it is the organization's directors who are performing the audit on the strategic decision-makers (the operating executives). And we must also recall that in the normal goal-setting process, certain constraints on means of obtaining any goal were passed down. In this sense, congruence merely asks about the extent to which the actions invoked by the strategic decision-makers remain within the normative bounds established by the directors. In short, were the means employed by the executives consistent with the letter or spirit of the procedural constraints that accompanied the original goal formulation?

We can see that a certain kind of discipline is available to us in making determinations about congruence. In this regard, consider Figure 3.3. There are basically three different types of procedural constraints which might be passed to the strategic decision-makers (executives). We already know something about them. Axiomatic constraints derive from logical or theoretical (e.g., philosophical) constructs—for example, capitalist economic theory, Marxian socioeconomics, Maslovian psychology, microeconomics, democratic political theses. These, in a sense, set the theoretical basis for rationality. Constraints that derive from nonlogical sources—from strictly subjective, aesthetic, emotional, or ethical sources—constitute the array of axiological predicates under which an executive might have to labor. Finally, the strategic decision-makers may be made responsible for not contravening any points of legislation, for obeying the laws of the land, so to speak.

To the extent that strategic decision-makers are searching for an effective strategy to employ in pursuit of some goal, we can see that they partition their search space in much the same way the goal-setters did. Recall that we equipped the

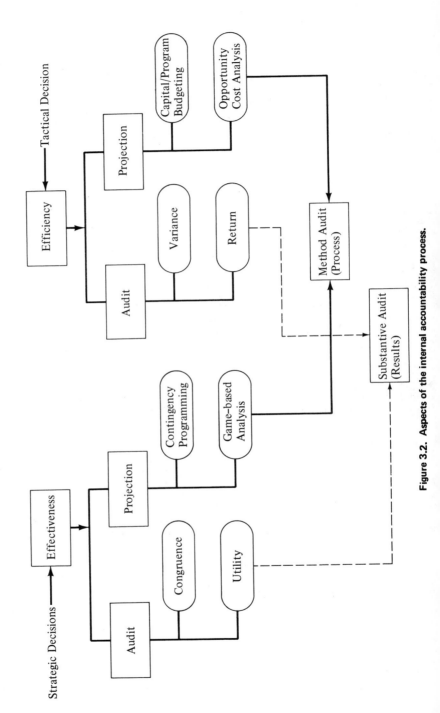

Figure 3.2. Aspects of the internal accountability process.

128

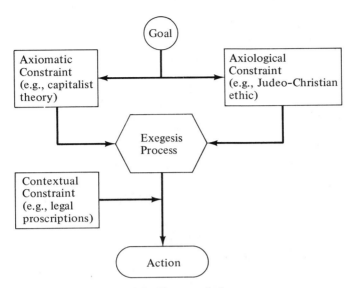

Figure 3.3. The exegetical process.

goal-setters with axiomatic, axiological, and visionary constraints, which eventuated in the reduction of the feasible goal search space (see Figure 2.1). We may do essentially the same thing for the strategic analysts, as in Figure 3.4. The figure suggests that any strategic search space may be partitioned into at least six generically different subspaces. We can, for example, let A and B indicate proscriptions on strategic alternatives that arise from axiomatic and axiological constraints, respectively. Subspace C might indicate strategic alternatives that are *a priori* preempted because of limits on the vision, imagination, or assiduity of the strategic decision-makers themselves. We can let D indicate the set of strategic alternatives that are excepted because they would contradict some

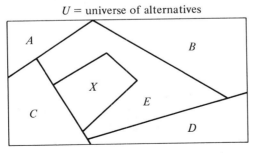

Figure 3.4. The strategic search space.

specific legislation. Note, in this respect, that the constraint set D is exogenous, whereas the others mentioned were defined internally or have their origin with respect to specific personnel occupying directorial and executive positions within the organization. The two remaining subsets, E and X, thus have the following interpretation. Existing all around the perimeter of the axiological, axiomatic, and legislative constraints is a gray area, the subspace E. Here we would find those strategies, which are not *a priori* condemned, but which would have been if the directors or legislators had thought of them. That is, these are strategic alternatives that can usually be tried only once and that are promptly excepted once they are actually employed. Subspace E is thus the domain of nonnormative alternatives, the arena of opportunism. This leaves us with subspace X, which then is the region of normative strategic alternatives, and hence becomes the most probable location to search for a stratagem to implement any goal. Note that this normative strategic partitioning would precede the substantive strategic partitioning illustrated in Section 2.1.2.

These subspaces have different implications for the strategic decision-makers, the most important being the need for an exegetical process of some sort, for this is the key to the establishment of subspaces A and B. Exegesis is essentially a variation on deductive analysis, because it usually involves reasoning from the general to the particular. This is usually required because both axiomatic and axiological proscriptions may exist in rather abstract form (the dictates of optimality, the golden rule, the tenets of the Judeo-Christian ethic, the socialist conventions reported by Marx or Mao, etc.). Thus, axiological and axiomatic referents will tend to proscribe classes of actions, or generic categories of alternatives, but in general do not offer explicit proscriptions (as would legislative codes). Therefore, the partitioning of a strategic search space must generally start with the strategic analysts or planners or decision-makers trying to lend specificity to abstract principles within some given decision context. Therefore, each alternative strategy—or class of strategy—must be set against axiomatic and axiological references and reviewed for consonance. Perhaps a couple of examples might help define the partitioning process more fully, although we cannot go into much detail here.

Let us suppose that we are strategic decision-makers who have been given the following reflective goal: improve our existing share of market to x percent by 19xx. We would realize from a casual logical analysis that we have essentially three generic strategic classes of action open to us, or three rudimentary dimensions on which we may operate: price, quality, and competition. If we can reduce the price of our product relative to our competitors' prices (while not dramatically reducing quality), we can expect our share of market to increase (given a degree of elasticity in the demand function). Or, if we can increase demonstrable quality while maintaining a price in the neighborhood of our com-

Table 3.2. Strategic partitioning.

Strategic Alternatives	Target	Assigned Subspace	Implication
Exclusion of competition	Competition	A	Proscribed by principles of capitalist theory
Exploitation of labor	Price	B	Proscribed by the Judeo-Christian ethic
Bribery, coercion	Competition	D	Specifically proscribed by criminal legislation
Monopsonization	Competition	E	Usually proscribable only after the fact, as neither theory nor legislation adequately treats the implications of industrial integration or constraint of supply

petitors' prices, we should capture an increased market share. Or we may operate directly on the competitors themselves, and seek to put them at a disadvantage. The partitioning of the strategic alternatives available to implement this goal might result in a partitioning such as shown in Table 3.2. Now, of course, the extent to which this partitioning will be effective depends on the sensitivity and sophistication of the strategists, and on the extent to which they may be held effectively accountable for the congruence of their actions. This, in turn, depends on the strength of performance criteria relative to normative criteria operating within the organization—the extent to which directors are willing and able to determine procedural congruence (which, in turn, expectedly depends on the willingness and ability of outside interests to hold the organizational directors accountable for organization propriety). In summary, the extent to which the partitioning of the strategic alternative set is operational may be the best indicator of the *character* of managements.

The reader will note that we did not treat the normative subspace (X) in the previous table, nor did we concern ourselves with subspace C (the set of alternatives proscribed by visionary constraints, etc.). But by redrawing Figure 3.4, we can see that subspaces C and X are related in a complex way, as Figure 3.5 illustrates. It is the composite spaces Y and Z that concern us here. The implication for Y is this: it contains normative alternatives that would be available to the strategists were they not bound by constraints of vision, imagination, or assiduity, and so on. Space Z would then be believed to contain nonnormative alternatives that the strategic decision-makers will neglect because of such constraints.

For the case at hand, we can see clearly what this implies, with respect to Y. Specifically, if we review the table of proscribed alternatives (Table 3.2), we find

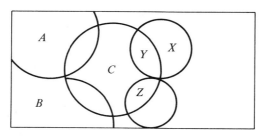

Figure 3.5. Endogenous constraints.

three strategic options that are not mentioned: innovation, advertising, and operational efficiency. These are all generic members of X, the set of normative (feasible) action alternatives. Yet they are all subject to limitations endogenous to the decision-makers—they are functions of imagination, wit, vision, and the like. Thus, the set X contains those strategies available to the decision-maker *a priori*. It thus becomes the major focus of strategic analysis to enlarge set X at the expense of C, for this is the way in which strategic decision-makers *extend the bounds of rationality*. In short, the absolute (if elusive) measure of the success of a strategic analysis exercise is lent us by the ratio of Y to X. And, reminiscent of what we did with the goal-setting process in the last chapter, we can see that the *latitude* allowed an organization's strategic decision-makers is given by $A \cup B \cup D/U$, or by $X \cup E/A \cup B \cup D$, the proportion of the strategic universe that is *a priori* proscribed. By extension, the expected *quality* of the strategic decision-makers is available to us from C/U. Again, the success of a strategic analysis process will be given by the difference between $([Y \cup Z]_{t-1} - [Y \cup Z]_t)$. Finally, we may summarize our concern with strategic congruence in the following way:

Any $S_i \in A \cup B \cup D \rightarrow$ incongruence (e.g., the strategy S_i is a member of a proscribed set)

Any $S_i \in E \rightarrow$ impropriety (via opportunism, for example)

$\forall S_i \in X \rightarrow$ congruence (e.g., S_i falls within the normative search space)

where S_i indicates any strategic alternative elected for implementation. For multiple strategies implemented in response to any goal, the degree of incongruence of the strategic decision-makers would be available by examining the proportion of S_i's falling into $A \cup B \cup D$, and so on.

Within the context of performing an audit of strategic decisions, we may turn briefly to the concept of utility. We may be brief because the concept is simple in its own right, and also because it has already been well treated within existing decision science literature.[3] We know at this point that utility is to be used as a measure of the performance of the strategic decision-makers, whereas congruence was used as a measure of the performance of the strategic decision-makers and of their propriety. As we have seen, the easiest goal to measure against—and hence the easiest type of strategic objective to evaluate—is a reflective one. For example, the incremental change in share of market or rate of return on investment or profitability, relative to a historical value or the values pertaining among competitors and so on, should be readily accessible. To the extent that a strategy has been invoked to obtain a properly formulated reflective goal, then strategic utility may be assessed within the framework of normal quantitative analysis. We merely take the target, assign it a value of 1.0, and then take the actually achieved objective and assign it a proportional value. The general audit procedure may then be taken either as a normal accounting exercise (an essentially deterministic function), or as an exercise in simple statistical inference. The difference between these two audit procedures is that accounting involves a consideration of all information in the universe of concern, whereas statistical inference finds us making utility calculations on the basis of a statistical sample. In either case, for a reflective goal, utility becomes a simple proportion.

Yet, while utility calculations are simplest and most direct in the face of reflective goals and reflective strategic objectives, rhetorical and absolute goals must also be dealt with. And they demand some variations on the normal utility calculation processes. Particularly, rhetorical goals and objectives, which are somewhat vague or perhaps even ambiguous, will demand that we approach the problem of utility using certain logical procedures. Absolute goals, although involving a greater level of rationality than reflective goals, complicate the accountability process and take us to the point where we must employ surrogates, because utility cannot be assessed directly.

One area in which rhetorical goals seem predominate is international relations, particularly foreign policy. This is the vehicle by which any nation seeks to protect its sovereignty, or perhaps project its influence; the former is often seen to imply the latter. In the United States, the agent of these interests is a department of state, which acts as the provider and implementor of strategic actions designed to effect the goals set by the president. In this sense, it is organization *qua* strategic decision-maker and as such is subject to accountability based on the utility it provides relative to the goals assigned it. Yet these goals are unlikely to be properly formulated.

Part of the reason for this is obvious: elected politicians are seldom schooled in the technology of proper goal-setting. Therefore, both the U.S. Congress and the presidency are likely to be occupied by men and women who are sensitive primarily to rhetorical formulations. A more subtle reason is that the president may not want the Congress to know what strategies are actually being implemented. As the agent of accountability for foreign affairs, Congress is thus frustrated in its access by such as vehicles "executive privilege" of "national security." The final reason is that proper goals are sometimes difficult to come by in such an area. For example, an oft-heard reflective goal is this: *foreign policy acts to keep America the strongest nation in the world.* But the difficulty is that "strongest" is not subject to precise measurement, nor could it be tested by experimentation (except at considerable peril). Or the State Department's goal might be set contingently: *the purpose of foreign policy is to carry out the national interest.* But this implies that the national interest is defined somewhere and properly formulated. Were the national interest ever defined at all, it might be formulated as follows: *America should be secure, respected, and loved.* Clearly, such a formulation wouldn't help us much.

Now, to the extent that a goal remains unspecified—so that criteria for strategic success remain ambiguous or subject to after-the-fact qualification—those responsible for exacting accountability from the State Department for the utility of their resource expenditures are in a difficult position. In fact, the U.S. congressional committees that have been formed to conduct accountability exercises are notoriously unsuccessful in reaching any conclusions on the subject. Their defense is, of course, that they are denied the relevant information. But a more accurate reason for their failure to exact accountability from the State Department may be that they have not used a proper approach. Particularly, when goals and objectives are rhetorical, or when relevant information is largely lacking, one may still attempt to get a utility measure through logical means. This is the court of last resort as it were, and usually provides only a crude measurement, but is to be preferred to no accountability at all.

For the case at hand, we suggest that the attempt at accountability be made at the point where the State Department seeks to renew its financing—in short, at the initiation of the budgeting process. In a rational world, future levels of support should reflect, at least in part, historical cost-benefit levels.[4] That is, an organization is to be rewarded for its successes and condemned for its failures. If cost-benefit levels are becoming more favorable, we have a *prima facie* case for advancement of the budget; where levels are unfavorable or declining, the presumed preferable alternative is to decrease the budget level, on the understanding that the funds could be used better elsewhere. This is a very crude picture of budgeting rationality, and one we will considerably modify and elaborate in the next chapter, but it serves as a starting point for us here. We will suggest that Congress act to make the new budget level dependent upon some logical utility index, one developed perhaps in the way discussed in the following paragraphs.

As an example of how this might be done, we can manufacture a very artificial and greatly oversimplified example. First of all, consider that the functional domain over which the State Department has control is diplomacy. Now, if we pose the supragoal to which the State Department is to respond as *the protection of the sovereignty of the United States*, then diplomacy is one of the three major strategic vehicles available to us. (The others are defense and development.) For the purpose of our illustration we may leave aside many important qualifications and equivocations (and some logical alternatives) and made some admittedly simplified assertions like the following:

(1) Defense seeks to protect the cause of sovereignty by discouraging aggression, presumably through the ability to retaliate in kind.

(2) Developmental initiatives might seek to protect soveriegnty by eliminating material causes for attack or aggression, perhaps by seeking to reduce imbalance in amenities between foreign states and the subject country.

(3) Finally, diplomacy may seek to discourage aggression by directing attention away from the subject country, by introducing a positive sentiment toward the subject country, or by seeking to solve disputes before they can accelerate into causes for aggression.

Now, in our much simplified example, the probable sovereignty of any nation is related to the relative strengths of these three interrelated and covariant dimensions. Any particular probability of sovereignty may be had by many different combinations of defense, developmental, and diplomatic initiatives. The presumption is, for example, that a poor country needs less defense and can benefit less from diplomacy simply because no one wants its resources; or that a nation with excellent and clever diplomats need not spend as much on national defense as would a country with ineffective diplomats (to achieve a given level of security); or that a nation with immense military power can presumably achieve a given level of security with less diplomatic effectiveness, even in the face of rather severe developmental imbalances. That is, sovereignty (accessible to us as projected national security) is a complex trade-off function of three variables acting simultaneously. That is, when there is an aggregate budget limit, diplomacy, defense, and foreign development efforts will be in conflict with each other for scarce resources. Investments in these three sectors should thus be on the basis of their comparative cost-benefit ratios, a point we will amplify in the next chapter.

For the case at hand, we have presumed that the accountability authority (the Congress) has been denied access to cost-benefit data (because of the nature of the goals involved and the pretense of security). But at this point, we at least know the function of the State Department (diplomacy) and its relationship to the supragoal (national security). So now we may ask about the expected *effects* of diplomacy. And we must here take recourse to utility logic. Let us first suggest that international relations may exist in three broad categories: amicable, inimical, and neutral. We would initiate our analysis by developing a probability

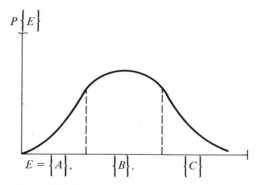

Figure 3.6. Distribution of relationship classes.

(frequency) distribution that reflects the conditions existing at some initial point in time.* Arbitrarily, we will begin with a normal distribution (although it could have taken any form). Consider Figure 3.6. Our probability construct is easily translated into set formulation, as in Figure 3.7. Here, *B* may be the set including all nations with a neutral relationship to the United States, *A* would include all nations with whom the United States enjoys an amicable relationship, and *C* would include those nations that are hostile. The set representation may, of course, be made proportional to the populations in each category.

Now, the effects of diplomacy become accessible to us as movements among these various sets or as shifts in the morphology of the probability distribution. Thus, Figures 3.6 and 3.7 represent starting-state conditions (those existing at *time t*). Let us suppose that this *time t* is the initiation of the previous operating period (e.g., the previous fiscal year, the last tenure of office) for the organization in question. In this respect, good and bad diplomacy could be indicated roughly, as in Figure 3.8.

The situation described in Figure 3.8a represents a case where the security of the United States has been improved, while Figure 3.8b indicates a case where security has been palpably weakened. We can measure the effective increase or decrease in security by taking the *expected value* associated with the original distribution (Figure 3.6) at *time t* and comparing it with the expected value of the distribution at *time t* + 1. This expected value calculation will reflect the probability of aggression and the expected costs of aggression, given the shifts in sentiment toward the subject country, a calculation we will look at shortly. Thus, the skewed-left morphology of Figure 3.8a puts most weight into the amicable category relative to the original distribution, and therefore would represent in-

---

*As we will see, this "point in time" should really be the beginning of the last full period of operations.

U = set of all nations

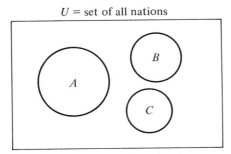

Figure 3.7. Set formulation of relationship classes.

herently less risk to national sovereignty. Here, then, we have the basis for a cost-benefit analysis of the operations of the State Department, for this reduction in risk may be assigned a manipulable "value."

But the valuation process is not direct. We may, however, assign utility indexes to the various events in the probability distribution. For example, we could let the condition of complete amicability yield an index of 1.0; open hostility could yield the utility value zero; and a perfectly neutral relationship could be assigned a 0.5 utility index. Depending on the skill of the qualitative analysts, the different nations involved in U may all be assigned an index value somewhere within this range. But these utility values will really be judgmental and categorical in origin, and hence will be treated as *interval* rather than point estimates. For example, we might be content to partition each of the three supercategories into three subcategories: very amicable (1.0), moderately amicable (0.9), adequately amicable (0.8), neutral but potentially alienable (0.4), weakly hostile (0.3), moderately hostile (0.2), openly hostile (0.0). The expected value for the relationship distribution thus involves the summation of the frequencies of appearance of nations in each of the nine subcategories, times the utility indexes (f_i, u_i). The higher

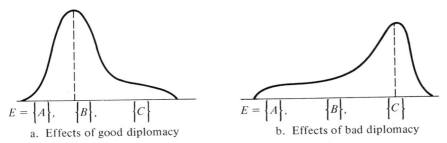

a. Effects of good diplomacy   b. Effects of bad diplomacy

Figure 3.8. Morphological transformations in qualitative distributions.

the expected value of the utility index V, the lower the threat to national security on the basis of diplomatic initiatives. The cost-benefit calculation would thus involve

$$V = \frac{(E.V._t - E.V._{t+1})}{R}$$

where R = the resources expended by the organization during the period bounded by t and $t + 1$.

We could, of course, do essentially the same thing using our set formulations. What we could be interested in here is the relative size of subpopulations at t and $t + 1$. For example, we might calculate

$$V = \frac{\left(\dfrac{A_t}{U} - \dfrac{A_{t+1}}{U}\right)}{R}.$$

But we can be a little more disciplined than this. First of all, we might keep the utility indexes we assigned the various subsets in the preceding example (e.g., very amicable = 1.0, moderately amicable = 0.9). Thus, we would have nine subsets instead of three, with each member of that subset carrying the utility index assigned that subset as a whole. However, in addition to these primary utility indexes, we might want to assign each nation in U (the universe of nations) another kind of index, such as a *threat factor*. A nation with strong potential to hurt us or endanger our sovereignty would be given a high value. In this situation, the *benefits* derived from the operations by the State Department over some interval would be accessible as

$$B_t = \sum_{L}^{g} \sum_{j}^{m} f_i \times u_i \times t_{i,j}$$

where

  i = the relationship category
  j = the jth nation in i
  f = number of nations in i
  u = utility index for i
  t = threat index for j^{th} nation in i.

Here, the benefit level increases as the more threatening nations are induced into set A or away from C. Thus, a high B value is more favorable than a low. And using this formulation, we then take the cost-benefit ratio as

$$V = \frac{(B_t - B_{t+1})}{R}.$$

Most practicing decision scientists are well-equipped to conduct such exercises in the face of rhetorical goals and objectives. Although such exercises consume much time, energy, and effort, they may be worth it where particularly critical functions are involved, as with the State Department. But there are often logical shortcuts we can take, which yield considerable information about utility with minimal expenditure of accountability costs. For the example at hand, a most interesting logical artifice can be advanced. Suppose that we concentrated only on those nations that have inimical relationships among themselves. We would emerge with a set of pairs of nations that are avowed enemies: $([w_i, w_j] \in W)$. In short, we are concerned here with a much smaller population of nations than in the previous exercise.

Now, using certain types of judgmental sampling disciplines (the Delphi method, for example)[5], it is possible to generate a subjective qualitative partitioning, such as the following:

State Alternatives	Implication (Qualitative Value)
$(w_i, w_j) \in A$	→ Superior Diplomacy
$(w_i, w_j) \in B$	→ Effective Diplomacy
$(w_i) \in A;\ (w_j) \in C$	→ Adequate Diplomacy
$(w_i) \in B; (w_j) \in C$	
$(w_i, w_j) \in C$	→ Dysfunctional Diplomacy

We might then develop a probability distribution around these four alternative states, employing an opinion-survey technique. The results might look something like Figure 3.9. It is assumed that our experts agree that enormous diplomatic skill would be necessary for the United States to remain friendly with two nations that have an inimical relationship (e.g., to have positive relations with both Turkey and Greece). Slightly more probable, but still admirable, is the case where we can maintain an effective neturality with two enemies, such as India

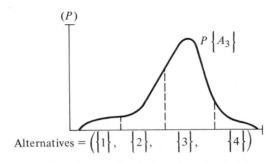

Figure 3.9. *A priori* distribution of relational states.

and Pakistan. The most probable situation is alternative 3, where we split our relationships (e.g., we are on friendly terms with Israel, but in an inimical relationship with one of its enemies, such as Iraq). Finally, it almost defies the laws of probability to have a situation where we are the enemy of two nations, which are themselves die-hard enemies (e.g., to have an inimical relationship with both Russia and China, both Greece and Turkey, both India and Pakistan). Yet, as some critics have suggested, this is precisely the result of the nonnormative (e.g., opportunistic, "realistic") foreign policy followed for the last several years by the United States. On the basis of this evidence, the Congress may legitimately presume to cut appropriations for the State Department, because we could not do this poorly *if we had no diplomatic force at all*. Therefore, we must suggest that the utility of the strategies implemented by the State Department is extremely low.

We can determine just how low accessible is—in imputation at least—by assigning utility indexes to the various state alternatives (e.g., let alternative 1 = 1.0, alternative 2 = 0.75, alternative 3 = 0.5, and alternative 4 = 0.25). Combined with a *threat index* associated with each nation, we could again compute a benefit index, and use it as the denominator in a cost-benefit index, which would be very unfavorable indeed. The point is that, by using such a logical artifice, we have considerably reduced the calculations required to determine a cost-benefit ratio. In fact, we have reduced them by the amount W/U, as W is a much reduced subset of the universe of nations we dealt with in our previous utility measurement. Thus, for the clever accountability authority, there are ways in which economies may be introduced even in the face of ostensibly very complex situations. And, of course, when we reduce the expected costs of accountability exercises, we increase their probability of occurrence.

3.3 EFFICIENCY, RETURN, AND PRODUCTIVITY

As is to be expected, the task of auditing *efficiency* in the tactical decision domain is much simpler than measuring strategic utility. A truly staggering amount of economic and business administration literature is available to those concerned with managerial-level decisions and their results. In the first place, as the decision latitude allowed tacticians is usually quite circumscribed, we have little real concern with matters of propriety. Clearly, the strategic decision-makers will pass down some procedural constraints, but the exercise of determining normative congruence will be much simpler in the tactical than in the strategic domain. In short, the subset of normative alternatives available to the tactician (the set X, given in Figure 3.4) will be expectedly quite small and will contain alternatives that tend to cluster around a single generic tactic.

Again, tactical decision-makers tend to be accountable primarily for efficiency. Efficiency generally means the rate of expenditure of scarce resources—time, money, talent, material, and so forth—in pursuit of an objective passed down by the strategic analysts. It is, of course, possible to employ utility calculations at this level, but *dimensioned* decision criteria are generally available to us and are to be preferred.

Utility, as we have seen, is largely a logical artifice, driven by judgment, subjective probabilities or disciplined imputations. As we will later show, such devices are largely appropriate for the relatively broad, often ill-structured problems with which strategic decision-makers deal. Particularly, strategic utility involves a larger domain of inquiry, and a farther time horizon, than does tactical efficiency. The ramifications of tactical decisions are more localized in both time and space, and therefore more amenable to empirical observation, quantitative measurement, and immediacy of assessment. Therefore, we have less excuse to take recourse in logical or judgmental modalities of accountability. Just as the tactician becomes primarily concerned with decisions involving quantities and clustered decision alternatives (e.g., members of the same qualitative set), so also may those to whom tactical decision-makers are accountable, i.e., the strategic decision-makers or organizational executives *per se*.

The executives or strategic decision-makers must initiate the accountability process properly and thus must establish proper targets for the tacticians to pursue. In our vocabulary, we have seen that organizational directors are concerned with goals; these goals then become translated into strategic objectives; and strategic objectives become translated into tactical targets.

As Figure 3.2 indicated, we are concerned with efficiency on two dimensions: *variance* and *return*. Of the two, variance is the simplest to comprehend. Particularly, variance becomes the focus of accountability whenever some "management by objectives" scheme is in force. Recall that management by objectives sets targets through a bargaining process. In the present instance, the tactical manager would attempt to set a performance target more favorable to him (presumably one with a high probability of attainment), while his superior would by trying to get him to agree to a target involving some challenge. At any rate, at the end of the year, accountability would consist of measuring the variance between expected and actual results. Presumably, when this variance is quite significant, the manager becomes susceptible to sanction of some sort. Where the target was met, he is presumably immune to objective sanction. The problem with such an approach is, of course, that it is generally reflective in the most explicit sense of the word, for targets may tend to be set only with respect to historical performance (e.g., increase performance by x percent over last year). Also, there may be no attempt to develop a *distributed* measure of performance, which may operate at all levels of management of across all functions of the organization. Finally, there may be the "apples and oranges" problem, with different functionaries accountable for very different criteria, even within the same level of management. In many cases, then, reliance on management by objectives may merely reflect a lack of sophistication among an organization's administrators, and not the rationality that is so often pretended for the scheme. Some variations on the theme are, however, of immediate interest.

In particular, there is the accountability system, which involves the partitioning of the organization into various *profit centers*. Here, a common target (distributed criterion) is set for all tactical operations: the rate of return on invested resources. That is, each manager of each profit center becomes accountable for some specific contribution to the overall earnings (or profit) base of the organization. Theoretically, we are here offered the opportunity to employ absolute targets (e.g., optimality criteria), but it is an opportunity often foregone due to technological problems. How, for example, might we calculate the impact on the aggregate rate of return associated with the janitorial department, the accounting department, the public relations office, or a research and development office? Indeed, to the extent that an organization has a large number of *support functions*, in contrast to directly productive functions, the promise of the profit center and the distributed accountability target becomes difficult to realize. The partial answer—and one often employed, with varying degrees of success—is to set up some sort of internal pricing system.[6] Here, the maintenance department, the accounting department, or the computer center will bill other units of the organization for services rendered. This requires a sophisticated cost-accounting scheme, but even so it does not answer for efficiency, as the internal pricing scheme will itself usually be reflective, being based on historical budget and expense figures for various service departments. (Occasionally, however, the internal price will be set on the basis of the best price that the consuming unit could obtain *anywhere*.)

Again, even in the framework of profit-center analysis, we arrive back at the point where optimality criteria are often displaced or neglected. Moreover, the profit-center concept opens the organization to certain types of political problems. Support units will attempt to get the highest possible price for their services. But because the price is a "shadow" function—a budget artifice—arguments cannot be resolved deterministically (solely on the basis of accounting data). Therefore, actual internal prices often involve a judgment, and therefore may be biased by factors of personality, corporate politics, and so forth. To partially correct this, there is the option to employ some sort of *value-added* scheme. This is useful, mainly in the face of sequential manufacturing or service operations. The principle is that each organizational unit, when it passes a semi-processed product on to the next department, bills the receiving department for the work done. But, this billing process, similar to the internal pricing scheme, computes the value added only as a function of historical costs. Ideally, all these costs would be related to the primary distributed target (rate of return on invested resources), but in practice we encounter the same old problem: what is the contribution to profit of the workers who sweep the plant floor or handle the payroll for the employees in the lathe department? Usually, all such support and service operations are lumped together into a *pro rata* overhead figure, and then added to the fixed (or direct) costs of the profit center or value-added unit (perhaps leading to evaluation on the basis of return on gross assets [ROGA]). As a result, there is no way to assess the profit impact of the support and indirect administrative functions; therefore, a significantly large proportion of actual organizational expenditures (investments) become effectively immune to accountability in terms of return criteria.

Thus, even for an organization that pretends to rationality through the use of profit centers, value-added analysis, internal pricing schemes, or the ultimate attempt to tie every expenditure (investment) to aggregate rate of return, there is always this problem: there is usually not a single person in such an organization who could hope to compute the real value of adding another accountant or janitor to the staff, of purchasing another computer. Nor could they accurately report the profit impact of new carpet in the marketing vice president's office, of sending supervisors to sensitivity-training sessions, or of industrial lunches given by the public relations director. Indeed, as many critics have suggested, partitioning the organization into profit centers, and distributing overhead expenses *pro rata*, often obscures the amount of corporate investments that go into indirect or nonproductive investments. In short, the aggregation of the corporation's operations into some overall rate of return on investment says little about the degree of optimality of the organization, or about the absolute rationality of management. As we earlier suggested, this is symptomatic of all occasions when reflective goals take precedence over absolute goals and optimal criteria.

Certainly, the concept of return on invested resources is superior to the use of simple measures of "variance" between desired and actual managerial performance. And, if these are faults with the profit-center scheme, or with the attempt to tie all functions to an overall performance index, they also have distinct advantages. With certain modifications and expediencies, accountability via return calculations may lend considerable discipline to an organization. Moreover, such discipline is not restricted solely to manufacturing firms or to private commercial enterprises. It also has a place in public and governmental enterprise, even where the goals of the organization as a whole are relatively immune to precise accountability or quantification, or where the functions of the organization are ostensibly such that accountability itself is a moot ambition to begin with. To make this point clear and to give us a working familiarity with the mechanism for auditing performance on the basis of return, we will now examine how we might tackle the very controversial problem of measuring return on investment within the context of higher education. And if we can do something about accountability in this context, our technology will be even simpler to apply in commercial or general government contexts.

Basically, we will have to develop some sort of variation of the profit-center theme and manipulate the concept of rate of return in certain ways. Moreover, we will also have to introduce surrogates into the accountability process. But before we can do that, we have to treat the initial problem that emerges in so much of public and governmental enterprise: the absence of a proper, actionable organizational goal. Knowing something about the criteria for proper goals, we quickly suggest that any college or university (and by extension, many service enterprises) might employ a goal-formulation something like this: *maximize the return of unallocated resources*.

Such a goal is a relatively pedestrian alternative to the grandiloquent statements of purpose and direction we have been led to expect from most service organizations. Most frequently, and with apparent seriousness, their missions are cast in such terms as ministering to the needs of people, serving as a husband of Western civilization, and helping to integrate the individual into the community. The whole gamut of service organizations (hospitals, universities, colleges, theater or artistic groups, charitable agencies, religious organizations, improvement societies, and most social-service arms of government or community) express their ambitions in generally vague, suasive terms. This contrasts sharply with the very practical, pervasive problem faced by most such agencies: they are all in competition for scarce resources, for share of what might be called "social overhead." However, their objective *right* to a share of such funds usually remains in doubt.

The primary reason for this is that the effects or benefits of service functions are often virtually incalculable using normal analytical, statistical, or accounting techniques. For example, what is the real and ultimate "benefit" to society from an educational institution? Do we measure it by the number of degrees granted? If so, is a degree in medieval French literature worth more than one in engineering? Is a master's degree in business administration worth more to the community than a Ph.D. in mathematics? More than a bachelor's degree in economics? There is also the horizon problem. At what point do we attempt to measure educational effectiveness? At the termination of study? Five years after graduation? Ten years? And then, what do we look for? The graduate's income level? Psychological health? Imputed level of happiness?

The same problems emerge if we try to calculate the benefits (effectiveness) of a church or a little theater, a medical clinic or a public defender's office, a welfare agency, or a community organization such as the Boy Scouts. All will claim to perform an invaluable service, and all will try to portray themselves as indispensible to society. Given their predilection for rhetorical goals, most service organizations will also pose themselves as relatively immune from accountability. They proclaim, and for the most part rightfully, that they cannot be treated like a shoe manufacturer, an automobile company, or any other profit-making entity. Thus, in the name of academic freedom, even if it were able, a university may not be willing to account for its resource's utility to the state legislature or alumni who support it; a charitable organization meets its accountability requirements simply by making a year-end income-and-expense statement available; a community hospital will do the same thing, perhaps indexing expenses with information about the patient population or other service parameters. In almost no case is any attempt made to produce a cost-effectiveness (or utility/resource expenditure) index. This, of course, immediately raises the critical question: with no attempt at linking expenditures to utility, how are internal allocations of resources made? They are often made in either of two ways: (a) on the basis of a flat percentage increase or decrease geared to historical budgeting levels for the organization's various departments or units ("inertial budgeting"), or (b) on the basis of casual (e.g., intuitive) or political criteria. A majority of organizations allocate resources using some combination of these two reflective methods, although many organizations do indeed employ more sophisticated techniques, and the field of evaluative research is an increasingly important area for consultancy.

As long as we are concerned merely with reflective criteria of performance, the separation of resource expenditures (cost) from utility (effectiveness) is a more or less legitimate strategem. For, given that such organizations are competitors for limited support bases, then we may presume that the organizations with the highest comparative return flow of resources among a group of similarly dedicated institutions are those that the community (or society) judges to be most productive or most valuable. Thus, the aggregate level of support (taken over some interval) is a *surrogate* for actual effectiveness, which usually remains inaccessible to us because of the complexity of the "outputs" of service organizations.

But we can see that using resource levels as a surrogate for genuine effectiveness has its problems. Particularly, there are very obvious ways that growth and effectiveness can be separated. A service organization with an effective lobby at the state or federal level may obtain funds using political leverage, with no utility criteria introduced. Or an institution with a clever public relations department may use emotional leverage to increase capital flow independent of investment utility. Or, as often happens, a service organization may have an effective monopoly (e.g., be the only community hospital or the only state university). Finally, as with the earlier commercial examples, reflective measurements give no real indication of the extent to which any service organization is the best possible destination for public or community funding (or for contributions or charitable support). Indeed, using comparative funding levels as a surrogate for effectiveness would simply tend to suggest that one organization is superior to another, but neither may represent an optimal investment of social overhead.

Although indexes of optimality are difficult to construct and interpret (as we will see in the next chapter), we can at least approach three critical subordinate issues within the framework of the accountability audit: (a) what mechanism is available for rationally allocating internal resources within a service organization? (b) what procedures are available for disciplining collective bargaining within the social-services sector? and (c) how might we rationally allocate societal resources among competing investment opportunities within the same service domain? Our goal formulation—suggesting that service agencies act to maximize unallocated resources *per capita*—sets us on the road to the answers. For it is the level of unallocated resources *returning* to a service agency that allows it to better serve its clients or constituents.

We can readily see why this is the case. Let us consider the ration s/y, where x is the funding level of the organization (the resource base) and y is the population the organization serves (e.g., the number of students in a university, of patients in a hospital, of welfare clients in an urban service program). The result of this ratio, z, give us the *per capita* expenditure level. When we consider that service (utility) is positively correlated with *per capita* expenditure levels, the three things that can happen to the s/y ratio at the initiation of any new operating period would have the following implications:

(1) $\dfrac{x_t}{y_t} > \dfrac{x_{t+1}}{y_{t+1}}$ Indicates an erosion in the *per capita* service level and hence a dilution of the imputed effectiveness of the organization

(2) $\dfrac{x_t}{y_t} = \dfrac{x_{t+1}}{y_{t+1}}$ Indicates a proportional change in the ration, which signifies no change in the organization's service posture

(3) $\dfrac{x_t}{x_y} < \dfrac{x_{t+1}}{y_{t+1}}$ Indicates a proportional increase in the *potential* level of service the organization is able to deliver.

In the first case, the aggregate support level has declined relative to the population to be serviced; this means less for everybody, assuming that services are distributed across the population symmetrically. In the second case, *per capita* service levels need not be affected. And in the third case, the resource base has increased at a faster rate than the client population (on the client population has decreased more rapidly than the resource base). In either case, the organization is left with a more favorable *per capita* situation.

The relationship between *per capita* resources (z) and organizational effectiveness should be clear. Subject to the conditions in Figure 2.8 (where we considered the problem of diminishing returns to scale within the context of the school-board problem), a higher z assumes that the organization can make a relatively greater contribution to its clients' welfare. For example, it can have more books or laboratory equipment for its students, and more drugs, physicians, nurses, or janitors per patient; it can give its welfare clients higher payment, more food stamps, or more counseling. Presumably, the *more* services an organization offers its clientele, the more effective it is. In short, a university with a lower faculty-student ratio, a relatively large library, and more laboratory equipment per user may be presumed to do a more effective job than a competitor with less services to offer each student. We must qualify this, of course, and suggest that this would demand that the services per student be rationally structured and distributed; we will introduce this qualification in a moment. Even so, when the organization's executives increase the *per capita* expenditure level, they increase the *potential* effectiveness of their organization. Therefore, in the service sector, it is possible to measure the potential *utility* of an organization (and hence the unqualified *performance* of its executives or operating officers) by looking at the time-dependent changes in the x/y ratio. In almost any case, an executive may be said to have failed his organization (although not necessarily the community at large) when the x/y ratio is allowed to fall, even if it reflects increased efficiency at the operations level.* From the parochial perspective we are adopting here, "more is always better," although we will later qualify this considerably.

What about the restrictions on the use to which an incremental increase in z may be put? Generally, we would have to consider two possibilities: (a) the funds are *categorical*, granted only to perform specific functions, and (b) the funds are *unallocated* and may be spent at the discretion of the organization's executives.[7] Now, categorical funds are to be used in a specific way: to educate American Indians over the age of 40; to give maternity benefits to welfare mothers; to build a statue on the campus in memory of an alumnus; to add modern French lithographs to the community art museum; and so on. Of course, the categories are virtually limitless. *A priori* dedicated inputs may therefore vary considerably in their impact on the effectiveness level of the organization. As a rule, they should always be accepted. They automatically carry a *zero opportunity cost*, for they are not available for any other purpose from the standpoint of the receiving organization. They may represent relatively idle investments, but they do not cost the organization anything. Thus, categorical increases in the funding base may or may not advance effectiveness, but in no case might they be expected to reduce it.

*In this case, if reductions in resources are proportional to increases in efficiency, the level of service is not revised upward, and gross effectiveness thus remains unaffected.

Unallocated funds are the most promising because they are potentially available to be invested in zero-opportunity-cost investments without *a priori* restriction. The executives would now be expected to search throughout the entire organization for the best uses for the funds, so that the most productive investment could be made. Thus, unallocated overhead funds or resources should enable the organization's executives to actually increase its effectiveness level. In the context of rationality, these funds should be used to maximize the incremental utility-resource ratio. But, to the extent that the organization's executives lack either wit or integrity, the incremental increase in z may be used poorly. In fact, it may be used to feather the executives' own nests—new carpeting, larger expense accounts, new office buildings—in much the same way that overhead could be employed in commercial enterprise. And what often happens in the service sector—perhaps even more frequently than in commercial or industrial enterprises—is that incremental increases in overhead merely expand the administrative structure at the expense of directly productive service functions. Thus, either ignorance on the part of the executives or the lack of an adequate accountability mechanism can act to deteriorate the productivity of any funding increases.

Such a point is gratuitous. But the question of accountability as a control on organizational quality is central to our interests. At this point, we must investigate the relationship between organizational effectiveness and efficiency. For, as is clear, the net effectiveness associated with any x/y ratio will depend upon the rationality of the resource allocations made internally. Thus, the *per capita* expenditure level is the strategic parameter for us in the service sector, but tactical considerations now force us to look at the productivity of x. In short, we must ask about the extent to which the *potential* of any x/y ratio is actually realized.

We know that potential benefits will increase as the x/y ratio increases (Figure 3.10a). But when we consider tactical efficiency, we also know that there will be a range of benefits (b_i's) associated with any given x/y level, as in Figure 3.10b. Thus, our analysis here is consonant with our earlier remarks about the relationship between strategic and tactical decisions. Particularly, the x/y captured by an organization's executives sets the potential benefit level (the "ceiling" effectiveness or utility index) for the organization; however, the quality of the tactical decisions will determine the actual benefit levels associated with any give x/y, with the expectation that the b_i's might be distributed more or less normally across any set of competitive service organizations (e.g., any set of hospitals or colleges in a region).

Clearly, the attribute working in Figure 3.10b is *decision rationality*. Specifically, more sophisticated decision-makers are expected to obtain results consistently in the more favorable segment of the distribution of b_i's. To make this clearer, and to show how accountability and decision rationality may reinforce each other within the confines of a service organization, we turn to our example.

Potential Benefit Level
(Effectiveness)

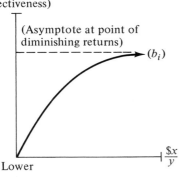

Probability

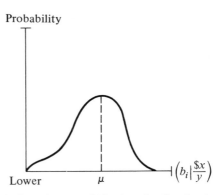

a. Potential effectiveness levels
relative to funding levels

b. Distribution of b's given funding level

Figure 3.10. Potential and actual benefit levels.

Recall that we will be working with some prototypical university, given a goal formulation directing the organization to "maximize unallocated *per capita* resources." Given such a goal, the first step is to identify the various sources of inputs (e.g., funding bases). A typical university may have a mix such as that in Table 3.3.

The input sources in the table are more or less obvious in their implications. Formula budgets pertain mainly to public-supported or sectarian (e.g., religious)

Table 3.3. Funding partitions (input sources).

Sources	*Per Capita*	*Categorical*	*Unallocated*
Formula Budgets (F) (from an external agency–state, community, church, etc.)	X	–	–
Contract Funds (C) (for either directed or free research, program development, etc.)	–	X	[X]
Student Tuition (S) including fees and profits on internal operations–cafeteria, book-stores, etc.)	–	–	X
Alumni Donations and Bequests (D) (including proceeds from any endowments, etc.)	–	X	[X]
Public Fees (P) (admission to athletic contests, concerts, special lectures, etc.)	–	–	X

institutions of some kind, where inputs are generated on a *per capita* basis, with the *per capita* funding base sometimes unrelated to actual costs. Contract funds, such as those made available by governments, foundations, private agencies, and corporations, are tied to some output; that is, they exact some performance from the university. In some cases, however, some latitude may be associated with the expenditures; hence, the bracketed check mark in the Unallocated column. For example, the funds may be for free (or pure) research, for curriculum development, or some sort of subject-free innovation in instructional methodology. In other instances, the contract inputs may be disposed of at the discretion of the university itself, in which case they are *a priori* unallocated. Student sources provide both tuition and fees (which again may be unrelated to actual costs) and also offer a potential for profit on internal services such as cafeteria, dormitory, and book fees. There are generally no external constraints on the disposition of tuition and fees, and so forth. Alumni donations and other bequests are usually categorical, but not always. In some cases, a bequest may carry no constraints as to its uses and, hence, may be spent at the direction of university officials. Finally, fees charged for university-sponsored events are usually available for free allocation.

These various inputs eventually find their way into the support of the several *functions* performed by the normal university. Table 3.4 identifies three major functions, with notes on their basic outputs. Inputs devoted to functions go directly into the development of the resource base of a university, perhaps consisting of:

(a) faculty (for teaching research, etc.)
(b) administrative and staff positions (management, secretarial, etc.)
(c) infrastructure (plant, equipment, facilities, etc.)
(d) student support (fellowships, grants, scholarships, etc.)

Table 3.4. Function and output relationships.

Function	First-Order Outputs
Teaching	Structure of education offerings, curricula, degree structure, degrees and certifications granted, etc.
Research	Advances of subject knowledge attributable to studies by faculty (and sometimes, students)
External Services	Accessible as the events (athletic or cultural, etc.) sponsored by the university; as the products associated with any contracted projects (e.g., government studies, corporation consulting projects); as the schedule of services offered by faculty, staff, or students to any external agency (e.g., addresses to the Rotary Club, journalistic efforts, consultation to civic governments, activities on academic associations)

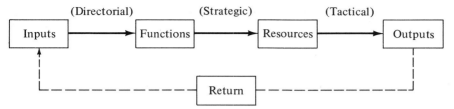

Figure 3.11. Transformation functions.

The actual outputs (or products) of a university thus ultimately depend on how the preceding resources are distributed across the major functions and on the quality of the resources (e.g., the amenities of plant or grounds; the prestige or teaching effectiveness of faculty). In the simplest sense, then, the decision structure of our prototypical university might look something like Figure 3.11. Particularly, it is the general responsibility of the university's directors (its board of governors, regents, or trustees) to determine the *mission* that the institution is to carry out. This implies responsibility for developing what we will call a functional configuration for the organization. In the present case, three generic configurations as illustrated in Figure 3.12, concern us.

Now, these various configurations may either be imposed on the university exogenously, or they may represent a deliberate choice on the part of the institutional executives. For example, a decision to emphasize teaching may, in some instances, be taken by default. If the institution has an unfavorable resource ratio (a low $\$x/y$), then it will have to employ virtually all its resources in the direct education function; this is typical of many local or community colleges, especially those with open enrollment. Such a school is not likely to be big in football, nor will it fund many concerts or have a well-developed research capability. However, some institutions will have to emphasize research. For example, they may be categorically endowed to do research (e.g., Rockefeller University),

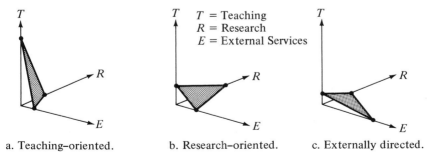

a. Teaching–oriented.   b. Research–oriented.   c. Externally directed.

Figure 3.12. Functional configurations.

or they may have a mandate for graduate education, with its implied research support, (e.g., as with a state university as opposed to a state college). Finally, some institutions must attend to external services, especially those that depend largely on alumni endowments; therefore, athletic programs at the University of Southern California and Notre Dame demand considerable emphasis.

Any of these configurations, in the absence of such exogenous imperatives, may be deliberately invoked. A school may emphasize teaching in an effort to minimize the student-faculty ratio and therefore gain a reputation as "humanistic" (and perhaps become a school of "social significance" as well). A university might seek to develop and emphasize a research capability because of market conditions (e.g., there may be a great demand for graduate education in the region that is not met by other institutions). Finally, a school may seek to amplify its external services, again perhaps because of local market conditions or because the university is the *only* source of cultural or athletic interest in a region.

At any rate, the basic functional configuration simply sets gross constraints on the use of whatever resources are available to the university (to the extent that they are unallocated). For example, teaching implies the maintenance of faculty, construction or maintenance of an educational plant, and certain administrative functions (e.g., the registrar's office, academic recordkeeping, dormitory management); it may also imply the dedication of some inputs to support student-teachers. On the other hand, a strong external services dimension would imply certain other resource loadings. For example, an athletic program would probably raise the demand for coaches, uniforms, equipment, a ticket office, a press relations officer, student scholarships, and the construction of spectator facilities. A research orientation might imply the need for a high-level faculty, many graduate assistants, expensive and sophisticated laboratory facilities, and a strong grants administration and research support office. The strategic allocation decision thus always involves the determination of a dedication of blocks of resources to potentially competitive functions, within whatever normative constraints are provided by the board. For, in most cases, a faculty position employed in one functional area (one mission domain) leaves it unavailable for other uses; a dollar used to support classroom education is a dollar lost to the football team or the physics laboratory. Therefore, strategic resource allocation is of critical importance in the service organization and is the counterpart of the major product or service decisions made in commercial enterprise (e.g., determinations of what businesses we are in).

These aggregate (strategic) allocations may be made either casually or with significant scientific discipline. A casual approach is simply to take existing aggregate allocations and expand or contract them according to increases or decreases in total resource availabilities for the coming period (e.g., the inertial budgeting scheme). Or, resource allocations may be subject to political or axiological criteria (e.g., a member of the board may be very fond of football and *a priori* illdisposed toward biogenetic research; or the president may be a mediocre scholar and, for subjective reasons, may act against the interests of fundamental research). Obviously, there are no limits to the irrational procedures by which allocations to basic missions may be made. But there are distinct limitations on the proper scientific approach to basic mission loadings (strategic allocation decisions). Rational allocations would first of all demand calculation of the direction and then the magnitudes of the relationships between the several functions (missions) and the resource-providers (input sources), perhaps as follows:

$$U.\,I. = f(F,C,S,D,P)$$
$$G = (U.\,I._{t+1} - U.\,I._t)$$
$$G = (\Delta\ [F,C,S,D,P] = f\ [T,R,E])$$

where

$U.\,I.$ = unallocated income as a function of the several input sources
$\quad G$ = the incremental change in $U.\,I.$ as a function of the several missions
$\qquad$ (teaching, research, external service)
$\quad F$ = formula budget
$\quad C$ = contract research funds
$\quad S$ = student fees, tuitions, etc.
$\quad D$ = donations, bequests, etc.
$\quad P$ = public fees (for events, publications, etc.).

The general function for our purposes is thus

$$MAX\ [G] = f(I_{i\ [t+n]}\ |\ E_{j\ [t]})$$

where

$\quad I$ = the set of all input sources for the next and all subsequent periods
$\quad E$ = the set of all missions (functional areas) for the current period.

Were we interested simply in maximizing the resource base, without regard to unallocated funds, then the decision-makers would simply replace G with X, the undifferentiated resource base.

Now, we have to assign each functional area (or mission) a utility index that reflects its expected *leverage* on unallocated inputs. This utility function U is the operator that relates the functional loadings to inputs:

$$[I]\ U_j\ [E]$$

where

U_1 = teaching function
U_2 = research function
U_3 = external service function
$\sum U_j$ = 1.0.

We are thus searching for a master relationship to be evaluated, which for the present context is

$$E.V.(G) = (W_{i,1}U_1 + W_{i,2}U_2 + W_{i,3}U_3)$$

where

$W_{i,j}$ = resources devoted to the jth function

and

i = 1 implies faculty
i = 2 implies staff (administrative) support
i = 3 implies infrastructure (*pro rata*)
i = 4 implies student support (scholarships, fellowships, etc.).

We can see, then, that the recommended strategy is to allocate resources to the several functions proportional to their utilities (that is, their expected leverage on input sources):

$$\frac{W_j}{W} = \frac{U_j}{1}.$$

Our real problem at the strategic analysis stage is thus to get reasonably reliable estimates of the U_j's, as these are the direct determinants of our actual allocations and hence the basis for the actual ($G = f[W_j]$) that eventually emerges. As a matter of practice, the calculation of utility values in the context of the service organization is an enormously demanding task. But we know something about the components of the appropriate utility index. Specifically, we will have to be concerned with three dimensions: direction of influence, order of effect, and magnitude.

The direction of influence simply refers to the qualitative relationship between an input and a function—e.g., does an incremental increase in the loading of a function (for instance, an increase in teaching effectiveness or level of education) yield a positive (P), negative (N), or indeterminate (I) effect on the input source? Order of effect reflects the fact that some impacts may be *lagged* through time (e.g., some effects are immediate, others take time to develop and operate through intermediate functions). Finally, magnitude measures the strength of the impact of a functional area on an input source—the "rate of return," as it were.

Table 3.5. Dimensions of a strategic allocation analysis.

	Input Sources														
	Formula Budget (F)			Contract Funding (C)			Student Inputs (S)			Donations, Bequests (D)			Public Fees (P)		
Function/Mission	a	b	c	a	b	c	a	b	c	a	b	c	a	b	c
Teaching (T)	I	2	$m_{1,1}$	P	3	$m_{1,2}$	P	(1)	$m_{1,3}$	I	3	$m_{1,4}$	P	4	$m_{1,5}$
Research (R)	I	3	$m_{2,1}$	P	(1)	$m_{2,2}$	P	2	$m_{2,3}$	P	4	$m_{2,4}$	P	4	$m_{2,5}$
External Service (E)	I	3	$m_{3,1}$	P	4	$m_{3,2}$	P	2	$m_{3,3}$	P	2	$m_{3,4}$	P	(1)	$m_{3,5}$

In any strategic allocation problem, it is useful to develop a master matrix, with a "cell" assigned to each of the possible critical relationships. For the problem at hand, we have a matrix like that in Table 3.5.

The entry in column *a* for each input source and functional pair specifies the expected direction of relationship, while the column *b* entries reflect our expectations about order of effect. In practice, these two dimensions are highly interdependent. Therefore, to suggest something of our logic in these assignments, we will elaborate on the implications of the increase in teaching effectiveness (T).

(a) Cell (1, 3):* The increase in teaching effectiveness (or level of educational service) is expected to have an immediate and positive impact on S; particularly, it is expected to lead to greater enrollment demand and to subsequently higher tuition and student fees in the next period.

(b) Cell (1, 1): Presuming a positive effect of T on S in the first period, the impact of T on F in the second period is *a priori* indeterminate. The impact is delayed and indeterminate because we do not know whether the increase in funding from student sources (following an increase in T) will cause the funding authorities to adjust downward the *per capita* formula budgeting rate, to compensate for the increase in S. That is $[T, F] = I$ because $[F, S] = I$. To eliminate this indeterminacy, we would have to try to get a commitment from the funding authorities that would guarantee the formula budget rate over some range of increases in S.

(c) Cell (1, 3): Here we presume that an increase in T led to an increase in S in the first period, with some portion of ΔS being available to hire new faculty with research ambitions; these then permit us to exert leverage on contract research funds in the third period (via cell 2, 2).

(d) Cell (1, 4): Given an increase in S responding to a prior increase in T, we have an indeterminacy in the third period with respect to $[T, D]$. For example, there is a possibility that alumni and others will lessen their do-

*For example, Cell (1, 3) would be the element at the conjunction of the first row and the third column, and so on.

nations and bequests as student enrollment grows. Their intentions would have to be evaluated very carefully to eliminate the redundancy, and we would of course have to develop a magnitudinal measure, $m_{1,4}$, given that there was a possibility of a negative donation level in response to an increase in S. The general expectation is that $[T, D] = P$, assuming that the growth in student population may be expected to develop new donors at a faster rate than old donors are alienated, etc.

(e) Cell (1, 5): We assume, here, that the ultimate impact of an increase in T on P is positive, but significantly lagged. Our logic is this: assuming that an increase in S accompanies an increase in T in the first period, we have some unallocated resources to invest based on S. We may elect to invest these, for example, in the development of an athletic program in the second period. This would imply hiring a coaching staff, purchasing equipment, and starting recruitment. A team may thus be fielded in the fourth period (or perhaps even the third), and a claim laid to fees for attendance at the games, television royalties, and so on.

We emerge with a strategic trajectory for each of the rows of the master matrix. The first row might be diagramed as in Figure 3.13. The various segments of the network in Figure 3.13 each carry a probability index (in brackets) and a directional operator (in parentheses). At the point where we are concerned about the relationship between $[F, S]$, we enter a *stochastic node*. This suggests that there is some probability $(1 - p)$ that F may be reduced to negate the increase in S. If this occurs, then we do not have the unallocated inputs to devote to increasing the research capability (to generate $\Delta R \overset{(+)}{\leftrightarrow} \Delta C$) or to developing the external service dimension (implying $\Delta E \overset{(+)}{\leftrightarrow} \Delta P$). Given this stochastic node (assuming that it cannot be *a priori* eliminated), we have two possible utility calculations

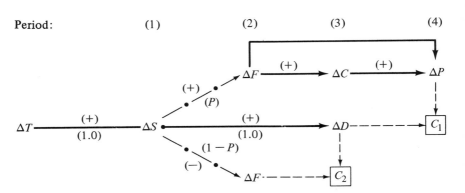

Figure 3.13. Strategic network diagram.

to consider:

$$U_T \equiv (\Delta G \mid \Delta T) = c_1 \mid (F, S) = P$$
$$= c_2 \mid (F, S) = N.$$

Of course, the condition where $(F, S) = N$ is tantamount to a punishment for success, which perhaps is not an unusual condition in the public sector. But generally, we can see that when missions are properly defined so that they are all correlated positively and are mutually reinforcing, then we can improve any one of the functions and eventually be able to improve them all. Thus, where unallocated resources are available for rational investment, and where organizational missions are properly defined, our service organization becomes comprehensible as a *positively reflexive system* (one that can move secularly along an upward spiral in terms of potential effectiveness over some considerable range of inputs). Consider Figure 3.14. We can readily see that the development of these strategic networks to evaluate the impact of major missions can consume considerable time and resources. But there are often some tricks to reduce the scope of the strategic analysis process. Such a trick is available here when we recall the dictate that the service organization should act, at the strategic level, to $MAX (\$X/Y)$. Consider that the fundamental utility of any mission will be measured with respect to this objective, so we get the following:

$$U_j = p_1 F + p_2 C + p_3 S + p_4 D + p_5 P \mid \Delta W_{j(t)}.$$

The coefficients (the p_i's) reflect the proportion of the increases in any of the inputs that are expected to be unallocated. Now, we may simplify our strategic

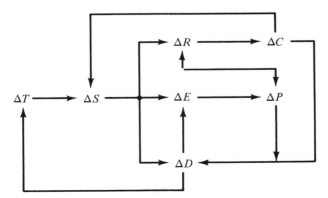

Figure 3.14. Array of reflexive functional relationships.

analysis by recognizing that

$$p_1 \to 0$$
$$p_2 \to 0$$
$$p_5 \to 1,$$

yielding a simplified utility formulation,

$$U_j = p_3 S + p_4 D + P \mid \Delta W_{j(t)}.$$

The logic behind this simplification is direct. The formula-budgeting input source tends to be fully allocated on the basis of real costs of educating a student (plus some fixed and usually minimal overhead contribution). If F were the only funding source available to the university, then $\$X$ and Y could increase (or decrease) only proportionally, and the strategic allocation problem would thus be moot. In short, the proportion of inputs from a formula (*per capita*) budgeting system that are unallocated goes to zero. So, as a rule, do inputs for the contract research function, for the C is predicated on the real costs of performing the research called for by the contracting authority (again with a minimal overhead loading). Therefore, p_2 also approaches zero. Funds drawn from external services (P) will, on the other hand, be totally unallocated, so that p_5 approaches unity and thus disappears. There may be some sort of internal contract that specifies that a certain portion of public fees (for example, from a football game) would revert to the athletic department, in which case we would have to compute p_5. But when such internal protocol is not in force, then the totality of public fees may generally be considered allocable at the discretion of the organizational authorities themselves.

The simplification of the basic calculation function becomes extremely important when we move into the zero-sum game, where an increase in resources devoted to one function (mission) implies a reduction in the resources available for the other missions. In such a case, an evaluation of the *cross-impact* conditions is required. A strategic network would have to be developed for each of the mission areas (e.g., development of a network for R and E, in addition to the T network already illustrated). The analytical requirement is that cross-impact conditions be evaluated by *superimposing* the several networks (mathematically or logically), and searching for the optimum trade-off point or neighborhood— the point where the marginal product of funds allocated among competing functions is maximized. Although this task may sound onerous, many econometricians and system analysts are well-equipped to undertake it. The general technology would be a simulation program that can evaluate the "staged" redistribution of resources, so that we attempt to converge on the optimum through several different periods rather than make dramatic, one-shot redistributions.

(Indeed, much of Chapter 5 will be devoted to explaining the techniques available for forcing functional innovations while minimizing the risk of unsought consequences or dysfunctions.) At any rate, when we have to work in a zero-sum-game context,[8] we are looking for the *net* utility for any function (the effect that is adjusted for the detrimental consequences of decreasing the loadings on other missions). The simplified utility formulation just developed helps us here, for our simulations will have to operate on three factors instead of the original five. Thus, the policy that asks service organizations to emphasize return in terms of unallocated resources has some analytical advantages directly at the strategic level.

The basic allocative strategy, however, is the same, irrespective of the method of calculating utilities (e.g., with or without cross-impact calculations). Suppose, for example, that we have an unallocated increment, ΔX. This increment will be distributed across several missions: $\Delta X = \sum X_j$. The formula for determining the actual allocations is thus:

$$X_j = U_j (\Delta X).$$

When we translate this funding increment into specific resources, we get the formulation we suggested earlier,

$$W_j = U_j (\Delta W).$$

It is worthwhile to note the obvious corollary: the strategy for *reducing* resource allocations in the face of a net decrease in the funding base. Expanding on the logic just developed, it is clear that reductions should be allocated with respect to the *reciprocals* of the utility indexes, as follows:

(a) $(X_t - X_{t+1}) = Y, \quad Y > 0$

(b) $Y = \sum Y_j$

(c) $Y_j = F \dfrac{1}{U_j} (Y), \sum \dfrac{1}{U_j} = 1.0.$

We have yet to mention an obvious qualification to what we have done with respect to utilities. In many cases, we will not be able to develop specific numerical utility values (at least not without engaging in a possibly elaborate and certainly extended "learning" exercise, of the type described in Section 5.4). Therefore, in practice, we may have to content ourselves with a *ranking scheme*, in which we are satisfied that, for example, the utility for one mission is significantly greater than that for some other. That is, our utilities now become "ordinal numbers," which merely reflect comparative positions in a continuum of rankings. The advantage of considering utilities in their ordinal form is that we may perform the strategic allocation analysis using essentially judgmental or subjective data, taking recourse in quantities (e.g., actually measuring the coefficients in Table 3.5) only when no consensus of judgment yields a clearcut ranking. And as we will suggest in the next chapter, there are methods available for dealing "scientifically" with subjective inputs, so there is no inherent disgrace in employing ordinal rather than cardinal utilities.

We now move on to discuss the tactical allocation decisions within a service organization (and here there is a strong correspondence with the allocation process as it would be conducted in the prototypical commercial or profit-oriented organization). We know at this point that the allocation of resources according to mission utilities—determined on the basis of their relative leverage on unallocated inputs—leads to: $MAX (G) \equiv MAX (\$X/Y)$. But at this point, our strategic allocations were really based on an expectation operator: $E.V. (G)$. Assuming that our strategic allocation decisions were properly (rationally) developed, $E.V. (G)$ becomes an *imputed optimum*, and the extent to which actual input leverage (actual G) approaches the imputed optimum depends on the rationality with which the tactical decision-makers allocate resources *within* the missions defined at the strategic levels (and subject to the utility constraints developed there). Therefore, the major performance index for the tactical decision-makers is

$$\frac{G}{E.V. (G)}.$$

Consistent with the outline of the accountability logic presented in Figure 3.2, the tactical decision-makers can use the facilities of the accountability system to try to converge on a favorable G. That is, allocations at the tactical level—within missions or functional sectors—become subject to some *a posteriori*, empirical discipline, *given* an adequate accountability system. For the case at hand, allocations should be made to individual units (or programs) on the basis of their *demonstrated productivity*.[9] Therefore, the tactical allocation process becomes coextensive with the accountability system.

As in nearly all accountability situations, we are concerned with two dimensions, *quality* and *quantity*. Obviously, the best of all possible worlds is where each unit of the organization does a large amount of high-quality work. However, it is common to think of quantity and quality as competitive targets, as in Figure 3.15. Both the curves in the figure reflect the trade-off condition. Yet, curve I_1 is clearly superior to curve I_2. There is still a competitive relationship between quantity and quality, but it is softer (less elastic) for the former curve. Thus, under curve I_1, given any particular quantity of output, the associated quality is higher than on curve I_2. For any given level of resources (e.g., a budget ceiling), the unit associated with curve I_1 will deliver a greater level of productivity than a unit associated with the curve I_2. Thus, the curves become intelligible as *productivity functions* (when we consider productivity as a given

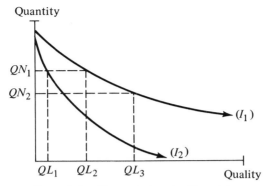

Figure 3.15. The tactical trade-off model.

quantity of services delivered at some specific level of quality). So, the unit associated with curve I_1—because it makes more efficient use of *whatever* resources are allocated to it—becomes the preferred recipient of any incremental resources, up to the point where it can be demonstrated that diminishing marginal returns set in. (Because productivity functions are comparable only within some specific *range* of input values, it is very important that all cost-benefit projections for proposed programs be put in the form of a proper production function and not merely posed as tabular data.)

Within the context of our university example, we have a tautological issue at hand. When we ask how one unit might achieve a more favorable productivity curve than another, the answer that emerges is straightforward: because it has higher-quality resources to begin with. That is, a "better" teacher is one who can realize greater educational effectiveness in a larger class than can a "poorer" teacher; a "better" researcher turns out more work at any given level of quality than a "poorer" researcher. Thus, the major factor determining the overall output structure for any university, and hence the value for the guiding function $G/E.V.$ (G), is the *quality* of the resources employed in the various units. The tactical accountability problem becomes the maintenance of the highest-quality personnel (and perhaps, equipment) base across all units. In this respect, the allocative decisions made in service organizations may sometimes reflect different criteria than those made by industrial firms. With the latter, increases in the quality of resources are generally accompanied by proportional increases in the cost of resources, which therefore permits a whole family of trade-offs. In service organizations, because of the difficulty of precisely measuring utility contributions, the relationship between quality and cost may be less elastic.

But, service organizations often face a problem that is not present to the same extent within commercial and industrial enterprise. Particularly, many employees of service agencies tend to gain a form of tenure, which insulates them from re-crimination for all but the most heinous activities (e.g., moral turpitude, embez-zlement). A considerable portion of a university's personnel thus might be rela-tively immune from the effects of accountability. To this extent, as in the civil service in general, tenure may be an institutionalized detriment to organizational efficiency and effectiveness. Of course, the essential argument for tenure is that it protects employees from managerial caprice. We hope to show that a proper accountability system can do the same thing, without guaranteeing sub-optimality. But to the extent that tenure exists, the university or general service organization should be prepared to pay more attention to selection and appoint-ment of personnel. Once an individual is appointed, or granted tenure, he is dif-ficult to remove or control. Therefore, the proper accountability system should also serve as a guide for the selection decisions of a service organization. That is, individuals seeking an appointment should be subject to the same accountability criteria as those seeking promotion or tenure, and so on. In summary, every unit as a whole—every department, every college, every division—and every indi-vidual seeking membership, promotion, or tenure should be required to demon-strate their probable contribution to the major missions of the university. Re-source allocations would then be directed to those individuals and units, which, among all alternatives, exhibit the highest productivity indexes.

For our purposes, the productivity indexes may take the form of utility values, perhaps computed according to a master function such as the following:

(a) $u_{i,j} = \sum a_{n,i,j} U_n$

    where

        $n = 1$ = teaching function
        $n = 2$ = research function
        $n = 3$ = external service function.

(b) $MAX\,(u_{i,j})$ is the objective function.

(c) $W_{i,j}/u_{i,j}$ or $(\$_{i,j}/u_{i,j})$ is the cost-benefit function (where w or $\$$ indicate resources allocated to the jth unit of the ith collectivity)

    where

        i indicates a collective unit
        ($i = 1$ = department
        $i = 2$ = division
        $i = 3$ = college
        $i = 4$ = university)

and

j indicates a lower-order unit within a collective unit
  ($j = 1$ = individual
   $j = 2$ = department
   $j = 3$ = division
   $j = 4$ = college).

For purposes of the university illustration, we would then have

$$u_{i,j} = (a_1 U_T + a_2 U_R + a_3 U_E)_{i,j}$$

In short, every operating unit is expected to act to maximize the utility function. The components are relatively simple to explain. Initially, we must suggest that U_T, U_R, and U_E may be constant across all operating units, for they carry the generic utility values assigned at the strategic level (reflecting expectations about the relative importance of each of the three functions to the organization as a whole). In this way, the executives (strategists) of the organization can make their judgmental determinations take effect at the tactical (managerial) level. For the higher weighting of the preferred function means that a given utility index (point value) can be scored there with a lower performance rating (a smaller coefficient) than in one of the lower-weighted functional areas. It is hoped, then, that individual operating units may be gradually "nudged" into aligning themselves with the strategic priorities of the organization's executives. This implicit form of control may often be quite important, for there are sometimes distinct limits on the ability of higher management to directly control behavior of lower-level units. Therefore, the weighting of functions within the accountability framework is generally an exercise in suasion, and a legitimate control device when coercion or direct determinacy are either unavailable or impolitic.

In some instances, the accountability mechanism may operate on a regional basis, so that there will be several different macroentities under a central authority (e.g., a state's department of higher education, the chancellor's office of a multicampus system). In such a case, it is possible for the different units to be assigned different functional weightings by the central authority. That is, the generic utility indexes may be determined exogenously. The preferred practice would be to set certain ceilings on one of the functions. For example, the central authorities may want a state college to concentrate on mass education. Therefore, they might set a ceiling value on U_R and U_E. This would not bar the state college from investments or research or external service, but it would a priori limit the point contribution associated with such functions. By the same token, a state university might be expected to be all things to all people;

therefore, the central authority might restrict its ability to concentrate excessively on any single function. For example, the university might not be allowed to assign any single function a utility value greater than 0.5. The same thing may be true *within* an institution, for certain units may be especially concerned with one or another function. An evening college, for example, might be expected to concentrate rather fully on teaching; a graduate program, on the other hand, might be expected to strongly emphasize research. Therefore, we have to give executives the opportunity to impose certain floor and ceiling limits on the utilities associated with any major function, as follows:

$$\text{Teaching} \quad (t_1 \leqslant U_T \leqslant t_2)$$

$$\text{Research} \quad (r_1 \leqslant U_R \leqslant r_2)$$

$$\text{External service} \quad (e_1 \leqslant U_E \leqslant e_2)$$

where $U_T + U_R + U_E = 1$. This imposition of ranges on utility values may, however, not merely restrict latitude, but may protect the integrity of certain specialized units, which would suffer a real loss of effectiveness were all three functional dimensions weighted equally $(U_T = U_R = U_E = 0.333)$.

The heart of the accountability process, given the assigned values or ranges for the generic functional utilities, is the matter of assigning specific quantitative values to the coefficients in the master equation: the a's. These will, as a rule, be utilities in their own right and should therefore range between 0 and 1.0. But from what we earlier suggested, we know that each coefficient will really be a productivity index, with two major components: quality (L) and some quantity measure (N).* Now, to allow some latitude to operating units, we may let these variables be indexed by subcoefficients, so that we get a formulation such as the following:

$$a_{i,j} = gl + kN$$

where $(g + k) = 1.0$. In short, the use of the g and k factors allow us to assign different weights to account for different levels of responsibility within any unit. For example, a graduate-level instructor may be responsible for fewer students, yet be expected to deliver high-quality education. Therefore, we might escalate the g value relative to k (which compensates for the inherently smaller classes that exist at the graduate level). Or a researcher, who is at work on a long-range project, might have little opportunity for publishing immediate (or intermediate) results; therefore, we might assign him a higher g value than we would someone whose research area permits a more favorable publication date. Of course, where

---

*These reflect the magnitude of achievements by a unit in one or another of the functional areas.

no clearcut predilection for quantity or quality exists due to structural or contextual considerations, the g and k values may be removed from the formulation, or set as $g = k = 0.5$. At any rate, we must try to get a value for the coefficients themselves on both subdimensions (quality and quantity). In this respect, consider Table 3.6.

We may go through each of the components of the table very quickly. First, quantity indexes for all three functions are first of all matters of a raw count (e.g., number of students taught for a certain number of hours, number of publications, number of external appearances). These are, however, subject to qualification on the basis of certain subfactors. For the teaching function, for example, we might be concerned about the number of different preparations the instructor has. The instructor who teaches four sections of the same course still has only one preparation and would therefore have the expected capability to handle a larger student population. Some courses require a lot of student counseling (e.g., professional seminars, laboratory courses, terminal or capstone courses); other courses—notably undergraduate survey offerings—require little counseling. Therefore, the teacher with a lower counseling load might be expected to handle a relatively higher number of students. Finally, the evaluation of students differs considerably from one course to the next. For example, it is relatively easy to grade mathematics homework, for the right answer is usually objectively determined and clearly accessible; essay or creative writing courses, on the other hand, make great demands on the instructor and reduce the student population he can be expected to handle adequately.

As for teaching quality, several evaluation schemes can be implemented. Probably the most direct is asking the students to "grade" the instructor's performance. However, we might want to qualify this effectiveness index by considering the subject to be taught or the nature of the student audience. For example, we may readily expect students to be more enthusiastic about an elective course than a required course. Moreover, if the author were looking for a handsome grade from students, he would generally prefer to teach something about sex or abnormal psychology than to teach integral calculus or general system theory. As for audience (enrollment properties), some classes will be filled by more enthusiastic students to begin with, especially where enrollment is restricted because of certain prerequisites or where there is a strict limit to class size, on a first-come, first-served basis. Finally, scheduling might affect students' evaluation of their instructors. For example, a class scheduled at 8 A.M. or at 9 P.M. might be expected to labor under inherent detriments that are no fault of the teacher. But there are also some relatively objective data that might be used to estimate quality of instruction. For example, in a free enrollment system, students will tend naturally to gravitate toward the best instructors in a field; therefore, under certain conditions, relative enrollment may

Table 3.6. Tactical evaluation criteria.

Coefficient/Function	Quantity (N)			Quality (L)	
	Base	Qualifiers	Base	Qualifiers	
a_1 (Teaching)	Student contact index = Courses × Enrollment × Credit hours	(a) Preparation schedule (b) Counseling imputations. (c) Evaluation requirements, etc.	Student evaluation of instructor performance through questionnaire; relative enrollment, schedule; drop figures	(a) Subject area (b) Distribution of enrollment properties (c) Scheduling data	
a_2 (Research)	Number of publications	(a) Book = x_1 (b) Monograph = x_2 (c) Article = x_3 (d) Book review = x_4 (e) Editorial = x_5	Data available on sales, reprint requests, citations, book reviews, etc., essentially measuring impact and visibility	(a) Publisher/journal (b) Subject area (c) Progress reports	
a_3 (External services)	Number of appearances	(a) Address (b) Lecture (c) Reading (d) Consultation	Data available on attendance, reviews, acceptance, etc.; return of contacts or requests for services, etc.	(a) Sponsoring organization (b) Impact	

reflect quality. Or, again assuming free enrollment, the best instructors may have their classes filled to the limit before less favorable instructors, on the basis of word-of-mouth advertising among students.* Finally, the number of drops in a course (relative to other sections of the same course) may be an indication of the instructor's quality. At any rate, these are just some of the criteria that might be employed in setting the performance coefficient on the teaching dimension.

As for the research function, the number of publications would be indexed by a point-value assigned the different types of publications one might produce. For example, a book would generally be expected to rate higher than an article, an article would imply more effort and prestige than a book review, and so on. As for research quality, we might employ many surrogates. With respect to a book, we might want to look at the quality of the reviews it received (and assign a qualitative value such as "excellent," "poor," etc., with different points associated with each value). Or we might judge a book's quality by the volume of sales. A good surrogate for the imputed quality of an article or scholarly paper is the number of reprint requests, whether it is republished as part of a collection, and so forth. The number of times a publication is cited and praised by other authors is often an indication of quality. (As a qualifier, however, we would have to adjust for the possibility that works critical of established practices may be attacked by a majority of reviewers.) But there are also qualifications that might be raised to lend a subjective amplification to research quality. For example, members of a specific discipline might get together and rank the different journals of a field, so that some are ranked higher than others. The same is true of publishing houses. Thus, a publication in a more prestigious journal or by a "better" house would earn the author more points than publication by a lower-ranking journal or house. Moreover, some subjects are more open to publication than others. For example, geriatrics, racial studies, and studies of the "work ethic" are quite easy to publish at the current time. Inquiries into pure mathematics or other erudite studies are always difficult to publish. Finally, there may be an internal consensus about the expected impact of the study or investigation, perhaps in an effort to protect those who are working on long-range projects. Such consensus would presumably be made on the basis of progress reports submitted to a review committee, which might then be used to evaluate research performance where there are no publications. This would be especially important in the appointment of newly graduated faculty, who would probably not be published and could only offer a research plan or a prospectus.

Essentially the same investigatory logic holds true when we move to the external services dimension. For example, a major address to the American Asso-

*However, we would want to factor out "cinch" courses, and so forth.

ciation for the Advancement of Science would earn the author more points than a lecture given to the college French club or a luncheon speech to the local Rotary Club. Consultation for a major branch of government on a critical problem would count for more than a week's work for the local bakery or the occupation of an honorary position on the board of the local sewer authority. Coaching a football team with a winning season would earn the coach more support and affection than would a losing season. At any rate, when we move to the area of external service, we usually will have to relay most heavily on judgmental performance indexes—point assignments that are essentially subjective in origin.

We hope that the basic features of these tactical accountability criteria are reasonably clear, although they are offered here strictly to further our illustration and not as a set to be immediately introduced into any operating situation. But the major point of the entries in Table 3.6 is that, wherever possible, quantitative data are sought, supplemented where necessary (or desirable) by subjective data. These subjective data, which result in the assignment of points on the basis of opinion rather than direct measurement, are not to be looked at askance. For as this accountability system would be employed, the subjective assignments could be made by a specially designed, disciplined qualitative analysis. This would minimize the probability of "irrational" factors entering the calculus, e.g., prejudice, personality, jealousy, internal politics. Moreover, subjective indexes may be developed with significant precision. For example, recall that the "quality" of a publication is to be measured in part by the imputed quality of the publisher. Let us assume that we are interested in sociology. In this case, a committee of sociologists would be formed either in a single location or as part of a correspondence team (perhaps with members from outside the particular department or university). They would be given a list of all sociological journals and asked to rank them as to imputed prestige, with this ranking perhaps reflecting something about the rejection rate for manuscripts, exhaustiveness of the review process, legitimacy of the particular journal as a source of sociological opinion, and so on. Thus, the assignment of point values to other journals could be a very disciplined process indeed, and need not be casual or arbitrary. Indeed, as many sophisticated analysts well know, there are techniques available for injecting "objectivity" into subjective analyses.[10]

We need not spend any more time on the calculative aspects of the model, as they are open to modification and imagination from many different directions. But the major point—that performance indexes can be developed to lend substance to our accountability coefficients—should be beyond dispute. The question now is: what do we do with these indexes after we have developed them? The answer, of course, is that they are the primary base for resource allocation decisions at the tactical level.

Particularly, we must note that, given an actual point score (utility) index for any unit of the organization, we may quickly develop a cost-effectiveness index. Recall that the utility index is the output of a performance audit conducted according to the following formulation:

$$u_{i,j} = (a_1 u_T + a_2 u_R + a_3 u_E)_{i,j}.$$

Now, we can usually identify the costs associated with the maintenance of any unit (e.g., salary and benefits paid to an individual, budget and overload associated with a department or division). Therefore, we have at hand the following:

$$\text{Cost/benefit}_{i,j} = \$i,j/u_{i,j}.$$

And, of course, cost-benefit ratios may be aggregated for any level of the organization. For example, the cost-benefit index associated with a department would be the aggregate of the indexes for the members of that department. A division's cost-benefit index would be the aggregate of the indexes of its departments; the aggregate cost-effectiveness index of a college might be arrived at by aggregating those of the divisions and departments under its aegis:

$$u_i = \sum \sum a_{n,j} U_n.$$

Given this, we can compute the aggregate cost-benefit index for any macrosystem (collectivity), such as a university. While this would give the directors a reading of the overall effectiveness and efficiency of the organization, it could also be used for the rational allocation of resources among competing organizations within a regional educational system, (e.g., between the state university and the several state colleges, or among several state colleges).

Thus, the three major allocation decisions of any system may be lent discipline by the result of the accountability process:

(a) Allocation of increases in x/y
(b) Allocation of cuts associated with a decrease in x/y
(c) Allocation of existing resources under the zero-sum game context in the hopes of maximizing G (the increase in unallocated overhead inputs between operating periods).

In Figure 3.16 several different units within some collectivity (i) are all competing for shares of some aggregate budget. These competing units (the $x_{i,j}$'s) are arrayed according to their performance (utility) indexes. Now, the optimum allocation schedule can be found in such a way that a "directional threshold" is established. Entities to the left of this threshold would receive proportionally larger allocations relative to demand than units to the right. In other instances, the resource allocations made to the units falling to the left of the threshold might be expanded, at the direct expense of the units to the right of the threshold (the zero-sum game context), using the relative utilities to weight

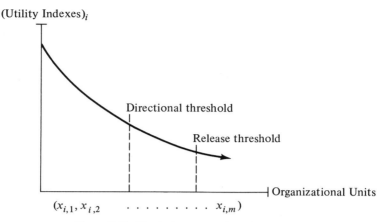

Figure 3.16. Tactical resource allocation curve.

the redistribution process. Finally, a release threshold might be established, so that units falling below some absolute performance level are automatically deprived of their allocations (e.g., disbanded or retired). For selection and promotion purposes, we might establish definite utility thresholds above which an individual must rise if he or she is to become a serious candidate. If there are scarce positions or promotional dollars, these would be allocated to the candidates with the highest utilities. In short, the decision-maker with a fair command of standard cost-accounting and a rudimentary knowledge of basic optimization procedures should be able to considerably *rationalize* resource allocations throughout the service organization or throughout some regional collection of organizations, given the output from an accountability process such as that we have described.

For purposes of collective bargaining and personnel compensation within service organizations—and, of course, service enterprises have been increasingly subject to strikes by and recriminations from their employees in recent years—the accountability model might also provide an answer. It is possible to develop a simple "map" of the relationships between costs (compensations or allocations) and performance, as shown in Figure 3.17.

The origin of the rational relationship is simple. We merely develop a scatter diagram of the various cost-performance rations that emerge for each operating unit. To the extent that resource allocations (costs) completely reflect performance, we should get a positive and directly proportional relationship. Departures from the rationalized relationship might be indicated were a regression curve such as the nonnormative trajectory to develop. Here, as we can see, costs (resource allocations) are in a significantly inverse (but roughly proportional) rela-

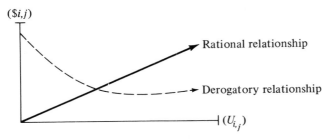

Figure 3.17. Utility/resource map.

tionship to performances. In short, through seniority, tenure, inertial budgeting, or some other device that insulates compensation from contribution, we have arrived at the situation where the greatest consumers of resources are the least productive users of those resources.

There are, of course, many other uses to which accountability data can be put, but we must now move on to the other aspects of accountability. Before we go, we should see that the overall strategic objective of service organizations, their operational objective, and the tactical objective are all equivalent:

$$MAX\ (\$x/y) \equiv MAX\ \frac{(G)}{E.V.G.} \equiv MAX\ (u_{n,i,j}).$$

In the short run, it is always possible to achieve the first objective without benefit of the third.* But if proper accountability processes were operating across the service sector, then we would expect the various funding sources to make their aggregate allocations according to the utility criteria, and thus make the connection between effectiveness and efficiency that rationality demands. To the extent that organizational directors—and the resource-providing agencies themselves—do not demand accountability in service organizations, there is no way to guarantee that allocations at any level are related to productivity criteria. In short, it is possible, in the absence of proper accountability mechanisms, for executives of an organization to achieve their objective (*MAX $s/y*) without having to enforce rationality at the tactical level. We will return to this problem (and pose a tentative solution to it) in the last chapter. For now, we must examine how we might inject *a priori* discipline into decision processes—that is, how we might control the quality of our decision-making before it has committed us to a course of action and before it is too late to correct errors.

*Through the mechanisms that allow an organization to abrogate the relationship between growth and efficiency.

3.4 NOTES AND REFERENCES

1. See the interesting article by Taylor Branch, "The Trial of the C.I.A.," in the *New York Times Magazine* (September 12, 1976).

2. Of course, the problem of arriving at a consensus among different interested parties is enormously complex. There is always the issue of the extent to which any majority orderings may be actionable. In this regard, see Niemi and Weisberg, *Probability Models of Collective Decision Making* (Columbus, Ohio: Charles E. Merrill, 1972). For a clever analysis of the ordering problem, see Kenneth Arrow's *Social Choices and Individual Values* (New York: John Wiley & Sons, Inc., 1951).

3. A nice, neat introduction to utility logic is given by Ferguson and Gould in Chapter 1 of their *Microeconomic Theory* (Homewood, Illinois: Richard D. Irwin, Inc., 1975).

4. As we will see in Chapter 4, this is a distinct simplification of the precepts of rationality. For future allocations may, in some cases, be rational only to the extent that they are *divorced* from historical performance criteria. However, this assertion would be practical only in the face of rather particular and seldom-exercised budgeting systems. In the normal context, historical performance should indeed be used as an allocative criterion.

5. Perhaps the best collection of essays on the application of the Delphi process to disciplination of opinion and subjective data is *The Delphi Method: Techniques and Applications*, eds. Linstone and Turoff (Reading, Massachusetts: Addison-Wesley Publishing Co., Inc., 1975).

6. See Jack Hirschleifer's "Internal Pricing and Decentralized Decisions," in Bonini et al., *Management Controls: New Directions in Basic Research* (New York: McGraw-Hill, 1964).

7. For more on this, see my *Managing Social Service Systems* (New York: Petrocelli Books) 1977.

8. Both zero-sum and positive-sum games will concern us in this volume, although not in great detail. A good report on these two gaming contexts—and others—is given by Anatol Rapoport in *Two Person Game Theory: The Essential Ideas* (Ann Arbor, Michigan: University of Michigan Press, 1966).

9. The responsibilities of the tactical decision-maker within the context of most service organizations is really more complicated than is suggested here. For they must generally allocate resources not only on the basis of historical performance criteria, but also in a way that will deal with demand problems. For example, there may be a low inherent demand for a particular service, yet its maintenance at some level might be considered absolutely necessary (perhaps even legislated). Such necessary but unfavorable services become exogenous constraints on the tactical decision-maker, and might thus set a "floor" under the aggregate efficiency he might achieve. However, resources allocated to these *a priori* fixed programs or units may still be undertaken within the rationality framework developed here. At any rate, we will have more to say about exogenous constraints on allocation processes in the next

chapter. Moreover, we can adjust tactical performance measures to reflect factors over which they have no control.

10. For example, see my paper "Attacking Indeterminacy: The Case for the Hypothetico-Deductive Method and Consensus Statistics," in *The Journal of Technological Forecasting and Social Change* 6 (1974).

4

Aspects
of Decision
Discipline

4.0 INTRODUCTION

We now have some idea of how the quality of decision-making processes may be reflected in the results they produce. But waiting for the results of a decision process is sometimes a luxury we cannot afford. So we must discuss how we might evaluate decision processes before they are completed, and thus before we are committed to a course of action.

In other words, we must be prepared to audit the methodology of decision-makers. For the way they perform the various decision functions is really the only timely clue we have as to the expected utility of their results. To be able to assess the appropriateness of the methodology of decision-makers, however, we have to have a very firm idea of the way decisions *should* be made. We need, as it were, some normative referents against which real-world decision-making exercises may be compared.

This chapter will be concerned with providing these normative referents, with setting out the "oughts" and "shoulds" of decision-making. In short, we will try to establish decision science as a proper discipline and thus as a practical instrument for enhancing administrative rationality.

4.1 THE METHOD AUDIT

We can see that the audit aspect of accountability operates only after a decision has run its course. Moreover, as we saw in the last chapter, trying to assess or control decision quality by looking at the results of decisions can be a troublesome exercise, especially when organizational goals or strategic activities are the focus of our efforts. Either of two things may confound the decision audit and dilute the concept of controlling decision quality through results. First, there are some occasions when a decision problem is so complicated and has so many ramifications that we simply do not know how to identify and evaluate results. That is, some decisions resonate far out into the environment and have too many implications for us to control or capture. Second, some decisions will have a horizon that is very distant; that is, they will not ultimate until far out in the future. As a result, a decision-maker may be insulated from a *timely* audit.

The probability of either of these confoundations occurring is, of course, related strongly to the level of decision-making we are trying to assess and control. We have already suggested, for example, that goal-oriented decisions tend to have effects widely distributed in time and space. Therefore, the rectitude of a goal decision may not really be accessible to us except in the distant future; even then, it may be accessible only indirectly because of the many factors and relationships that would have to be audited. As we move downward in the organization, complexity and horizonal factors will tend to become more favorable, eventuating at the point where the results of deterministic decision exercises may become almost immediately and completely available. In short, we expect a situation such as illustrated in Figure 4.1. What we mean by "utility" is *the ability to reduce the overall value of decision errors throughout some interval*. We will later define this concept more fully; here, it may be taken simply to mean the extent of our ability to put a timely stop to suboptimal or erroneous decision processes. Indeed, the explicit use of decision audits of the type described in the last chapter was in their ability to identify inept decision-makers so they can be removed, or to identify faulty decision processes so they can be amended.

The ulterior implication of Figure 4.1 is that the utility of the decision audit is related to the nature of the problems solved at the various levels of enterprise. Thus, the diagram may also be read as suggesting that directors—occupied with

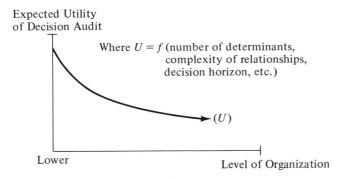

Figure 4.1. Utility of the audit modality.

essentially indeterminate problems—are less susceptible to decision audit than supervisors occupied with more narrowly bounded, precisely defined deterministic problems, and so on. When we recognize that our earlier definitions of the various problems types (e.g., indeterminate, severely stochastic) were built around the number of determinants to be considered, the complexity of relationships among the determinants, and the horizon for the problem, (its time frame), we can see why the audit modality would begin to fail us.

For example, the results of the decisions of long-range planners or mission analysts will not become available to us until the actions based on their planning recommendations have ultimated. This may be many years in the future. This implies that we might have difficulty in evaluating the performance of these long-range planners at any time during that interval. If we have to wait many years until the results of the decisions are known, much loss and waste may occur in the meantime. If the horizon factor is important, the matter of complexity is also critical. For example, how might we adequately assess the rationality of a group of economic policymakers concerned with controlling certain economic parameters of a large system? Ostensibly, we should be able to evaluate whether their policies have resulted in the effect they sought (e.g., was inflation reduced? did unemployment drop? is industrial investment increased?). In all but the most simple cases, it is very difficult to accurately capture the resonating effects of an economic policy decision, simply because there are so many intervening variables, and really no adequate constraint on the types of relationships that might develop among those variables (even in the relatively short run). We would have the same problem were we to try to directly measure educational effectiveness, the utility of a neighborhood welfare clinic, or the implications of a foreign-policy decision. Of course, using techniques indicated in the last chapter, the effectiveness of decisions taken in these arenas may become at least partially accessible to us through utility surrogates; however, the precision of the accountability process is bound to suffer. At some point, the complexity may be so significant that the imputed reliability of any decision-audit data falls so low that it becomes unactionable; that is, we cannot use it to determine a best course of action with respect to the decision-makers or decision processes involved. It was in this sense, then, that we suggested that many strategic decision-makers and goal-setters may find ways to elude the implications of the after-the-fact decision audit.

Even though the potential inability of audit-oriented accountability processes to capture the real ramifications of high-level decisions is of great concern, there is another, entirely different liability of the accountability audit. By concentrating only on the results of decisions, we have no control over the effects. That is, the best we can do is to recognize errors, not *prevent* them. In short, by the time a dysfunctional or suboptimal decision has run its course, the adverse effects are seated and beyond our control. Thus, the audit modality of accountability virtually assures some cost of error, with the level of cost usually related to the level at which the decision in question is taken. If we assume that the goal of the decision sciences is to reduce the incidence, severity, and frequency of decision error, then the audit modality is not really favorable except for deterministic decision exercises, and to a somewhat lesser extent for tactical issues.

It was thus that we introduced a second, parallel dimension to accountability in the last chapter, the *projective* dimension. The projective audit will have two focuses. On one hand, the projective discipline may simply involve the decision-makers' efforts to show that the action they contemplate is favorable with respect to a particular variable. On the other hand, they may have to demonstrate that the *decision process* they used was rational. There is an enormous difference between these two focuses, a difference that is very critical to our work.

In our original outline of the accountability process (Figure 3.2), we made specific entries under the tactical and strategic trajectories for the projective dimension. We suggested that some sort of *impact programming* would be the device available for projecting the effects of strategic decisions and that the tactical decision-makers might involve themselves with a projective technique such as *capital budgeting*.[1]

Both technologies are relatively well-known instruments for implementing the variable-based projective modality. For example, impact programming would be the attempt to evaluate strategic action-alternatives with respect to a specific goal. In general, as was earlier suggested, impact programming will employ mainly logical devices as the source of discipline—subjective probabilities, "fuzzy set" theory, qualitative analysis using axiomatic or axiological (normative) bases. Several of the problem illustrations we have used previously have given us an idea about the way in which strategic analysts might perform their functions. The point is, however, that the strategic analysis exercise will yield the expectedly most effective solution in terms of utility indexes distributed across the several action-alternatives, with utility acting as a variable with real-world imputations. Again, the action that is finally taken is that which emerges with the highest expected utility index—the most favorable imputed "impact."

On the tactical level, we have the well-developed and widely practiced capital-budgeting concept to draw on. For the most part, at least in the industrial and commercial sector, capital budgeting asks that we array all potential investments in terms of their expected return on investment. Investmental and allocative rationality is thus served to the extent that the expectedly most favorable alternative is selected and implemented. Theoretically, virtually any investment of resources is subject to discipline through capital budgeting. Of course, there are problems. It is very difficult, for example, to assess the expected profit impact of new carpet for the sales manager's office or the expected rate of return on an investment in a new computer (or another lathe, or another accountant). But, when an organization produces a tangible product—with an inventory value and accessible demand and cost functions—perhaps a majority of precedented allocation decisions may be disciplined by the capital-budgeting process.

As for those cases where inputs and outputs are more difficult to measure or correlate—or where unprecedented activities are to be considered—we have ostensible recourse to devices such as program budgeting or the now popular zero-base budgeting mechanism.[2]   Most of these extensions to the capital-budgeting process dictate a set of procedures such as the following:

1. First, the various missions (functions) that the organization is to serve must be specified. As a general rule, missions should be specified in such a way that they become cross-correlated; that is, like the teaching, research, and external service functions of our prototypical university, they are mutually reinforcing (or related positively).

2. The strategic decision-makers will presumably have set generic utility indexes on the several functions, as did our university executives. These strategic weightings may or may not be known to the unit managers.

3. Given these functional specifications, each unit manager, department head, program director, etc. is asked to submit activity specifications for the coming period, suggesting what he wants his unit to do. As a general rule, the activity proposals (program statements) should meet the following criteria:

   (a) They should correlate to one or more of the strategic missions of the organization.

   (b) They should express performance criteria with respect to effectiveness (or utility).

   (c) They should not be identified exclusively with any specific operating unit (that is, they should presume no organizational structure *per se*).

   (d) They should carry a projected cost-effectiveness index, showing the different levels of output (effect) associated with different resource levels, e.g., a specification of the expected functional relationship between inputs and outputs.[3]

4. The various activity proposals are all collected and then arrayed across the various missions, giving the *a priori* (or gross) benefit configuration for the organization, such as shown in Figure 4.2. The actual activity aggregates submitted by the array of unit managers must then be compared against the desired mission weightings developed by the strategic decision-makers (presumably as the output of their impact programming analysis). In Figure 4.2, we see that the subordinate decision-makers gave more weight to mission 1 than was desired and less to missions 2 and 3. The more serious the deviation between tactical and strategic benefit configurations, the more radical must be the revision of the program (activity) schedule.

5. The correction between actual and desire weightings will, of course, be resolved through the resource allocation process. That is, the budget con-

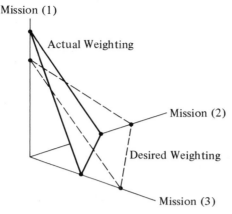

Figure 4.2. Benefit configurations.

figuration—representing the proportional allocation of resources to the several mission areas—will be isomorphic with respect to the desired configuration, not the actual. However, when the desired and actual are very far apart—and relations between strategic and tactical decision-makers are not amicable—then the adjustment to the desired mission orientations may be made gradually, perhaps over several iterations of the program-budgeting process.

6. To arrive at the budget configuration, we do the following:
   (a) We eliminate all redundant program or activity specifications, so that we have a set of mutually exclusive alternatives.
   (b) We then rank each of the proposed activities (programs) according to their apparent cost-effectiveness ratios, within the several mission categories.
   (c) Where an activity (program) purports to support more than one mission, it is ranked according to its distributed effect (that is, according to aggregate cost-effectiveness). At any rate, any given activity will appear in the program array only once.

7. At this point, we will have an ordered array of programs pertaining to each of the n-functional areas, as in Figure 4.3. Now, we will have previously partitioned the aggregate resources (or aggregated budget) into segments reflecting the expected utility of the various mission areas (functions). These represent the *ceiling* investment levels for each functional area:

$$B = \sum_{i=1}^{n} b_i,$$

where $\dfrac{b_i}{B} = T(U_i)$, $\sum U_i = 1.0.$*

*See Section 3.3.

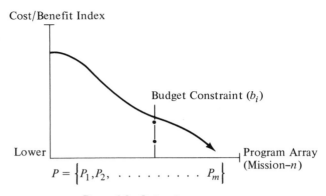

Figure 4.3. Ordered program array.

8. The procedure is then to allocate resources, up to the ceiling b_i, according to the resource demands of the ordered programs. Resources associated with mission 1 are thus dedicated initially to the most apparently favorable investments in terms of some return function (cost-effectiveness). When the budget ceiling is reached, the programs that remain unfunded are simply not implemented. When this has been done for all missions (functional areas), then the ostensible objective of the program-budgeting process has been met, that is, the most favorable allocation of resources has been achieved.

Thus, both capital- and program-budgeting processes, in their various guises, appear to be significantly rational from the standpoint of decision science. And, in their theoretical pretentions, they are indeed rational. But there are numerous problems that can interfere in practice to dilute the benefits of such projective discipline. The most significant problem may be that the accuracy of the individual cost-effectiveness indexes assigned to the various activity (or program) alternatives may be very low, because the unit managers lack the necessary analytical discipline to make "rational" estimations. This situation becomes more serious as the various activities or programs considered become more and more unprecedented—in short, as the organization departs more and more from historical behavior. This is because most unit managers or program analysts will only be able to project cost-benefit indexes on the basis of historical information—for precedented programs. (The reason for this concentration on projective techniques is one mentioned in Chapter 1—the lack of formal deductive skills among most operating managers.) In other words, their analytical skills will be primarily extrapolative (inductive). In normal circumstances, the cost-benefit calculations for successively more significant departures from historically precedented activities are successively less satisfactory. When this happens, the whole purpose of the program- or capital-budgeting process becomes subverted. For, to the extent that the individual cost-benefit assignments are in error, so will be the resultant resource allocations. In fact, they will usually depart from an optimal set of allocations to the extent that the individual program projections are in error.

In some cases, we may in part discount the expected effect of estimation errors by suggesting that the process just described results in an adequate *ranking* of the various programs. That is, the cost-benefit indexes—as numerical values— may be in error, yet we will still be able to make assertions about the *relative* value of the programs. And, to the extent that we allocate resources on the basis of relative cost-benefit criteria, then we will still be behaving rationally. But the problem with this reasoning is, of course, the matter of the *magnitude* of estimation errors. In this respect, consider Figure 4.4. We can see that the situation in the left-hand diagram is quite favorable. Particularly, the accuracy of the estimation process was such that there is no probability of P_i and P_k taking on the same value; in short, P_i is significantly associated with cost-benefit level 1, which is presumed superior to cost-benefit level 2. In the right-hand figure, however, the error of estimate is sufficiently high to cause a potential confoundation, for there is a *well-populated intersect* between the probable cost-benefit values assigned the two programs. That is, there is some probability that P_k might have a higher cost-benefit value than P_i, for CB_1 falls within the expected domain of P_k and the reverse. Now, to the extent that large-magnitude errors occur in the individual estimation processes, then the relationship between any capital- or program-budgeting exercise and allocative optimality declines accordingly. In such a case, neither budgeting process may be considered an agent for decision rationality.

As suggested, estimation errors are more likely to occur (at any given magnitude), the less well-precedented the program or activity at hand. For, empirically (historical) supported cost-benefit indexes will generally carry a higher probability of error than those that must perforce be a product of judgment or speculation

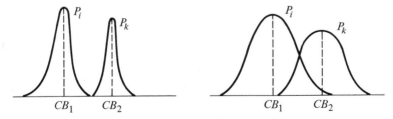

Figure 4.4. Cost-benefit distribution configurations.

(as they must usually be for unprecedented or significantly innovative activities). Therefore, the expected utility of capital- or program-budgeting mechanisms is highest for relatively stable, conservative organizations. As the organization's missions vary from an historical emphasis, both program and capital budgeting decline in apparent utility because of the expectedly higher errors of estimate made by the unit managers or activity analysts. The disturbing corollary is that, for any well-behaved, stable, and conservative organization, the results of any capital- or program-budgeting process are likely to look a lot like the results of more traditional and less pretentious budgeting technologies. Particularly, programmed allocations will tend to increase or decrease relative to historical budgeting levels. Obviously, we would expect precisely this were we dealing with a stable, conservative organization. There is something of a grand irony here. Specifically, the more analytically sophisticated, demanding program- and capital-budgeting mechanisms were originally developed to improve on the processes of line or proportional budgeting, especially in the face of organizational innovations (and under zero-based budgeting logic, the organization is supposed to wake up in a brand new world every period). But as we have seen, the real utility of these procedures declines in the face of significant innovations because of the degree to which estimations errors may concatenate. Therefore, their fundamental "rationality" in the very contexts for which they were originally designed may be very much in doubt.

We can see, carrying out this logic, that the extent to which a projective mechanism such as capital or program budgeting can contribute to the quality of organizational decisions at the allocative level depends on the quality of the decisions made at the program- or activity-analysis level. So, as with so many other decision artifices, program and capital budgeting do not compensate for any intellectual deficiencies that might be present among the decision-making personnel. They simply channel errors into a different direction, but with the same net effect as if these procedures were not employed at all. Given this realization, we now have two conditions under which the second type of projective instrument, the concentration on the decision *process*, becomes our major (if not our only) accountability instrument:

(a) where the decision at hand is one where results will not be readily available to us because of complexities or extended decision horizons.

(b) Where the errors of estimation associated with projective analyses may be significant, so that any point projections become improbable as surrogates for reality.

In either case, about all that we can really hope to audit is the *method* by which decisions were made. And in the general sense, auditing decision methodology is the only way to prevent decision errors, for results-oriented accountability processes do not even go to work until after an error has already been committed.

The *method audit* thus becomes perhaps the major source of accountability and organizational discipline for higher-level decisions, and also for allocative decisions that are not appropriately handled within the framework of the normal (data-driven) capital- or program-budgeting framework (e.g., decisions about unprecedented or significantly innovative programs or activities). For the target of the method audit is that key decision parameter we mentioned earlier, *the expected value of a decision error*. In tne normal workaday world, this is all that is accessible to us *before* an action has been committed, or when results are too widely distributed in time and space. Therefore, the method audit and the expected value of decision error become the major focuses for accountability, and hence decision discipline, for a significant number of real-world decisions. The expected value of decision error is thus the central variable in the modern decision sciences.

Before we define and elaborate this critical variable, we might discuss the implications of the method audit itself. What is asked, in effect, is that decision-makers be prepared to defend the *method* they use to arrive at a particular decision. In short, it is errors in procedure and method rather than errors in actual results that become focuses for us here. Decision-makers thus become accountable for the rationality of their analytical behavior, and errors become intelligible in two guises:

(a) *Legitimate errors* are those for which the administrator cannot be blamed. For, although a dysfunction resulted from their actions, the procedures used to decide upon that particular course of action were essentially above reproach. Thus, the error may be attributed to exogenous factors (those beyond the control of the decision-maker).

(b) *Illegitimate errors* are those for which the decision-maker is properly to be blamed, for an audit of the procedures used in the face of some error indicates a failure to apply the analytical instruments and approaches congruent with the problem at hand (which means, as we will see, that the expected value of a decision error was not reduced to its effective minimum). In short, some substance of the error or dystunction is endogenous to the decision-maker himself.

Again, in those cases where the outputs of an organization are irreducible to precisely evaluable terms—or where the "events" of a decision action are simply too complex, ill-structured, or confounded to be accurately calculated—capital- or program-budgeting techniques are often impotent, and results-oriented audits gratuitous. With only these in our accountability arsenal, many higher-level decision-makers are entirely within the bounds of propriety in suggesting that there is really no equitable, rational basis for evaluating their performance. When we shift focus from the results of decisions to the methods by which decisions were arrived at, then no functionary can become immune to accountability, no matter the complexity of the environment in which he operates or the elusiveness of the "outputs" of his enterprise. When an error results from a decision exercise, and the decision-maker suggests that he "did his best," the method audit could determine if indeed he really did make a "rational" effort. In the same way, when an administrator blames forces beyond his control for an error, his defense will depend on the audit-trail he left to indicate if that is indeed the case—or at least that there is substantial probability that uncontainable exogenous factors caused the error. If the decision-maker does not leave a method audit-trail available to those who will review his performance, then there is a *prima facie* case for dereliction. Under the method-audit system, then, the decision-makers (especially those working in particularly ill-structured areas) now become responsible for providing *evidence* of the degree of rationality they employed in performing their duties. If this imposes an onus on them, it is at the direct expense of the possibility of their being unfairly or capriciously blamed for errors that are really not their fault. In short, the method-audit is a two-edged sword. Cutting one way, it promises to eliminate offenses against rationality that result from lack of capability or assiduity; but, by the same token, it will of necessity disallow recriminations stemming from abjectly political or nonobjective origins.

Thus, the members of Congress who suggest that their vote on a particular bill reflected the majority opinion in their districts should be prepared to give evidence that this is the case. The appropriate evidence would be an indication that a proper sampling procedure was used in the solicitation of sentiment. If the secretary of agriculture suggests that wheat sales to the Russians will not affect domestic prices in any measurable way, we have the right to demand that he support that assertion with a disciplined collection of projections and expert opinion should the contrary emerge; if objective defenses pertinent to method cannot be produced, then that should be the swan song for the secretary, with "cause."

The list of areas to which the method-audit is appropriate and promising is endless, and very few functionaries would be able to legitimately escape its implications. But the ancillary advantage of this type of accountability mechanism is that it might force sorely needed revisions in the recruitment and selection procedures of major institutions, especially in the public sector. We have long suspected—and we are certainly not alone is this—that the study of law is not necessarily the best preparation for members of the Congress or Senate, who are forced to make decisions about social, economic, technological issues. By the same token, we seriously question whether 30 years as a military officer is adequate preparation for a position as a regional counselor within the Department of Health, Education and Welfare, or whether a career as a business entrepreneur or bond-salesman *a priori* qualifies one to head the Atomic Energy Commission or to assume a position on the board of governors of the Federal Reserve System. Reason would dictate that if propriety of method becomes the *prima facie* evidence for acceptability of performance, then candidates for public office should be required to present evidence that they are capable of employing an analytical sophistication appropriate to the position they seek (or for which they are proposed). Thus, party loyalty would hardly be a criterion for the position of attorney general, nor would a large party contribution presume a capability for an ambassadorship to Africa or a seat on the House Appropriations Committee. Nor should the issue of relevant experience be allowed great latitude; for example, a career as a marketing executive for an oil company has little bearing on the responsibilities, much less the analytical requirements, necessary for a position on the National Energy Board. Not only are the ostensible aims of the agency entirely different from those of the marketing arm of an oil company, but the problems to be handled bear almost no resemblance to those encountered in commercial marketing. (Nevertheless, the "technical" marketing executive will indeed have a subset of analytical skills valuable for operations in the public domain.) In the same sense, being heiress to a cookie fortune is not a palatable preparation for the role of national consumer advocate.

This is not at all to suggest that all public officials be Renaissance scholars, completely at home with all areas of expertise and knowledge that might be called upon in the course of their duties. But neither can we nor any reasonable people accept the proposition that public administration is nothing more than an art form, with no scientific, methodological, or disciplinary bases—and that the only qualifications are a glad hand, a winning smile, and a facility for avoiding contentious issues. Thus, while we cannot ask that all decision-makers hold Ph.D.'s in the general sciences, we can ask that they give evidence before they are allowed to enter office, that at least they are aware of where specific knowledge may be found and that they are sensitive to something more than merely political or rhetorical arguments. And, even if some officials do not demonstrate adequate preparation, the least we can expect is that a method-audit process set a limit to their tenure.

But, while the desirability of the method-audit process as a means of exerting accountability within complex organizations may not be disputable, there may be some doubts about its feasibility. For its concentration on the methodology of decision-making implies that someone knows how decisions *should* be made. It implies, in short, a normative reference against which real-world decision behavior may be measured. It is the task of the remainder of this chapter to advance these normative criteria and, in the process, to define the dimensions of decision discipline.

4.2 THE DECISION ANALYST AS MODEL-BUILDER

The path by which a decision-maker arrives at an effective minimum value for expected decision error may be long and tortuous. We know from the introduction that the decision process, in greatest abstraction, involves at least the stages

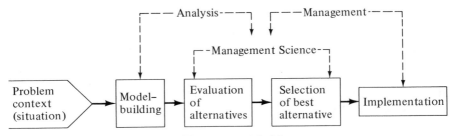

Figure 4.5. The abstracted decision process.

depicted in Figure 4.5. This is a static and considerably simplified portrait of the decision process, upon which we will elaborate considerably in coming sections. For now, we at least see the basic areas of interest of the three major aspects of administrative science. First, the analysis process involves model-building, evaluation, and sometimes selection. Management science, on the other hand, is concerned most directly with the selection of alternatives (according to certain criteria, such as maximization or *minmax** once the alternatives have been defined; indeed, in most management science texts, both the problem context and the alternatives to be selected among usually appear as "givens").[4]

Finally, management (as, for example, the "art of getting things done through people" or as the "distillation of experience") will be primarily responsible for implementing the selected alternative, subject to the sociobehavioral properties of the organization.

In some cases, depending on how administrative responsibilities are distributed within an organization, the decision-maker may simply be the person who selects the action alternative to be implemented, from among a collection of alternatives made available by the analysts (i.e., the technical staff). In other cases (and we believe this is to be preferred), the decision-maker is responsible for all three analytical functions (model-building, evaluation, and selection), with the organization's managers *per se* responsible for implementation. Thus, the decision-maker, as we have suggested, has primarily intellectual responsibilities, while the manager or administrator is concerned with the "management" of individuals and resources, i.e., the socioeconomic functions. The decision-maker, on the other hand, manages ideas and information. These dual responsibilities may fall on the same individual, but in the normal organization, the implementation functions are most likely to be passed on to people of primarily rhetorical persuasion, at least in the near future.

In general, however, the decision-maker must develop a *model* of some process system, entity, or phenomenon that he is interested in controlling, acting upon,

*Choosing the alternative with minimum maximum loss or, conversely, with maximum minimum gain (in terms of expected value).

or otherwise influencing (or to which he is expected to respond). Obviously, this model—allegorizing the structural and dynamic properties of subject of a decision-making exercise—is the initial and single most important output of the decision-analysis function. From it, all the information that eventually leads to a commitment of action—to a decision *per se*—will be developed. Subjects will, of course, expectedly differ for the several decision domains. For example, we have assigned the goal-setters (the organizational directors and chief officers) the responsibility for authoring the organization's interface with the world around it, and with the farther future. Therefore, the "model" of concern to them must allegorize the properties of the organization's milieu at that future point in time. Strategic analysts (operating at the executive level) are concerned primarily with a reduced segment of the environment, particularly the "neighborhood" that the goal-formulation process has defined as the feasible strategic search space. Moreover, their relevant "future" is nearer than that of the goal-setters, as they will tend to set objectives to be achieved in sequence along the path toward the ultimate destination designed by the directors. Thus, the strategic analysts may be interested in approaching a goal in stages, with their attention focused on each stage in turn. The efforts of the strategic analysts, as we have seen, even further constrain the situations faced by tactical analysts. If the goal-setters are looking 10 or even 20 years ahead and the strategic analysts look perhaps 3 or 5 years into the future, the tactical analysts (the organization's managerial staff) may be looking ahead only to the next period of operations, e.g., the next fiscal year. Moreover, their domain of interest is decidedly less broad than that faced by the strategists, and is particularly reduced to just one qualitative partition among the several (or perhaps many) that originally faced the strategic decision-makers. Finally, as we arrive at the deterministic level, we reach the point where both decision horizon and domain collapse considerably. The supervisor may be concerned with just a single process and perhaps proceed on a quarterly time horizon, or perhaps even day-to-day. In very simple terms, what we expect then is the situation illustrated in Figure 4.6. Our different administrative functionaries thus operate in the face of distinctly different (e.g., discrete) decision contexts. Yet, each decision-maker faces the same set of functional responsibilities:

(a) He must develop a model of the subject of interest within his domain, one setting out both the structure and dynamics of the process(es) or system(s) resident there.
(b) Using this model, he must define the various courses of action (alternatives) open to him.
(c) He must then evaluate the expected effects of each of the action-alternatives, usually by trying to predict the differential outcomes associated with each.

Thus, the example, the goal-setter's model will involve specifications of the range of factors or entities expected to affect—or be affected by—the organization at

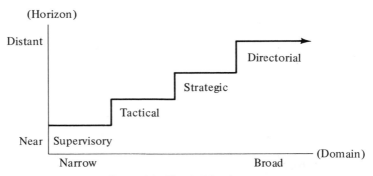

Figure 4.6. The decision focuses.

the interval of interest (the decision horizon). The goal-setting process thus consists of trying to isolate the best possible position for the organization to be in with respect to various environments and time horizons. In the formulation of goals illustrated in Chapter 2, the goals took the form of a particular point in space (the domain) at a particular point in time (the horizon). In the goal-setting process, then, we would have expected the directors to evaluate the benefits and liabilities of the wealth of alternative "states" available to the organization in the far future. To perform such a process well, the goal-setters would have had to have a "model" setting out the likely social, political, economic, and other contextual properties of the relevant environment. Using this as a base, they would then try to *simulate* the results of adopting one goal alternative as opposed to another. The point, then is that both the identification of action alternatives and their evaluation demand that there be a model base allegorizing the properties of the domain at some point in time. This then allows the decision-makers to *predict* the outcomes associated with the various actions they might impose on that environment.

Models used by strategic decision-makers must be able to capture and project the properties of the feasible search space left them by the goal-setters. Thus, their domain of interest will usually be some subset of that sought over by the directors, and their models will thus usually be somewhat less broad in implication, less encompassing, and confined to a nearer time frame. The strategic models must, however, be able to answer for the qualitatively different situations that might accompany the implementation of any of the several strategic alternatives occurring to the decision-makers. Thus, strategic models, must also have both descriptive and predictive capabilities (serving to allegorize the properties of the domain of interest and simulate the effects of imposing certain action-alternatives on that domain). The operations of the tactical decision-makers are similar, except their domain is expectedly still more confined and the alternative actions are all members of the same qualitative set (and the alternative outcomes associated with those actions also belong to the same qualitative set). Finally, the deterministic decision-maker will have a search space that is very constrained, and an action latitude so small, that his search for a best alternative may usually be found through a trial-and-error stroll (i.e., a "random walk") over the search space; or, he may take recourse in expedient analytic techniques (e.g., engineering formulas or linear programming constructs). In short, by the time we reach this level, the probability of *not* finding the right* answer is very slight, for the models required here are usually simple to construct and manipulate.

Again, it is the successive collapse of the feasible search space (the reduction of the domain of interest) and the gradual shortening of the time horizon that lend the different decision domains their attributes of major interest for us here. For the implication of these two conditions, as we move from higher-level to lower-level decision functions within the organization, is that the *modeling task becomes simpler*. The reason for this emerges from the consideration of just what modeling entails. For our purposes here, we may think of any proper model as involving specifications on at least four levels:

(a) At the *state-variable* level of analysis, we would attempt to enter all the major structural determinants present in our domain of interest.

(b) At the *relational* level, we try to capture the basic dynamics of the state-variables, particularly by suggesting the dominant ways in which they interact. Generally, this level of analysis will confine itself to determining interface conditions (what variable connects with which others) and the directions on influence at these interfaces.

(c) The *coefficient* level of analysis sees us trying to measure the "magnitudes" of the relationships identified in the preceding level.

(d) Finally, as we move to the *parametric* level of analysis, we are interested in assigning actual point-in-time (or interval) values to the state variables, where the relevant point in time is usually taken to mean the decision horizon.

To make the relationship of these levels of analysis somewhat clearer, let us take a highly artificial, greatly oversimplified example of a problem-solving process. We can refer to an example we used in Section 1.2, the surtax-inflation problem. For illustrative purposes, we will go through a highly simplified model-building process, beginning with the following:

$$F = f(M, I, T, D, E, S)$$

*Right, that is, in terms of the prior goal, strategic and tactical constraints.

where

   M = money supply
   I = interest-rate structure
   T = tax-rate structure
   D = disposable personal income (DPI)
   E = expectations operator
   S = savings propensity (rate).

The implication is that F (the inflation rate) will be some function of these six state variables, which thus serve to set the initial constraints on the domain of inquiry. We may now move to the point where we will look at relations. Recall that we are usually interested in two things at the relational level: (a) are the state variables in any way related? and (b) if so, what is the direction of influence? Thus, again just for illustrative purposes, we might emerge with a schedule of relationships something like the following:

State-Variable Pairs	Expected Relationship
(M, I)	N
(M, T)	U
(M, D)	P
(M, E)	I
(M, S)	P
(I, T)	U
(I, D)	N
(I, E)	N
(I, S)	N
(T, D)	N
(T, E)	N
(T, S)	N
(D, E)	P
(D, S)	P
(E, S)	I

where

   P = positive correlation
   N = negative correlation
   U = uncorrelated
   I = indeterminate

and the number of pairs is the combination: $\dfrac{6!}{2!\,(4!)} = 15$.

Here we have a combinatorial listing of the six state variables, taken in simple pairs, with each pair assigned a relational attribute (quality). Given these, we may then try to get a tentative answer to the issue we are concerned with: what is the expected effect of raising the tax-rate structure (T) on the inflation (F)?

Again, operating with unwarranted simplicity, we can *resonate* the effect of an increase in T by doing some simple subpartitioning, as follows:

Given $T\uparrow$:

$$(T, D) = N \longrightarrow \begin{bmatrix} (M,D) = P \\ (I,D) = N \\ (D,E) = P \\ (D,S) = P \\ (M,E) = I \\ (I,E) = P \\ (E,S) = I \\ (M,S) = P \\ (I,S) = N \\ (D,S) = P \end{bmatrix} \longrightarrow \begin{bmatrix} M\downarrow \\ I\uparrow \\ E\downarrow \\ S\downarrow \\ M? \\ I\uparrow \\ S? \\ M\downarrow \\ I\uparrow \\ D\downarrow \end{bmatrix} \longrightarrow \begin{bmatrix} M\downarrow \\ I\uparrow \\ E\downarrow \\ S\downarrow \\ D\downarrow \end{bmatrix} \longrightarrow \Delta F.$$

with $(T,E) = N$ and $(T,S) = N$ also feeding the central listing.

Note that we have not worked with the variable pairs (M, T) and (I, T), as they were initially considered uncorrelated. By resonating out the implications of the three remaining T-dependent variable sets, we were able to arrive at the point where we find that, as we increase the tax rate, the money supply, disposable personal income, savings rates, and expectations all decrease. But we also have now established, by surrogate, the originally neglected relationship between the tax rate and interest rate (I, T). Particularly, we now assume that the tax rate and interest rates are positively correlated, being mediated through the secondary relationships $(I,D), (I,E)$, and (I,S).

There remains, of course, the second aspect of the relational analysis. Particularly, we now have to assess the direction of the relationships between the several mediating variables (M, I, E, S, D) and the inflation rate (F).

For example, we might suggest the following:

$$\begin{aligned}
(F,M) &= P \longrightarrow M\downarrow \longrightarrow F\downarrow \\
(F,I) &= N \longrightarrow I\uparrow \longrightarrow F\downarrow \\
(F,E) &= I \longrightarrow E\downarrow \longrightarrow F? \\
(F,S) &= N \longrightarrow S\downarrow \longrightarrow F\uparrow \\
(F,D) &= P \longrightarrow D\downarrow \longrightarrow F\downarrow.
\end{aligned}$$

We can see now that we have two problems, each of which must be solved in a different way. First, the failure to resolve the relationship between (F, E) is the most serious. So we must now develop a submodel of the way in which expectations operate across our economic system, thus attempting to answer whether the decrease in expectations will act to increase or decrease F.

As events proved in the late 1960s in both Great Britain and the United States, adverse expectations may be said to have actually fueled inflation. That is, the relationship between E and F became negative within some substantial range. The reason for this lies farther back in the model, at the point where we left the relationship between expectations and the savings rate unspecified ($[E, S] = I$). The strategic (qualitative) issue we failed to resolve was whether adverse expectations operate to increase or decrease the savings function. The answer that emerges from empirical history of economic systems is sometimes yes, sometimes no. It really depends on *how bad* expectations are. Thus, we must attribute certain qualitative classes to E, as it is a complex variable, e.g., very bad, moderately bad, good. If expectations are only moderately adverse, so that a consumer sees a possibility of being temporarily unemployed, he might cut back on spending and thus reduce inflationary pressure (at least that exerted from the demand side). On the other hand, if his expectations are severely adverse, so that he foresees the collapse of the economic system, or a radical reduction in across-the-board disposable personal income, or a dramatic increase in prices, then he might very well elect to draw down his savings and spend like a lord while his savings are still worth something (or he may effect the same thing by increasing his credit burden). In such a case, adverse expectations would result in a decrease of savings, which, given $(F, S) = N$, would suggest that the inflation rate might actually rise. Therefore, to avoid very serious errors of analysis, *all* indeterminate qualitative (directional) relationships should be fully specified at the relational stage. But, as we earlier suggested, the real-world analysts who worked on this problem, and hence gave impetus to the strategy of the surtax as a deflationary instrument, made the most serious of all errors. They failed to include expectations as a state variable and therefore guaranteed a dysfunctional decision.

Note that, in our example, relationships were simply concerned with directions of influence. Thus, we took each pair of state variables and asked about the condition $S.V_{.j} \, r \, S.V_{.k}$. The relational operator, r, could assume only a limited number of qualitative values (positive, negative, etc.). In other cases, we may be interested in relationships on another level entirely. Particularly, we may be interested in the *mathematical* nature of the relationships, so that r may take on any of the following "values" ($+$, $-$, $\div$, $\times$, and any power). The issue of whether we use the qualitative or mathematical relational sets is important, for it determines what we do at the coefficient level. For example, where r specifies only directions of influence, then the coefficients we will assign will be measures of the *magnitude of the intercorrelation* between the state variables. That is, pairs of state variables will be related by ar, where r is the directional operator and a is a magnitude. In nonlinear allegorizations, using mathematical or arithmetic relationships, the coefficient determination will most often involve assigning numerical values to the connectors, e.g., given $S.V._i^a \ ^{S.V.k}$, this would mean determining a point-in-time (or possibly constant) value for a.

For illustrative purposes, however, we may presume that the state variables are linearly related, and we are therefore interested in assigning values to the coefficients in a formulation like the following: $F = aM + bI + dD + eE + fS + R$, where R is an error term. The coefficients (a, b, d, etc.) measure the strength of the relationship between the dependent variable (F) and the independent variables, and thus are true regression values. In short, we must here measure the *sensitivity* of the inflation rate to the several determinants. But note that in the real-world, model-building exercise we would also have to measure all the interrelationships or covariances; moreover, we would have to assess the strength of the relationships between T (the change agent) and all the other state variables, yielding a set of values for dM/dT, dI/dT, etc. In short, we would emerge with a *system* of either linear or differential equations (depending on the nature of the original relationships). This would then constitute the model as developed at the coefficient level.

But to our simplified illustration, suppose that we simply emerge with the equation just given, so that we have values for all the coefficients and for R (the latter being a measure of the *unexplained variance* in F, given our formulation). As a general rule, R may be used as an index of the quality of our model. The higher the unexplained variance (residual error), the lower is the descriptive sensitivity of the model, and therefore the more perilous its use in a predictive capacity.[5] Indeed, when R is very large, we might want to test some other modeling algorithm, perhaps nonlinear regression analysis or difference analysis, etc. At any rate, we can see that the values for the coefficients would come from evaluation of historical-empirical data. This would give us the values for M, I, D, E, and S that prevailed with respect to different levels of F (and secondarily, T).

We are now prepared to enter the last stage of the model-building exercise. Under parametric analysis, we would assign specific point-in-time (or interval) values to the state variables M, I, D, E, and S. Thus, our symbolic variables now disappear and are replaced with numbers or "fuzzy" categorical terms. For example, it would be very difficult to cardinalize the expectations operator, E. Therefore, we might have to rest content by providing a qualitative parameter (e.g., excellent, very poor) or ordinal rankings. At any rate, we are now ready to use our model to proceed to the *selection* aspect of the decision process.

To do this, we need to use the parametric values assigned the state variables to compute:

$$E.V. \ ([M, I, D, E, S] \mid \Delta T).^*$$

*Note that were we operating with a system of equations, than all the cross-relationships would also have to be evaluated with respect to $\Delta T \ldots \Delta M \mid \Delta T$, etc.

That is, we are interested in assigning estimated parametric values to the state variables, given some incremental increase in the tax rate (a specific surtax). Given these new parametric values and the coefficients earlier assigned to the state variables, we can evaluate:

$$E.V. \ (F \mid \Delta T) = aM + bI + dD + eE + fS.$$

That is, we now have an expected value for F, given the particular surtax rate being tested. Depending on circumstances, we might evaluate the F rates for some range of T's, or, given the properties of the model, it is possible for some authority to simply specify the desired reduction in inflation (ΔF) and then let the model determine the required ΔT value automatically. At any rate, if we ignore the residual error term in the coefficient-level formulation, then we now have reduced the problem to a deterministic one. If, however, we want to retain the error term (so that each ΔT is really a range function comprising different point estimates of greater or lower probability of occurrence), then our analysis remains a stochastic exercise.

Now, even this somewhat artificial and much simplified example allows us to make a point critical to our subsequent investigation of decision discipline. To assist us here, consider Table 4.1. Table 4.1 shows the way in which we may re-interpret our basic problem categories and decision functions given our inquiry into the model-building process. As for the model-dependent definitions of the problem categories, we find that indeterminacy is now characterized by the situation where we do not even know the basic constituents of the system or process with which we are concerned. In short, we must construct the basic state-variable array. This, of course, determines the basic domain of inquiry (a subset of the universe or variable) and was essentially the task performed by our goal-setters in Chapter 2. Now, at the point where we do not even know the fundamental composition of a process or entity, these would be expected to meet the criteria for an indeterminate problem first given in Figure 1.3; given the starting-state information available (which in this instance lacks even state-variable specifications), we are completely uncertain about what the system or process might do or become. Thus, what we have in the model-dependent problem definitions is the *static* counterpart to our originally dynamic definitions. In short, given the static conditions outlined for the several problem categories in Table 4.1, the dynamic (behavioral) implications of Figure 1.3 are expected to hold.*

As we move on, we can see that a severely stochastic problem is one for which we lack the specification of fundamental relationships. In short, for the case at hand, we knew only what variables were involved (i.e., M, I, T, D, E, S), as these were given to us as the output of the state-variable analysis. But we did not know

*See Section 1.1.

Table 4.1. Associations between modeling and decision functions.

Problem Category	Model-Dependent Definitions	Levels of Analysis			
		State Variable	Relational	Coefficient	Parametric
Indeterminate	The composition of the system or process is unknown. The array of state variables must be developed.	Goal-setting			
Severely Stochastic	The relationships among the state variables are unknown and must be supplied.		Strategic analysis		——(Unspecified)——
Moderately Stochastic	The magnitude of the relationships must be calculated	—(Given)—		Tactical analysis	
Deterministic	Parametric values for the state variables must be provided.				Instrumental analysis

the direction of influence among these variables, or even which ones interrelated. Thus, we had to engage in a qualitative analysis exercise, which resulted in the directional specifications given earlier in this section. Before doing that, we were in a position where the dynamic criterion for severe stochasticity was met: we did not know whether raising the tax rate (T) would result in (a) no change in F, (b) reduction in F, or (c) increase in F. Note that with only the starting-state conditions at our disposal (only the state-variable specifications), any increase in T could have led to either of these three qualitatively distinct situations. By the time we had completed our relational (strategic) analysis, however, we should have had only one of these three qualitatively unique outcomes assigned any significant probability of occurrence, say alternative b. In making this assertion, we are ignoring the expectation operator in the same way the real-world analysts ignored it; were this problem to be resolved for other than illustrative purposes, however, we would have to spend considerable time evaluating (F, E) and would also have to be particularly concerned about the effects of (fS) in our coefficient formulation. For if (F, E) is sufficiently positive, or if f is sufficiently strong, then alternative b would be an unlikely outcome given an increase in T. Again, it was not the outcome at all in the real-world version of this problem; rather, alternative c was the actual result.

Nevertheless, assuming that a single qualitative outcome was seized upon, the problem was ready to be passed down to the coefficient level. Here, the analysts were concerned only with the domain defined by alternative b. Their task was then to put magnitudes to the relationship of ultimate interest, dF/dT, or ($F = f [\Delta T]$). As we saw in the previous chapter, this was the type of decision function performed at the tactical level. Finally, it remained only to pick a particular T, and here the problem passed to the parametric and final level of analysis. The deterministic (instrumental) decision-makers merely had to exercise the model itself to get the set of all feasible (F, T) alternatives, so that some higher-level decision-maker could select a particular T value for implementation. Or again, there was the possibility that the instrumental analysts would be given a desired ΔF, and then would simply direct the model to return the appropriate ΔT. At any rate, at this level, the analysis was characterized by significant closure of domain, and by the availability of an analytic solution (provided by the mechanical quality of the model itself at that level). Again, this was the kind of task that was passed on to our operational or "algorithmic" personnel in Chapter 2.

We can now see the "envelope of certainty," which passes down the various decision levels, in a new light. Particularly, again with respect to Table 4.1, the entries along the major diagonal represent the *vector of decision congruence* — that is, the various decision functions (levels) associated with their correlative levels of analysis. As these levels of analysis are passed through, what was done at the previous level of analysis now becomes a *given* for the subsequent level. Finally, we can see why, again, it is more serious to make a higher-level decision error than a lower-level one. For, if the state-variable analysis task is ill-performed, all subsequent model-building tasks will be error-ridden. If an error in specifying basic relationships is made by the strategic decision-maker, it will concatenate into the coefficient and parametric analyses. If an error is made at the coefficient level, then the parametric analysis will be thrown off, as will the ultimate rectitude of the answer the model finally returns (or the action-alternative it recommends). But the *degree* of error caused by an ill-calculated coefficient (or ill-measured parameter) will not be as great as that which would result from a state variable being misdefined (or neglected), or a basic relationship being set erroneously (or neglected).

Finally, we can see that the level of detail of the model increases as we move downward through the several model-building operations (gradually taking the problem from indeterminacy to determinism, at least to the extent it will permit). And, again, we can see that as we move downward from the state-variable and strategic analysis (relational specification) stages, there is more opportunity to replace judgment with fact and to replace speculation with calculation. Moreover, we can now see why we earlier suggested that, as the problem at hand approaches indeterminacy, the probability of decision error and the expected value of a decision error tend to increase. And we can also see why, in the strictest terms, it is more difficult to audit the results of higher-level decision exercises, and therefore why the "method audit" becomes so critical. But the model-building process also gives us the clues we need to inject a normative aspect to decision-making, this being the key to the operational feasibility of the method-audit process. We may now move toward the normative content of decision science.

4.3 THE EXPECTED VALUE OF DECISION ERROR

We suggested at the initiation of our work in this volume—and have since repeated several times—that the rational decision-maker seeks always to minimize the expected value of a decision error associated with some decision exercise. To define this concept operationally, we must return to the aspects of the model-building process described in the previous section. Particularly, in terms of the scenario we have been constructing, the decision-makers will have built a model of the process (or subject) of interest. They will then have used this model to identify alternative actions they might impose on the subject or process, and to evaluate the outcomes associated with each of the action-alternatives. At this point, they will have emerged with a specific action-alternative (A_i), which, among all others, is expected to be most favorable with respect to the decision objective being sought. That is, on the basis of the analysis process just completed, one alternative action will be recommended for implemented as best goal, most promising strategy, or optimal tactic, etc.

But, in all likelihood, this A_i will not completely dominate the array of action-alternatives. There will usually be some doubt about its optimality relative to other alternatives. In short, A_i will be a member of a probability distribution, as shown in Figure 4.7. (The distribution may, of course, take any form, not just the unimodal, normal used here.)

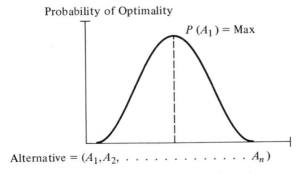

Figure 4.7. The distribution of action-alternatives.

Here we have simply suggested that there is not total agreement (of data or opinion) that alternative A_i will prove to be the optimal action to take in the face of the problem at hand. Rather, it is simply the alternative that is expected to be most productive in terms of the objective being sought. The strength of this expectation is reflected in the morphology of the distribution, which in turn reflects the dispersion of either empirical or judgmental inputs.

Still within our decision scenario, the element of doubt about the optimality of A_i would be followed by some element of doubt about the *outcome* (or effect) it will have if actually implemented. That is, there may be more than one significantly probable outcome associated with A_i, each unique outcome being indexed with some expected probability of occurrence. Therefore, we must consider a second event-probability distribution, one for each A_i, as in Figure 4.8.

Now, the expected value of a decision error will be reflected in (or determined by) the *morphology* of this distribution of outcomes, i.e., the shape of the event-probability distribution across which the alternative outcomes associated with a decision action are arrayed. In symbolic terms, the event-probability distribution is structured as follows:

$$(A_i) \rightarrow (p_1 e_1, p_2 e_2, \ldots, p_m e_m),$$

where the p_i's are the probability of each outcome and $\sum p_i = 1.0$, and the e_i's are all outcomes that have been assigned a significant probability of occurrence. These several probability coefficients are thus one component of the expected value of a decision error, associated with the problem at hand. A_i is the action-alternative that was assigned the highest probability of being the most effective and efficient means for achieving the decision-maker's end (e.g., the supposedly optimal goal, the most favorable strategy, the most promising tactic). And e_i is the outcome most likely associated with that action-alternative.

The second component of the expected value of a decision error is rather straightforward. Basically, we ask about the costs or losses we might expect to incur were A_i, when implemented, not to return with the expected outcome e_i. The computational problem is thus to assess the implications of each $e_k \neq e_i$. In

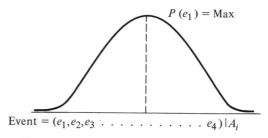

Figure 4.8. The distribution of action outcomes.

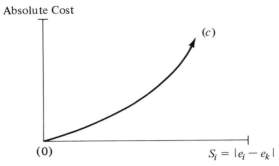

Figure 4.9. Cost of error.

general, we would expect a functional relationship such as that shown in Figure 4.9. That is, we expect that the absolute cost of an error will depend on the expected (and desired) outcome, e_i, and the other alternatives carrying a significant probability of occurrence, the e_k's. As the absolute value of this difference increases, the absolute cost expectedly increases, at least when alternative outcomes are "normalized" about the mean or most probable outcome.

In the usual decision calculus, this increasing cost function is usually dampened by a decreasing probability function. Particularly, we expect that increasingly large departures of e_k from e_i become increasingly improbable, as in Figure 4.10.* We can see, immediately, that this figure reflects the implications of Figure 4.8, assuming that we arrayed the various outcomes in terms of their assumed difference with respect to e_i (although, of course, we need not use a normal distribution *per se*). At any rate, the expected value of a decision error may now be calculated by multiplying the absolute cost associated with each ($[S_i = | e_i - e_k |] \rightarrow C_i$) by the probability ($p_i$) of an error of that magnitude occurring:

$$\text{Expected Value} \mid A_i = \sum p_i c_i, \quad \text{for } \forall s_i,$$

where Expected Value $| A_i$ is the cost of error expectedly associated with the implementation of action A_i. In the normal decision situation, then, we view the expected value of a decision error as a *force vector* function, which looks something like Figure 4.11.

Finally, if we wish to be more strict in interpreting the expected value of decision error, we may perform the following calculation:

$$\text{Adjusted Expected Value (E. V.)} \quad \Big| \; A_i = \frac{E.V. \mid A_i}{P(A_i)}.$$

*Note that this expectation is less true for goal-setting or strategic problems than it is when we are dealing with tactical or operational matters.

Probability of Error

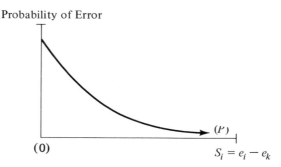

$$S_i = e_i - e_k$$

Figure 4.10. Probability of error.

In short, we use the probability of A being the true optimal action (as taken from the distribution in Figure 4.7) to inflate the expected value calculation made on the basis of the distribution shown in Figure 4.8. The greater the probability of optimality associated with A_i relative to all other action-alternatives included in A (all $A_k \neq A_i$), the smaller will be the inflation factor. We may, of course, compute either the adjusted or unadjusted expected value of a decision error using discrete distributions (in which case the weightings of the outcomes and alternatives become frequencies rather than probabilities) or using continuous distributions and the integral calculus.

Given this formulation for the expected value of decision error, we can immediately see how it may be reduced for any decision problem. Particularly, it can be reduced to the extent that we can transform the distributions of action-alternatives (the A_k's) and the distribution of outcomes associated with any A_i (the e_i's) into a more favorable configuration, as in Figure 4.12. We can see

Expected Value

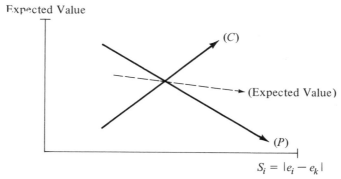

$$S_i = |e_i - e_k|$$

Figure 4.11. Expected value vector.

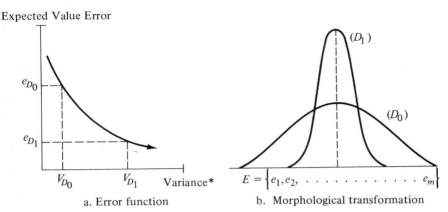

a. Error function   b. Morphological transformation

Figure 4.12. Error transformations.

*Variance is, in effect, a measure of the degree of difference (qualitative or quantitative) among the e_i's, similar to the concept of the coefficient of variation $\left[\dfrac{x}{\sigma_x}\right]$.

immediately why the transformation of distribution D_0 to D_1 results in a reduction of the expected value of error. The more extreme event-alternatives have been removed. This means, in essence, that the more costly absolute errors (computed as $c_i = f\,(s_i) = f\,|\,e_i - e_k\,|$) now do not enter our calculus, for the subset of e_k's associated with D_1 do not contain the larger s_i's. In short, what remains are much less significant errors, which virtually exhaust the relative probabilities. The implication is simply this: distribution D_1 represents a situation where we are more sure about our problem than was the case with distribution D_0. Ideally, this transformation from D_0 to D_1 is driven by proper *information* (as opposed to irrational factors). When this is the case, the value of information becomes imputedly equal to the difference between the expected value of decision errors associated with the two distributions:

$$\text{Value of Information} = (\text{E.V. Error}_{D_0} - \text{E.V. Error}_{D_1}).$$

Finally, we can see immediately what we need as a measure of the *efficiency* of a decision-making process under the method-audit scheme. Particularly, we want to evaluate $e = dE.V./dR$, where R is the resources expended in pursuit of a reduction in expected value (e.g., analyst's salaries, computer time, costs of data acquisition). This is the measure that would be the counterpart of the type of measure we would employ were we using the decision-audit accountability modality of the previous chapter. Were we operating in the *a posteriori* mode (i.e., traditional orientation on historical outcomes [results]), we would be looking at something like the following:

$$e = | e_i - e_a |,$$

where e_a is the *actual* outcome and e_i was the predicted (expected) outcome. But this measure would not be available to us until after the decision action has been implemented and run its course, whereas the method-audit efficiency measure is available to us beforehand. Given this measure, we need not wait for the results of a set of decision exercises to make an assertion about a decision-maker's efficiency.

But there is another dimension of the decision function to consider, *effectiveness*. We can see that the appropriate measure of the effectiveness of a decision-making process would be the extent to which the expected value of a decision error exhausts the potential for the problem at hand, or $q = E.V._a/F$, where F is the floor level to which expected value of decision error could have been lowered for the particular decision instance. Of course, this F value may be inaccessible to us most of the time, as it is an optimal criterion. But we know something about what to expect for the ideal-type problem categories we defined earlier. In this respect, consider Figure 4.13. These performance curves are merely abstract references, suggesting the relative levels of efficiency and effectiveness the different problem categories permit. Initially, we can see that the efficiency curve for the indeterminate problem is the most *inelastic* of the four, indicating that:

(a) Each unit of information pertinent to an indeterminate problem is expectedly most expensive to obtain.

(b) Probability of error diminishes least rapidly as magnitude of error ($s_i = | e_i - e_k |$) increases; thus, in the indeterminate problem domain, even quite significant errors still have a relatively strong probability of occurrence.

(c) Because indeterminate problems tend to emerge at the apex or highest level of a decision process, errors made there will have the highest concatenation factor, and therefore carry the highest absolute cost. That is, errors in goal-setting (or errors in the definition of a state-variable array during a model-building process) are the most costly of decision dysfunctions.

In short, for indeterminate problems, *the cost of error will tend to rise most rapidly with respect to magnitude of error, while the probability of error tends to fall least rapidly with respect to size of error*. Thus, the performance curve for the indeterminate problem category will be the flattest, indicating the least strength of relationship between expected value of decision error and expenditure of analytical resources.

Expected Value of Error, E. V.

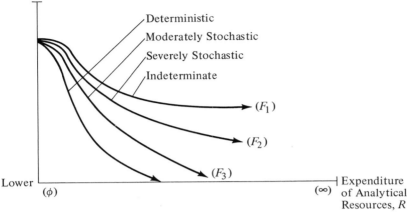

Figure 4.13. Differential decision performance curves $\left(\dfrac{d\,E.V.}{d_R} \right)$.

Moreover, the "floor" to which we might hope to reduce expected value of decision error for an indeterminate decision problem will still be quite high relative to the minimal feasible values for the other problem types. Indeterminate problems were defined as those where any outcome we might preidentify would have only minimal probability of being the true state of the system at any future point in time. Such a definition is consonant with our earlier assertion that, for most complex organizations, goal-setting operations tend to be undertaken within the indeterminate context.

The deterministic problem is, of course, the effective antonym of the indeterminate, which the performance curve adequately indicates. Clearly, the sensitivity of expected value of decision error to expenditure of analytical resources here reaches a relative maximum. The implication is that the cost of error associated with a deterministic process rises least rapidly with respect to size of error, and that probability of error falls most rapidly with respect to error magnitude. This merely reflects the fact that deterministic problems are, by definition, very susceptible to quick, expedient, and direct solution, as they have the least capability for surprising us. In sum, if the indeterminate domain is the worst of all possible worlds in which the decision-maker may find himself, then the deterministic domain is relatively comfortable indeed. The deterministic domain is also the only one where we allow the expected value of decision error to fall to zero (although it might come quite close for moderately stochastic decision problems); again, this merely reflects the original definition of the deter-

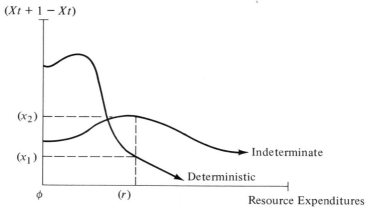

Figure 4.14. Information production functions.

ministic problem as one where only one outcome from among all alternatives can be assigned any significant probability of occurrence. Thus, the morphology for the distribution of outcomes around a deterministic problem would reach a most favorable configuration; it would, in effect, be practically vertical at the single most probable alternative.

The obvious question—and a distinctly operational one—is: how do we know when we are getting close to the floor error level for a decision process? The answer is that the floor is getting close when changes in the emerging information stock we are developing begin to dampen sufficiently—when $(X_{t+1} - X_t) \rightarrow 0$.* Within the confines of the decision scenario we have been constructing, this is also the point where $dE.V./dR$ begins to become less and less significant. In short, it marks the point where diminishing marginal returns begin to set in (such that the marginal cost of obtaining the next increment of information is expected to be roughly equal to its marginal value).

In general, then, we may conceive of an information production function of some kind. But, for our purposes here, we would be more interested in the rate of increase in the information stock associated with some problem, relative to the cumulative expenditure of analytical resources. In great simplification, we might get a mapping something like that shown in Figure 4.14. As expected, the "learning curve" for the deterministic problem-solver is more elastic than that for the person facing an effectively indeterminate problem; it goes rapidly toward maximum productivity, and moves even more rapidly toward the point where

*We here use X as a variable measuring the information base pertinent to a problem. Operations with information bases, and an elaboration on measures of information production, are discussed in Section 5.2.

additional resources provide essentially no change in the information stock. The indeterminate curve, on the other hand, is very soft throughout a very wide range of resource expenditures. Thus, were we to enter any budget (or time) constraint, r, the deterministic problem's information production curve always leaves us in much better shape than does the indeterminate. In short, point x_1 is much superior to point x_2 because we can make the following assertion: the model-building process will have proceeded further, at r, for the deterministic decision analyst than for the indeterminate analyst.

Thus, there is an important if tacit association between the information production function and the expected value of decision error. Particularly, as the degree of completeness of a model we are building—the extent to which exhausts the relevant properties of the problem, process, or subject being allegorized— increases, the number of alternative events or outcomes that must be assigned significant probabilities of occurrence decreases. As we have seen, this is the factor that forces a reduction in the expected value of decision error. Now, the generally acceptable ancillary implication is this: as the rate of increase in the information stock associated with some model-building process dampens toward zero, the probability of our approaching the "floor" level of decision error approaches unity (1.0), because the dampening of the information production function is the best operational indication we have that our decision model is nearing completion.* From another perspective, we might simply suggest this:

$$\left(\frac{E.V.}{F} \right)_t = q\,(x_i)_t,$$

where $x_i = dX/dR$ as evaluated in the neighborhood of t. Again, we tend to operationally measure the completeness of the model we are building by evaluating x_i during some interval $(t \rightarrow t + 1)$. We tend to assess this value by looking at the nature of the changes that are introduced into our model at any or all four of the levels of analysis: state variable, relational, coefficient, or parametric. More particularly, if we tend to measure completeness relative to the total model configuration, then we are relatively sure of approaching the point where x_i will dampen toward zero when we have completed the parametric specifications, as they are generally subject to our having completed the higher-level model-building tasks. From still another direction, we may consider the output from the model we are building as being a set of state specifications (S). In this sense, we are interested in evaluating $S = f(x_i)$. Thus, depending on the particular model-building process we are employing, there may be several different ways of measuring the rate at which it is nearing completion. But, in general, the *preferred* measure is the reduction in the number of alternatives having significant proba-

*We will elaborate on the uses of information production functions in Section 5.2.

bilities of occurrence at all points in the model—the extent to which we have forced distributional transitions such as those shown in Figure 4.12b at all four levels of analysis.[6]   In summary, *as the model-building exercise becomes more complete, the problem at hand tends to become more deterministic*, subject to the floor error constraints that might exist.   And as the problem becomes more deterministic, the expected value of decision error is forced to decline, eventually reaching an effective asymptote at the floor.   We will have more to say about this in the next section when we look at the dynamics of the decision process.

First, however, we must consider the operator q, which relates the analysis (information production) function and expected value of decision error.   Obviously, it is not merely the degree to which our model is complete that is important; it is also the degree to which it is *accurate* (where accuracy reflects a model's real-world sensitivity, not its internal properties).   That is, a model may be complete, but also be completely wrong.   So the question for us now is this: how do we operate to ensure, to the extent possible, the accuracy of the models built during a decision-analysis process?   The ancillary question is: how do we ensure that the expected value of decision error at which we arrive is a valid estimate of the real properties of the problem, and not an irrational estimate that bears little relationship to the real-world situation?   The answer is, of course, that we cannot ensure accuracy.   All that we can do is to try to gain a rough idea of the quality of the decision-analysis process by comparing the analysts' performance against the *criterion of analytical congruence*.   This criterion asks, simply, that the decision analyst be as careful as possible to use the right instrument at the right time toward the appropriate effect.   In short, both decision efficiency and effectiveness are intimately tied to the concept of analytical congruence.

4.4 ANALYTICAL CONGRUENCE

The concept of analytical congruence is, of course, at the heart of the disciplinary implications of the decision sciences.   In a sense, it is perhaps the major source of *normative* propositions about the way decisions should be made.   To clarify the concept, however, we must return briefly to the concept of the decision analyst as a model-builder.   Obviously, the quality of the solutions posed for organizational problems—the effectiveness and efficiency of the action alternatives selected for implementation by decision-makers—depends ultimately on the quality of the model developed by the analysts.   This, after all, is the origin of the action-alternatives and the primary vehicle for their evaluation.   Now, when we try to evaluate the quality of a decision model, we might look at four dimensions:

(a) *Reflectivity*. Fundamentally, this is the extent to which the model under construction reflects the degree of complexity inherent in the subject, process, or system being allegorized. That is, the uncertainty the model displays should mirror the uncertainty inherent in the subject's structure and/or behavior.

(b) *Exhaustiveness*. While the above criterion demands that no model be allowed to artificially simplify a subject's properties, exhaustiveness demands that we lose no opportunity to inject the full complement of determinism that the subject permits. This criterion, of course, operates with respect to the floor error level we discussed earlier.

(c) *Elegance*. This demands that the model be as parsimonious as possible, taking advantage of every opportunity to deliver the most information with the fewest manipulations of the fewest structural components.

These three criteria apply to virtually every model, built for whatever purposes, within essentially any discipline. But for the models built by decision analysts—for use by decision-makers—we must add a fourth criterion of quality:

(d) *Actionability*. This demands that the model produce decision premises (information outputs) that, to the greatest extent possible, recommend a specific action to be taken in the face of a problem. That is, every model used for decision-making purposes must be *prescriptive*.

The enforcement of analytical congruence is the surest means available for controlling the quality of the models we build. But before we discuss this point, let us briefly elaborate on the preceding criteria.

Initially, reflectivity warns us against analytical expedience and oversimplification. In any model-building exercise, there is always the tendency to artificially eliminate complexity in order to hasten the completion of the exercise, or to restructure the problem in a way that permits our preferred analytical instruments to go to work. In almost all cases, this means the introduction of unwarranted *assumptions* about a problem's properties, or the neglect of some properties that are particularly difficult to work with or entertain. Within the context of our illustrative model-building exercise (the inflation problem), we gave an example of how nonreflectivity can enter. Initially, we saw that the state-variable array for the inflation problem was unwarrantably foreshortened through the real-world analysts' failure to include the "expectations" operator. Second, we saw that the failure to evaluate certain relational aspects of the problem led to an ultimately false recommendation (e.g., that the imposition of a surtax would actually reduce inflation). Reflectivity is most often sinned against at the state-variable and relational level, simply because most analysts will have the least skill in normative or qualitative analysis, but also because of a very natural reluctance to incorporate uncertainty into our models. That is, decision models are supposed to answer questions, not ask them. However, to the extent that we do not properly perform the reflective task, the question we eventually "answer" is very likely to be the wrong one. Thus, whenever we assess the degree of reflectivity of a model, we must concentrate on the possibility that some real complexities were wished away, or artificially eliminated in the name of analytical expediency. As the reader might expect, nonreflectivity is most often associated with models developed by empiricist, "scientific" decision analysts, who have at their disposal only a limited set of quantitative instruments. In this instance, we would tend to recognize nonreflectivity when there is a distinct absence of qualitative determinants, or a large number of exogenous variables. These later serve to constrain the model from outside, and therefore reduce the number of model components that are to be treated simultaneously. Any model constructed by members of a single discipline only—economists, sociologists, political scientists, etc.—is also likely to have a relatively high proportion of exogenous to endogenous variables. As this proportion increases, the likelihood of nonreflectivity increases. Any model, for example, that tends to allegorize economic processes using only economic variables (with behavioral and sociological determinants introduced exogenously, if at all) is very likely to be a contradiction of the dictate of reflectivity. In short, we become sensitive to the possibility of nonreflectivity whenever we find a model that seems to introduce more determinacy into a problem than it apparently deserves. And because nonreflectivity tends to operate at the highest levels of the model-building process—at the point where we are developing an array of state-variables or determining interfaces and directions of relationships—nonreflectivity is usually the most serious source of procedural error (the most telling and important detriment to model quality).

If lack of reflectivity is most often associated with parochialized or quantitative model-building exercises, lack of exhaustiveness is usually indicated by a model that does not take advantage of whatever quantitative discipline and precision is available, or a model that is shy of logical elaboration. In short, nonexhaustive models tend most often to be developed by rhetoricians. The most obvious indication that we are dealing with a nonexhaustive model is when there are few specifications at the coefficient or parametric levels of analysis. That is, virtually all model components are left in a "fuzzy" specification, irrespective of the opportunities available for injecting numerical values. In short, such a model will be well-elaborated only at the state-variable and relational levels, but will lack specification of the magnitudes of the relationships or the time-dependent values that state-variables assume. This low level of specificity at the coefficient and parametric levels simply reflects the rhetorician's lack of affection for quantitative analysis or lack of mathematical or statistical skills. In summary, we tend to recognize either nonreflectivity or nonexhaustiveness by an *imbalance* in the levels of analysis. In nonreflective models, there will usually be elaborate specification at the coefficient and parametric levels, but perhaps only a few, highly selective state-variables and directional relationships. Nonexhaustive models, on the other hand, tend to have a great scope of inclusion at the higher levels of analysis, but be largely bereft of detail at the lower levels.

In general, nonexhaustiveness is a less serious model complaint than lack of reflectivity. In the terms we have been using, a nonexhaustive model that is nevertheless reflective may still take us along the proper strategic trajectory, even though we may travel that path somewhat inefficiently. But in some instances, nonexhaustiveness can rob our ultimate decision action of any effectiveness (strategic utility) whatsoever. This can happen whenever we leave a coefficient without a numerical value, or whenever we fail to give a state variable a proper parametric value. For example, harking back to our earlier attempt to model the relationship between increase in tax rates (T) and decrease in inflation (F), we can ask what would have happened had we not troubled to evaluate the coefficient linking these variables: $T \, r \, F$. To the extent that we understate the value of r, any given incremental increase in T may have a greater than expected impact on F. Therefore, it is very possible to increase T to the extent that it produces the dysfunctional antonym of inflation, deflation. In short, we would have failed to realize that different coefficient values can effect different qualitative outcomes, or to consider that the desired relationship between incremental tax increases and incremental decreases in the inflation rate operates only within some *range*. If we were equipped with only the directional specification of the relationship (i.e., $T\uparrow, F\downarrow$), then it is possible to implement an action, recommended by the model, that obviates the therapeutic treatment we sought to introduce.

An even clearer example of the danger of nonexhaustiveness to us is available from our illustrative model-building exercise. Recall that we were ultimately interested in the relationship between expectations and inflation. Also recall that the relationship between these two factors is indeterminate when we fail to equip the expectations operator with a point-in-time parametric value (some sort of ordinal value). The normative expectation was that adverse expectations would lead people to save against the future and therefore ease demand (with this easing of demand pressure causing a reduction in inflation). In short, we assumed the following directional relationship: ($E\downarrow, F\downarrow$). In this case, the magnitude of the relationship between these two variables (the value of the coefficient relating them) is really less important to us than the fact that the presumed directional relationship operates only within certain limits. As suggested earlier, when expectations are very bad indeed, then we would get the opposite effect ($E\downarrow, F\uparrow$) through dissaving and expansion of credit. Clearly, the effect of expectations on inflation rate is conditioned by the *magnitude* of the expectations operator at any point in time. Thus, the failure to assign a parametric value to this state-variable could result in our obtaining exactly the opposite effect we hoped for. Thus, we suggested earlier that a proper (rational) model-building exercise is one that results in specifications at all four levels of analysis. The failure to adequately treat any of these levels may sometimes introduce serious decision dysfunctions. In particular, as we have just suggested, it is very important to assess the possibility that magnitudes of relations or parameters may have an effect on the direction of relationships (the qualitative components of the model). Obviously, the strict rhetorician is just as ill-equipped to do this as is the strict "number cruncher."

The matter of the elegance is considerably important, but we can treat it only briefly here. The concern with elegance may be either academic or very pragmatic indeed. In all cases, it refers to the attempt to inject efficiency into the model as an information-producing artifice. In the academic domain, elegance is measured by the extent to which we have "honed Occam's razor," i.e., the range of implications that can be derived from a single theoretical construct. In the decision domain, however, we are interested in the conservations of scarce analytical resources. In virtually all cases (except for those instances of government study grants or other categorical funds devoted exclusively to analytical ends), the funds available for analysis are funds that are not available for other functions. Therefore, there are usually practical economic constraints on the analysis function. We will later see what this implies in procedural terms. Here, however, we can see that it is incumbent upon the analysts to maximize the relationship between the input of scarce resources and the informational output: $MAX\ d\ E.V./dR$ (maximize the reduction in expected value of decision error relative to analytical expenditures). We are more likely to get the resources to conduct an analysis when we can promise a significant return relative to investment, or when our analytical exercises have a history of high productivity. In another sense, given any budget constraint, the ultimate utility of the information we produce is a function of the efficiency of the model-building and evaluation tasks we performed. In the decision domain, analytical efficiency becomes coextensive with analytical elegance.

We can immediately see that there is potential competition between reflectivity and efficiency and between exhaustiveness and efficiency. But we also know that reflectivity and exhaustiveness must usually take precedence, as they are more directly related to the ultimate utility of our analytical exercises than is efficiency. To the extent that reflectivity and exhaustiveness are not unduly damaged or derogated, however, we can usually inject some elements of efficiency into our analytical exercises by obeying such dictates as:

(a) Wherever possible, avoid developing parochial (original) data bases; make every possible use of secondary information.
(b) Wherever possible, employ analytic (e.g., deterministic) instruments in

favor of heuristic or stochastic instruments, and try to minimize the frequency of resource-consuming search or simulation processes.

(c) Use, to the extent possible, any analogic algorithms that might be available. (This minimizes the need for developing original constructs.)

(d) Never collect data without an *a priori* (theoretical) model used to guide and discipline the collection process (e.g., the popular process of trying to elicit theoretical or normative positions from previously collected data bases is usually a prime source of analytical inefficiency, unless the problem is simple enough to permit the use of some sort of nonalgorithmic, trial-and-error process).

(e) Partition a model, to the extent possible, in such a way that you have the fewest state-variables to manipulate simultaneously. The cost of computation usually varies almost logarithmically with respect to the number of variables to be optimized in any single process.

(f) Always establish a criterion for the entry of state-variables or relational factors, reflecting the expected or actual resource limitations associated with an analytical exercise. That is, every state-variable and every relation should be evaluated with respect to some threshold for inclusion. This threshold would reflect the *degree of significance* that a variable or relation must have before it is to be entered into the emerging model. Greater resources usually permit us to use a lower threshold level (that is, we can usually accommodate more variables, and thereby hope to produce a more comprehensive model). Obviously, some budget constraints may be so severe that a proper analysis simply cannot be performed because our state-variable and relational sets would be so restricted as to dilute utility.

There are, of course, many other tactics that might be suggested. But the dictate of greatest strategic importance is this: efficiency in analytical exercises is best served by doing a lot of thinking before we do any manipulating. To the clever and sensitive analyst, this thinking is always directed toward the maximization of the *information leverage* of a model. This, in essence, means that we want to try to develop models in such a way that any calculation we make resonates as far as possible across the model domain, determining automatically as many other values as possible, given any degree of partitioning. That is, we look for all possible sources of analytical or logical *preemption*.

Of the preceding suggestions, possibly the most contentious is the matter of trying to *a priori* minimize the number of state-variables (and therefore the number of potential relations) our model will accommodate and operate on. As we add state-variables or basic relationships, the resource requirements of our analysis exercise will increase dramatically. Therefore, we must always be alert to the matter of the threshold. The general logic is to assess the potential strength of impact of each state-variable candidate (see Table 5.1 for a note on how this can be done). A good analyst will be able, in many cases, to estimate the costs of a model-building and evaluation exercise if you can tell him the number of state-variables to be included and give some clue as to the array of relationships that must be determined. But, as a rule, the decision as to whether to include a specific state-variable must be a matter of disciplined judgment, for all the determinants in the domain of a decision problem will expectedly differ in the degree of impact they may be expected to exert. Beyond some point, this probable level of impact becomes sufficiently small relative to expected costs of inclusion to warrant the neglect of that factor. But, again, the greater the analytical resources we are able to command, the lower may be the exclusion threshold. In some cases, imagination may serve to soften the relationship between the number of endogenous state-variables and analytical costs. Particularly, we should pay attention to the possibility of developing regression relationships among state-variables. When this can be done, the evaluation of a single variable may lead directly (through simple analytic techniques) to the evaluation of other factors related to the master variable. In some cases (as our model-building exercise indicated), we can set up a *reflexive* system, so that a parametric value assigned to any member of the state-variable array operates through relational coefficients to determine the value of all other state-variables.

As for actionability, this really concerns the nature of the interface between a decision analyst and decision-maker (or between the two hats worn by a single individual responsible for both functions). This is where the interests of the decision analyst and decision-maker may diverge. Given the criteria of reflectivity, exhaustiveness, and elegance, the decision analyst (*qua* model-builder) may consider his exercise successful if he has outlined *all* possible events and outcomes associated with a decision process. In short, the broader the range of outcomes to which he assigns probabilities of occurrence, the lower is the probability that he can be condemned for an analytical error. But, as a general rule, the decision-maker's affection for any model will be related to the fewness of the alternatives it offers. And much acrimony is born in the interstice between these competitive conditions. Two examples might help clarify this point.

Suppose we are responsible for making an investment in manufacturing equipment to produce a certain quantity of a product for the next operating period. In such a situation, a "model" of the market must be developed to give us an idea of potential demand. Given this figure, we may then make the needed investment in manufacturing equipment. To effect a demand estimate, the decision analyst will develop a forecasting model. For illustrative purposes, let us suggest that the model finds that the firm's expected sales are a function of the GNP. In short, GNP estimates are used as the regression variable against which investment decisions are determined. Now, no one can really expect to estimate GNP with complete accuracy. Therefore, the analysts will probably return with some *range* function; for example, with the conclusion that they are 95 percent sure that GNP will fall somewhere between x and y billion dollars for the coming period. Now, the analysts may always improve the probability of being right by setting x and y extremely far apart. But, when this range becomes very large, it becomes unactionable. What the person responsible for making the investment decision often wants to a single estimate against which can be measured the investment requirements, not a large set of alternatives. Therefore, he might press his analysts to return that single estimate, or to narrow the range of alternatives, a command that increases the analysts' peril. For, if analysts understate GNP (and therefore underestimate demand), the firm will forego opportunity profits associated with the amount it could have sold but did not produce; if the analysts overstate GNP (leading to an expected demand figure that is too high), the firm will have unsold goods to contend with at the end of the period—a direct loss. At any rate, the analysts are the appropriate individuals to make the range collapse into a point estimate (perhaps, for example, by selecting that GNP figure with the highest expected value), for they have the technical statistical skills. They will, of course, try to protect themselves by introducing dilutive probabilities, but they may still be held responsible for the point estimate despite their disclaimers. For the decision-maker—the person responsible for determining investment levels—cannot do the job unless the analysts are willing to risk their own reputations and welfare. There are many occasions, then, when the analysts' preference for a range-based result and the decision-maker's demand for a point estimate will conflict.

Who should prevail in this conflict? Only when the investment decision must be taken at once and cannot be spread over a period of time, should a point estimate be used. If it were possible to commit only some fraction of resources to immediate investment, and to delay the remainder, then the analysts would be doing the decision-maker a disservice by returning a point estimate instead of a range. In short, the point estimate, considering the potential volatility of GNP, would be unreflective of the real complexity of the demand-determination problem. The preferred situation would be for the analysts to make the decision-maker aware of the nature of the probability distribution surrounding GNP, and to initiate what is called a *sequential decision process*. Here, for example, the analysts might develop several alternative trajectories—one leading to the lowest feasible GNP level, another to the highest, and a third toward the GNP value carrying the highest expected value from the probability distribution emerging from the forecasting model. The decision-maker would then be counseled to make some minimal investment (e.g., that which would support the lowest demand level were the lowest GNP estimate to emerge as the true parameter). They would then wait until some empirical information is available, e.g., say the actual GNP projection taken at the end of the first quarter of the operating period. This actual value would then be compared against the values that refer to the three reference trajectories. More specifically, it would be used to revise the original probability distribution (estimated demand schedule) on the basis of new information. The technology available to us here is the well-known, widely practiced *Bayesian* transformation function.[7] At any rate, the revised probability distribution might point more clearly to one or another of the trajectories, and the cumulative investment would be raised according to the revised probabilities. In this staged, sequential analysis-decision process, the aggregate expected value of decision error may usually be reduced below that which would be realizable were the investment to be fully effected without benefit of empirical (*a posteriori*) information. In short, where circumstances permit, commitment of irrecoverable resources (or irrevocable actions) should be delayed as long as there is still an opportunity to reduce the expected value of a decision error. As we will later see, however, many practical factors may deny us this opportunity. Thus, despite their own predilections, decision analysts may often have to go under the gun and return a specific prescription even when their own interests might better be served by fudging or returning an array of possibilities. Yet the staged, sequential decision process—when not perforce denied us—usually allows the interests of the analyst and decision-maker to become identical (and thus best serves the cause of decision rationality).

Another simple example might help clarify actionability still further. Suppose we are in the position of a military commander who has been given responsibility for defending some position from enemy attack. His problem is to partition his defensive forces in order to maximize the probability of success against the attack. So he delegates to his analysts (staff) the responsibility for determining the most likely locale for the attack. Knowing well the penalties for being wrong, they are determined to maximize the probability of a successful (correct) analysis. Therefore, they develop many alternatives and return them to the commander. In short, they have attempted to be as analytically correct as possible, and not to neglect any possibility. Now the commander has a problem. Were he to partition his forces to cover all the alternatives his staff returned him, no single locale would be adequately protected. Now, he can try to force the risk on his staff, perhaps by having them select the two most probable alternatives from among the entire array, and then dividing his forces in two. Or he might assume the responsibility himself, and simply pick one, two, or several locales that appear most probable to him on the basis of experience, intuition, etc. Or, he might decide on a third alternative, one that makes use of the probability distribution developed by the staff: he might ask his analysts to locate the centrix, so that his defensive force would be located in a neighborhood determined (topologically) by the probabilities assigned the various alternatives. In

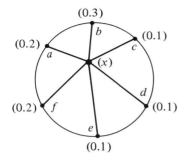

Where x is the location offering the lowest expected value of error (and the radii are given a distance that is a function of the reciprocal of their probability of occurrence).

Figure 4.15. The centrix solution.

short, he would position them as shown in Figure 4.15. In Figure 4.15, the centrix (x) is the product of the probability distribution developed by the analysts, and is therefore that particular point in the defensive zone that has the highest expected value of proving functional. Where the terrain or resources does not permit such a centrix solution, then the commander might want to initiate a sequential decision process. He would do this by seeking empirical information, much as did the decision-maker in the investment example we just went through. He might send out reconnaissance parties, develop intelligence about enemy movements, or otherwise do everything possible to displace a less favorable *a priori* informational state (with a consequently undesirably high probability of decision error) with a more favorable *a posteriori* state. But the sequential process demands time to develop the empiricial data base, just as the centrix solution demands a specific type of terrain (e.g., relatively flat and accessible) and a certain type of resources (e.g., troops and equipment of great mobility). Thus, the actionability of the output of a model-building exercise cannot be determined without some data about the decision context. But, as a general rule, we can again suggest the terms of the trade-off: (a) the probability of the analysts' expectations being wrong is inversely related to the number of different alternatives they offer (e.g., the range of recommendations); but (b) the expected utility of any output from an analysis process to a decision-maker is directly related to the narrowness of the range of options or alternatives or recommendations developed by the analysts; and (c) where exogenous constraints (e.g., factors of timing, resources, or information availability) do not demand an immediate and total commitment to a single alternative, decision rationality usually dictates that we devise a procedure that will allow the decision-maker and analysts to simultaneously realize their different ambitions; that is, a decision procedure that, under the criterion of selectivity, takes advantage of the uncertainty and conservatism of the analysts. (Of course, analysts should always be required to return a point estimate or a single action prescription in the face of an inherently deterministic decision problem, as there is no real "decision" to be made in the sense that we have been using the concept.)

Now, to return to our central question: how can we ensure that all the criteria of analytical quality are met to the fullest extent, despite the existence of some competitivity among the objectives of reflectivity, exhaustiveness, elegance, and actionability? Again, the answer is to be found by elaborating on the concept of analytical congruence. Particularly, given the several different problem categories we earlier defined, and considering the type of analytical instruments available to the modern decision analyst, it is possible to develop a vector of analytical congruence, as in Table 4.2.

The point of the construct is that certain instrumental categories tend to be associated with certain problem categories; that is, we may partition the instruments of analytical science into subsets that respond directly to different problem properties. The class of "algorithmic" instruments, broadly defined, means that we have a ready-made recipe for solution; in short, we plug in the appropriate numbers and the solution (a single answer) appears directly. Many of the laws of hard science represent algorithms, and some instruments of management science (e.g., inventory optimization models, linear programming constructs) are algorithmic. Although there are attempts to associate proper algorithms with more complex problems, the recipe-orientation gradually disappears and the procedures become more and more subject to interpretation. Therefore, proper algorithms tend to be isolated in the company of essentially deterministic problems. The inductive instrumental category is very large and imposing and well-developed, and fundamentally serves whenever we are trying to predict a future that is likely to be some function of the past, or whenever we are trying to generalize from

Table 4.2. The vector of analytical congruence.

Instrumental Category	Problem Categories			
	Deterministic	Moderately Stochastic	Severely Stochastic	Deterministic
Algorithmic	Optimization		Domain of Ineffectiveness	
Inductive		Extrapolative/ Projective (statistical)		
Hypothetico-Deductive			Contingency Programming Process	
Metahypothetical	Domain of Inefficiency			Heuristic and Normative Analysis

particulars (e.g., develop inferences about a population from a sample). The hypothetico-deductive class of instruments are generally those of philosophy, logic, qualitative analysis, or all the other tools available to discipline the attempt to bring a generalized order to a specific situation or context. In short, the hypothetico-deductive techniques are the primary instruments in the arsenal of the "soft" sciences. Finally, there are very few instruments to deal with indeterminacy—the metahypothetical category is very ill-populated. But, essentially, metahypothetical techniques would impose an artificial and tentative order on a chaotic context, and therefore serve as the initiating instrument for a long-range "learning" exercise. We will elaborate these points shortly.

For the moment, however, it is the concept of congruence that concerns us. Those particular instruments that are entered along the major diagonal of Table 4.2 represent congruent treatments for the problem category indicated. Any attempt to use an instrument falling to the left of the diagonal would result in a condition of *inefficiency*—a lack of *elegance*. Simply, the problem at hand is not complex enough to warrant the use of such an instrument (e.g., trying to attack an effectively deterministic problem using a hypothetico-deductive technique would be a waste of resources). The area to the right of the vector of congruence, the main diagonal, is the domain of *ineffectiveness*. Here the instruments are not sufficiently powerful to resolve the problem at hand; in short, our analytical solution is likely to be either *nonreflective* or *nonexhaustive*.

We will give but a brief defense of this construct here.[8] Initially, the association between optimization techniques and deterministic problems is very direct and clear. For optimization methods will locate the single solution available for any deterministic problem. They will do this in one of two ways. First, there may be an analytic technique available that will directly return the solution on the basis of the input specifications we define. Probably the most widely employed technique of this sort is linear programming.[9] The fundamental requirement for a linear programming solution is that we have a process or subject where the state-variables are related linearly, a specific objective function (e.g., maximization, minimization), and a domain that may be gradually closed by successive linear constraints. In short, we have a very well-behaved problem, for which there is only a single completely correct answer, given the constraints we develop. Many instruments of system engineering (i.e., finite-state system analysis) and microeconomic derivatives (e.g., inventory-control models) may also return the single correct answer to a deterministic problem. And, as we earlier suggested, many of the instruments employed by industrial engineers are properly members of the optimization category, as they are capable of identifying the single best production process for a simple manufacturing task, the optimal plant layout, or the optimal assembly process for some simple product, and so on. In the latter cases, it is not merely that the processes or subjects involved are inherently well-behaved that permits us to use optimization techniques, but also that the problems lend themselves to controlled experiment (perhaps through trial and error). Finally, most optimization techniques—even those involving reasonably complicated search patterns—are predicated on relatively efficient computational algorithms, many of which are available as preprogrammed packages on computer systems. As a rule, then, optimization techniques are the "cheapest" analytical instruments to employ.

As the above construct suggests, however, optimization techniques are appropriate only in the face of inherently deterministic problems. As soon as we move into the stochastic domain, these optimization instruments lose their utility. We have already suggested why: both moderately and severely stochastic problems involve subjects or processes that are capable of initiating several different outcomes to any action we might implement, or that are inherently ill-behaved in their own right. Therefore, were we to attempt to cast such a problem in a framework that would permit optimization instruments to go to work, we would be artificially wishing away the real complexity of the problem. For example, suppose we were enamored of the expediency and neatness of some optimization instrument, and tried to force a stochastic problem into the mold that would permit its use. To use it, we would have to introduce some constraining assumptions at the relational level of analysis. This would automatically inject an error into the model-building process, an error that would eventually concatenate through the coefficient and parametric levels to possibly seriously erode the relevance of our decision analysis. However, in some cases it is important to recognize that optimization instruments generally have a distinct cost and time advantage over the more sophisticated instrument categories, and this advantage must be set against the error expected to be associated with analytical expediency. The general calculation involves the attempt to *concatenate* the potential cost of error due to the oversimplification of the problem, and then to assess this relative to the expected savings in cost of analysis. And as suggested, the entrance of the error here will usually be at the relational level of analysis. In this respect, consider Figure 4.16.

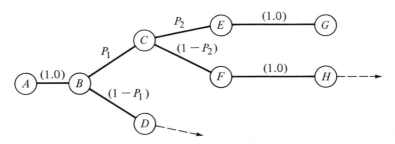

Figure 4.16. Illustrative relational configuration.

Now, to use an optimization instrument, we would have to eliminate all but one of the component paths. Were $(p_1 \gg [1 - p_1])$ and $(p_2 \gg [1 - p_2])$, then the path of greatest likelihood would be: $A \rightarrow B \rightarrow C \rightarrow E \rightarrow G$. For this particular case, let us suggest that A is a starting-state condition, e.g., some action that we are going to impose on a process. Were the problem inherently deterministic, then none of the stochastic nodes would exist. That is, the probability that A implies G significantly approaches 1. $P(A \rightarrow G) \rightarrow 1.0$. But we can see that the potential error in this assumption would be a product of the probabilities associated with the trajectories $(A \rightarrow D)$ and $(A \rightarrow H)$. At any rate, given such a relational "tree,"[10] we can eventually assign an event-probability distribution around the possible outcomes associated with A, and then take the expected value of error. For a simple case such as the preceding, this would be computed as:

$$E.V._e = \sum_{P_i C_i}, \quad \forall \, (A - X_i; \; X_i \neq G).*$$

That is, we take the product of the cost associated with each outcome other than G, and the probability of each outcome other than G, and add them to get the expected value of the decision error associated with the neglect of the stochasticity inherent in the problem. This $E.V._e$ is expected cost of implementing an analytically expedient modality, rather than employing the congruent instrument.

Now, where decision analysts have a sufficient experience base on which to draw, they may also be able to calculate some estimate costs of using the expedient as opposed to the congruent instrument. We have already mentioned, for example, that the costs of analysis will increase as we include more relationships to be evaluated (and they increase even more rapidly, as a rule, when we increase the number of state-variables to be included). Now, employing the expedient assumption (probability that $[A \rightarrow G] \rightarrow 1.0$) allows us to eliminate some relationships from our calculus. This implies that we will have fewer components to our model, and fewer calculations in our evaluation exercises. If $\$Y$ is the expected cost of analysis for the inclusion of all probable relationships, and $\$Z$ is the cost of the expedient analysis (using only $A \rightarrow G$), then we would want to look at:

$$E.V._e / \$W$$

where $\$W = (\$Y - \$Z)$. If $E.V._e$ is less than $\$W$, then the criterion of efficiency would dictate that we employ the expedient analytical technique, because the value of the additional information to be obtained from the use of the congruent instrument is less than the incremental cost of employing it.

*The set X would here contain D and H, given Figure 4.16.

We can see, of course, that we can assert certain expectations about the value of the above ratio. Initially, the value of the probability pairs at the stochastic nodes of the relational "tree" tells us something about the concatenative error prospects. For example, where p_1 relative to $(1 - p_1)$ is very high, and p_2 relative to $(1 - p_2)$ is also very high, then we have only mild uncertainty to contend with and the value of $E.V._e$ is expectedly going to be quite low relative to $\$W$.* In short, were we to impose an event probability distribution around the various trajectories, it would be of a favorable morphology—a tall and lean one, with low variance. However, as the primary probabilities (p_i's) begin to fall, the relational distribution would flatten out and inhere greater variance. In this case, the $E.V._e$ factor would tend to become more serious. (In some cases, it may be so high that we are not permitted to use an expedient instrument, for the probable accuracy of our ultimate decision premises would fall below some desired confidence level, which we will discuss in the next chapter.) Although explicit calculations of the cost associated with analytical expediency are sometimes very difficult to make, the going concern (one that has certain types of recurrent decision problems) may find it worthwhile to make some *referent* calculations for the most common decision instances. Were these available, then the analysts might be able to decide *a priori* whether the problem at hand, given some variance estimate, would be economically served by an expedient instrument.

The analysis we just went through also has applications when we are considering selecting from among instruments that all belong to the same category. For example, linear programming exercises are almost always cheaper to conduct than nonlinear optimization exercises. In fact, there are serious limits on the number of state-variables we can accommodate in a nonlinear optimization process, even given a very large and powerful computer. Therefore, the analysts might try to estimate the concatenative error that would be associated with the introduction of artificial assumptions of linearity in the face of an inherently nonlinear problem. Now, both being optimization techniques, the linear and nonlinear instruments would both return a single answer (a point value). Therefore, what we would be interested in here is the expected deviation between the value returned by the expedient instrument (the linear programming technique) and that expected to be returned by a nonlinear optimization instrument, relative to the incremental increase in costs associated with using the nonlinear alternative. Certain procedures are available for determining the effect of assuming linearity, some of the most simple being analytic techniques in their own right (based, as a rule, on some application of Taylor series operations).[11] And we also may generally gain a fairly good idea of the cost of search-based optimization techniques as opposed to an analytic technique like linear programming. As a general rule, both the expected error effect of assuming linearity and the incremental

*See Section 5.4 for a discussion on superimpositional probabilities relative to uncertainty.

cost of nonlinear analysis are related to the size of the restricted (linearized) search space relative to the search space defined by nonlinear constraints, and to the number of constraints. The ultimate effect that we are trying to measure here would be the difference between the system state defined by a set of linear equations, and the system state that would emerge were we to cast the problem in terms of, for example, difference equations. While such an analysis is oftentimes quite complicated, it is fortunately an operation with which many analysts have some experience.

The general point, however, is that there are means available for deciding just how important it is to obey the dictate of congruence in any specific decision situation, and that we also can exercise some discipline in deciding which particular instrument to use *within* some specific category. Obviously, in the illustration just mentioned, the use of a linear instrument to approach a nonlinear problem (within the optimization category) would transgress the principle of reflectivity (e.g., we would be unlikely to be able to "reflect" the real uncertainty or unpredictability of the problem were we to impose linearity as an analytical assumption). By the same token, the decision to employ an optimization instrument in the face of a severely stochastic problem would transgress the principle of exhaustiveness. Yet, as we hope we have shown, these generic principles are always subject to qualification on the basis of the criterion of efficiency, which introduces the economic factors. Therefore, our "vector of congruence" merely suggests how we might reduce expected value of decision error to its effective minimum by ensuring gross compliance with reflectivity and exhaustiveness. But when we introduce efficiency (and sometimes actionability), we find that rationality might sometimes dictate an expedient as opposed to the normative (congruent) analytical approach.

The arguments and conditions we raised with respect to the conjunction between a deterministic problem and optimization instruments also appear in the other contexts. Harking back to our original definition of moderately stochastic problems, we see that they are those where the alternative outcomes (given some contemplated action) are all members of the same qualitative set (e.g., the different levels of demand that might be associated with an advertising program; the several different productivity indexes that might be associated with some new manufacturing modality; the range of different profit rates that might be associated with the introduction of some new product line; the range of different values that might emerge for GNP during the next period). Again, moderately stochastic subjects inhere the capability for surprising us only within very narrow limits. In the world of enterprise—public or private—such problems abound. Indeed, virtually all logistics and normal forecasting exercises fall into this category (and become, in the popular management science jargon, matters of calculable risk). As a result, virtually every organization requires a strong capability (i.e.,

statistical procedures) in the analytical category associated with moderately stochastic problems. The instruments of statistical analysis that are most often used
in the face of moderately stochastic decision problems are those that are grouped
generally under the heading of projective or extrapolative processes. These would
include instruments such as regression and correlation (both linear and nonlinear),
Markov processes, statistical inference procedures, econometric "shock" models,
most Bayesian processes, and the range of numerical approximation techniques.
Indeed, this instrument category is almost as well-populated as the optimization
category. All these techniques differ somewhat in the specific context in which
they become appropriate. For example, Markov processes manipulate state
transformations; Bayesian processes allow us to combine historical with contemporary data and to combine, in certain instances, subjective with objective (empirical) probabilities; regression and correlation techniques allow us to determine
relational strengths. However, all produce a "range" of possible solutions (although the ranges are sometimes dropped in favor of a single likelihood estimator,
existing within an *implicit* confidence interval) in place of the single point
solution produced by their optimization counterparts, or they develop "neighborhood" solutions to effect *sufficiency* where optimality is inappropriate as a
decision objective. And, like the optimization instruments, they generally require numericalized inputs (although, as we suggested, these may sometimes be
surrogates for qualitative attributes).

As we move into the severely stochastic problem domain, we leave the well-
populated, relatively mature instrument categories behind us. For, as we ask
about the instruments congruent with severely stochastic problems—where processes may produce broadly different outcomes in the face of any action we impose or where subjects themselves inhere the capability for very protean behavior—
we must considerably increase our analytical sophistication (and with that, the
costs of analysis and the "floor" error level we will have to tolerate). Particularly,
as soon as we move into the severely stochastic domain, we are in part denied
recourse to the three most important and popular sources of decision information:
experience, observation, and experimentation. Experience may be limited in its
utility because severely stochastic subjects, by definition, inhere the capability
to develop unprecedented states—to emerge in the future in a form that is different from any function of historical properties or states. Here, then, there is the
possibility that our experiences will have been had in a context that is largely
"irrelevant" with respect to the situation at hand. By the same token, because
severely stochastic problems have reasonably distant horizons and may involve
many determinants and complex relationships, there may be a problem getting
access to relevant, timely empirical data via observation. In the first place, we
might not really know what data to collect. In other cases, data may be a problem because we are in a *strategic* relationship with an entity of interest; that is,

it will seek to deny us access (or must be expected to try to react unpredictably to any action we might implement). Finally, all the preceding factors tend to make severely stochastic processes unlikely candidates for experimentation; they will simply not "fit" into a laboratory framework because of their sprawling nature or because of our inability to protect against confounding factors. In other cases, we may face a situation where there is no way to move without a total commitment; that is, limited or sample information will not really answer for the ultimate utility of some strategy (e.g., one does not drop bombs on an enemy to see how many it will take before the enemy will retaliate).

At any rate, as the ability to employ hard data derived from experience, observation, or experiment deserts us, we have to turn more to alternative sources of decision information: disciplined judgment. In short, we begin to make a significant change in the configuration of the models we develop. The criteria of analytical congruence would suggest that the informational bases of the models we develop alter in certain predictable ways, as shown in Figure 4.17.

We can see that deterministic problems permit us to develop models that have

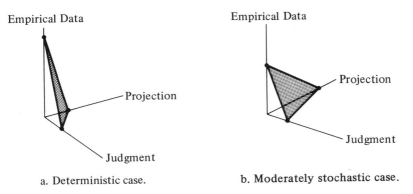

a. Deterministic case.   b. Moderately stochastic case.

c. Severely stochastic case.

Figure 4.17. Informational configurations.

a significantly high reliance on empirical data. Very little judgment is required (or desirable) in the face of such problems. Moreover, we usually employ the data directly, without bothering to put it through projective models (which will serve to expand or generalize a data base, as when we use a statistical sample to make assertions about the behavior of a population as a whole or where we use historical information to project future conditions). But as expected, projective information dominates in the face of moderately stochastic problems, but a significiant empirical data base is required as the input to any projection process. As a rule, the impact of the projective aspect of analysis would be a function of the distance of the horizon toward which we are projecting, the size of sample relative to the population with which we are concerned (e.g., the "degree" to which we are generalizing), or other factors pertinent to statistical data manipulation. Finally, the contribution of hard data sinks very low as we challenge severely stochastic problems, with the brunt of the informational burden now borne by judgment.

But the question for us now concerns the quality of the judgmental information we may apply to a problem. As we suggested earlier, there is a significant difference between casual speculation (perhaps driven by simple exegesis or by the crude imposition of unvalidated assumptions on a problem domain) and scientifically conditioned judgments. As a rule, these latter emerge from a particular type of analytical process, the hypothetico-deductive method. This process is outlined in Figure 4.18.

Very briefly, we here employ certain aprioristic predicates to develop an array of logically probable hypotheses (event-alternatives), with these alternatives then established in an array that distributes them according to their logical (subjective) probability of occurrence. Next, to meet the requirement for actionability, we attempt a consensus as to a most probable alternative, which will then be used to direct the decision-maker toward a specific strategic action. Wherever possible, this selected action-alternative should be implemented in an experimental context, with the results of the limited experiment being fed back to adjust our hypothetical constructs; however, as we already suggested, opportunities for direct experimentation are often very limited in the severely stochastic domain. As the reader might note, the hypothetico-deductive process is very similar to the inductive process that we think of as the *normal* scientific method. The fundamental differences are that, here, the hypotheses (or state alternatives) are not elicited from facts but from *a priori* predicates, and that we substitute subjective probabilities for the objective probabilities demanded by inductive (or empirical) exercises.

As for the instruments available to us in the hypothetico-deductive category, those that enable us to perform disciplined *contingency* analyses are most important. Generally, these contingency programming instruments would allow us to

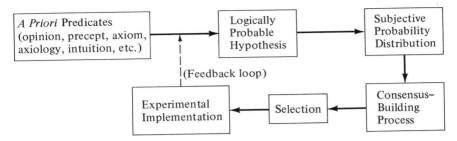

Figure 4.18. The hypothetico-deductive process.

identify the several qualitatively unique states a severely stochastic system might enact, and to evaluate the various strategic options (action-alternatives) available to us should any one of these state alternatives appear as the actual condition. Dynamic and adoptive programming techniques are useful in this respect, and are being employed with increasing (if still limited) frequency.[12] The "war game" simulations (stochastic-state simulations) that have become popular in military contexts are now available for translation into either business or public administration contexts. Network formulations (many based on topological or modern algebraic formulations of great sophistication) are basically elaborations of the simple relational "tree" exercise we went through earlier, but can generate and manipulate large numbers of relational alternatives (trajectories). To provide the input into these instruments, we can use variations on the Delphi theme to structure opinion or subjective predicates, and use certain statistical techniques to engineer a consensus."[13] To increase the precision with which we define and manipulate qualitative information, we may turn to such logics as Boolean algebra and predicate calculus and to the emergent discipline of "fuzzy set" theory.[14] The logics permit us to be sure we have exhausted the full range of relational alternatives available to us, whereas operations on "fuzzy" data allow us to generate important and sometimes quite strict relationships between quantitative and qualitative operators and attributes.

As a set, these instruments allow us to allegorize very complex processes, systems, or subjects, and to gain some structured comprehension of what they will do, either on their own or in response to some action (or stimulus) we introduce. Clearly, these instruments are difficult and expensive to operate, and a great premium must be placed on the sensitivity and imagination of the analysts. Yet, as our congruence construct indicated, the attempt to employ projective or extrapolative instruments here would most likely lead to analytical *ineffectiveness*, because the future of a severely stochastic system will generally not be any calculable function of its past, and is therefore beyond projection. Again, where economic or time constraints are very severe—or where one from among all qualitative state alternatives seems primarily probable as being the actual event—we may sometimes find it to our advantage to assume that a single state will emerge and avoid the demanding hypothetico-deductive processes. But we should never forget that the unwarranted treatment of severely stochastic problems as moderately stochastic has been perhaps the key cause of our most dramatic administrative failures. As we suggested earlier, the proper use of hypothetico-deductive instruments for strategic decision-making is perhaps the single most important step in extending the bounds of administrative rationality. Particularly, they allow an organization operating in a complex environment to become something more than the passive victim of circumstances, and may permit it to shift away from the generally suboptimal reactive management postures that have dominated for so long.

The last of the instrumental categories is of course the least well-developed, most sparsely populated, and most analytically demanding—and therefore the least frequently exercised. But the demand for skills in normative analysis—the means by which we seek to *create* a favorable future—is increasing. For one thing, modern technology has given us some leisure to think about events of the far future, freeing us from constant attention to basic material needs. Other events have made this imperative: acceleration in the reduction of available natural resources; increased moral (and practical) concern over developmental imbalances among nations and regions; availability of apocalyptical weapons of war; increased interdependency of events and peoples through the offices of modern communication and transportation technology; the realization that even highly localized actions (decisions) can have increasingly far-reaching and important ramifications due to this greater interconnectedness; increased interests in matters of ethics and morality in the face of the Watergate scandal and other breaches of integrity by officials in both public and private enterprise; demand that businesses begin to internalize certain social costs that could once remain unconsidered, most especially ecological impacts; increasing recognition that the economic, social, and behavioral dimensions of any societal system are intimately and inextricably intertwined, so that the traditional partitioning of political and governmental functions (and decision authorities) becomes increasingly unpalatable.

Various scholars have tried to meet this demand for a highest form of analytical sophistication, and for the development of instruments that can encompass enormous amounts of time and legions of determinants all acting in concert. As is to be expected, these scholars have had to do largely without the benefit of mathematical tools because of the complexity of their subjects. The normal (projective) forecasting techniques are also perforce denied them, except in very rare instances. So they have had to create a fundamentally new discipline, which might be called *metahypothetical* analysis. This is basically an amplification of the hypothetico-deductive method just outlined. Rather than using deduced hypotheses, however, the metahypothetical analyst may have to content himself with *scenarios* of very broad implication. These scenarios will be composites of many different hypotheses, all interconnected—hence the use of the phrase "metahypothetical"—with these interconnections taking place at a still higher level of abstraction. Rather than having any neat analytical strategies or algorithms at their disposal, the decision analysts working at this level will probably have to be content with broad *heuristics*—largely artificial procedural trajectories that seek to provide us with some initial, tentative constraints on the search space within which desired societal or organizational "states" are expected to be found. They may also provide procedural constraints on our attempts to travel from a less favorable current system state to a more favorable future state.[15] And, because the future is where contemporary constraints disappear, the work of most metahypothetical analysts takes on distinctly *normative* implications; it is, in short, strongly conditioned by matters of "ought" and "should." Those employing heuristic and normative techniques, and who are concerned with the far future and the wide environment, often call themselves "futurologists." It is among these that we must look for practical guidance in dealing with indeterminate problems.* Fortunately, there are an increasing number of futurologists at work, and their technological innovations are becoming increasingly accessible to those who would employ them in the service of some specific, real-world organization.[16] Because the complex organization is likely to have to face problems from all four generic problem categories, its decision functionaries should be able to employ instruments from all four categories (either individually or in concert). In short, a familiarity with optimization, projection, contingency planning, and heuristic (normative) analysis constitutes *the minimal intellectual preparation for the modern scientific administrator*. Analytical congruence thus becomes not only the key to decision rationality, but also the crucial component in any accountability system that can operate across all the decision domains of a complex organization.

Moreover, we should now have a fairly clear idea of the relations among the major focuses of our discussions: problem categories, decision functions, instrumental categories, and analytical techniques. To make idealized associations somewhat clearer, we have developed a typology of *static* associations, as shown in Table 4.3.

The specific implication of the above construct is that the specific analytical skills dictated for the several problem categories should be exercisable by the decision functionaries responsible for solving problems at the level indicated. That is, we expect the goal-setters of an organization to have some facility in norma-

*The intellectual and operational basis for work with metahypothetical instruments seems, however, to be tied most intimately to the field of *general system theory*.

Table 4.3. General decision typology.

Decision Function	Associated Problem Category	Associated Instrument Category	Selected Instruments	Functional Implications
Goal-Setting	Indeterminate	Metahypothetical	(a) Heuristics (b) Scenario-building (c) Normative system architecture	Extremely long-range planning, mission analysis, general system analysis, etc.
Strategic Planning	Severely stochastic	Contingency programming	(a) Game analysis (b) Stochastic state simulation (c) Dynamic programming	Competitive operations; new product (or service) innovations; midrange forecasting, market analysis, functional (benefit) scheduling and allocations
Tactical Planning	Moderately stochastic	Projective analysis	(a) Markov processes (b) Regression-correlation (c) Bayesian analysis	Short- and intermediate-term forecasting and logistical analysis, demand analysis; production scheduling, budget projection, etc.
Operations Programming	Deterministic	Optimization	(a) Industrial engineering instruments (b) Linear programming (c) Finite-state system analysis procedures	Plant layout, production engineering, transportation and routing problems, inventory control, manufacturing design, etc.

tive and heuristic analysis; we want strategic decision-makers and analysts (e.g., executives and their staff) to have a strong capability in qualitative analysis, and to be prepared to employ the instruments associated with contingency programming, etc. But, as suggested, this is a static construct.

4.5 DYNAMICS OF THE DECISION-ANALYSIS PROCESS

The dynamic aspects of the decision-analysis process become apparent when we return to the concept of administrative decision making as a problem-solving process, and to model-building as a requisite component in this process. In this context, analytical resources are expended in an effort to take an initially intractable, ill-comprehended problem (with an extremely high probability of decision error), and transform it into a more tractable, more predictable entity. That is, while the functional implications of the above typology tend to hold for certain recurrent types of problems (e.g., extremely long-range planning tends to remain an *inherently* indeterminate exercise), there is also a large population of problems that represents special, one-shot demands for decision-making. With respect to these, consider Figure 4.19. The process begins at the point where some decision problem emerges. This problem may, of course, reflect the properties of any of the problem categories. But for our purposes, let us suggest that it is effectively indeterminate (that is, we have very little comprehension of its structure or behavioral potential). As our criterion of analytical congruence suggests, this problem should be attacked at this point by using instruments from the metatheoretical category, e.g., heuristic analysis. Now, when we consider the decision-analysis *process per se* we can see that the heuristic analysis exercises are really concerned with initially defining the feasible solution (or search) space for the problem at hand. This will most often imply the specification of the state-variables expected to be determinants of the problem. Thus, heuristic analysis supports the goal-setting decision function, which also was interested in tentatively partitioning some universe of destinational possibilities for an organization, thereby reducing the feasible solution space.

   Now, to the extent that the heuristic analysts have properly performed their function—and to the extent that the problem at hand is not an *inherently* indeterminate one—we may proceed to the operations at the relational level. The heuristic analysts must be expected to at least deliver the state-variable array, which, as we have often explained, reduces the search space over which strategic analysts must wander. And, given the state-variable array, the strategic analysts may now exercise their contingency analysis instruments to develop the several qualitatively unique "states" the problem might effect over some interval. These "states" are of course, developed by prescribing the various relations among the state variables. Given these, the problem has now been reduced to a severely sto-

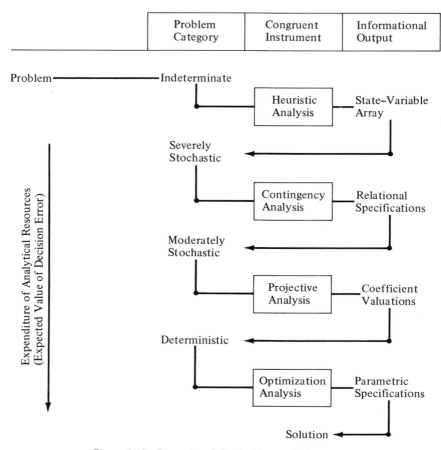

Figure 4.19. Dynamics of the decision-analysis process.

chastic one, with a reduced array of logically probable outcomes (events) being defined where initially there was no dynamic constraint at all. The contingency-analysis instruments may also be exercised to equip each of the state-alternatives with a probability of occurrence, with this index generally being a product of subjective rather than objective (empirical) probabilities.

As a general rule, the strategic (contingency) analysts must make some assertion at this point about the *most likely* of the state alternatives. That is, they will tend to treat one or another of the qualitative alternatives as the *null hypothesis—* that event which is, indeed, most likely (given the logical probability distribution surrounding the alternatives).* When they do this, the severely stochastic problem has now been transformed into a moderately stochastic one, with one strategic outcome being assigned a significant probability of occurrence. If the strategic analysts cannot make a decision about a most likely system state, then the problem at hand may very well be *inherently* severely stochastic, and incapable of being reduced or disciplined any further. If this is the case, then the strategic decision-makers must be prepared to develop contingency actions associated with each of the probable alternative states, and try to set up signals that can forewarn them as to which of the several alternatives is currently most likely to represent the true state of the problem. That is, the analysis process is, to all effects, completed at this point. Those responsible for dictating action must now take over. However, as mentioned earlier, it is desirable to try to delay commitments of resources and actions until as much *a posteriori* information as possible has been collected.

Assuming, however, that the strategic analysts were able to isolate a single qualitative state as significantly probable, then the tactical analysts can try to estimate the magnitudes of interaction associated with the relational trajectory passed down to them. As a general rule, estimation of magnitudes of relationship is best performed using projective (statistical) instruments, although, for deterministic entities, we may use analytic techniques or attempt to measure them directly through trial-and-error experimentation, skipping the moderately stochastic phase altogether. At any rate, once the relations between the problem determinants have been assigned specific coefficients, the problem has been reduced to a moderately stochastic one. In the process, a much reduced expected probability of error is associated with any decision we might make at this point (as contrasted with the condition that would have prevailed had we had to make a decision at some earlier stage of the decision-analysis process).

It is, of course, possible for the strategic analysts to ask the tactical analysts to evaluate coefficients associated with several different qualitative (relational) trajectories. This is an important option, for sometimes (as we have seen) assigning magnitudes to the relational alternatives does have an impact on the relational level, perhaps making certain relational trajectories more probable than others. In such a case, the emerging model for the problem at hand would involve several different relational "modules," each with its own coefficient specifications. This would be the case had we, for example, chosen to evaluate and develop all of the trajectory alternatives in the little relational "tree" model we earlier introduced.

---

*Note, however, that this "null hypothesis" will be a tentative construct, and subsequently exposed to empirical validation exercises. But the single, tentative "system state" is required to meet the criterion of actionability in a decision problem. For more on this, see Section 5.4.

This procedure is recommended whenever there is no singularly significant state-alternative, and where we have the resources or time to engage in a *learning* process. The tactical analysts would merely set up certain indicators to be evaluated periodically. These indicators would be used to determine which of the several relational trajectories is currently most probable. Again, we have the option, when constraints permit, to try to develop an *a posteriori* information base to complement the *a priori* decision-analysis exercises. In the development of this empirical data base, we would expect that the quality of the model would be improved, and the expected value of decision error correspondingly reduced. We will elaborate upon this point in the next chapter.

The other responsibility that might devolve on our projective instruments is, of course, the assignment of point-in-time values to the state-variables—the parametric specifications. And when we have completed our coefficient and parametric levels of analysis, we are in a position to decide whether or not the problem is an inherently deterministic one. If, for each of the relational magnitudes and each of the parametric values, there is a single point estimate that appears to dominate, then we have a deterministic situation. However, where there is significant doubt about the appropriateness of any single value, so that we have to remain at the moderately stochastic level and equip the doubtful coefficient and parametric entries with a *range* function. This means that we are perforce denied access to optimization techniques, and must rest content with an *approximately* optimal solution—with the "statistical" rather than "mathematical" optimum. At any rate, our model of the decision problem is now complete, and may be used to generate the evaluation of the various action-alternatives and to select among them. In short, the decision problem has been solved.

Although we will amplify this discussion considerably in the coming chapter, we can here suggest some of its operational implications. Initially, the task of identifying and specifying a problem to be solved—and the terms of its solution—is roughly the equivalent of the goal-setting process we described earlier. The point of association is this: every decision problem is equipped with an *objective function*. This objective function not only sets out the state-variables (or determinants) of the problem, but also sets a *goal* for the analysts, e.g., to maximize or minimize the function. At this point, the analysts will usually set about constructing the *structural equations* associated with virtually every real-world decision process. For example, suppose that we were told by the goal-setters to maximize the productivity in some manufacturing process. The process variables now become state-variables, and the goal is explicit maximization. The structural equations will now be developed to express (allegorize) the nature of the process. Simply, we establish the incidence and direction of influence among the process components. Here we also note some of the basic characteristics of the process to be maximized; e.g., is it linear or nonlinear? is it finite-state or stochastic state? is it stationary or perturbable?

The next step in a real-world decision-analysis exercise is generally to introduce *constraints*. The structural equations merely allegorize the process. The constraints will tell us within what limits we must operate, and what practical limits there are on our process (e.g., what production ranges are feasible given expected demand; what the total budget resources are for purchasing equipment or labor; what spatial (layout) restraints may exist). The development of the constraint functions usually involves equipping the structural equations with coefficient and parametric values, with the constraints being interpreted as the "limits" associated with these values. In short, they take the generalized process model generated by the structural equations and lend it a point-in-time significance, thereby entering the actual (or imputed) realities of the situation at hand. In the process, these constraint functions thus further restrict (and hopefully close) the feasible search space for the enactment of the objective function. The nature of the structural equations and constraint function then serve to determine the nature of the *solution algorithm* we may employ. For example, if the structural equations are all linear—and if all parametric and coefficient values are point estimates—the appropriate solution algorithm would probably be a linear programming instrument of some sort. On the other hand, if the structural equations were nonlinear, indicating that the manufacturing process is nonadditive, then we would have to use a nonlinear programming algorithm to find the optimum. Or, where the constraint functions are assigned "range" estimates for coefficient and parametric entries—reflecting their inherent stochasticity—then we would probably have to turn to a probabilistic (approximative) solution algorithm, perhaps to a simulation instrument. At any rate, the components of the decision-analysis exercise and the various levels of analysis are usually related as follows:

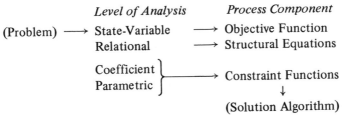

As a final note to this chapter, we must add that the dynamic aspects of the decision-analysis process impose one final criterion for analytical congruence: the decision analyst must be very careful about when he shifts from one instrumental category to another; about when, for example, he abandons his heuristic instruments for contingency programming techniques, or about when he moves from the severely stochastic to the moderately stochastic domain. The timing and appropriateness of these modality shifts will affect the aggregate effectiveness and efficiency of any decision-analysis exercise in which we engage. But there are many aspects of the decision-analysis process that we have left hanging in this chapter. We will attend to these in Chapter 5.

4.6 NOTES AND REFERENCES

1. We will have more to say about impact programming in the course of this chapter. As for the implications of capital budgeting, this is a very widely known and well-practiced instrument. A generalized discussion of the procedures is given by Newman and Logan in Chapter 13 of their *Strategy, Policy and Central Management* (Cincinnati, Ohio: South-Western Publishing Company, 1971).

2. The fundamental principles of program budgeting are elicited from the generally fine essays in Lyden and Miller's *Planning Programming Budgeting* (Chicago: Markham, 1972). As explained later in our text, zero-base budgeting is a simple evolution of program budgeting, which itself may be said to have evolved neatly and directly from capital budgeting.

3. That is, they should be required to show some definite range over which their productivity projections operate, and perhaps to show the points of increasing, proportional, and diminishing marginal returns to scale, etc. This would give us a mathematical check on the quality of their projections, even if it would not, of itself, allow us to answer for their substantive relevance.

4. That is, perhaps from a somewhat distorted concept of what is "scientific," most management science authorities generally eliminate the problems of normative analysis from their texts. We suspect that part of the problem is that the normative aspects of decision-making are also the most difficult areas to discuss and discipline, and are much less safe ground to walk than matters of technique. At any rate, the obsession of many operations researchers and management scientists with tools is under attack from many quarters, some of them quite august indeed. In this respect, see the challenging remarks by Ida R. Hoos reprinted in the IEEE *Systems, Man and Cybernetics* newsletter 5 no. 5 (October 1976).

5. In short, the R here would have the same purpose as the *measures of dispersion* used in normal statistical estimation (or correlation) exercises.

6. For more on the matter of levels of analysis in actual problem-solving processes, see Chapter 6 of John W. Sutherland, *Systems: Analysis, Administration, and Architecture* (New York: Van Nostrand Reinhold Company, 1975).

7. For a fine introduction to the elementary uses of Bayesian analysis, see Robert Schlaifer's *Analysis of Decisions under Uncertainty* (New York: McGraw-Hill, 1969). For a mathematical based discussion, see Chien and

Fu's "On Bayesian Learning and Stochastic Approximation," *IEEE Transactions on System Science and Cybernetics* **SSC-3** no. 1 (June 1967).

8. For a more detailed defense of the construct, see Sutherland *Systems*, Chapter 5.

9. A good introductory treatment of this instrument is given by N. K. Kwak in *Mathematical Programming with Business Applications* (New York: McGraw-Hill, 1973).

10. Relational analysis may be as simple as the development of decision trees, or as complex as the applications of graph and network theory that derive from concepts of topology and modern algebra. For an interesting discussion of network concepts, see T. C. Hu, *Integer Programming and Network Flows* (Reading, Massachusetts: Addison-Wesley Publishing Co., Inc., 1969). For an introduction to some theoretical implications of modern graph theory, see Claude Berge's *The Theory of Graphs* (New York: John Wiley & Sons, Inc., 1962).

11. See Chapters 1 and 2 of Arden and Astill's *Numerical Algorithms* (Reading, Massachusetts: Addison-Wesley Publishing Co., Inc., 1970).

12. An excellent introduction to the concept of Bayesian-driven dynamic programming processes is given by Martin J. Beckmann in his *Dynamic Programming of Economic Decisions* (New York: Springer-Verlag, 1968).

13. See John W. Sutherland, "Attacking Indeterminacy: The Case for the Hypothetico-Deductive Method and Consensus Statistics," *Technological Forecasting and Social Change* **6** (1974).

14. For a quick but interesting look at the role of formal logics, see Sanford S. Ackerman's "Symbolic Logic: A Summary of the Subject and Its Applications to Industrial Engineering," *Journal of Industrial Engineering* (September-October 1957). What has come to be known as "fuzzy set theory" is discussed by L. A. Zadeh in "Outline of a New Approach to the Analysis of Complex Systems and Decision Processes," IEEE *Transactions on Systems, Man and Cybernetics* **SMC-3** no. 1 (January 1973).

15. For a brief discussion of heuristic analysis, see Sutherland, *Systems*, Section 5.5.1.

16. Much "futurology" is built up from the Delphi process. Some good articles on the subject are given in Linston and Turoff, eds., *Delphi Method: Techniques and Applications* (Reading, Massachusetts: Addison-Wesley Publishing Co., Inc., 1975).

5

Managing
the Decision
Function

5.0 INTRODUCTION

In this final chapter of our inquiry into administrative decision-making, we will shift our focus to the setting in which decision functions are resident—the complex organization. This will not be any radical shift of perspective, but it will allow us to make some assertions about the practicality—the operational feasibility—of the kinds of decision procedures and propositions we have been promoting.

Quite honestly, I do not believe that we are ready to usher in an age of rationality. There is too much work to be done, particularly in translating concepts and normative precepts into working programs that can be put directly to use by real-world organizations. Yet, despite the immaturity of our field, there are still many benefits to be gained were only some small portion of the recommended procedures put to work, and were decision-makers merely willing to give some passing attention to optimality as a feasible criterion.

We will be concentrating on these interim advantages in the coming pages. The central lesson is this: the operationalization of rational decision procedures cannot be engineered simply by technical or instrumental (analytical) innovations. Rather, there is a fundamental requirement for rethinking basic managerial strategy, and for the role that science can actually—and immediately—play in the conduct of complex enterprise.

5.1 THE DECISION SYSTEM

As we move toward the conclusion of our inquiry into decision-making, we should consider the way in which the decision-making function fits into the normal organizational structure. As has been our premise throughout this volume, it is useful to distinguish between the intellectual and the coordinative or people-

236

oriented tasks of enterprise. As we have seen, the various decision-making functions act to determine the "intelligent" behavior of the organization, passing on dictates to the coordinative functions (whose forte is "getting things done through people"). The advancing of propositions about how to organize and control and motivate people is the proper domain of the human relations school of management. Decision science—as the broader envelope within which management science and operations research reside—is concerned with the organization and control of information and ideas. But, as suggested, some organizations may make no distinction between individuals charged with decision-making and those with coordinative (implementation) functions. In other cases, decision-making exercises may be conducted by individuals who have effectively no coordinative responsibilities as such, or even by select committees whose sole function is decision-making. In still other cases, the decision-making function itself will be broken down into two parts: the decision-analysis function, performed presumably by technical or specialized staff, with decision-makers usually serving only to select among action-alternatives provided by the analysts. In either case, it is possible to describe and relate the components of a typical decision system, as in Figure 5.1. As a general rule, the cause of decision efficiency within the decision system is best served by assigning specific decisions to those individuals who require the *least additional information*.[1] But there are some other general propositions we can advance within the framework of this model:

(1) Decision information (cast in the form of decision premises) is always a product of some elements from a data base being operated on by some instruments from the model base. That is, the data base contains "raw" data, which only becomes information *per se*, after it has been manipulated by an analytical instrument.

(2) The model base should contain instruments appropriate to all the different generic categories of problems to be faced by the organization. For the complex organization, the model base would have to contain representatives from all four instrumental categories:

   (a) heuristic instruments (perhaps including the programs to produce Delphi-based judgmental constructs or the basic logical instruments available for guiding normative analysis or initial state-variable definition).

   (b) contingency programming instruments, including game-theoretic and stochastic-state simulation constructs, etc.

   (c) the instruments to support projective or extrapolative analysis, including standard forecasting and time-series analysis tools, statistical inference models, analysis of variance techniques, Markov-based algorithms, etc.

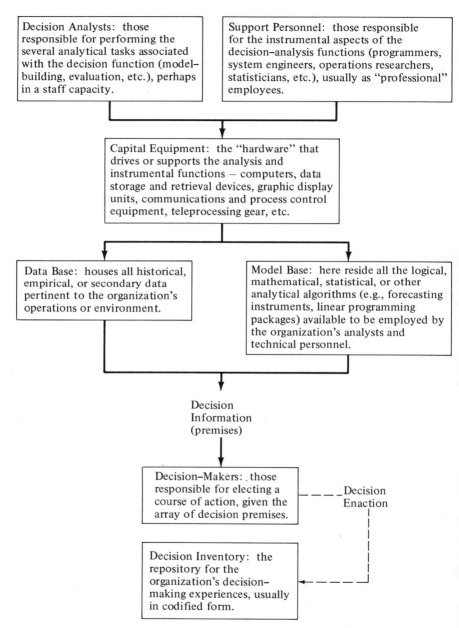

Decision Analysts: those responsible for performing the several analytical tasks associated with the decision function (model-building, evaluation, etc.), perhaps in a staff capacity.

Support Personnel: those responsible for the instrumental aspects of the decision-analysis functions (programmers, system engineers, operations researchers, statisticians, etc.), usually as "professional" employees.

Capital Equipment: the "hardware" that drives or supports the analysis and instrumental functions — computers, data storage and retrieval devices, graphic display units, communications and process control equipment, teleprocessing gear, etc.

Data Base: houses all historical, empirical, or secondary data pertinent to the organization's operations or environment.

Model Base: here reside all the logical, mathematical, statistical, or other analytical algorithms (e.g., forecasting instruments, linear programming packages) available to be employed by the organization's analysts and technical personnel.

Decision Information (premises)

Decision-Makers: those responsible for electing a course of action, given the array of decision premises.

Decision Enaction

Decision Inventory: the repository for the organization's decision-making experiences, usually in codified form.

Figure 5.1. Components and relations in a decision system.

(d) instruments of normal optimization analysis, including industrial engineering models, linear programming packages, etc.

(3) The structure of the model base—the way the various analytical instruments are partitioned—should reflect the nature of the problems to be solved, not the structure of the organization *per se*. That is, assigning specific models to specific operational divisions or departments (on geographic or functional lines) should be avoided, so that redundancy can be minimized. The components of the model base should thus be as general as possible, with specific operating units developing models appropriate to their own needs by selecting (eclectically) from among the generic instruments. That is, specific divisions or departments should be discouraged from developing parochialized models.

(4) To the extent possible, models should be kept data-independent. This serves the cause of their generality of utilization, and also reflects the fact that we would tend to update the components of a data base more frequently than we would alter the basic analytical or processual instruments of the model base. For the most part, data-independence requires that we use the data base as the source of supply for coefficient and parametric specifications, with the different models being fixed with respect to the type of state variables than can be accommodated (or the number of factors that can be operated on) and the nature of the permissible relations —e.g., linear programming algorithms generally set a fixed limit on the number of independent variables and specify linearity. At any rate, to the extent that the components of the model base are not data-dependent, we increase the generality of the instruments and act to reduce analytical redundancy. Thus, this prescription complements the above, for when models are both nonparochial and data-independent, we have injected maximum *parsimony* into our model base (permitting the smallest number of instruments to serve the largest user population).

(5) Finally, every complex organization should maintain a *decision inventory*. This, as suggested in the diagram, is where we reposit the results of all previous decision exercises. The essential purpose of the inventory is to provide direct (analogic) solutions to recurrent or precedented decision problems, so that our analysts need not constantly "reinvent the wheel."

Now, as we have so often suggested, categorically different decision problems tend to emerge at different levels of the organization. Therefore, the decision system will assume a fundamentally different "character" as it is called upon to operate at these different levels. Particularly, the personnel requirements alter. For example, those analysts skilled in qualitative analysis or in the simulative techniques may be called upon most frequently in the face of severely stochastic problems that emerge at the executive level; the support personnel, with very little input from the decision analysts, may handle the majority of deterministic problems with which the organization must contend.

Obviously, the type of instruments called into play will also respond to the level of organization at which the decision system is exercised. For example, the instruments in the optimization category will be called upon most frequently at the lower levels of organization, whereas contingency programming instruments might be used almost exclusively by those analysts serving as staff to executives, etc. Thus, we may expect significant changes to occur as the decision system is called upon to serve the different levels of organization, as summarized in Figure 5.2. With this construct, the decision system becomes intelligible as what is more commonly referred to as a *management information system* (which is really the decision system minus the decision function *per se*). Thus, we may continue with the development of our array of propositions, but those that follow here concern only the information aspects of the decision system:

(6) As we move from higher to lower levels within any complex organization:

    (a) There is less reliance on components of the data base, and more reliance on the manipulative instruments of the model base. In terms of a concept employed earlier, the "degree of projection" increases, indicating the reduction in the relevance of empirical or historical data to higher-level decision problems.

    (b) There is increased frequency of access to the system, reflecting the fact that lower-level decisions tend to occur with greater frequency than do higher-order decisions.

    (c) The interval over which the system is allowed to respond to a request for decision information (the time allowed it to produce a set of decision premises) generally decreases, indicating the ten-

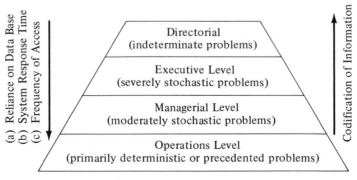

Figure 5.2. Organization-dependent characteristics of the decision system.

dency for lower-order decisions to *mature* more quickly than higher-order decisions (e.g., the time between the recognition of the requirement for a decision and the point at which it must be enacted is generally shortest for operational decisions).

(7) As we move from lower to higher levels within the complex organization:

(a) Access to components of the decision system becomes successively less restricted, reflecting the increased decision latitude associated with higher-order decisions, and also the greater sensitivity (e.g., proprietary value) of strategic data and models. That is, degree of access tends to increase as the level of decision responsibility increases.

(b) There is increasing codification of information, reflecting the greater reliance on breadth of perspective—and the decreasing interest in detail—as we move from the operational to the directorial level. That is, information made available to higher-level decision-makers tends to become successively more "abstract."

Given this set of general propositions, we may now recast some of the arguments we earlier raised about the type of information that tends to be associated with the various problem categories (and therefore with the different decision domains). Here we are interested in the extent to which the decision premises for problem categories may be said to be a product of one or another of the components of the decision system itself. Particularly, any information base (set of decision premises) will owe something of its substance to any or all of three separate sources: (a) the data base provides the fundamental input on which the components of the model base will operate; (b) the models tend to recast, project, or otherwise manipulate these raw data, producing an output that is something "more" than the raw data—it is the contribution of the model base; and (c) the decision-makers or decision analysts may always interject (or impose) *a priori* or judgmental inputs, which may either amplify or in part determine the substance of the decision premises. Thus, as a restatement of a construct we used earlier, we can set out two polar situations, as in Figure 5.3. Drawing on our familiarity with such constructs from earlier pages, we may add the following propositions to the array we have begun:

(8) As the problem at hand begins to depart from the criteria established for determinacy, reliance on the contributions of the data base declines. This is because strategic and goal-oriented issues are likely to be unprecedented, and have ramifications too broad to be completely exhausted by observations or experimentation, etc. Lower-level decisions, on the other hand, are likely to be either recurrent (precedented) or sufficiently narrow in ramification and short in horizon to permit observation and experimentation, and to therefore induce greater reliance on hard data.

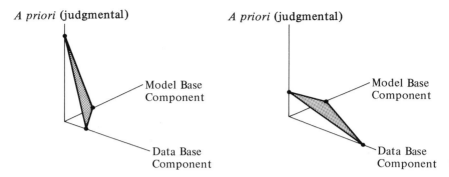

A priori (judgmental)   *A priori* (judgmental)

Model Base
Component

Model Base
Component

Data Base
Component

Data Base
Component

a. Higher–order (e.g., strategic) problem.   b. Low–order (e.g., operational) problem.

Figure 5.3. Origins of decision premises.

(9) The contribution of the model base is expected to be highest in the range of stochastic problems . . . strategic and tactical. The difference is that the relative strength of the data-base component is stronger in the face of moderately stochastic (tactical) problems, than for strategic issues. In the face of the latter, more of the substance of any decision premises we develop will owe its origin to the manipulative or projective aspects of the models themselves, with the data component being much diluted or "disguised." This is because we tend to use deductive models at the severely stochastic level of analysis, and deductive models generally tend to alter the input data much more significantly than do the inductive instruments we tend to employ in the face of moderately stochastic problems.

(10) The information configuration for very complex, far-ranging problems will tend to have a significant contribution of *a priori* assumptions and constraints, which are instances of judgmental influence. This reflects the normative content of goal-setting operations and may also reflect the necessity to impose certain logical, theoretical, or axiomatic restraints to close the search space for some types of strategic problems (e.g., those where the number of different qualitative states that might emerge is so great as to be unmanageable without some sort of artificial closure).

Returning to an assertion we made and tried to defend much earlier,

(11) As the judgmental contribution begins to dominate any set of decision premises (any information base), the expected accuracy of these decision premises declines. Therefore, the expected value of decision error we must be prepared to tolerate is expected to increase as does the complexity of the problem at hand, which in turn is expected to increase with the level of organization at which the decision-maker operates.

When we turn to consideration of the *decision inventory* present in the decision system, we get another critical proposition:

(12) The cost of servicing and maintaining the decision-making and decision-analysis functions within any organization will depend upon the relative frequency of legitimate access to the decision inventory.

This proposition requires some elaboration, as it refers to issues we have not yet approached.

We may begin this elaboration with a quick look at the procedural aspects of the decision system as we represented it. The procedures in which we are particularly interested are diagrammed in Figure 5.4. Very briefly, when an organization has a decision inventory available to it, any decision problem that emerges is subjected initially to some sort of abstraction process. This usually involves stripping away the contextual properties of the problem, and trying to isolate its *generic* properties (e.g., is it basically an allocation problem? a trade-off problem? is it deterministic or stochastic? linear or nonlinear?). When the problem has

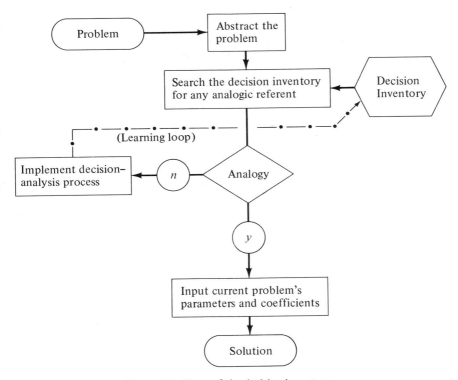

Figure 5.4. Usage of the decision inventory.

been reduced to generalized properties, we may begin to search the decision inventory. What we will be looking for is a decision problem we have already dealt with that might be sufficiently close in nature to the current problem.

In short, the decision inventory allows us to try to capitalize on our experience. The problems entered in the cumulative decision inventory would also have been stored in generic terms, codified in order to facilitate a match. Moreover, each generic decision problem would be associated with the results of previous solution attempts. Thus, we would have a record of the problem model(s) developed, the type of solution posed, and testimony regarding the accuracy of the model and the efficacy of the solution. For example, suppose we are a tactical decision-making unit with responsibility for predicting and securing a sufficient labor force to support next-period production levels. This is the type of *recurrent* problem for which we should have an entry in the decision inventory. Presumably, historical decision-makers, faced with the same type of work-force projection problem, would have developed a model that would have incorporated the relevant state-variables (e.g., the various production centers, the workflow stages), considered and coded the nature of the relationships (what process leads to what output in what order, etc.) and probably would have developed a set of relevant coefficients relating output levels for the various processing stages with work-force requirements. That is, we would have a generic production function for each processing center suggesting that changes in rate of output are associated with incremental changes in the local work force.

Now, when we are given the required output levels for each of the processing stages (or centers), we may apply these already existing production coefficients to yield the personnel requirements, assuming that the fundamental state-variable, relational, and coefficient specifications remain essentially unchanged. This would require, for example, that the configuration of production equipment remain essentially the same between the historical and current context (e.g., we have not introduced new machinery or processing procedures), and that the network of productive relations among the various processing centers remains essentially unchanged. To the extent that this is true, we may then employ the previously developed model and solution algorithm in an *analogic* framework, and pursue a solution directly.[2] All that we would do would be to supply the current output requirements (as parameters), and let the historical-generic model yield the answer we require. In such a case, we would not have to exercise any of the decision-analysis tasks except the lowest-order one: supplying parametric values to a model that is already structurally and dynamically deemed appropriate as a source for a direct analogic solution.

The decision as to whether to employ a direct analogic solution would generally involve an evaluation of the cost of creating an entirely new model and solution algorithm relative to the possible cost of error associated with employing an analogic solution. As a rule, the expected value of any analogic solution involves an evaluation of the variance between the current and historical decision contexts, and an evaluation of the extent to which the generic or analogic model has been in error. With respect to our illustration, we would ask to take a look at the historical accuracy of the work-force estimate yielded by the generic model, and the extent to which the previous generations of users might have refined the model, as well as at the increases in accuracy that might accompany any structural or instrumental changes we might make. As a general rule, the advisability of developing an original solution, and architecting a context-specific model, will increase either as contextual variance increases, or with the historical error characteristics of the generic model. Contextual variance generally implies that we will have to make adjustments in the generic model, for the analogy between historical and current situations is incomplete. For example, we might have to revise coefficients in order to use the existing model for current purposes, or we might even have to introduce some fundamentally new relationships (e.g., modify the direction of influence among the state-variables). In some cases, we may even introduce new state-variable arrays, and leave the relations and coefficients unchanged. All sorts of possibilities exist, but we can see that the efficiency and economy associated with the employment of analogic solutions decreases as the strength of the analogy decreases. Beyond some point, then, the expected error associated with the use of an analogic model—or the expected costs of reworking it—become unfavorable with respect to the decision-analysis alternative of creating an entirely new model and solution. At this point, the decision inventory ceases to be of immediate benefit.

But it still may have potential benefit. The original model and solution that we develop (to a current problem lacking an historical analogy) will be entered into the decision inventory, for possible future reference should this or a kindred problem ever recur. Thus, we set up the "learning loop" in Figure 5.4, and thus we can suggest that *precedented problems tend to become deterministic* with cumulative experience. The analogic solution is thus the same expedient, direct process as is the development of an analytic solution to an effectively deterministic problem; we simply supply the parametric values, and let the analytic model itself grind out the answer we require. Through time, even quite complicated, wide-ranging problems may gradually be reduced to more tractable ones, as succeeding generations of decision analysts chip away more and more obscurity and unpredictability. Thus, as we will later show, the decision inventory is one of the prime vehicles available to us for reducing (secularly), in the long run, expected costs of decision error, and for injecting *mechanisticity*—and hence efficiency—into the decision-making function.

Now, getting back to the proposition we advanced about costs of decision-making being related to the frequency of legitimate access to the decision inventory, we can see its rationale immediately. Analogic solutions allow us to avoid the decision-analysis process altogether (or at least in part, depending on the strength of the analogy between a historical and a current problem), and therefore allow us to move most directly from the emergence of a decision problem to its solution. The key qualifier here, of course, is "legitimate" access. Most of us—and especially rhetorical decision-makers—tend to overvalue experience as a source of decision discipline, just as technicians might tend to consistently overvalue the resolution power of those particular instruments with which they are most familiar and comfortable. Therefore, we must be alert to abuses of the decision inventory, and to the natural tendency to recast problems into terms that permit analogic (or analytic) solutions, even at the expense of rectitude. Rather, the decision to employ an analogic model should always be undertaken with rational ambitions, and involve the calculations we earlier mentioned (the cost of original solutions relative to the expected value of error associated with the analogic solution). At any rate, we may now conclude the set of propositions we have been constructing in this section:

(13) The proportion of administrative expenditures devoted to the decision system will reflect the proportion of decision problems for which analogic solutions are available.

(14) Analogic solutions tend to become available as the proportion of precedented and/or deterministic problems in an organization's decision mix increases.

(15) The expected proportion of precedented and deterministic problems in an organization's decision mix will reflect the extent to which the organization's viability is dependent upon innovation.

In general, the extent to which a problem is precedented sets up the level of *demand* for a generic ("canned") solution, and decision or management scientists or operations researchers will tend to supply solutions to more widely distributed problems. As a rule, operational and tactical problems tend to emerge with greater frequency than strategic or goal-oriented problems, and therefore are more likely to be precedented. It is no accident that there are more ready-to-use algorithms or models available for moderately stochastic and deterministic problems than for severely stochastic or indeterminate problems.* In short, science tends to provide us with the analytic models for simpler problems, while our decision inventory promises to provide us with direct, analogic solutions to

---

*As anyone who attempts to set up a model base for a decision system will quickly find out. It is also, of course, fundamentally easier to develop generic or analytic solutions for simple problems, something that our discussions on model-building technology should make amply clear. Thus, the higher-order models or instruments of organizational model bases tend to become more *proprietary*, and less likely to have been lifted from any scientific literature or general secondary source.

precedented problems, thus yielding a constant complementation between theory and experience.

But the key determinant of the extent to which precedented or deterministic (or simpler problems in general) will emerge within an organization is the matter of the extent to which the organization's viability is a function of innovation. For innovative behavior tends to be unprecedented and required only in the face of certain conditions external to the organization. In this respect, consider the following relational set:

(a) $R_a = R_d + R_c + R_o$

Total administrative expenses (R_a) are the sum of decision-oriented expenses (R_d), coordinative expenses (R_c) and any other overhead components (R_o).

(b) $R_d/R_a = f(P_p + P_e/P_u)$

The ratio of resources devoted to the decision system relative to all administrative expenditures is a function of the proportion of precedented (P_p) and deterministic (P_e) problems to unprecedented or nondeterministic problems (P_u) emerging during some period.

(c) $P_u = f$ (viability $= g$ [innovation])

The proportion of unprecedented and nondeterministic problems is a function of the strength of the relationship between organizational viability (e.g., effectiveness) and innovation ... $P_u = f(g)$.

(d) $g = h$ (environmental properties, competitive structure, etc.)

The value that emerges for g is determined by the nature of the environment in which the organization is resident, by the nature of the competitive relationships among systems resident there, and probably other factors as well.

(e) $E.V.$ error $= k(g, p_u)$

The expected value of decision error associated with the aggregate of an organization's decision-making exercises is thus ultimately a function of the demand for innovation, and more directly a function of the frequency with which unprecedented decision problems emerge.

From the preceding, we find that a key determinant of the ultimate expected value of decision error we must be prepared to tolerate, and of the expenses of the decision-making function, is the nature of the environment in which an organization has been forced (or in which it has elected) to operate. For example, an enterprise participating in the high-fashion market or operating in technologically accelerating areas such as aerospace or electronics must be expected to rely considerably on product innovation, and therefore assume some considerable risk, because significant product innovations imply, directly, a fundamental lack of precedent. As such, product innovations will generally be undertaken within the severely stochastic framework, and consume considerable research and analysis resources (and even so leave us with some significant risk of loss). Even firms where product innovations are perforce obviated (as with extraction or primary industries) might have to rely for their competitive viability on strong and constant innovation in the means of production, as processual innovation is the key to increasing efficiency, which is the key to growth and health in basic manufacturing, agriculture, etc. And while processual innovations are usually of a lower-order of significance (and therefore risk) than basic product or service innovations, they nevertheless imply considerable recourse to decision-analysis functions. On the other hand, a firm enjoying a local monopoly (so that competition is preempted) and dealing in a stable, precedented product with an inelastic demand—e.g., milk products or electricity—would be expected to have an extremely high $P_p + P_e/P_u$ ratio, a low (g) value, and consequently a high frequency of access to either analogic or analytic solutions. As such, its proportional expenses for decision functions (R_d/R_a) should also be relatively low.

In general, as the environment in which an organization is resident increases in complexity, or as the relations among the organizations resident there become more intensely competitive, or both, innovation becomes more and more an imperative, and less a luxury.[3] And as innovations are demanded more frequently, the organizational decision-makers will be called upon to make more higher-order decisions and thus to face a greater proportion of indeterminate or severely stochastic problems. And as this occurs, as we well know by now, the frequency of decision error and the cost of decision errors will tend to increase. Because it is precisely this situation that is of greatest interest to us in this volume, we will have to spend considerable time suggesting how the relationship between innovation and error may be softened and made less elastic. In fact, the remainder of this text will deal with this problem, beginning with another look at decision discipline and analytical congruence.

5.2 A GENERALIZED DECISION PARADIGM

The existence and maintenance of the decision inventory provides for *institutional learning*; it seeks, over significant intervals of time, to reduce aggregate decision error within the enterprise as a whole. But, as we have seen, aggregate error is a composite of our performance on individual decision exercises. Therefore, our concern is still with ways to reduce expected value of decision error to an effective minimum, given a single decision context. And we may enter a learning provision for individual decision efforts by simply restating and reorganizing some of the points and prescriptions developed in previous sections.

To begin with, we may abstract the concept of decision information, suggesting that there are really four distinct informational states (or stocks) with which we are concerned in the context of any decision exercise:

(1) The *real* informational stock houses the decision-maker's expectations about what will be required to solve the problem. In short, it serves as the residence for the problem definition, and thus sets the specification for all subsequent decision activities through the generation of a decision context and goal. The real informational state, then, may usually be seen as a proper heuristic.[4]

(2) The *a priori* information stock contains all the information we think we already possess about the problem at hand—that which is seen to exist prior to the inauguration of any formal, dedicated decision-analysis exercise.

(3) The *a posteriori* stock(s) is (are) the residence(s) for the information produced during a formal decision-analysis exercise—information that costs us something in terms of time and/or analytical resources expended. This *a posteriori* information is usually empirical (objective) in nature, although in certain situations the data employed may be subjective, logical, or judgmental.

(4) The *actual* informational stock is not available to us until after a decision action has been taken, and run its full course, for it represents the ultimate true state of the world, which all our analysis exercises aimed at uncovering.

Given these four different informational stocks (or states), we may introduce a very simple, very direct decision-making paradigm, which will allow us to summarize the arguments we have raised about the nature of the decisions *internal* to the decision-making process itself. Figure 5.5 provides us with the major points of choice available to decision-makers and decision analysts within the context of a decision exercise. The story Figure 5.5 tells is very simple:

(1) Initially, a decision-maker may perceive identity between the real state and the *a priori* state. As such, he suggests that he already has all the information he needs about the problem at hand. Usually, this is an illegitimate move, except where the problem at hand is essentially deterministic or well-precedented (so that the *a priori* state contains an analytic or analogic solution that may be applied directly) or where the problem itself is essentially trivial (so that the worst possible cost of error would still be in-

250

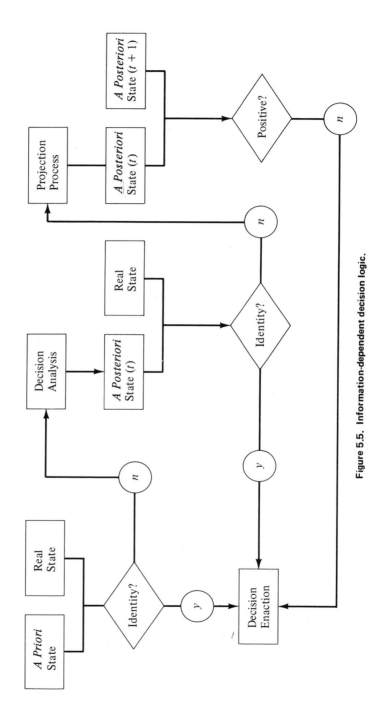

Figure 5.5. Information-dependent decision logic.

significant). In either case, given this identity, he will proceed directly to the enactment of a decision, with the decision premises being drawn entirely from the *a priori* informational stock. If there is not a perceived identity, then he would inaugurate a decision-analysis process.

(2) The decision-analysis process produces an *a posteriori* informational state (t). At each iteration of the analysis process, the existing *a posteriori* information stock is compared against the requirements of the real. To the extent that an identity is perceived (such that the existing *a posteriori* information stock is seen to exhaust the properties of the real), the decision-maker will move toward enactment, generating decision premises that are drawn from the existing *a posteriori* stock.

(3) However, the determination of whether to pursue analysis (to produce an information stock for time - $t + 1$) depends on the nature of the information projection function: is the production of the next increment of information deemed to be worth it? is it expected to carry a positive marginal productivity index? If the answers are yes, then the analysis process proceeds. If, however, the learning curve is seen to be dampening, or if it appears that we have pretty well exhausted the *a posteriori* information potential (i.e., that we are approaching the floor), then the decision-maker may elect to take action.

Now, given these simple internal decisions that have to be made, and our informational-state definitions, we can see that three types of error might emerge:

(1) *A priori error* occurs when the postulated real-state fails to adequately reflect the properties of the actual state (which causes us to solve the wrong problem).

(2) The incidence of *a posteriori error* reflects the extent to which the existing *a posteriori* informational stock fails to exhaust the properties of the real, the extent to which our informational objectives are left unfulfilled.

(3) *Opportunity error* occurs to the extent that the *a posteriori* information stock from which decision premises are drawn fails to exhaust the informational potential (fails to reach the "floor").

These various informational states and error types operate within the context of the several phases of the decision process, as in Figure 5.6. From what we already know, the *a priori* error is likely to be the most serious. Its effects will concatenate all through the process. And, to the extent that the properties of our real state (the basic referent for the subsequent decision-analysis process) fail to exhaust the properties of the actual, the magnitude of ultimate decision error will increase. It will also increase as the emerging *a posteriori* states fail to exhaust the requirements of the real. And the expected value of decision error will in-

Decision Requirement		Analysis Process	Decision Enaction	Ultimation
Real state	*A priori* state	*A posteriori* state(s)	Decision premises	Monitoring

$$t_0 \qquad\qquad t_1 \cdots\cdots\cdots t_n \; t_e \cdots\cdots\cdots t_u$$

Time and/or Expenditure of Analytical Resources

Figure 5.6. Phases of the decision process.

crease as the decision analysts fail to exhaust the informational potential available for the problem at hand—as they operate at levels above the feasible error "floor."

Therefore, it is extremely important that the real state associated with any problem (except perhaps very simple, directly deterministic ones) be treated as a variable set, and be made responsive to the emerging *a posteriori* information base ($R_t = f \mid X_t \mid$). The purpose for this is shown in Figure 5.7. In Figure 5.7, the error classifications are the following:

$(X_1 - X_0)$ = opportunity error
$\quad X_1 = $ *a posteriori* error ($= f [R - X_e]$)
$\quad X_2 = $ *a priori* error, given a variable real state ($= f [R_t] = f [X_e]$);
$\quad X_3 = $ *a priori* error given an invariant real state ($R_0 = $ constant).

From the figure, we can see again that is is the expected value of decision error that is of major interest to us during the decision process, as true error, represented

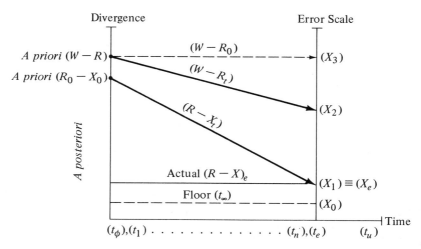

Figure 5.7. Informational state relations.

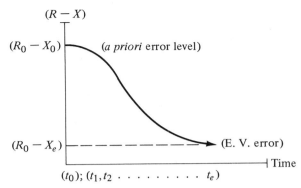

Figure 5.8. Information and error function.

as $(W - R)$ will not be available until long after a decision has been enacted and run its course (at t_u). Therefore, our key control on the decision process is the relationship between R and X, a relationship that has direct implications for us in terms of expected value of decision error, as in Figure 5.8.

Again, the emerging values for $(R - X)$ yield only an expected error component. True error will thus be comprehensible as $T.E. = f([W - R]; [R - X])$. The decision discipline we have been trying to induce will simply seek to reduce the value for $(R - X)$ to zero. There is no real measurable control over the other element of the function, the $(W - R)$ component. But there are two procedural prescriptions that seek to induce a decline in divergence: (a) the real state should not be held constant, but should be made responsive to the emergent *a posteriori* information stock, $R_t = f(X_t)$, and (b) there should be a constant effort to increase the interval $(t_0 - t_e)$ and to reduce the interval $(t_e - t_u)$, for:

$$P([W - R] = 0) = f(t_e - t_u) \quad \text{and} \quad P([R - X] = 0) = f(t_0 - t_e).$$

As for the first of these suggestions—that the real state be transformed from a constant into a variable—the rationale is self-evident: for all but the simplest problems, our expectations about the nature of the problem to be solved and the degree to which it can be solved can always be improved as we actually undertake the analysis and solution process itself. In short, the problem-definition function should be contained *within* the decision-analysis process, and not remain entirely exogenous. But to the extent that there is a division between the decision-makers and the decision analysts within an organization—so that the decision-maker dictates the terms of solution to the analysts—the feedback relationship between the *a posteriori* information stock (X) and the real state (R) may not emerge. Thus, the *a priori* error remains fixed as a function of $(W - R_0)$. This is generally unfavorable and unnecessary, and contradicts a proposition we advanced long ago: all *a priori* components of a decision process should be considered as both *tentative* and *hypothetical*, and hence subjected to empirical validation to the extent the problem context permits. We will have an opportunity to restate this assertion in even stronger terms in a later discussion.

Of the two little equations we just developed, the first states that the probability that the divergence between the real and actual states will decline to zero is a function of the interval $(t_e - t_0)$. This interval is what we earlier described as the decision *horizon*, that is, the time between the enactment of a decision (the imposition of some action) and the point at which the last repercussions of that action have run their course or dampened beyond recognition. But we know that the decision horizon we must be prepared to tolerate is largely a function of the nature of the decision problem at hand. For example, we earlier suggested that goal decisions entail a far horizon, while operational decisions tend to mature or run their course very quickly, and so forth. Therefore, it would appear that the interval $(t_e - t_u)$ is effectively beyond the control of the decision functionaries. And to a certain extent this is true, for it can really only be manipulated to the extent that we can introduce certain significant procedural and organizational changes, which represent major policy innovations, into the normal organization. We will suggest just what these are, and the nature of their effect on the decision horizon, in the final section. For the moment, however, we may assume that $(t_e - t_u)$ enters any decision process as an exogenous constraint, and thus concentrate our immediate attention on the interval $(t_0 - t_e)$.

Of these two factors, (t_e), the point at which we elect to enact a decision, using the decision premises currently available, interests us most. From what we have seen in Figures 5.7 and 5.8, the degree to which we are able to reduce the value for $(R - X)$ depends on the duration of the decision-analysis process (the $[t_0 - t_e]$ interval). Now we are not really interested at all in the (t_0) factor, so we must ask about the determinants of (t_e). We already know what they are from previous discussions, but will restate them here:

(a) First, the (t_e) factor may be set at the point where we perceive we have exhausted the *a posteriori* information available for the problem at hand.

(b) We may choose to enact a decision at the point where the expected value of the incremental information we might obtain turns unfavorable with respect to the costs of obtaining it.*

(c) There are some cases where (t_e) will be set as a trade-off between the cost of delaying a decision and the informational advantages associated with delay.

*For very trivial or extremely well-precedented problems, we may not even get into the *a posteriori* phase; rather, the decision-maker may perceive that the insignificant cost of error recommends taking the decision action using premises derived from the *a priori* information stock.

(d) There may be situations where behavioral factors act to determine the (t_e) factor, these behavioral factors acting to determine some desired level of confidence for the decision-maker. We will explore the implications of each of these determinants.

For the case where we aim to fully exhaust the informational potential for the problem at hand, the real state (R) serves merely as an idealized reference, and our functional control turns to a factor we mentioned in an earlier section: the value of successive first differences obtained for *a posteriori* information stocks. In this respect, consider Figure 5.9. Here we simply continue to amass information until the successive first differences between information stocks approaches zero, indicating that we are nearing the point where the *a posteriori* information for the problem at hand is exhausted, irrespective of the value for $(R - X)$ pertaining at that point.† In short, we look for the point where $dX/dt \to 0$, so that further analysis produces essentially new information, which would be reflected in the fact that incremental changes in the specifications of the problem model we are building cease to appear. At any rate, we would tend to use this criterion for setting (t_e) whenever we are unconcerned about the productivity of our information-generation exercises, and merely concerned with reducing expected value of decision error as low as possible. As a general rule, we would not expect to find time-dependent or the $(X_t - X_{t-1})$ factors being used to discipline decision processes in anything other than academic exercises.

The more probable criterion will be the second of our determinants of (t_e): productivity. Whereas in the previous case we attempted to hit the *floor* error

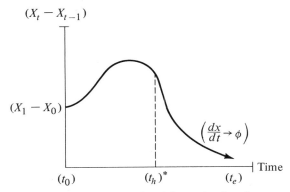

Figure 5.9. Time-dependent information function.

*(t_h) indicates the possibility that, under some circumstances, we may simply run out of time, making further delay impossible.
†See Section 4.3.

level, here we are concerned about taking action at the point where the information-production function turns uneconomic, as in Figure 5.10. Here we have two curves on the graph, a cumulative and a marginal. The cumulative curve simply reflects the increase in the information stock (X) associated with all levels of expenditure of analytical resources (C). The information stock keeps increasing until it hits the *ceiling*, which is equivalent to the point where $(X_t - X_{t-1})$ approached 0 in Figure 5.9 (corresponding to the point where the *a posteriori* information potential is effectively exhausted). Thus, at the asymptotic ceiling we achieve the maximum mass for the *a posteriori* information stock (X_{max}). This is the optimal point where productivity constraints are neglected.

The marginal function, on the other hand, seeks the marginal optimum, that is, where the expected value of the next increment of information is expected to be worth approximately what it will cost to obtain it. Recall from Section 4.3 that we calculated the value of information *per se* in terms of its effect on the expected value of decision error associated with a problem at hand. We worked there to show that increased expenditures of resources could reduce the variance associated with our decision expectations, and thereby reduce expected error. Translating this logic into our present circumstances, we can suggest that:

$$\text{Worth of Information } (c - c_{-1}) \equiv (\text{E.V. error}_c - \text{E.V. error}_{c-1})$$

That is, the expected worth of information for the interval of expenditures bounded by c and $(c - 1)$ is equivalent to the difference in the expected value of decision error over that interval. We would thus continue to add to our informa-

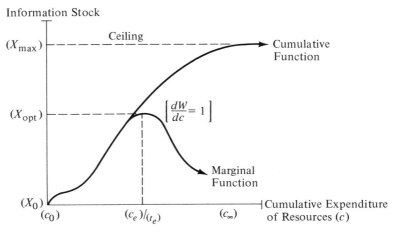

Figure 5.10. Resource-dependent information function.

tion stock (X) up to the point where the relationship between cumulative expenditure of analytical resources produces the situation where $dW/dC = 1$. This point is marked on Figure 5.10 and suggests then that we enact a decision (i.e., cease analysis) at the point where resource expenditures have reached (c_e). And as resource expenditures are some function of time, this would establish a specific (t_e) for us. At this point, our information stock has been optimized with respect to productivity criteria, and we would thus expect to tolerate an expected value of decision error that is a function of $(R - X_{opt})$. This will be higher than that which we would obtain were we to use $(R - X_{max})$, but producing the maximum information stock is not expected to be worth it in terms of the cost.

The third way in which a point of decision enaction may be determined is through the use of a calculated trade-off between advantages of further analysis and disadvantages of further delay in commitment. This situation is familiar to those who have studied the range of speculative decisions as they emerge in such fields as arbitrage and commodity futures, and to some extent in the investment of securities and common currencies. From the simplest perspective, the speculator's objective is to gain control of some quantity of a commodity (Q_i) at a forepurchase price (p_f) lower than that which will prevail at a future point in time (p_1). When he transfers ownership or control of the commodity at the point (t_1), his profit is determined crudely by $(Q [p_1 - p_f])$, with a loss occurring were $(p_f > p_1)$. Such decisions are enormously complicated, but we can get a rough idea of the quandary facing the speculator by looking at Figure 5.11. In the figure, the lettered curves (e.g., Q_2, $+s_1$; Q_1, $-s_3$) are indifference

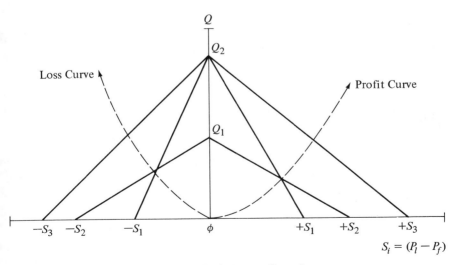

Figure 5.11. Profit-loss configuration.

constraints; they indicate the different Q and $(P_1 - P_f)$ combinations yielding the same loss or profit value. For example, the net loss associated with Q_1, $-s_2$ is the same as that associated with Q_2, $-s_1$. The quadratic function, which yields loss or profit depending on the sign of $s = (P_1 - P_f)$, may be thought to have been graphed through a number of these indifference curves to yield a loss-profit function. (In actual practice, such functions are unlikely to be simple quadratics.) At any rate, the speculator must make sure that $(P_1 > P_f)$ to avoid a loss, and then select some Q; for any given profit level, Q must increase as $(P_1 - P_f) \rightarrow 0$. The speculator's decision thus becomes comprehensible as the commitment to a certain quantity at a certain time, Q_{t_e}, where

$$Q_{(t_e)} = f(E.V. \ s_i) \mid P(P_1 > P_f)_{t_e}$$

That is, the quantity to be purchased and the time of enactment (t_e) is a function of the expected value of the magnitude of the difference between P_1 and $P_f \cdots$ E.V. [s], given some probability that P_1 will be greater than P_f at (t_1), the point in time where the speculator must actually pay for the commodity contracted for at (t_e).

Now, a decision problem like this is fraught with trade-off conditions, so we may set out a generic configuration such as Figure 5.12, and make the attributions listed therein.

$C_1 \rightarrow$ (a) $P[P_1 > P_f]$ $C_2 \rightarrow$ (a) $E.V. (s)$ $T \rightarrow$ (a) Q
      (b) P_f (b) $(R - X_t)$
      (c) Opportunity loss   (c) Expected loss
      (d) P [type-I error]   (d) P [type-II error]   (d) E.V. error

The set of trade-off curves presented in the figure can serve any of four different situations. We may work through the logic very quickly. The major source of difficulty here is the trade-off between information and risk, and therefore the inherently positive relationship between risk and profit. The real state of the

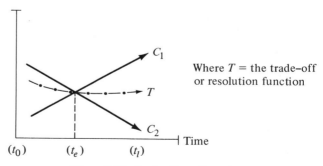

Where T = the trade-off or resolution function

Figure 5.12. Trade-off configuration.

speculator (R) may be thought to specify the determinants that he thinks will determine the actual state, and provide some guidance on how to evaluate those determinants. The actual state (A) in this situation will contain only one piece of information, the forepurchase price for the commodity $(P_f)_t$. If we could know P_1 —which we clearly cannot—then the major risk, the possibility that P_1 will be less than P_f, the forepurchase price, could be eliminated, and we would have to take a direct loss.

Now, as we can see from our trade-off configuration, we expect that as we delay t_e, we can increase the probability that $(P_1 > P_f)$, and therefore reduce the probability of taking a loss, or increase the probability of making a profit, for any Q. But as already suggested, the decision to commit to some $Q_{(t_e)}$ is itself a trade-off–conditioned decision, for as we delay commitment, the expected divergence between (P_1) and (P_f) decreases, meaning either a lower profit or a lower loss, for any Q, depending on the strategic condition—whether s is ultimately positive or negative. The reason for this is that as we delay our decision waiting for more information (an increase in the *a posteriori* information stock, X), the forepurchase price is steadily increasing. That is, the longer we delay making a commitment, the greater will be the parity between the forepurchase price (P_f) and the ultimate price (P_1). In short, the speculator who commits to a purchase early can generally expect to realize a larger gain (or loss) than those speculators who delay. For as the interval $(t_e - t_1)$ decreases, the expected value for $(P_1 - P_f)$ decreases, with the decrease in $(R - X_t)$ also acting to reduce the probability that $(P_1 < P_f)$. In short, we have to be prepared to pay an *opportunity loss* for each interval of delay, with the expected value of the opportunity loss increasing as the probability of an error decreases with respect to direct costs. Thus, the speculator's situation is uncomfortable indeed, for when he tries to minimize the probability of taking a direct loss (given that the forepurchase price is higher than the ultimate price), he also erodes the potential profit he can expect. Therefore, the expected value of decision error—the critical decision-variable determining a specific (t_e)—is the resolution vector between two antipodal error curves: (a) the type-I error curve, representing the opportunity-loss function, is the cost of *not* purchasing some Q at any t_e, given that $(P_1 > P_f)$ and (b) the type-II error curve, which represents the direct cost that would occur in the face of any Q_{t_e} commitment were the actual state to emerge as $(P_1 < P_f)$.

Now, we can see that the actual $(t_e - t_1)$ interval, and thus the $(t_0 - t_e)$ interval, is now determined by an inescapable trade-off, whereas we determined it directly by either time-dependent or resource-dependent criteria in previous cases. But we may now expand the illustration at hand to introduce the fourth way in which (t_e) may be determined: by a *behavioral* factor. The particular determinant of (t_e) that we are after here is the *desired level of confidence* of the decision-maker, as this may force a commitment independent of any of the objective criteria we have thus far discussed (e.g., the floor error level, productivity, or the condition of the information-loss trade-off).

Desired level of confidence is always a complex variable, having both an objective and subjective component (with the subjective component sometimes being very elusive. Very simply, when we consider the desired level of confidence, we get the following:

$$P \text{ (decision)} = f(c)_t \rightarrow (t = t_e)$$

$$c_t = s_i \left(\text{E.V. Error;} \; \frac{dX}{dC} \; ; [X_t - X_{t-1}] \right)_t$$

$$(R - X_e) = f(t_e) \rightarrow \text{E.V. error}$$

Here we are suggesting that the decision to take action and abort analysis is now a function of the desired level of confidence (c_t) pertaining at some point in time. At that point, the desired level of confidence is determined by a behavioral operator (s_i) operating on whatever objective criteria are available: the actual expected value of error, the productivity function evaluated at t, the nature of the first differences between successive *a posteriori* information stocks, etc. Finally, we know that the expected value of error (E.V. error) will be a function of the extent to which the existing *a posteriori* information stock (X_e) exhausts the properties of the real (R) at t_e.

The tacit and critical factor, however, is that the desired level of confidence tends to make its presence felt in the real state, in R. In short, as expected, behavioral variables tend to enter the decision process as *a priori* determinants. For example, the decision-maker who knows that he will not be audited is likely to underestimate error properties, and be less inclined to inaugurate decision analysis than the decision-maker who is under careful scrutiny (and who can expect to be held accountable for a decision error). But the simplest, most direct implication of a behavioral variable is the well-known dichotomy between the *risk-taker* and *risk-averter*. In general, we tend to distinguish between these two ideal-type decision-makers on the basis of the preference for a type-I or type-II error. The risk-averter is generally more interested in avoiding a type-II error (which we just defined as the error that leads to a direct cost; e.g., he purchases some Q when the forepurchase price was actually higher than the ultimate price). The risk-taker, on the other hand, will generally be more interested in avoiding a type-I error—failing to make a profit. We may always be more rigorous and define precise intervals over utility functions,[5] but for our purposes we can set the implications with reference to the speculator problem we just treated. Consider Figure 5.13. The two curves superimposed on the opportunity-loss and expected-cost curves represent the function P [Decision] for the risk-taker and risk-averter, respectively. At all points, the risk-taker is more willing to commit

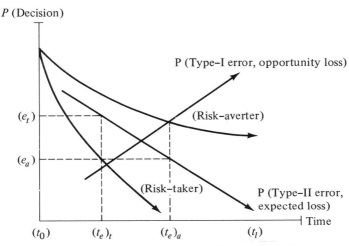

P (Decision)

P (Type–I error, opportunity loss)

(e_t)

(Risk–averter)

(e_a)

(Risk–taker)

P (Type–II error, expected loss)

Time

(t_0) $(t_e)_t$ $(t_e)_a$ (t_l)

Figure 5.13. Decision characteristics of different risk preferences.

than the risk-averter; hence, the $(t_e)_t$ for the risk-taker appears much earlier with respect to (t_l) than does the enaction point for the risk-averter. We can also see that the risk-taker is willing to enact a decision at a higher risk of direct cost than is the risk-averter, etc. The general implication is that the risk-taking specu-lator will purchase earlier than the risk-averting speculator, given that opportunity loss is his primary avoidance target.

Finally, we can develop the implications of the two risk categories with respect to our central variable, expected value of decision error. Consider Figure 5.14. Here, using expected value of decision error as the control factor, we see that the risk-taker is at all points more willing to take a decision—and cease analysis—than the risk-averter. In fact, beyond the point (e_h), the risk-averter will not make a decision at all, which suggests that there are certain types of decision functions for which he is simply inappropriate.[6]

At any rate, this discussion of the various determinants of (t_e)—and hence of the intensity or scope of the decision-analysis process as a function of $(t_0 - t_e)$—has given us the information we require to summarize the conditions under which a decision-maker will seek to acquire additional information:

(a) There is a significant difference between the existing stock of information (either *a priori* or *a posteriori*) and the postulated real stock—that which is desired.

and

(b) There is still a significant first difference between successive *a posteriori* information stocks . . . $(X_t - X_{t-1} \gg 0)$.

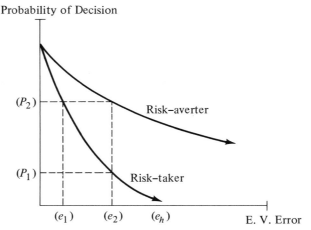

Probability of Decision

Figure 5.14. Decision functions for risk classes.

or

(c) There is no requirement that the decision be made immediately (e.g., t_e is to be determined endogenously).

(d) There is expected to be a positive marginal product associated with the next increment of information, relative to the expected costs of obtaining it . . . $(dX/dC \gg 1)$.

(e) The cost of delaying decision under the trade-off terms is perceived to be less than the expected worth of the information to be obtained during the next interval of analysis.

The final and obvious requirement for the continuation of the analysis process is that sufficient analytical resources are available; that is, no budget constraint exists to force a suboptimal conclusion to the analysis process.

Figure 5.15 indicates what happens when a budget constraint is entered. There are three major curves on the diagram. First, there is the cumulative information curve, which shows how the *a posteriori* stock increases with cumulative increases in the expenditure of analytical resources. The marginal curve shows the productivity of the analytical expenditures, the incremental increase in X associated with an incremental increase in expenditures (c). Finally, there is the $[R - X]$ curve, which is equivalent to the E.V. error curve; this factor is expected to be reduced as $(R - X)$ decreases. We know from our earlier analyses that the economically optimal resource expenditure level is c_{opt}, determined at the point where dX/dC approaches unity (1.0). This point yields, by way of the cumulative curve, the total information stock X_{opt} and consequently the E.V. $(e)_{opt}$ level.

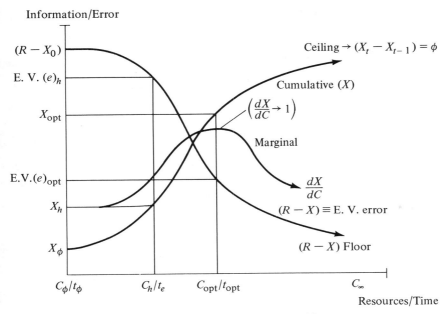

Information/Error

$(R - X_0)$

Ceiling $\rightarrow (X_t - X_{t-1}) = \phi$

E. V. $(e)_h$

Cumulative (X)

X_{opt}

$\left(\dfrac{dX}{dC} \rightarrow 1\right)$

Marginal

E.V.$(e)_{opt}$

$\dfrac{dX}{dC}$

X_h

$(R - X) \equiv$ E. V. error

X_ϕ

$(R - X)$ Floor

C_ϕ / t_ϕ C_h / t_e C_{opt} / t_{opt} C_∞

Resources/Time

Figure 5.15. Effect of budget constraint on decision process.

The real state is not exhausted by the *a posteriori* at that point ($[R - X_{opt}] > 0$), but further expenditures are expected to produce a declining marginal product with respect to the possible reduction in expected value of decision error that could be realized. We can see the suboptimal situation that results with the entrance of a (t_e), an enaction threshold, at the point (c_h). This (c_h) is a budget constraint, which aborts the analysis process prematurely.

Thus far, we have been concerned with the probability of *decision* versus the probability of *analysis*—the explications of the conditions under which we elect to generate information or take action. But we have to recognize that there are internal decisions to be made *within* the analysis process: the decision on whether to move from one level of analysis to another, or to continue to exploit the information potential within a given level of analysis. Recall that our model-building technology implies four different levels of analysis: state-variable, relational, coefficient, and parametric. Clearly, the decision-analysis process will focus on each of these levels as we move through the interval $(t_0 - t_e)$. Thus, the arguments we have raised so far could apply to analysis operations at any of the four levels of analysis. That is, at each level of analysis we have to decide the following:

(1) For any of the four levels of analysis, we must first decide whether we have sufficient *a priori* information (X_0) to adequately discipline that aspect of the model we are constructing. This becomes more probable as the problem at hand becomes simpler or if the problem is precedented (for, the application of either an analogic or analytic solution is essentially the development of an *a priori* solution). It also becomes probable, but illegitimately so, the less analytically sophisticated the decision-maker is; for, as we tried to show earlier, the rhetorical decision-maker does not have much skill in bringing discipline to the areas of his concern, and therefore tends to discount the possible contributions of formal analysis.

(2) Given that we elect to inaugurate a formal analysis process, we must decide the duration of analysis at each level (in terms of either time or resource expenditures) by looking at the learning curve for that level of analysis. That is, we may elect to cease analysis at any level by going through the type of determinations we just set out; e.g., has the informational potential been exhausted? is the productivity curve turning unfavorable? has the desired level of confidence been reached?

That is, we would replace the generic determinants we just discussed with determinants that are level-specific, as follows:

Level-Specific Determinant	Implies
(a) $(R_t - X_t)_i \rightarrow 0$	We cease analysis at the point where the *a posteriori* stock associated with level-i is perceived to exhaust the real for that level; e.g., the desired level of confidence has been attained for the ith level of analysis.
(b) $(X_{i,t} - X_{i,t-1}) \rightarrow 0$	We cease analysis at the point where the first differences between successive changes in the specifications at the ith level of analysis dampen toward zero—we see that we are running out of available information at that level.
(c) $\left(\dfrac{dX_i}{dC_i}\right)_t \rightarrow 1$	We cease analysis at the ith level when the information productivity function (evaluated in the neighborhood of some t) begins to turn unfavorable relative to resources expended at that level (C_i).

The implication is that, as one of the above events occurs the rational decision is to *shift analytical modalities*, that is, move to the next level of analysis and employ the congruent instruments for that level. To the extent, however, that the learning curve, production functions, etc., do not approach the limiting condition, the probability is in favor of an *iteration* of analysis at the existing level of analy-

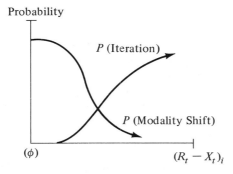

Figure 5.16. Probability of iteration versus modality shift.

sis. Using the first determinant as an illustration, consider Figure 5.16. When we make the modality shifts at the proper time, we can expect to make best use of the aggregate analytical resources devoted to a decision-analysis function, e.g., MAX (dX/dC). In very simple graphic terms, omitting discontinuities that might emerge in practice, we would want a situation such as Figure 5.17. This model is entirely consistent with our view of the decision-analysis process as a concatenative, sequential exercise. And the allowance for iterations within the various levels of analysis simply gives us a second-order "learning" opportunity within the confines of the process, the first-order learning condition being the dictate that the

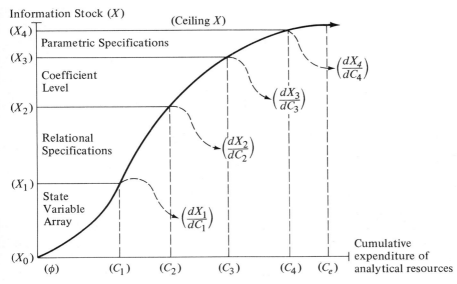

Figure 5.17. Modality shift logic.

real state be made responsive to the emerging *a posteriori* information stock $(R_t = f[X_t])$. But each level of analysis will introduce different types of iterative conditions, as Table 5.1 suggests.

We can see immediately some of the assumptions that affect this construct. First, the condition of *actionability* makes itself felt in the nature of the output objectives. Note that we are not concerned with passing on several different alternative state-variable arrays to the relational level, nor in passing on several different causal trajectories (relational configurations) to the coefficient and parametric levels. It is, of course, possible to do so, so that we would assign coefficient and parametric values to several different relational configurations, etc. But the assumption here is that we are dealing with an *inherently* deterministic problem, for which an ultimately optimal solution is available. But the problem may be inherently moderately stochastic, in which case we would have to content ourselves not with a single, sequential (linear) model, but with several different models, each with relational, coefficient, and parametric specifications peculiar to itself. Each of these models would be equipped with an *a priori* probability of occurrence, and some "monitoring variables" would be identified, which would, as they become evaluated at future points in time, act to make one alternative more probable than the others or perhaps dictate the development of a new relational, coefficient, and parametric set altogether. But the logic of this type of learning process awaits us further on. The other assumption is that neither time nor resource constraints will curtail the iterative process; if they did, we would not be able to let the information base exhaust itself, or obtain our desired level of confidence. But we are already familiar with the constraints that time or resource thresholds impose. Finally, we have not treated an ancillary selection problem; that is, *within* any of our four instrument categories, there are alternative instruments, each of which may purport to do the same thing. This is really not a significant problem, as a rule. For, in the "hard" science arena, we seldom find two instruments that are strict substitutes. Therefore, we have avoided the problem of intracategorical instrument selection altogether, although in some very rare circumstances there may be occasion to compare the expected productivity functions for two highly similar instruments; the technology to do this exists within the generic constructs we developed earlier.

There is a last assumption implicit throughout the construct, which is worth repeating here. In all the levels of analysis, we are interested in minimizing the expected value of decision error. The iterative logic serves this end, as described in Figure 5.18. Again, we have an event-probability map on the left-hand side of the figure, with three variants. Given earlier discussions, the distribution D_0 is least favorable (the *a priori* distribution), with the distribution D_2 being that associated with the lowest expected value of decision error on the right-hand side of the figure (e_{D_0}). The point here, however, is that this kind of transforma-

Table 5.1. Summary of iterative and modality-shift logic within the decision-analysis process.

Level of Analysis	Output Objective	Iterative Instrument	Modality-Shift Conditions
State Variable	To isolate that particular set of state variables that has the highest probability of fully exhausting the determinants of the problem at hand.	Where the problem is complex and unprecedented, the Delphi process or some other tool to discipline opinion must be used (developing arrays carrying subjective probabilities of accuracy)	At the point where a consensus has been reached on a particular array, and further iterations of opinion solicitation fail to increase consensus.
Relational	To define that particular relational configuration (e.g., causal trajectory) having the highest probability of reflecting reality.	Some sort of stochastic-state analysis using qualitative, network, or (for simpler, precedented problems) inductive instruments to isolate all causal and interface alternatives.	At the point where a single relational configuration is seen to carry the only significant probability of occurrence, or where further stochastic-state analysis fails to introduce either structural or probability changes.
Coefficient and Parametric	To equip all relational interfaces with a magnitudinal factor that is the best estimate of the true magnitude. To equip all state variables with the most probably accurate point-in-time parametric value.	We would probably use some sort of Bayesian (successive approximation) technique trying to force convergence on a single estimate for each coefficient or parameter; for simple problems, coefficient and parameter values may sometimes be found via trial and error.	At the point where, for each coefficient or parameter, we arrive at: $P(\bar{p} - p) \leq e$, where e is a tolerance limit; or, where successive iterations of the Bayesian transformation process fail to introduce significant changes.

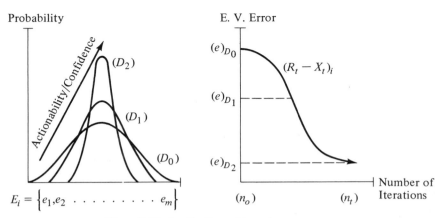

Figure 5.18. Implications of iterative processes.

tion takes place at all four levels of analysis; that is, E_i may be the set of all possible state variables, the set of all possible relational alternatives for a specific interface, the alternative values that some coefficient might assume, and so forth. In either case, our *confidence* in our analysis and the *actionability* of the output increase as the number of alternatives to be considered at each stage of a model-building process is reduced through an iterative analysis of the type described for the various levels of analysis in Table 5.1. That is, all components of a decision model become equipped with a probability index setting out their expected probability of occurrence; these act to determine the ultimate confidence with which we can enact a decision based on the premises supplied by the model.

We know from our previous discussions that we do not move directly from analysis to action. There are also action-alternatives to evaluate and a particular action-alternative to be selected for implementation. Implicit in these last two processes are two more "learning" provisions:

(1) The matter of evaluating alternatives consists of some sort of *simulative* process, where we use the model we have developed to project the differential effects (outcomes) associated with different actions we might impose in an effort to solve the problem;

(2) Once we have implemented an action—made a decision and imposed it on the problem context—we are responsible for *monitoring* the actual outcome—for continually evaluating the nature of the emerging relationship between our real state (R) and the actual state (W). We do this to minimize the duration of an error, subject to the logic we first developed in Section 2.3.

Thus, we are still trying to "learn" and avoid the consequences of error, for the monitoring process worked during the interval $(t_e - t_u)$ between enaction and

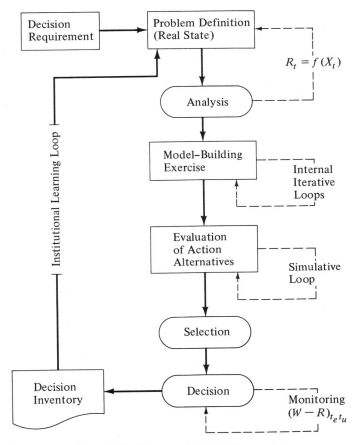

Figure 5.19. The generalized decision model.

ultimation. The scope of the monitoring process, and the resources we devote to it, should be conditioned by the residual level of error that emerged at the conclusion of the model-building process. Any error that remains in our problem model will dilute the expected accuracy of our evaluation exercises, and hence introduce a risk into the selection process. The strength of the monitoring process should reflect this risk. At any rate, we finally emerge with a generalized decision process such as Figure 5.19.

5.3 THE STRUCTURAL TRADE-OFF: DECISION SCOPE AND DECISION RECTITUDE

The ease, expediency, and economy with which we can move through the analysis process depends, of course, on the simplicity of the problem at hand, on its degree of analytical tractability. In short, for operational or tactical decision problems, we would expect to move almost linearly through the tasks of the decision paradigm, with fewer iterations at any of the "learning" levels and greater ultimate confidence in the results of the decision analysis, evaluation, and implementation exercises. But, as suggested earlier, the decision mix that any organization must face will depend to some extent on the nature of the relationship between organizational viability and innovation. When innovation is a critical contributor to enterprise effectiveness or integrity, then the decision mix will shift in favor of more complex, less tractable problems, and the number of unprecedented, nondeterministic problems will rise inexorably. But the nature of the environment in which the organization is resident is not the only determinant of the decision mix. To a certain extent, the organization has some latitude over the nature of the problems it will ask its decision-makers to attack. The way in which an organization exercises this latitude will become apparent as the degree of *centralization* associated with the decision system.

From the usual perspective (which we will later modify considerably), centralization becomes comprehensible in terms of the distribution of decision authority. Often, the degree of centralization a system exhibits will be a response to aprioristic (theoretical, normative, or philosophical-ideological) predicates. For example, looking at the matter from the highest perspective, theoretical capitalism dictates that a decentralized economic system is preferable to a centralized one. Leaving aside philosophical issues about human dignity, volition, and so on, we can see that the capitalist precept is that decentralized investment, production, and distribution decisions will *maximize clearance* of the market, which in turn minimizes waste in an economic system. That is, there will be the lowest possible level of production of goods or service for which there is no effective demand.[7] This implies that centralized allocation decisions tend to result in imbalances between supply and demand, and therefore in a certain inescapable level of diseconomic production (because of either the failure of the central planners to read the demand schedule properly, or the lag inherent in bureaucratic mechanisms).

The apologists for socialist systems offer a contrary argument. They suggest that the net welfare of the inhabitants of any economic system will be maximized only to the extent that economic decisions are concentrated in the hands of a limited number of nodal decision authorities, acting to deter any concentration of wealth, power, or prerogative. The socialist would consider the goal of market clearance subordinate to the goal of symmetry in the distribution of economic prerogatives. To a certain extent, the major variables of concern to the socialist and capitalist are different, with the latter primarily concerned about maximizing a growth coefficient, and the former concerned about symmetrizing the distribution coefficient. Thus, the level of argument is usually different for these two theses, with the socialists usually arguing from ideological premises and the capitalists usually building their case on quasi-axiomatic grounds.* In either case, the decision scientist may be indifferent to these positions, for both result in essentially the same decision context, even if they proceed from different directions. That is, there is a concentration of decision authority, but in the hands of different classes. In the protosocialist system, decision authority becomes concentrated in the hands of bureaucrats; in the *de facto* (as opposed to the *de jure*) capitalist system it tends to become concentrated in the hands of a limited number of private operatives. Both situations thus result in the demand for decisions of enormous scope and ramification, with very limited discretion left to satellite or subordinate decision-makers.

It is, of course, necessary to distinguish between theoretical (axiomatic or pure) capitalism and the capitalist structure that has actually evolved. In practice, the idealized situation of unfettered competition among a large number of limited producers has not emerged at all except in some primary industries; therefore, the ostensible responsiveness of supply (production) to demand cannot be postulated as an operational fact. Rather, there has tended to be a concentration of power in virtually all productive sectors (including agriculture, once thought to be the prototypical competitive domain). This concentration of power has raised the possibility that large firms, operating as *de facto* cartels, now act to *make the market* rather than respond to it. This concentration of power is often defended on the grounds of natural differences among firms' ability to produce efficiently, so that there is an implied correlation between size and efficiency. However, we have already suggested the mechanisms by which the relationship between size and efficiency may be abrogated, along with the abrogation of the normative relationship between risk and profit. At any rate, the most common defense of industrial concentration—advanced as a consistent argument for monopolistic or oligopolistic enterprises—is that large size permits an organization to take advantage of *economies of scale* that are perforce denied smaller firms. These economies of scale are supposed to permit (if not force) efficiencies in production, marketing, and so forth, and therefore make larger firms significant contributors to the general economic welfare. But economy of scale is a two-edged sword, even though apologists for capitalist concentration use only one. The other edge—as sharp as the first—suggests that *the larger a firm grows, the greater the probability that it will exceed optimal scale of plant and therefore represent an uneconomic investment of resources.* Thus, economy of scale is not a general defense for commercial titanism, but may often be posed as an argument against it.

The general condition under which we may recognize operations beyond optimal scale of plant is when a radical shift occurs in the ratio between organiza-

*For more on the difference between axiomatic and axiological decision premises, see Chapter 3 of the author's *Societal Systems: Methodology, Modelling and Management* (New York: Elsevier-North Holland, 1977).

tional overhead and direct investment. That is, beyond a certain size of plant, administrative and overhead costs begin to rise faster than accompanying increases in output. In short, the ratio of administrative overhead to aggregate revenue (output times selling price) begins to accelerate as scale of plant increases beyond a certain point. The relationship between size of plant and administrative costs is thus a function that is discontinuous at some point, except for very simple types of organizations.[8] And beyond some point, the direct economies of scale that may be associated with productive, marketing, or other line functions may be more than offset by the diseconomies introduced at the administrative level. Figures 5.20a and b summarize the points of concern.

Figure 5.20a simply illustrates that administrative expenses relative to output may not be proportional across the entire range of plant size (as a function of A). Beyond a certain point, as the solid curve $(\partial A/\partial T)$ indicates, administrative costs begin to rise proportionally faster than the increase in total costs (which would include all productive expenditures for labor, equipment, materials, etc.). At this point, investments in overhead and administrative functions become *diseconomic*, and some proportion of the resources devoted to maintain the level of output beyond the optimal level (O_{opt}) are therefore misallocated; they would be better invested in another organization altogether. Figure 5.20b suggests the same story, working from the platform of marginal productivity.

When an organization begins to exceed optimal scale of plant, several things happen:

(a) The ratio of staff to line positions begins to increase.

(b) The funding of indirect relative to direct supervisory functions accelerates.

(c) The ratio of salaried to hourly employees might begin to increase quite rapidly.

(d) Service operations (e.g., payroll, industrial relations) begin to increase more rapidly than production units.

(e) New levels of administrative structure are introduced, which attenuates the hierarchical structure of the organization.

(f) Administrative infrastructure (e.g., offices, buildings, furnishings, computer gear) tends gradually to be replaced more often than productive plant and equipment, so that administrative facilities tend generally to be newer than productive facilities, and geographically separated from them in some cases.

(g) New quasi-professional positions tend to be created, where profit impact becomes successively more diluted (e.g., we might find more public relations people; more human relations, community, and investment consultants; and some truly outlandish positions such as the corporate art director or the staff interior-design consultant).

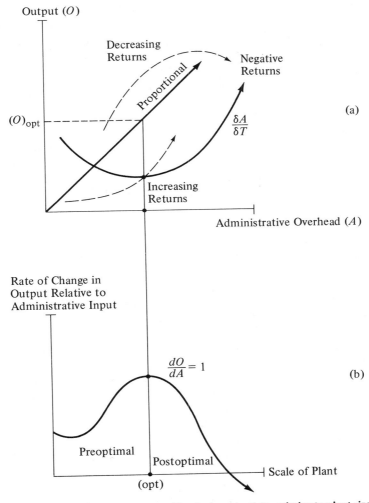

Figure 5.20. *a*, Returns to scale. *b*, Marginal productivity relative to plant size.

The net result, then, is that administrative and overhead expenses consume a larger and larger proportion of the total operating budget, with the net effect of increasing the positive opportunity cost associated with any incremental investment in the organization.

Thus, real profit (leaving aside returns generated by depreciation, goodwill, paper profits on security transactions, etc.) tends to decrease as a percentage of overall investment. This may not become immediately apparent to investors because of the confusion that reliance on retained earnings increasingly produces, and the different mechanisms for accounting for the equity base. Nor, given the generally reflective profit targets of oligopolistic firms, will any radical shifts in profit rates appear for any single firm. (Rather, changes in profit levels will tend to remain more or less constant for all firms in a concentrated industry over the long run, although individual firms may show some variation from year to year. However, this variation may not make itself felt in terms of the prime competitive coefficient, share of market.) This is to be expected, as one of the characteristics of corrupted capitalism is that firms in the same industry may tend to be structural-functional replicates of each other, despite differences in absolute size, and therefore have administrative ratios that tend to be constant.[9] The same symptoms of exceeding scale of plant affects enterprises in the public sector, with the major diseconomies perhaps being indicated by the tendency to put surpluses into infrastructure or other nonproductive amenities.

The real damaging effects of consistently exceeding scale of plant may not be felt with respect to any specific firm, not if the excesses are sufficiently widespread and pervasive. Rather, they will be felt structurally and secularly. First, the relatively greater proportion of resources going into quasi-professional functions and into administrative support positions means an increase in the white-collar work force at the expense of the blue-collar worker; in short, a secular increase in unemployment at the lower levels. Second, the necessity to keep profit rates constant in the face of increasingly unproductive scale of plant forces inflation; this is a natural and inescapable accompaniment of the erosion of the real asset base of an economic system that places successively more reliance on the fourth factor of production (management) than on the three direct inputs: capital, labor, and equipment. The increases in costs, which firms tend to pass on, and which add fuel to the inflationary fire, may thus be delayed reactions to the increasingly inefficient scale of plant associated with the major producers, which naturally make themselves felt in terms of secularly decreasing productivity at the functional level—for example, decreasing productivity with respect to labor and/or capital may have an indirect and ultimate cause in the decreasing productivity of administrative investments. In this way, the Phillip's curve may be abrogated, and an economic system may realize both secular inflation *and* secularly high unemployment. The third secular effect will be a decrease in the competitivity of the economic system's exports, which internationalizes the inefficiencies of the host producers. Here, a counterpart to the inflationary mechanism comes into play, *devaluation*. Like inflation, devaluation is the normative response to the decreasing productivity of an economic system's means of production, and also serves to obscure inefficiencies by manipulating them through fiscal artifices. But the net result is still a loss of jobs, loss of purchasing power of the host currency, and reduction in real asset value. Now, given the inherent inefficiencies that might be transmitted from operating consistently in the post-optimal area (in the region of decreasing returns to scale), the normative relationship between level of demand and prices may be abrogated; for example, prices will not tend to fall as demand falls. Moreover, labor may not decrease its price as jobs become scarcer, but may actually demand higher wages even as employment falls. The point behind these contranormative events is that, as inefficiencies tend to become institutionalized, the organizations and the input factors gradually reduce their horizon of interest, giving short-term outcomes complete control over long-term considerations.

These last assertions tend to operate through the mechanism of the capital-labor ratio. We suggested earlier that investment in a new plant and equipment may proceed faster at the administrative than at the production level, so that we get a secular increase in the obsolescence of productive infrastructure. Now, because administrative and overhead positions are increasing faster than productive positions (direct labor), the capital-labor ratio may look constant, even though its real productive implications are becoming diluted. This may be obscured as we move—in inflationary periods—to valuate equipment at replacement cost; this accounting technique, coupled with the reduction in labor force, artificially inflates the capital-labor ratio. The specter of secularly increasing capital-labor ratios, amplified by the threat of automation, tends to make labor rapacious in the short run, which makes the concept of displacing labor with capital equipment even more attractive. But the expected increase in demand for new equipment does not really materialize, for the increasing capital-labor ratios do not associate themselves with the expected increases in productive efficiency. This is because the capital-labor ratio, as currently constructed, is deceptive: we continue to construct the ratios using only direct labor in the denominator. But, for firms that have exceeded the optimal scale of plant, this labor factor will have been reduced at the expense of nondirect functionaries. It may be that if we were to include *all* organizational employees in the capital labor ratios, we would see that they have been secularly declining; the secular reduction in productivity would therefore become comprehensible in terms of normal economic expectations. Finally, the investment community reacts to all these economic anomalies by reducing its planning horizon and becoming more active share-traders. The far horizon of the market—its secular or long-term properties—becomes of less interest than trying to make short-run gains by anticipating the market, irrespective of the direction in which it is moving. This of course leads to an anomaly in its own right: the volume of trading and the alterations in the value of shares traded are maintained at a very high level, even while the economic system to which the market is supposed to respond remains sluggish and inactive. The movements of the stock market and of the economy thus tend to become disjoint, even when the lag between economic events and market response is considered. For when no economic "events" are occurring, the market tends to author its own movements, which may no longer be looked upon as representing forecasts of the future. The bull and the bear, as it were, are now at play on fields of their own demarcation.

To a great extent, these and other anomalies and dysfunctions of our quasi-capitalist economic systems become intelligible as natural responses to the domination of growth as an economic criterion, and the diminution of interest in optimal criteria (e.g., profitability or marginal productivity). Thus, contrary to popular opinion, economic growth does not necessarily imply an increase in effective employment opportunities nor in the level of general welfare; it may, when misdirected, actually effect a reduction in welfare and employment potential in an economic system.[10] We are concerned with concentration of economic power, but we have thus far considered only its adverse aspect (the increased danger of running afoul of the optimal scale of operations as an enterprise increases in size). Yet there is also a theoretical advantage available to economic systems where degree of concentration is high. This advantage, simply, is the increasing probability of making optimal aggregate resource allocations across a broad range of programs. Particularly, to the extent that a capable, nodal (*qua* central) decision authority exists, instances of both competitivity and redundancy may be resolved before any set of programs is funded. However, *concentration of economic authority does not always imply integration of decision functions.* To this extent, concentration is just an artifice of the organization chart, and what we really have is an agglomeration of more or less independent enterprises, joined together *additively* rather than synergistically. This, for example, is the situation with the majority of conglomerates; they become merely fiscal creations, with no real pretensions to effective integration except on the year-end combined income statement and balance sheet.[11] The same is true, to a certain extent, of what have come to be called "diversified" organizations. Here we may have a group of operations linked either horizontally or vertically, but the basic resource allocation and functional decisions may be taken independently for each unit. As a result, such organizations seldom become much more than the sum of their individual parts. The synergistic promise of the whole being more than the sum of its parts is not realized in practice. Another example where concentration does not imply integration is the commercial enterprise that exercises only *policy control* over its several more or less autonomous divisions. Within these very broad and often abstract policy constraints, each organizational unit operates more or less autonomously, and performance again becomes additive only. In short, financial integration is not the same thing as functional integration, and the former is a great deal easier to achieve than the latter.

The reason for this is a central thesis of this section: as the organization in question broadens in scope, effective functional integration becomes more difficult to achieve.* Specifically, we quickly run up against *analytical limitations*, which limit the extent to which we can cojoin all the various units of an enterprise into a working, integrated whole. Rather, as an organization tends to increase in size, decision functions tend to become more and more decentralized. This does not alter the fact that control over a large block of resources is effectively concentrated in the organization as a whole; it simply means that the decisions regarding the allocation of those resources may be decentralized *within* the organization, subject to any general constraints the senior organizational authorities might impose. The situation then is this: resources in the economic system tend to become concentrated into large blocks, but the actual uses of these blocks may be determined by a large number of essentially isolated allocation decisions. To the extent that allocation decisions tend to become decentralized within any organization, the expected loss associated with program redundancy and competitiveness increases, as does the opportunity loss associated with the failure to achieve whatever level of synergy might be available. When this occurs, we are left with only the disadvantages of centralization of economic power—the probability of institutionalized inefficiencies resulting from the consistency with which large organizations exceed optimal scale of plant.

There are, of course, some usually rhetorical arguments for decentralization. For example, it is suggested that individuals on the spot are better able to assess local opportunities than someone far away in a corporate headquarters; there are also the arguments against bureaucratic structure and hierarchical control that have become popular in certain social-science circles.[12] Yet we suspect that the actual degree of decentralization of decision authority within an organization is determined less by any policy or rhetorical considerations than by the very real analytical constraints that impose themselves. Simply, as the scope of a decision-maker's authority increases (as the number of units for which he is responsible expands), the probability that he will make rational, accurate decisions about the properties of those programs decreases. We can readily see why. The rational allocation of resources or the conjuncture of many different units into an integrated whole implies the existence of a "model" of the units as they interrelate and mutually affect each other; as the number of units to be entered in the model increases, the expected accuracy of that model will generally decrease. Therefore, we have the constant and troublesome trade-off between decision *scope* and *rectitude*. Simply, because of inherent limits on our ana-

*The limited qualification to this assertion may be that larger organizations have more effective demand for new computer and other coordinative technology, but analytical limitations may constrain its proper employment.

lytical technology, the quality of models may usually be expected to diminish as their elaborateness and size increases. That is, following our discussions in Section 4.4, the models will tend to become less reflective, less exhaustive, less elegant, and less actionable.

Now, the field of systems analysis has been developed in order to devise a technology for dealing with large-scale problems as an integrated whole. General system theory, in particular, has pretentions of being able to bring discipline to inherently complex, protean issues.[13] But the difficulty with the general trends in systems analysis and system theory is the same as with general administrative science. The models that are developed are either largely rhetorical and lacking in mathematical capability or precision, or they are mathematical in nature, with pretentions to quantitative discipline, but very restricted in their assumptions. Thus, for example, the most popular of the large-scale system models (those of Forrester, Meadows, Randers, et al.) are efficient only when the system can be allegorized in terms of first-order feedback functions and sets of difference equations.[14] Even the promise of the massive cybernetic management and control systems that are sometimes posed as the panacea for complexity diminishes rapidly in utility as the relationship between organizational effectiveness and the need for innovation (the demand for unprecedented responses) becomes stronger.[15] So, there are strong but subtle limits to an administrator's ability to borrow, out of hand, an existing generalized process model to guide his managerial responsibilities. And the point we will make in the final section relates directly to this quandary: rational decision-making in a complex organization cannot be obtained simply through analytical innovations; rather, basic shifts in managerial and organizational strategy are definite prerequisites.

For the moment, we may merely elaborate on the apparent competitiveness between decision scope and rectitude, and on the matter of *effective decision authority*. Here is where we are caught: we want to take advantage of the effectiveness that is associated with truly integrated operations as opposed to loosely articulated agglomerates, but analytical constraints may limit our ability to effect meaningful integration. Thus, the prerequisite for a functionally (as opposed to a fiscally) integrated system is an effective decision-maker at some nodal position; what makes him effective is the level of analytical sophistication he brings to his coordinative functions. Where such capability is missing, the various nodal positions that appear on any organization chart simply imply a reporting arrangement or titular (after the fact) authority. For example, at the federal level, the office of the president is responsible for an enormous number of programs. (Responsibility here implies control, not over the individual programs, but over their interfaces, i.e., their collective character.) Yet, despite the existence of the president as a nodal authority, the real level of integration of federal programs is stunningly low. To take one example, the U.S. Energy Research & Development Administration and the U.S. Environmental Protection

Agency exist under the same organizational umbrella. Yet, to a great extent, they pursue directly competitive ends, so that some functions performed by ERDA act to the detriment of the functions of the EPA. Thus, at least some portion of the resources devoted to these two agencies is ineffective. To this extent, the aggregate productivity of resources devoted to the federal government function is reduced, due to the competitiveness between these programs.

We may multiply this instance of competitive programs operating under a single organizational framework many times, and the waste of resources may rise to staggering levels. For example, there are programs to subsidize farmers for not growing certain crops in the same agency where research is being conducted into how to improve the yields of those crops; one program thus discourages crop expansion, while another encourages it. In many urban areas, there is a constant and debilitating competition between the local police authorities and the welfare (or human resource) programs, with the latter often frustrating police efforts to contain and convict criminals. At the state level, there are often programs to build highways, while resources are devoted to another agency whose express mission is to discourage private transportation. Instances of cross-competitiveness are very widely distributed in the public sector.

At any rate, there are really only two ways to resolve competitive interfaces among programs in an organization. The first demands considerable analytical sophistication. For example, given the conflict in objectives between ERDA and the EPA, a skilled analyst will be capable of finding a trade-off that effects a synergistic relationship between the two components. That such a synergistic balance can exist is obvious, for energy conservation implies environmental integrity. Yet, for the most part, ERDA seems to have interpreted its mission in ways that are contradictory—indeed, anathema—to environmental interests. For example, it has advocated cutting back on antipollution requirements for automobiles, as well as burning high-sulfur-content coal; it has had kind words to say about such destructive technologies as strip-mining. Such policies or strategies do not, of course, represent a formal or rational trade-off; rather, they are effected by one set of *a priori* references subordinating some other set through the offices of casual bureaucratic conflict. Thus, the prerequisite for calculated, considered trade-off solutions is significant analytical sophistication. When this is absent, we will find either blanket subordination or, more frequently perhaps, political compromise.

When competitive programs are looked at through the political lens, a very interesting transformation often takes place. Competitiveness ceases to be a problem *per se* and becomes instead an irreconcilable conflict of interests. For example, the conflict between energy and environmental interests is often described as an *ideological issue*.* This is followed by the popular presumption

*See the appendix to this chapter, *Ideologics.*

that ideological issues are irresolvable, and thus do not present an opportunity for solution. Rather, they are treated as inescapable symptoms of a democratic government or a free system. The practical response is to simply let the environmental and energy interests fight it out among themselves, rather than attempt to impose a solution as such. Thus, both agencies are funded and left to dilute each other's effectiveness, and the decision authorities feel neither remorse nor embarrassment at this diseconomic situation. But when we have only rhetorical decision-makers at the nodal positions, the political approach may not simply be the preferred treatment, but the only recognizable alternative. The analytically skilled administrator, on the other hand, recognizes that value-issues or ideological conflicts *are* capable of scientific resolution. But the technology appropriate to the resolution of such issues is not widely distributed. Basically, we would have to formulate a *syncretic* solution, which seeks to find a point of mutual interest among two competitive interests *by raising the issue to the next higher level of abstraction.* This implies being able to isolate the "background" assumptions held by the disputants, and then displacing their perspectives toward *substantive* as opposed to ideological issues.[16] And when substance begins to displace subjectivity, the various trade-off alternatives become apparent, as do the points where two rhetorically opposed interests may find common ground. But where the skills required to generate syncretic solutions are not available, competitive programs may not only continue to be funded and supported, but may often be pointed to with pride (e.g., the democratic government has something for everybody).

In general, then, when decision authorities lack essential analytical skills, having several programs under a single authority does not guarantee coherence and integration; the unskilled nodal administrator simply becomes a reporting agent, and the several programs might just as well belong to different organizations altogether. And the result, again, is simply a situation where the various operating units tend to be related only additively (and where it is possible that, given the potential for competition, some units may be related *subtractively*).

To make these points somewhat clearer, we can revisit a generic problem with which we have some familiarity, that is, making optimal resource allocations. The objective sought was, recall, the association of an effectively *zero opportunity cost* with the entire schedule of allocations (and therefore with the aggregate investment decision). Given the zero-opportunity-cost objective, it is possible to simultaneously maximize both organizational effectiveness and efficiency. Again, zero opportunity cost means that there is no better investment we might make with a specific resource block, given whatever return criteria might be in force. The aggregate rate of return on investment (AROI) refers to the overall productivity of *all* resources invested over a period by any organization, with the specific rate of return (SROI) referring to the productivity of any single investment measured in isolation. But from what we have just said, AROI cannot be considered merely the sum of the SROI's. Rather, we compute:

$$\text{AROI} = \sum_{}^{n} \text{SROI}_i - (C_{i,j} + R_{i,j})$$

The $C_{i,j}$'s would here indicate any competitive detractions among any pair of programs (for all interactive pairs), while the $R_{i,j}$'s serve as the repositories for any redundancies among all interactive programs. Thus, we must be able to compute the *cross-impact* conditions among all programs in a set. This, obviously, is the major technique available to us for guarding against suboptimal allocations, and for developing functional relationships among programs that optimize (expectedly) overall rate of return. In Section 3.3, where we discussed allocative decision mechanisms for the service organization, we showed essentially how these cross-impact calculations may be made.

The general requirement is an organizational model. Efforts have long been afoot to treat organizations as wholes, subject to the difficulties we earlier suggested with the operational aspects of system analysis. As a rule, these models are used to simulate the effects of various allocation strategies we might elect, and to account (endogenously) for possible redundancies or competitive relationships. But the development and use of such models is an expensive proposition, and becomes rapidly more expensive as the organization itself becomes more complex (e.g., as the number of processes to be allegorized increases, as the number of possible interface conditions expands, as constraints become nonlinear, as the interface between the organization and the environment becomes less selective or stable). Therefore, in Section 4.1, we suggested that we attempt to eliminate competitive relationships or redundancies at the logical or *qualitative* analysis level, at the initiation of any budgeting process. For example, we tried to anticipate the problem of competitiveness by developing major missions for the organization that were mutually supportive, positively correlated. Admittedly, these criteria would cast aspersions on organizations that are strictly fiscal artifices (e.g., many conglomerates, where only cash flow as opposed to functional integration is considered as a criterion for enveloping a new unit). The diversified firm, especially the horizontally enjoined enterprise, may also be inviable under this criterion, simply because horizontal extension is often undertaken in an effort to protect some eroding corporate base, which merely dilutes the productivity of the new acquisitions (usually by forcing the new units to pay for the profligacy of the old). Vertical integration is seldom "integration" in the sense that we have described. Rather, it may often be employed merely to frustrate if not outright transgress the principles of theoretical capitalism; it often further concentrates economic power and obscures inherent inefficiencies.

For example, take the matter of an integrated oil company. It might have a crude-oil extraction operation, and transportation, refining, and marketing functions. Now, it is unlikely that the same level of skilled expertise will be given to each of these functionally isolated ares. Rather, headquarters personnel may be able to pass on inefficiencies at any of the levels to the ultimate consumer—the target of the marketing function. Moreover, except perhaps for the internal accounting records of the organization, the comparative profit advantage of these separate entities will be largely obscured in the integrated fiscal reports. Thus, great efficiencies in the marketing function may offset relative ineffficiencies at the transportation or refining or extraction level. However, the issue of the absolute desirability of vertically integrated complexes may be resolved more easily in terms we have already discussed. Specifically, there is the significant probability that the organization as a whole has exceeded the optimal scale of plant and therefore has introduced institutional diseconomies. The *axiomatic* rationale is that the conjuncture of essentially separate functions, related sequentially under a single organizational envelope, *always implies the existence of a new level of administration that would not exist were the several units all isolated.* In short, all conglomerated and diversified enterprises automatically affect one of the systems of postoptimal size that we suggested earlier: all add administrative costs and functions that would not exist were the fiscal artifice not in effect.

Now, for the cruder forms of conglomeration (especially those that were popular in the 1960s), the relationship between the functional units becomes, again, effectively additive. For the more ill-conceived, vertically integrated firms, lower-level units simply provide inputs into the next higher-level function, under a strict and often unilaterally restrictive hierarchical configuration. Thus, in both the crude conglomerate and the hierarchical integrated firm, there is *no cross-impact to consider*, and therefore no opportunity for injecting synergistic relationships (which make the whole something more than the sum of its parts). The same thing is true, in a slightly different way, with horizontally integrated structures or conglomerates. Again, the conglomerate management—or the headquarters group of a diversified firm—simply represents an additional level of management, and therefore a source of expense that would not exist were the units separated fiscally (as they are indeed separated functionally). The addition of incremental management and overhead functions (e.g., a legal staff to review antitrust matters, a communication facility to enjoin the separated units) detracts from the rates of return that the individual entities might secure were they not forced to absorb the additional costs of fiscal integration.

But the defense of the conglomerate is really easier to undertake than the defense of the diversified (horizontally integrated) or vertically integrated enterprise. Diversification, as suggested, is often undertaken merely to protect an increasingly inefficient and inviable base function, and vertical integration simply implies a linear linking. But a conglomerate may often benefit the economic system as a whole, under a very specific restriction, that is, when the management of the conglomerate is able to reduce the administrative expenses of the units that they absorb, or otherwise increase productivity. Such instances may be rare, but they do occur (a good example is the Loews Corporation).[17] But the axiomatic consideration remains: once the individual unit's management has been improved, then the economy pays an opportunity cost for the additional expenses implied by the existence of the conglomerate's management. And, given the functional isolation of the units that comprise the usual conglomerate or the diversified enterprise, the centralized decision authority usually cannot expect to pay for itself by eliminating redundancies, dampening competitivity, or injecting synergy. Unless the functions of the enterprise are distinctly correlated and interactive, then the promised productivity of a nodal decision authority is obviated. Therefore, for the normal organization, the concentration on a limited set of functions (missions) that are clearly correlated is expectedly more beneficial to the economic system as a whole than to the development of enterprises that are integrated only at the fiscal level. For all such organizations, it is generally much less expensive to preempt competitive relations among programs at the qualitative-analysis level than to try to do so through the offices of a simulation analysis. When basic missions are properly defined, as we tried to show with our example of the educational system in Chapter 3, the qualitative relationships between the several functions all have the potential to be positively correlated, with the skill of the decision-makers determining the extent to which this potential will be realized in practice.

As for redundancy, we earlier suggested (within our idealized program budgeting model of Section 4.1) that all program proposals submitted to the allocative authorities be *organizationally independent*. That is, the programs should not be identified with any particular operating unit—any department or division, etc. —but rather only with one or another of the missions that the organization has elected to support (e.g., one or another of the strategic functions). This means that we can hope to largely eliminate redundancies before they become institutionalized. In short, we always want to be sure that *function takes precedent over* organizational structure (a point we will elaborate in the next section). When we make program proposals independent of existing organizational units, then we have the option to constantly readjust the structure of the organization to best fit emerging functional emphases, and we are unlikely to wind up with a large number of individual units all treating parts of the same problem, but located in different areas (and all jealous of their own prerogatives). This, of course, is precisely the situation that has drawn so much fire to the federal bureacracy.

Of course, in actual practice, the resource-allocation decision is always subject to determination from another direction, that of *transaction costs*. But this does not so much affect the commercial or industrial sector as it does the public domain. Transaction costs are those associated with actually allocating and disbursing funds. And, as the federal government may in some respects be looked at as a mechanism for resource redistribution, transaction costs are of great significance. Obviously, transaction costs are reduced to the extent that we do not conduct any analysis of the type suggested in these pages, and to the extent that we make a few, large allocations as opposed to many, smaller allocations. An extension of these arguments leads us to a defense for general revenue-sharing (although rhetorical arguments—e.g., regarding states' rights—must also be considered). General revenue-sharing, as a disbursement and allocation mechanism, must be compared with the categorical programs that control the major share of federal resources. Such programs specify the conditions for which funds are to be used, and therefore operate to impose catholic effectiveness criteria on local users. This requires layers of bureaucrats in Washington to evaluate requests for categorical funds, audit the propriety of their expenditure, and perform other functions that generally impose significant transaction costs. But the categorical funding mechanism does suggest the potential for centralized, nodal allocative decisions, which we have been applauding. To this extent, the additional transaction costs associated with centralized allocation decisions may be more than offset by savings in the elimination of redundancy and competitiveness, and in the synergistic effects of developing categorical programs that exert a positive (reinforcing) leverage on one another. In practice, however, there is no central control over categorical programs, and thus no effective mechanism for offsetting the additional administrative costs. (In short, the federal categorical budgeting complex is very similar to the conglomerate or the other fiscal artifices we find in the private sector). As such, we pay a premium for the categorical system, a premium that makes itself felt in the dilution of resources that actually reach the local level and are put to work. And redundancy and competitiveness are rife, which further dilutes the aggregate productivity of federal investments at the point of employment.*

The lack of an effective nodal decision authority thus makes itself felt in many ways, and the entire categorical budgeting system is eloquent testimony to the process by which analytical expediency is translated into very real, tangible dysfunctions. The allocative authorities may simply act as a conduit for funds (lacking the fiduciary mandate that attaches itself to a properly constituted finance committee of the type present in some private corporations). When this is the case, the "inertial" budgeting technology dominates, where across-the-

*For more on this, see the first chapter of the author's *Managing Social Service Systems* (New York: Petrocelli Books, Inc., 1977).

board increases or decreases in allocations are made in response to changes in the aggregate resource base. No attempt is made to spread reductions in allocations so that the effectiveness of the organization is diluted minimally; nor are incremental increases allocated according to utility valuations. Rather, if the budget increases 10 percent, so do the individual allocations. New programs may tend to be evaluated with respect to rhetorical or political criteria, so that the array of programs supported emerges as an *ad hoc*, ill-articulated collection of isolated functions. The tendency is also to make budget allocations sequentially, neglecting cross-impacts entirely, with a premium given to the aggressive, self-interested program manager. Moreover, the probable level of next period's funding may be related to the rapidity with which this period's allocations were expended, with effectiveness criteria subordinate to any of a number of contextual determinants of the type previously mentioned.

Of course, this sequence of unpalatable practices is perhaps a bit overstated, yet the categorical budgeting process is very widespread, despite much lip service given by the public sector to such techniques as zero-base budgeting. And it leads to some interesting ancillary practices. Once funds have been allocated to a program through the categorical process, they automatically become fixed with a zero-opportunity cost. Being restricted to a specific function, they are unavailable for distribution to other areas. And when no alternative uses exist, the designated area of use becomes an artifically optimal investment from the standpoint of those in local control of the resources. The local user might not be applauded for trying to return unused budget or for attempting to transfer them to a unit that he thinks has better use for them, because no mechanism exists, as a rule, for making intraperiod reallocations.

This tends to lead to a categorical "sink," a place where funds simply disappear. For example, suppose that we operate a local agency that depends entirely on categorical funds. Suppose that our mission, in response to the national emphasis, is to fight alcoholism among American Indians between the ages of 15 and 19. Now, we apply for funding based on our estimate of the client population to be served (e.g., categorical funds are often distributed on a *per capita* basis, as with the formula-budgeting system described in Chapter 3 for the prototypical university). In the meantime, the categorical granting agency in Washington, D.C., accumulates all the requests and prepares a block budget. Resources are then earmarked for this agency—put into federal "escrow," as it were. Now, given the level of analytical capabilities that may exist in small local agencies, there is very little likelihood of their forecasts being accurate; as a rule, they will tend to err on the "up side," by overstating demand. Therefore, the categorical funds placed in escrow are very likely to be underspent. But the rule is that an agency is to fully spend its funds by the end of the fiscal period. And given the constraint of transaction costs, the agency director might try to find some large allocations it can make. One of the best alternatives is to inaugurate a study, and allocate a large budget to an external consultant. Or, the agency may launch an advertising program to create a demand for its service. In either case, the expected productivity of these desperation allocations is likely to be of little concern. But it is also possible that an agency may be restricted from hiring consultants or mounting advertising campaigns. In this case, the unallocated surplus simply disappears. It is in escrow, probably not earning any interest, and remains there (perhaps automatically being transferred back to some general account at the end of the fiscal year). However, because the budgeting period begins far in advance of the close of the last fiscal year, the surplus is not known to the allocation authorities. And given the preference for inertial budgeting procedures, the agency receives a new budget that may actually exceed the old one, part of which went down the fiscal drain, as it were. But the new aggregate budget requirements, based on the aggregated "escrow" commitments, are summed by the budgeting authority and reported as part of the overall federal budget. To the extent that it is a deficit budget, this accelerates inflation and works its way through the broader economic system, even though an accumulated surplus may exist from funds unspent by categorical programs in prior periods. This becomes known to the general public only when the government announces that it has underspent its allocations, and this news is generally delivered very quietly indeed.

This entire categorical budgeting process is a tribute to political "entrepreneurism," which yields most of the detriments and few of the advantages of entrepreneurial operations in the private sector. For when practiced in the public domain, it merely adds more special, categorical programs to an already inflated, unmanageable list of social investments. As the list of programs expands, the ability to adequately discipline aggregate allocations—the probability of being able to operate in the neighborhood of an optimal AROI—declines accordingly. There is thus some legitimacy to the claim that the categorical budgeting process is the best we can do, given the complexity of the allocative decisions facing governmental units and large commercial enterprises. In short, the categorical budgeting process is a direct response to the constancy of the trade-off between decision scope and decision rectitude, which we proposed earlier. For, as we increase the number of different programs to be evaluated for cross-impact and optimized as a set, the interactive evaluations to be made would tend to increase as the permutation of the programs; computation time and would increase logarithmically with the number of entities to be considered simultaneously. Moreover, simple (deterministic) simulation exercises are usually inadequate to evaluate cross-impact, as the direction of influence among programs may often be dependent upon magnitudinal factors that remain undetermined at the point of modeling. Therefore, we are often driven to use very expensive and sophisticated stochastic-state simulation techniques, often beyond the reach of all but very large organizations. But this is as it should be. For larger organizations usually imply greater complexity, but also relatively higher resource bases; and it is only proper that the cost of making effectively optimal allocation decisions should reflect the absolute size of the allocations to be made. As the complexity of the organization increases, however, the model-building task becomes more complex, so that the decision premises used to discipline allocation decisions owe more and more of their substance to judgmental or subjective factors. And this, as we have seen, ultimates in a reduction of the expected accuracy (rectitude) of the resultant decisions.

But our purpose here is to seek a way to soften the relationship between decision scope and rectitude, a way of taking advantage of centralized decision systems without having to pay an enormous price in terms of expected value of error. And we still have a mission left over from an earlier section: the development of some strategies for easing the relationship between the demand for innovation and the expected value of decision error. Thus, the trade-off between decision scope and rectitude—and the trade-off between innovation and risk—become primary targets for the decision sciences. And we really already have some weapons at our disposal, particularly in the form of the precepts about analytical congruence and the other principles of decision discipline. However, the troublesome level of error, which seems doomed to appear whenever we try to manage a complex enterprise or try to centralize decision operations, cannot be reduced solely by analytical innovations. Rather, there must be fundamental changes in the basic strategy of management and the procedures of administrative problem-solving, changes that become more important as the organization in question becomes more complex, and as the environment in which it is forced (or has elected) to operate becomes more protean and unstable.

As we enter the final section of this volume, we are still concerned with complex enterprise. But this time we are asking that the innovations of analytical significance posed by the decision scientist be complemented by some very fundamental structural and processual innovations.

5.4 OPERATIONALIZING OPTIMALITY

The constancy of the trade-off between decision scope and decision rectitude is the most cogent argument I know against gigantism in the economic sector, and in the political as well. For the effective limitations of available analytical technology—and perhaps intellectual limitations as well—quickly set in to reduce the probability of approaching optimality as a system or organization increases in size, and/or as the environment in which it operates becomes more complex. The mathematical models that we can develop these days do not well comprehend the realities of complex situations, and their pretentions about directing even adequately optimal decisions are largely just that—pretentions. It is perhaps a sign of the general misconception about scientific potential that Nobel prizes have been awarded to economists whose models, econometric or otherwise, lack real significance; they are largely parochial (accommodating only economic parameters) and are sadly limited in the level of complexity they can resolve.* No individual firm—and certainly no broad-based economic system— could put them directly to work without courting considerable probability of analytical error, and hence dysfunction.

It thus appears that the critical constraints on the size to which individual organizations would be permitted to grow (under rational criteria) are the analytical sophistication of the nodal decision-makers, and the resolution power of the instruments of system analysis that science can make available. As things now stand, we believe these are very tangible and confining constraints indeed. But they will relax as more and more administrators become subject to a broader, more balanced education, and as science gradually raises its sights from the preoccupation with deterministic and projective tools (and its fascination with neat but trivial algorithms). And as these events occur, the size of the systems we will be able to rationally manage will also increase.

Yet the inability to effectively administer large-scale systems has not prevented their emergence, nor has the increasingly potent correlation between concentration and cataclysm. So we have no choice here but to attempt to show how we can bring all available discipline to the management of such systems, and exhaust the potential for effective optimality (given current analytical constraints). We know that neither the rhetorical decision-maker nor the traditional management scientist (facile mainly with only the lower-order instruments of decision analysis) can bring proper scientific discipline to the entire range of problems that emerge within a complex enterprise. But here's the rub: effective employment of the more sophisticated analytical techniques (the contingency and heuristic instruments, and even the Bayesian or dynamic-adaptive programming technologies) all presume a certain context of operation. For the most part, the normal organization as it is currently constituted does not provide the required environment. Therefore, before the range of sophisticated analytical techniques and algorithms can be put to work, certain alterations must be made in the structure and managerial procedures of the normal organization. In part, the nature of these changes is dictated by the kinds of argument raised in the previous section (especially with regard to the dysfunctional aspects of the categorical budgeting process and decentralized decision systems). The managerial strategies and organizational configurations adopted by many organiza-

---

*Although one may think more kindly of technical artifices such as linear programming and input-output analysis, which are at least innocent of any substantive pretensions.

tions, especially larger enterprises, frustrate our ambitions for rationality. Indeed, many organizational and procedural attributes are merely responses to the general disrepute into which optimality has fallen—a response to the rise of adequacy, sufficiency, or "satisficing" as a legitimate organizational objective. For example, the entire concept of categorical budgeting—or of the planning and budgeting systems that set targets far in advance of a situation and then impose rigid performance criteria—are contraoptimal. They simply do not reflect the speed with which opportunities emerge and disappear and reshape themselves in a complex environment. Periodic reviews (quarterly, annually, etc.) thus always cause the organization to lag behind reality. The general tendency to make decision exercises one-shot affairs—to commit and then simply sit back and steel oneself for the consequences—is completely contrary to the caution and humility that complex organizations and protean environments so richly deserve.

But there are several other areas where fundamental institutional changes are required if even a limited degree of optimality is to be achieved. Yet, they all represent something of a compromise, as we have not yet reached the point where we can deal with complex problems as unreduced wholes, or with organizations as "organic" entities (completely interrelated and integrated). Therefore, the strategic dictates that follow tend to become more important as the organization becomes more complex and massive, and more significant in its milieu. For each institutional innovation we recommend, however, the organization must be prepared to pay a price. But as decision contexts become more precarious—more susceptible to serious errors—the price begins to pale beside the advantages these dictates promise. In introducing these structural and procedural innovations, we may be very brief, for they are really just extensions of points we have already made.

(1) Delay all irrevocable commitment of resources and/or action until the last possible moment, subject to the rational constraints we suggested earlier (e.g., until the learning curve begins to turn unfavorable or until the information-production function becomes diseconomic). In short, we want the organization facing a complex decision problem to *make maximum use of* a posteriori *information*, and to employ gradualized, sequential decision schemes wherever probability of error is significantly high. Recall that delaying commitment implies an extension of the key analytical interval $(t_0 - t_e)$, with the consequent reduction in expected value of error associated with that extension (and with the informational transformations that occur when *a priori* assumptions are made subject to empirical validation).

(2) To lend substance and feasibility to (1), the complex organization must gradually reduce its reliance on periodic planning, budgeting, and review

schemes—with goals, strategic objectives, and tactical targets fixed over some significant interval—and *turn instead to a real-time, feedback-based decision technology.* This would enable the organization to make maximum use of emerging *a posteriori* information, and turn its gradualized decision exercises into a context-responsive sequence of most promising directions. Thus, the real-time scheme enables the organization to make maximum use of Bayesian decision logic, and improves the probability of obtaining effectively optimal performance levels (as objectives set yesterday, in a protean, rapidly changing milieu, are almost certain to be suboptimal today). In virtually all cases, an approach to optimality requires a "learning" process, and real-time learning is generally more favorable than those cases where we wait several months or even a year to recognize our mistakes, adjust trajectories, or so on.

(3) Given the gradualized, adaptive decision scheme and the real-time decision process, it becomes essential to *introduce the method audit* process for evaluating decision performance. This shifts emphasis away from results of decisions, which may reside far out in the future or be obscured in a protean environment, and concentrates instead on emerging rationality. Again, before a decision has ultimated, the only meaningful basis for control that we have is the rate of change (and direction of change) in expected value of decision error, perhaps coupled with careful attention to the "propriety" of the decision-makers. And the method-audit scheme, recall, was focused primarily on the expected value of decision error, and thus may also operate in real-time.

(4) As a structural complement to the procedural points just mentioned, there should be a deliberate attempt to *make organizational structure constantly responsive to changes in the functional posture* of the enterprise, whether private or public. One referent in this regard is the "adhocratic" system advocated by Alvin Toffler, or the many contrabureaucratic configurations that are being advanced by organization theorists.[18] In short, we want to inject considerable plasticity into the basic pattern of departmental or divisional relations, and into their resource-holding prerogatives.

(5) Every effort should be made to populate the now largely empty, analytical midrange between the rhetorician and the technical manager or administrator, possibly by inaugurating the kind of complementary educational scheme we suggested in Chapter 1. This would tend to *diminish the largely artificial discontinuity of preparation and perspective between lower- and higher-order decision-makers.* Moreover, it would permit us to relax the disruptive and often dysfunctional barriers between decision-makers and decision analysts, and therefore argue against a continuation of line and staff distinctions. Moreover, it would help introduce a much-needed mutuality of exchange between strategic and tactical decision-

makers, and thus act against the traditional hierarchicality of decision authority where authority runs unilaterally downward through the normal organization). Finally, it would tend to reflect that our assignment of certain types of problems to certain levels of organization (e.g., the association of managers *per se* with moderately stochastic problems and of executives with severely stochastic problems) is largely an academic artifice. For, in some organizations, strategic and tactical issues are distributed without regard to level of organization; thus, balanced education of administrators would help us where our ideal-type assignments might not hold.

(6) Finally, as an organization becomes more and more dependent upon innovation in the face of a complex, competitive environment, *there is an advantage to introducing modularity in the decision-making process*. The rationality for this suggestion is simple: in a very complex world, where both the probability of error and cost of error are consistently and inescapably high, organizational effectiveness may become more and more isolated from organizational efficiency. That is, within some range, effectiveness and efficiency tend to become competitive ends. Now, efficiency is always served to the extent that we develop a highly integrated, completely interdependent system (for this allows us to take advantage of whatever synergy is available among organizational components). But modularity (deliberately isolating certain components of the organization from others) may serve the cause of effectiveness in several ways. First, it will permit the organization to operate in a complex field via a process of disciplined, controlled experimentation. Second, it will allow us to buffer the effects of errors in any locale, preventing or dampening its transmittal to the organization as a whole. Third, modularity allows us to make rapid structural changes in one component of the organization without having to disrupt the structure of the entire organization; structural "plasticity" may then be isolated to those particular areas where it is most necessary. This simply reflects that not all areas in any complex organization will be equally precarious, or equally susceptible to error and dysfunction; rather, the organization will tend to have certain "leading edges" that push furthest into uncharted, unprecedented decision territory. Finally, we should note (and we will make this even clearer in a short while) that modularity is not the same thing as decentralization. Rather, modularity is an analytical artifice, but one with considerable implications for complex organizations.

All these propositions simply give operational significance to a central suggestion we made many pages ago, that the decision-making functions in a complex organization should all be set in a *disciplined learning context*. There are two reasons for this. First, it is only through the development of a learning context that we can generate the *decision inventory* with its potential for increasing the instance of directly analytic or analogic solutions to precedented decision problems. To the extent that this decision inventory is well-developed, the organization need not wake up in a new world every morning, and may inject considerable economies into its administrative operations. But these six policy dictates also offer us the key we need to reduce the expected error associated with complex unprecedented problems. For they permit us to attack initially intractable decision issues through the medium of *action research*. This scheme fits itself well into the workaday world of complex enterprise, for it recognizes that decisions must be made, even in the face of considerable uncertainty or risk. But it also gives credence to the fact that, for particularly complex problems, we should stretch out the information-generation and analytical processes as long as possible, in order to effectively minimize peril. Finally, it reflects a critical proposition: the only way to learn more about complex decision contexts is to make commitments, but in such a way that outcomes can be controlled or contained if they are unfavorable.[19] Thus, the six propositions just advanced reflect the dualistic nature of the demands facing the complex organization: *the complex organization must both act and learn!* The essential strategy behind the action-research approach to decision-making is simply to make sure that the actions we do take contribute to our learning, and that commitments are both tentative and revocable to the extent that circumstances permit.

But what of the price that action-research and the six policy dictates exact? Initially, decision-makers are going to have to yield some of the security and comfort—or at least the placid intervals—that accompany situations where goals, objectives, and targets are fixed over some significant interval. They must also become more reflective and less reactive, and learn to tolerate the intellectual demands of analysis. In effect, they will have to shift their basic emphasis, becoming more concerned with the avoidance of error and less concerned with "taking action" and letting things run their course. But the pursuit of decision rectitude demands great concentration, and is frankly rather dull compared to the wheeling-and-dealing, Wyatt Earp school of management in which so many of us were brought up. Moreover, administrators will have to refocus the basic loyalties to which they respond, becoming less closely associated with any particular structural component of the organization, and more associated with missions or projects—with broad functional referents. In addition to these sociobehavioral exactions, there is the economic price: generally, real-time decision-analysis and control activities will be more expensive to implement than periodic systems. And the fundamental prerequisite for action-research decision processes is the existence of skilled personnel and the consequent expenditure of analytical resources. In short, if our action-research decision activities focus on the range of allocation decisions an organization must make—throughout all levels of the organization—then we must expect that the *transaction costs* associated with the disciplined allocations will increase beyond those required for the operation of some simple categorical budgeting scheme (or even with more advanced program or zero-based budgeting processes). But, again, as the organization increases in significance and size, these additional transaction costs may be more than offset by the consequent reduction of the cost of misallocations (decision errors). At any rate, the decision as to whether to implement the scheme we have outlined—or any part of it—is necessarily a matter of local conditions and context-specific calculations.

But, as the fundamental viability or effectiveness of the organization becomes more and more dependent on a degree of functional innovation, the inherent risk of decisions increases. As such, the up-side optimality criteria (e.g., maximizing profits) become less important than down-side criteria, (e.g., minimizing expected loss). And the action-research modality promises to minimize the expected loss due to decision error, *given the necessity for innovation*. Again, we are facing a trade-off. The best way to avoid expected loss is perhaps to avoid innovation, but this increases the probability of incurring significant opportunity costs. When a sufficient number of opportunities have been foregone in an effort to repudiate risk, opportunity costs quickly become translated into real losses. Beyond a certain point, the failure to heed the demand for innovation and the unwillingness to tolerate risk is as sure a route to organizational dissolution as is undisciplined innovation (hysterical action in the face of unnecessarily high risk).

Such comments are probably gratuitous, for by now every reader must realize the necessity for action with caution. Yet it gives us the basis we need to suggest just what procedures are involved in an action-research decision approach. Its properties will certainly reflect virtually all of the normative propositions we have advanced, and will also allow us to bring together the analytical and operational aspects of decision-making. Therefore, the action-research paradigm is appropriately the last conceptual construct we will build in these pages. It is summarized in the Figure 5.21.

Initially, the requirement for a decision derives either from the goal-setting process or perhaps naturally from the environment in which the organization is resident. The normative first step is to employ our heuristic procedures to establish the initial, tentative properties of the problem, to generate what we have referred to as the *real* state. Fundamentally, this would give us an initial boundary on the problem by establishing an array of state variables, setting a decision goal, and thus restricting the context in which subsequent decision tasks will operate. Given this context, the strategists will go through the kind of qualitative analysis procedures outlined in earlier chapters to produce a most logically probable strategic alternative, which is *a priori* expected to be effective in meeting the decision goal. From the decision-analysis perspective, the strategic

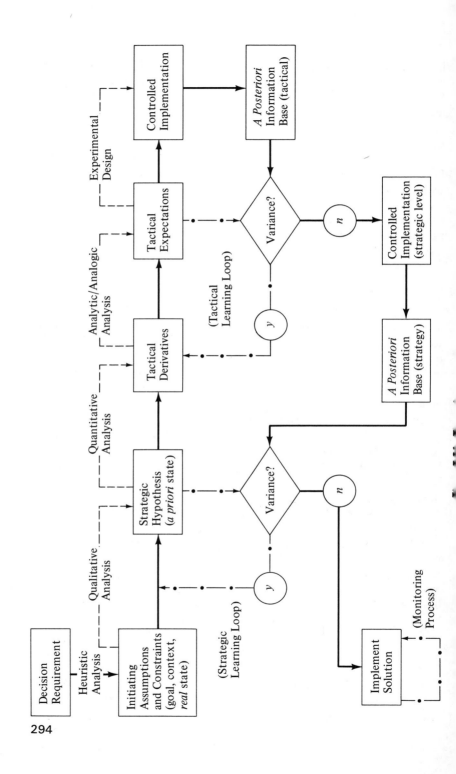

294

analysts will have developed a relational configuration for the problem (as described in Table 5.1), selecting a specific strategic alternative on the basis of a utility analysis of the type described in Section 3.3. In the action-research paradigm, this strategem becomes a *hypothetico-deductive* construct, which must be subjected subsequently to empirical validation. Yet, given the requirement for *actionability* in the decision-analysis processes, the strategists had to put forward a single alternative for the tactical analysts to work with.

Now, given any single stratagem (irrespective of its probable rectitude at this point), several distinct tactical derivatives may emerge for consideration. For illustrative purposes, let us suppose that we are a commercial organization whose directors have posed the problem of increasing market share to some specific point, within some specific interval, without decreasing the aggregate profit rate for the organization. Our strategic analysts might then have set about evaluating the various strategic alternatives (e.g., product innovation, differential advertising, preemption of competition). Let us suppose, however, that they arrived at the following strategic hypothesis as the expectedly most favorable action-alternative: share of market will be expectedly most responsive to a decrease in the price of our product relative to competitors' prices and, given that profit rates are not eroded, this would best be accomplished by increasing productivity. That is, given the state-variable and relational specifications the goal-setters and strategists developed, this particular strategy emerged with the highest expected utility (predicated most likely on qualitative analysis, and therefore having a significant subjective substance).

At this point, the problem is properly passed off to the tactical domain. Let us suppose that the tacticians developed several tactical alternatives associated with the strategic objective—e.g., productivity could be increased by eliminating the least efficient employees, introducing new capital equipment, introducing a motivational scheme such as job enrichment. But, let us suppose that only two tactical alternatives emerged with significant probabilities of proving efficient: (a) increasing the capital-labor ratio, and (b) inaugurating a piecework incentive remuneration scheme, so that employees are differentially rewarded for differential performances. Now, these two tactical derivatives would presumably have been selected on the basis of quantitative (or substantially so) calculations about the expected increase in productivity associated with each. In overview, what we might have is:

Strategic hypothesis: Market share = f (productivity)

Tactical derivatives: Productivity $(P) = g_1$ (capital-labor ratio)

g_2 (incentive scheme)

$$\text{E.V.} (P \mid g_1) = v_1$$
$$\text{E.V.} (P \mid g_2) = v_2$$

The two tactical alternatives have differential coefficients with respect to productivity (g_1 and g_2, respectively). Now, were one coefficient significantly greater than the other, we might proceed directly with that particular tactic. But for our purposes here, assume that (g_1) and (g_2) are sufficiently close in value so that a selection cannot be made at this point. In such a case, we might want to develop an expected value index, which would reflect how certain we are about the postulated value for the coefficients; it would reflect the variance in the information base used to develop the coefficient values. Particularly, we are concerned with how certain we are about the direction of the relationship (i.e., will the tactics produce the desired effect on productivity at the magnitude calculated?). The E.V. calculations then ask what is the expected value of productivity (P) given the two tactics? Now, the criterion of actionability asks that we put forward a single alternative to the next phase of the action-research process; otherwise, we have to set up parallel implementation exercises. Let us suppose that E.V. ($P | g_1$) $\gg$ E.V. ($P | g_2$). Therefore, we are going to proceed with the empirical investigation of the tactic of increasing the capital-labor ratio.

This expected value operator here has some interesting implications for us. Consider, for example, that the tactical analysts in the present problem tried to arrive at a best estimator for (g), the coefficient relating productivity to capital-labor ratios. A standard regression-correlation exercise might have been used or perhaps a nonlinear function of some kind (either convex or concave). We might thus have a situation such as that shown in Figure 5.22.

Let us suppose that our tacticians used the linear formulation [C_2] to arrive at a best estimator for (g_1). We would then compute the expected error of estimate in the normal way, by taking the least-squares variance. But suppose there was a disagreement on the linear formulation; e.g., some analysts think that a

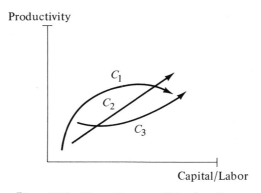

Figure 5.22. Alternative curve-fitting functions.

concave or convex nonlinear curve would be a better "fit." In practice, disputes about what formulation to use may often be resolved objectively (by noting the comparative variance). But where such disputes remain (especially for projective problems), then we have a *superimpositional* probability to consider. Not only will there be a primary error associated with the estimate (g_1), but also a secondary source of error, which is derived from the probability that the basic fitting algorithm was inappropriate: probability $(C_2) < 1$. That is, the expected accuracy of (g_1) would be deflated not only by the variance inherent in the distribution, but also by the probability of (P_2) being the proper formulation. Thus,

$$v_1 = P(g_1) \times P(C_2) = \text{E.V.} \, (P \,|\, g_1)$$

The problem that emerges is one in *experimental design:* how do we structure a controlled experimental situation that will give us *a posteriori* support (or detraction) for our tactical calculations? In short, we need to structure an experiment that will give us a real-world, context-specific estimate of the actual (g_1), against which we may compare our expected value. Derivatively, the experiment should confirm or deny, with reasonable precision, the validity of the tactical assumption that increasing the capital-labor ratio will indeed act to increase productivity. Now, given our concept of analytical congruence, the design we seek is that which promises to yield a most favorable information-production function, given the characteristics of the problem at this point. We also want an experimental design that entails the least risk of causing unexpected or undesired consequences (e.g., by rebounding to upset employees or by committing us to the purchase of a certain quantity of capital equipment should the strategic hypothesis or the tactical expectations prove false). Therefore, the direct task is to structure a *module* that is sufficient in scope to provide the level of information we need, but that is sufficiently insulated and economic to operate within the experimental context. As a general rule, the degree of elaboration of a module (its scope, cost, consequence, visibility, etc.) will increase as does the *heterogeneity* and *asymmetry* of the process under investigation. Heterogeneity, in the present context, might reflect the basic complexity of the production process with which we are concerned; for example, the number of different stages of production and equipment configurations involved, the degree of difference among employee properties. Asymmetry, on the other hand, would reflect the degree to which the production process in one location is similar to that in another location—the degree to which the same set of process properties prevail throughout the entire organization (e.g., is the production process for the product in question essentially the same at the Pittsburgh plant as at the Miami plant?). Of course, where the production process at issue exists at just a single location, then asymmetry becomes gratuitous. Yet as a general

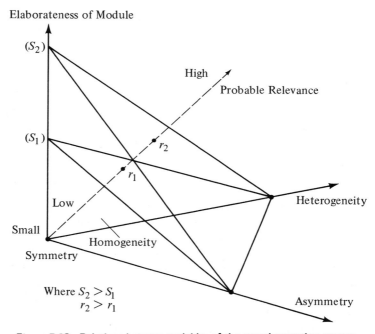

Figure 5.23. Relations between variables of the experimentation process.

rule, aspects of heterogeneity and asymmetry will both have to be taken into consideration. As heterogeneity and asymmetry increase, the elaborateness of the experimental module must increase if any given level of relevance is to be obtained (relevance here indicates the expected accuracy or rectitude of the results of the experimental output). Thus, we get a situation such as that shown in Figure 5.23. In short, the probable error that any experimental results will entail will decrease as the elaborateness (size, etc.) of the experimental module increases, given any level of heterogeneity and asymmetry in the process, subject, or system of interest.* The criteria for the development of an experimental module is thus essentially the same as those used to compute required sample size in a normal statistical experiment.

For the case at hand, this experimental module would be effected by isolating a certain portion of the production process, and increasing the capital-labor ratio within the module. Thus, we are now in a position to obtain empirical data that will be compared against our expectations. The target estimator is

---

*Subject to the asymptote that would be reached as the *a posteriori* information potential is exhausted.

(g_1), which postulates a certain functional relationship between capital-labor ratios and productivity. This (g_1), depending on the type of moderately stochastic instrument the tactical analysts employed, might be a regression variable, a derivative function (for the nonlinear situation), or perhaps a discontinuous function, in which case we would have a set of $(g_1$'s), each associated with a distinctly different level of the capital-labor ratio. In either case, our task is to use the experimental module to produce an actual coefficient (g_a), which will be compared against the estimator.

Following the logic for iterative analysis processes we developed in Section 5.2, we would probably introduce several different experimental capital-labor ratios, and thus generate the following:

$$P_i = g_{a,i} \mid (C/R)_i$$

Simply, we iterate the experiment with several different capital-labor ratios (C/R_i) and generate an *a posteriori* value for the associated productivity level (P_i), and therefore an *a posteriori* estimate for the coefficient $(g_{a,i})$. Now, if the relationship between productivity and the capital-labor ratio appears to be roughly linear, we might generate the ultimate (g_a) by taking a simple average:

$$g_a = \frac{\sum g_{a,i}}{n}$$

where n is the number of different C/R values used, i.e., the number of iterations. As is more likely, the production process will be nonlinear and/or discontinuous, so that g_a would require slightly more complex computation (using the calculus). At any rate, we would then be interested in the following:

$$\text{VARIANCE}_t = (g_a - g_1)$$

In practice, this (g_a) would be adjusted to reflect any internal variance—variance in the results of the different iterations—yet we would still have the basis for the critical test: $P(g_1 = g \mid g_a)$. This simply asks about the probability that our estimator (g_1) will be equal to the true coefficient g (a component of the actual state), given the value that emerged for the *a posteriori* coefficient (g_a). When this value is sufficiently high, we may usually assume that our tactical expectations are accurate, both in direction and magnitude. But where this value is unsatisfactory, we have to revise our tactical expectations, and perhaps consider another alternative altogether. This is the purpose of the "tactical learning loop" entered in Figure 5.21.

When we get a sufficiently low variance, we move on to the next phase of the action-research process. Particularly, we must now test the validity of the strategic hypothesis, the expectation that increasing productivity will increase market share. For this we would have to develop another experimental module (for the case at hand, the strategic experimental module would be developed according to the normal precepts of market research, considering matters of homogeneity and asymmetry or market conditions, and the caution against having an experimental situation lead to a commitment that is irrevocable in some respect or dysfunctional). At any rate, the output from the tactical level of analysis now becomes an input into the strategic analysis process. Particularly, a most favorable (effectively optimal) capital-labor ratio would have been located during the tactical process—that which yields the greatest increase in productivity at the lowest marginal cost (p). This (p) will imply a particular decrease in the price that we can charge for our product; for example, Δr. The strategic module would then be used to test the hypothesis that a reduction in price will dictate an increase in relative sales: $\Delta S = f(\Delta r \mid p)$. Note that the problem at this point is properly a severely stochastic one, for any of three qualitatively distinct events might occur:

(1) There could be no effect at all, indicating that the demand schedule for our product is highly inelastic in the neighborhood of $(\Delta r \mid p)$, or perhaps we are a victim of oligopolistic market conditions, so that our competitors immediately follow us down in price.

(2) Our strategic assumption could be proven correct—our price reduction does provoke an increase in market share (so that some "monopoly" profits may be expected until competitors can adjust their own productivity levels, which may be prohibited in the short run).

(3) The price reduction could actually rebound to our disadvantage by reducing our share of market; e.g., our competitors may be provoked into banding together and setting a preemptive price in order to drive us out of the market, or consumers might see the price reduction as a signal for a decrease in quality.

In other words, the experimental situation at the tactical level looks again for a variance between our expectations and the reality of a problem context. To the extent that variance is high, we should rethink our strategic assumptions, and perhaps develop a new strategy (and repeat the entire action-research process using the new strategic hypothesis). But where our strategic assumptions are substantially met, then we may proceed to actually implement our solution, monitoring the outcome at an intensity that reflects the degree of confidence we have been able to generate during the analysis phase. For the case at hand, this would mean lowering the price of our product according to the productivity increases. But even here we might want to pass the problem back to our tactical analysts. They might be asked to effect an optimal solution by evaluating the demand function $(S = f)$ for its optimal point. In this case, we would search for the particular r that yields maximum profits; r would then be used to determine a required productivity rate (p_{opt}), which would in turn determine the optimal capital-labor ratio. Thus, the action-research process keeps folding back on itself, and gains institutional significance when we deposit the results of our action-research exercises in the concatenative decision inventory.

As a final note, our movement through this action-research paradigm will ideally be disciplined at all points by the criteria of analytical congruence we developed in the previous chapter, and by the efficiency criteria (the time, resource, and productivity functions) we discussed in Section 5.2. And, the extent to which the action-research promise can be fulfilled depends in large measure on the degree to which complex organizations are willing to invoke the six procedural and structural innovations we suggested earlier. But most of all, the promise of rationality—the feasibility of optimality—depends on the work of others who are sure to follow what we have done here with efforts that are at once more elegant and more relevant. That these pages may somehow assist those men and women of greater wit and energy and insight is the highest ambition of this book.

5.5 NOTES AND REFERENCES

1. This is one of the key points made by Adrian M. McDonough in *Information Economics and Management Systems* (New York: McGraw-Hill, 1963).
2. For a general note on the use of analogic processes in scientific research, see Anatol Rapoport's "The Search For Simplicity," in *The Relevance of General System Theory*, Laszlo, ed. (New York: George Braziller, Inc., 1972).
3. For a classic work on the nature of the relationship between environments and organizations, see Emery and Trist's "The Causal Texture of the Environment," *Human Relations* 18 (1965).
4. Some work has been done on the concept of a Type-III error—solving the wrong problem. The implication is that the "real state" serves to house the possible biases of the analyst. See "On Measuring the Conceptual Errors in Large Scale Social Experiments: The Future as Decision," by Ian Mitroff and Murray Turoff, in *Technological Forecasting and Social Change* 6 no. 2 (1974).
5. For more on this, see the appropriate sections of Robert Schlaifer's *Probability and Statistics for Business Decisions* (New York: McGraw-Hill, 1959).
6. Particularly, he would be inappropriate in a position where there was little opportunity to reduce error, either because of enormous inherent complexity or because of the necessity for quick reactions. In short, where considerable risk is inescapable, the risk-averter becomes a decision-averter.
7. The essentially different levels of waste that can be theoretically postulated for the decentralized and socialized system generally would disappear were

we able to propose omniscience for the centralized decision authorities. The decentralized nature of the free market system does not require any pervasive assumptions about the "rationality" of consumers or producers other than the latters' responsiveness—with limited lag—to self-evident market properties. Yet as has been frequently pointed out, the "realities" of capitalist markets is seldom at all reflective of the normative (or idealistic) attributes. In this regard, see J. K. Galbraith's *Economic and the Public Purpose* (Boston: Houghton Mifflin Company, 1973).

8. For more on the size of organization in relation to coordinative and control modalities, see John W. Sutherland "Towards an Array of Organizational Control Modalities," *Human Relations* 27 no. 2 (1974).

9. This assertion is argumentative, for comparative structural data are not at hand as yet. The point, however, is that organizational magnitude may be less important as a determinant of organizational and administrative structure than the particular industry setting in which an organization operates. That is, there tends to be a "demonstration effect" at the structural level among competitive enterprises.

10. This point, in much elaborated form, is one of the key propositions advanced by Walter A. Weisskopf in his brilliant *Alienation and Economics* (New York: E. P. Dutton & Co., Inc., 1971).

11. For a note on additivity in systems, see Chapter 2 of John W. Sutherland, *Systems: Analysis, Administration, and Architecture* (New York: Van Nostrand Reinhold Company, 1975).

12. See, for example, Warren Bennis, "Beyond Bureacracy," *Transactions* (July–August 1965).

13. John W. Sutherland, *A General Systems Philosophy for the Social and Behavioral Sciences* (New York: George Braziller, Inc., 1973).

14. In this regard, consider the operational basis, for example, of Forrester's *Urban Dynamics* (Cambridge, Massachusetts: M.I.T. Press, 1969).

15. See John W. Sutherland, "System Theoretic Limits on the Cybernetic Paradigm," *Behavioral Science* 20 no. 3 (1975).

16. For a procedure to isolate and evaluate background assumptions, see Russell Ackoff and Fred Emery, *On Purposeful Systems* (Chicago: Aldine-Atherton, 1972).

17. See the editorial in *Business Week* (November 1, 1976): "How Loews' Lean Management Fattened the Profits at CNA."

18. See Chapter 7 of Alvin Toffler's *Future Shock* (New York: Random House, Inc., 1974).

19. For notes on the technology of action research, see the papers in *Experimenting with Organizational Life: The Action Research Approach*, Alfred Clark, ed., (New York: Plenum Press, 1976).

Appendix to Chapter 5

As we sought to show in Chapter 5, the failure to resolve significant issues—the metaproblems affecting our age—is not always merely a result of technological incapacities. Often, it reflects the tendency to consider issues as matters of "ideological" conflict, or as value disputes, or as the result of natural differences of opinion about different courses of action that might be taken. This tendency to translate issues into ideological conflicts means that the issues are not recognized as *real* problems and that no rational solution is sought. For, problems imply a solution, whereas ideological conflicts imply mere tolerance. This is unfortunate. Some attempts have been made to make ideological predicates explicit, so that issues may be resolved rationally. But the field is immature, and I have asked an expert on ideological theory to add a few comments to this text on this critical but intractable area. I hope the reader agrees that, in the near future, decision theorists must begin to deal with ideological issues and value-conflicts in a disciplined, precise way. How this might be done is the message this appendix offers us.

IDEOLOGICS by Stephen E. Seadler

One can reasonably aver that the most remarkable feature of administrative decision-making in the United States, as taught and as practiced, is the almost total neglect of the most pervasive and powerful domain involved in the real world with which those processes supposedly deal: namely, ideology.

Therefore, the need, to involve ideological considerations in a decision-science mode in business and industrial affairs is proportionately important, and in national and international affairs is critically urgent. In the process of such considerations, we will apply the principle expressed by the Alfred North Whitehead quotation in the preface, and thereby move toward resolution of a problem Whitehead expressed elsewhere in the cited work. "The problem is not how to produce great men, but how to produce great societies." The relevance of these

303

considerations for the business community, for its managers, executives, and directors, is succinctly expressed in still another Whitehead quotation, which is chiseled into stone at the entrance to Uris Hall of Columbia University's Graduate School of Business. "A great society is a society in which its men of business think greatly of their functions."

For brevity, we will begin these considerations by (1) accepting as demonstrated, at least upon some reflection by the reader, the pervasive and powerful nature of ideology, and (2) accepting any good dictionary definition of "ideology." However, the word "ideology" is confusingly tautological, in that it represents both process and substance: ideology is the study of ideology. Therefore, we will coin the term *ideologics* to denote this new science of the nature, structure, and dynamics of ideologies, especially of their roles in individual and societal phenomena, comprising both theoretical and applied branches, and intended to be primarily an applied science. Ideologics thus becomes one of the behavioral sciences, along with economics, psychology, sociology, and history. In the context of this volume, we distinguish the branch of *administrative ideologics* and, within that, ideologic aspects of decision science.

A good methodology with which to begin, because it introduces fundamental concepts, is ideologic cluster analysis. This is an adaptation of one member of the class of multivariate statistical analyses for the behavioral sciences. The objectives of this technique are different from those of other multivariate techniques, such as regression, correlation, discriminant, and canonical analysis, because it seeks to assess the similarities between observations of the sampled individuals.

For our purposes, "individuals" can be entities such as companies, industries, unions, mediants,* cities, regions, and nations. The observations (measurements) of these individuals on a number of characteristics provide a score for each individual on each characteristic, and each individual's scores provide a "profile" of him or her (it).

The measurements are obtained from a battery of m-tests, or a single test of m distinct parts, where each m contains a set of measurements representing a particular characteristic or dimension. A "test" can be such instruments or methods as survey questionnaires (oral or written) or content analyses of speeches, articles, and broadcasts. On the basis of such data, one can proceed to a number of cluster-analytic objectives, but for our purposes a key one is the ability to determine—without advance assignment of observations to groups—what clusters (groups) of observations (individuals) are "similar" with respect to their profiles.

Briefly, the procedure sets up hypothesis as to an individual's group membership in the form of a likelihood function, $P(H_j|X_i) = P_{ij}$; $j = 1, 2, \ldots, g$; $i = 1, 2, \ldots, N$; which reads: the probability of hypothesis H_j that individual i is a member of group j, given his score vector X_i, is P_{ij}. The centour (centile con-

---

*For convenience, we will refer to any individual member of the media—that is, any particular newspaper, journal, radio station, and so on—as a "mediant."

tour) approach to determining P_{ij} describes a multivariate normal distribution[*] of the m-test scores of the i individuals in terms of hyperellipsoids,[‡] each of which represents a centour, i.e., the locus of points of a particular frequency derived from x^2.

x^2 is called the "classification," and is a function $(X_i'D^{-1}X_i)$ of the distribution's dispersion (variance-covariance) matrix D and an m-element vector of deviation scores $X_i = (X_{1i} - \overline{X}_1.\ X_{2i} - \overline{X}_2.\ \cdots\ X_{mi} - \overline{X}_m)$, where, for instance, the last element is the deviation of individual i's score on test m from the mean of all scores on test m. Each test j in the battery of m tests assesses a different dimension, or characteristic, and is represented by one of the m orthogonal coordinate axes in the m-dimensional test space. The larger the value of x^2, the larger the size of the hyperellipsoid corresponding to it, that is, the larger the proportion of the group's membership that falls within it. Thus, the smaller an individual's x^2 for a particular ideological group, the closer he is to its centroid, and the more certain he is to be a member of it.

D is an estimate of the dispersion of the population from which the sample was drawn, and, within that, D_j is an estimate of the dispersion of the $j = 1$, $2, \ldots, g$ groups within the sample. An individual in the sample has a p_j, *a priori* probability of belonging (in terms of test scores) to group j, determined from estimated real-world relative frequencies of membership in groups.

Pulling all of the foregoing together, with the aid of Bayes' theorem, we obtain for the probability of group membership, in simplified functional notation, an expression of the form $P_{ij} = P(H_j|X_i) = f(p_k, |D_k|, x_k^2);\ k = 1, 2, \ldots, j, \ldots, g;$ $i = 1, 2, \ldots, N$.

The universes sampled for these determinations can be, for instance: union locals in an industry; union locals in a country; executives and directors of companies in an industry; executives and directors of companies in a country; employees of a particular company, industry, or country; labor and management combined; government officials above a certain rank, or all such engaged in certain domains of activity; and speeches, articles, and programs in all or particular types of media in a country, region of a country, or in regions of countries.

The reader should now be able to get at least the flavor of the following ideologic capabilities:

1. to define an ideology by computing membership in it in terms of its dispersion matrix and individuals' score vectors.

2. (a) to define and determine the number of significant (well-populated) ideological dimensions (from x^2-derived classifications of members), and the degree of significance of each dimension; (b) by exploding the dimensions in terms of their original measures, to deal in substantive detail with

---

[*]Moderate departure from normality is no more a constraint here than in much of applied statistics.

[‡]In two dimensions, an ellipse; in three dimensions, an ellipsoid; in more than three, a hyperellipsoid.

the issues involved; and (c) to know the vector impact of details on the whole.

3. to define and measure the distance between ideologies; an individual's position within an ideology; and an individual's distance from (a) the center (= centroid = vector mean) of his or her own ideological group, (b) the center of another ideological group, and (c) another individual in his own or another ideological group.

In cluster-analytic ideologics, the same m-test battery or m-part test is applied to all individuals in the sample; that is, no prior ordering or assignment of the m is made among the groups in the sample. The delineation of the m characteristics, however, is conceived and designed in advance on the basis of expert knowledge of the ideology (or ideologies) involved. In some cases, however, it is desirable to determine both the number and composition of dimensions after having conducted exploratory research, and, again, mathematico-analytic ideologic means are available. In this approach, expert knowledge is employed in the advance design of the detailed measures, but dimensionality is *subsequently* defined, this time by means of the appropriate method from among a set of multivariate techniques generically known as *factor analysis*, whose primary objective is, in our adaptation, to aid in determining the fewest, simplest, and most meaningful ideological dimensions latent in the set of measures. The resultant dimensions can then be employed in a wide range of applications, including cluster-analytic, regression analytic, and topological ideologics. Therefore, we now turn to this methodology.

We begin with a sample of N "individuals" i (same range of entities as before) that have been measured on n observed variables X by means of some test or battery of tests. That is, a "variable" can be a test, or any item or combination of items on a single test, such as a question or group of questions on some aspect of ideological belief, or an element of ideological content in media, speeches, articles, or broadcast programs, with values obtained by any of the many available rating or scaling techniques.

The value of variable X_j for individual i is represented by X_{ji}, which we treat by the usual statistical techniques to obtain its *standardized value* z_{ji}. The set of z_{ji} for all i ($i = 1, 2, \ldots, N$) is the variable z_j in *standard form*. The intercorrelations among all the variables are then computed, and the resultant correlation matrix R becomes the primary datum, the foundation for analysis of the ideological domain of concern.

This genre of analysis can best be conceptually conveyed by describing one of its methods, *principal components*, which is based on the simple model consisting of n linear equations

$$z_j = a_{j1} F_1 + a_{j2} F_2 + \cdots + a_{jn} F_n$$

which express each of the n observed variables in terms of n *uncorrelated* components, or factors, $F_1, F_2, \cdots F_n$, and their "loadings" a_{jp}. Geometrically, this means that the standardized values (scores) of the N individuals on variable (test) j locate a point for that variable in the N-dimensional sample space, that a line from the origin to that point is the variable's vector representation, and that the cosine of the angle between that vector and the vector for any other variable is the correlation between the two variables.

The N-dimensional sample space is thus reduced to an n-dimensional test space in which the test scores (variable values) form a hyperellipsoid. Principal-components analysis then seeks the principal reference axes, or components, that uniquely define the factors F_p, which the variables are measuring in common. These factors will, upon content-based expert interpretation, comprise the ideological "constructs," or dimensions, that we are seeking in the domain of concern.

This is accomplished by finding that axis of the hyperellipsoid along which the projection of variable-points produces maximum variance; then constructing a second axis orthogonal to the first along which the remaining variance is maximized; then constructing a third axis along which, etc.; and so on until new axes produce only insignificant amounts of variance. Thus, not only have the principal axes (= components, factors, dimensions) of the ideological domain been located, but they have been reduced to the smallest number required to define the domain.

Expert content knowledge now reenters the procedure to interpret the meaning of the resultant factors F_p on the basis of their loadings a_{jp} in relation to the variables z_j. In the event that the first set of derived principal-component axes is not considered substantively satisfactory in terms of ideological interpretation, they can be rotated, repeatedly, until a substantively satisfactory set is located. A variety of rotational schemes have been devised for this, differing in objectives, criteria, and properties.

Whether we focus primarily on delineating ideological groups, as with cluster analysis, or on delineating ideological dimensions, as with factor analysis, we become involved with sets of elements. These elements can be analyzed and dealt with from another, quite different perspective, that of set theory and topology. Ideologic topology can also serve as a more directly perceivable and handy methodology by itself, for both analytic and operational purposes.

While derived from general topology, ideologic topology bears a fundamental difference: rather than developing as a pure (mathematical) science, ideologic topology develops as an applied science, and, furthermore, as a mission-oriented applied science. Ultimately, a thoroughly rigorous formulation may evolve, and if so, the progression would be similar to that of other branches of science—for example, probability theory evolving from games of chance, and the related trio (number theory, set theory, and topology) evolving from everyday affairs involving 10 fingers and the arrangement of objects in places.

An essential difference in the ideologic topology progression is that it does not start with raw experience and then creatively abstract and mathematize, but starts with already highly developed, rigorous mathematics and then deliberately adapts the mathematics in order to achieve a predetermined operational goal. The goal is to develop real-world ways of dealing with a particular phenomenological domain—the "dealing with" being ideologics, the "domain" being ideologies. The motivation for choosing this approach is the critically urgent need for ideologics, as averred at the outset. This, in turn, leads to the need for an operational ideologic topology.

We begin by defining the "universe of discourse" U_Ω and its hierarchy of sets and elements, as illustrated in the following hierarchy. For brevity, some knowledge of topology on the part of the reader will be assumed. The uninitiated will nevertheless be able to gain some feeling for the approach.

Tier U_Ω

where specific subscripts are represented by an ordered n-tuple $< >$ (e.g., $j \epsilon < j >$, $< j > = 3, 7, 15, 16, 119$).

Induction:

3 $\theta_{jk1} = \{\theta_{jk}\}$

2 $\theta_{jk} = \{\theta_j\}$

1 $\theta_j = \{\alpha_i\}$

0 α_i

Reduction:

-1 $\alpha_i = \{a_h\}$

-2 $a_h = \{b_g\}$

-3 $b_g = \{c_f\}$

At any level of the hierarchy, a class of sets is denoted by θ with primed subscripts, e.g., θ_j', $j' \epsilon < j' >$, and a family (collection) of classes by C_k, θ_j'. This provides for substantive specificity while maintaining notational economy. Reduction of the set elements α into successively lower components is also provided for by an archeoarchy of more primitive elements, represented by lower-case Latin letters. The collection of all functions f operating in U_Ω is represented by $F(\Omega)$, and of all functions f operating among θ's by $F(\theta)$.

Now, some sets in U_Ω will have properties that distinguish them as *ideological*, and are denoted by ϕ, with the same induction-reduction schema as for θ's. Classes and families are similarly denoted by Φ and $C\Phi$ with primed subscripts.

Some functions in $F(\Omega)$ operate so as to generate ϕ's from θ's, and others operate solely among ϕ's. Both of these types comprise *ideological functions*, and their collection is denoted by $F(\phi)$. That is, $F(\phi)$ includes functions of the type f: $\phi_{j_1} \rightarrow \phi_{j_2}$ and f: $\phi_{j_1} \rightarrow \phi_{j_2}$. $F(\Omega)$ also includes functions that generate θ's and ϕ's from α's, i.e., f: $\{\alpha_i\} \rightarrow \theta_j$ and f: $\{\alpha_i\} \rightarrow \phi_j$.

In standard fashion, a class τ of subsets of a set θ defines a *topology* on θ if τ satisfies certain axioms, and the members of τ together with θ, i.e., the pair (θ, τ) defines a topological space. In special fashion, however, some sets and their topologies have properties that distinguish them as *ideological topological spaces* (ϕ, τ), or ideological spaces, or, simply, *ideologies*.

This then brings us to the search for *functional continuities* and *homeo-morphisms*, for *bases* for ideological topologies and hence for ideologies, and for set *connectedness*, among other properties. Metricization is sometimes feasible and desirable, and sometimes neither.

Development of this topology proceeds, broadly speaking, from two families of resources: (1) deduction and induction based on expert knowledge of ideologies, and (2) formal results and cues from multivariate procedures such as those described earlier.

Although the foregoing would have to be developed at much greater length before proceeding to an operational demonstration, we can nevertheless gain at least a sense of operationality by means of a highly compressed and simplified example. For this, we will employ a scenario approach in a business-economic context, and begin by formulating a hypothetical situation.

Business conditions had long been stubbornly "stagflated." Factions existed within both the government and the business community on both sides of the policy question of whether the administration should be more "interventionist" or should leave matters to "market forces" for correction. As the national debate wore on, severe adversary relations developed, measures were debated, statistics were adduced, statistical interpretations diverged, prognoses diverged, decision-making became confounded, the Phillips curve went limp, and coherent strategic and operational consensus became more distant within and between government and business. A joint congressional committee, beleaguered as well as divided, called in the Nu Group, an ideologic consulting firm known to be of no partisan persuasion. Due to certain circumstances, the committee could allow only 10 calendar days for the group's report, but compensated for this by means of a cost-plus contract with a generous not-to-exceed. The group was charged with doing whatever it could to meliorate the national atmosphere so that work could progress toward improving business conditions. The group's operations then proceeded as follows.

One of the firm's principals, acting as project leader, called his five top colleagues into a quick huddle. They decided on a high-speed topological approach, called in 10 assistants who were waiting in the wings in local hotels, and repaired with them to a room full of administration, congressional, and business reports, speeches, transcripts, publications, and so on, which the committee had provided. They divided these among the five ideologicians in five offices, and equipped each with cassette dictating machines, which were connected to the project leader's "mission control" office via closed-circuit television, for instant conferring. They raced through their respective stacks of source materials, dictating preliminary α, θ, and ϕ components as they occurred, numerically keying them to the materials. In so doing, they utilized their extensive backgrounds in politico-economic ideology, including cues from prior cluster-analytic and factor-analytic studies.

Runners, also provided by the committee, ran the finished cassettes sequentially to the 10 assistants in other rooms, where the assistants typed them via visual tele-word-processor terminals directly into their home-office computer-system's off-line memory. Hard copies were produced simultaneously, and the work was monitored by the project leader in his office via 10 CRT screens, whereupon he dictated notes for subsequent discussion or corrections.

Toward the end of the third day, they packed their materials into numbered footlockers, sent them "air freight special" to home base, and followed on various flights that night.

By noon the next day, "Genie," their computer configuration for ideologic topology (or "ideotop") had alphanumerically translated the teletyped preliminary α, θ, and ϕ components into machine language, worked those inputs against the huge set bank in the U_Ω memory, which housed the U_Ω θ-structure and U_Ω ϕ-structure, comprising the U_Ω-structure; and produced the preliminary U_ω-structure (a reduced U_Ω-structure) for the project. Home staff then mapped the printouts onto large "top grids," and mounted them in the "war room," where they also distributed reproduced copies of the printouts to each work station, each of which was electronically connected to backup specialists in various staff offices.

After a series of full team conferences in the war room and successive computer runs spanning 3 days, the report was drafted. In 2 days, the final version was printed, bound, crated and air-freighted to Washington. The original six-person team caught a later flight and was at the committee for the scheduled 10-o'clock presentation the next morning. What the group had accomplished can be described in summary fashion, as follows.

In overview, they had explicated the ideological labyrinth in which the factions were wandering, and had indicated ways out, while neither taking substantive positions nor weighting the options.

In summary detail, they had found and defined ideological sets ϕ_1 and ϕ_2 such that class τ_1 of subsets of ϕ_1 represented one faction and class τ_2 of subsets of ϕ_2 represented the other faction, such that (ϕ_1, τ_1) and (ϕ_2, τ_2) formed ideologic topologies, or spaces, for the two factions. This provided essential structure on the basis of which further valuable considerations could proceed.

They then searched for, found, and defined classes β_1 of subsets of τ_1 and β_2 of subsets of τ_2 that formed bases for the respective topologies. With this, they were further able to construct topologies (β_1, τ_{11}) and (β_2, τ_{22}), and define a function $f_{\beta_{1,2}}$ within $F(\phi)$ such that the two β spaces were homeomorphic. That is, the two factional spaces were ideotopologically equivalent.

Continuing in this vein, the group was ultimately able to demonstrate how these and other ideotop findings formed foundations for reconciliation and conjoint development of macroeconomic and microeconomic measures. The factions had the option of conducting such development in the explicit context of the ultimate ideotop, or of factoring its components out of their considerations altogether, or of using the ideotop as bounds for their considerations, or some combination of these.

In particular, the group had provided disciplined, formal procedures for communicating and negotiating the factions' ideological differences. Although not covered in the report (because they decided that it was unnecessary and would be confusing in this case), one of the unique and invaluable features of ideologic topology is that it allows, *in extremis*, for changes in the topological procedures themselves, and provides procedures for negotiating changes in those procedures. Such changes, however, would be rare, due to their potentially enormous ramifications, which would be at least partially apparent at the time.

During the course of their work, the group had also noted that at a lower ϕ-set tier there appeared to be a problem concerning an *ad hoc* "freedom" space, which had been formed for test purposes, labeled ϕ_{F7}. It included components labeled "free market," "laissez-faire," "perfect competition," "competition," and "free enterprise," among others, which seemed to contain disconnected subsets. The problem was tentatively diagnosed as due to α's such as "compete," "struggle," "rivalry," "control," "zero bargaining," "zero cooperation," "perfect information," "strategy," "control of state variables," "price taking," and so on. Furthermore, there appeared to be $F(\phi)$ problems in mapping over from economic θ's involving "general equilibrium theory" and "utility theory," which sets, in turn, involved lower-tier θ's that included deterministic mathematics.

The group decided, however, that the objectives of this project permitted working entirely at higher tiers, and left the $f: \theta \rightarrow \phi$- and ϕ_{F7}-connectedness problems to subsequent research. They had also noted a possible mapping and topology involving "degrees of freedom" from the statistical mechanics θ and the classical mechanics θ into the $\phi_{1,2}$-space that might prove quite helpful in meliorating the ϕ_{F7} problem. Again, however, they agreed that this would require much careful work to define and legitimate, so it was deferred for subsequent research.

The group's report included Part I, Objectives and Findings, translated into lay language and keyed to the technical Part III. (Part II set forth project procedures.) It was enthusiastically received by the committee, which provided a prefatory statement, and printed and reprinted in accordance with widespread demand. In a brief time, factions found common ground, cooperation within and between the public and private sectors was facilitated, work by primary participants was enhanced, measures were passed, and the economy began to prosper. End of scenario.

Despite the brevity of this discourse, the reader may now have some sense of the prospects: that with ideologics it becomes feasible to deal with explicit ideological issues, and to surface and deal with unrecognized implicit ideological components of other issues, as called for by several passages in this volume. Ideologics also interfaces with other aspects of administrative decision science, as developed in these chapters, and thus becomes an essential, integral component of administrative rationality, in both the public and private sectors.

From another perspective, we are all Minotaurs wandering in ideological labyrinths—built by the ideological Daedali among us. However, we too can build wings to escape—from wandering, from dead ends, and especially from malevolent pathways. It is primarily due to those malevolent pathways that the most urgent need for ideologics is in the administration of international affairs and national defense, particularly for the development of ideological defense systems; that is, defense systems that are designed to operate along the ideological dimensions of conflict. Such systems include rhetorical, educational, programmatic, political, informational, and analytic dimensions, and are based in large part on principles, practice, and findings of ideologics. Highest priority should be assigned to their becoming integral components of United States national strategic planning, tactics, operations, and intelligence. Had this been so for the past decade, the United States would not have been confronted in December 1976 with a "grim," "somber" national intelligence estimate of Soviet strategic objectives; those estimates would have been so all along, and our present circumstances would be less grim.

Index

Index

Abstraction (of decision arguments), 280
Accountability, 108–175
  concentration index, 92
  determinants, 174ff
  foci (dimensions), 108f
  process characteristics, 128
  projective aspects, 182
  public versus private context, 121ff
Actionability, 66, 207–213, 266, 295
Action research process, 292, 294–301
Administrative functions, 6
  general typology, 228
  goal-setting, 52–60, 129–136
  operational programming, 85–89
  overhead analysis, 271–275
  strategic processes, 60–76
  tactical processes, 76–85
Allocation analysis, 155f, 166–171,
  178–182
Analogic processes, 32, 240–245
Analytical congruence, 216ff
Asymmetry (in decision distributions), 297
Axiological predicates, 61
Axiomatic predicates, 62

Bayesian process, 267, 288–301
Benefit formulation, 179
Block investors, 116f
Boards of directors, 53, 115–118
Boolean logic, 44, 73
Budget configuration, 152
Budget process (idealized), 178–184

Capital-labor ratio, 273–275
Capital budgeting, 177
Categorical budgeting, 147, 282–286
Centralization (decision concentration),
  270, 276
Centrix formulation, 215
Cluster analysis, 305ff
Concatenation (of decisions), 90
Coefficients, 189
Complementarity of decision skills, 46, 290
Confidence-level analysis, 247–262
Congruence (of decision instruments),
  127, 196
Constraints, 61f, 73, 130–133, 233
Contingency programming, 214, 224–230,
  237
Correlative (directional) analysis, 209
Cost-benefit analysis, 57, 126f, 155–171, 178f

Data-base characteristics, 102f, 237–243
Data independence, 239
Decentralization, 277ff
Decision-analysis functions, 5
  deterministic, 85–89
  normative, 52–60
  phases (stages), 252
  strategic, 60–76
  tactical, 76–85
Decision auditing, 108
Decision configurations, 90, 93f
Decision congruence, 196
Decision control, 153
  action-research paradigm, 294–301

313

Decision domains, 6–12
  administrative implications, 52
  functionaries, 52
Decision horizon, 90
Decision integration, 269–272
Decision inventory, 237, 242ff
Decision-making processes, 2
  abstracted, 186
  action-research base, 294
  analytical limitations, 277
  dynamics, 230
  generalized, 269
  in relation to model-building logic, 195
  paradigmatic representation, 249–269
  typology of components, 228
Decision system (components), 238–260
Decompositional analysis, 148–153
Delphi technique, 44
Determinism, 15
Devaluation, 274
Directorial functions, 52–60

Effectiveness (system), 124ff
Efficiency, 140
  in decision processes, 250–258
Elegance (of models), 207
Empirical predicates, 73
Envelope of certainty, 88
Error (in decision contexts), 11, 250–255
  characteristics, 85–95
  computations and transformations,
    197–206
  floor, 104, 254–258
  legitimate versus illegitimate, 183
Exegesis, 39, 129
Exhaustiveness (of models), 207
Expected value formulations, 136, 197ff
  of decision error, 12, 197–206, 247
  of estimate, 97

Finite-state machine, 16
Functional structure of decision models,
    233
Funding categories, 149
Fuzzy-set operations, 44, 193

Game theoretics, 44, 237
General decision logic, 250
Goal-setting, 8, 52–60, 129–136
  goal maps and partitioning, 61ff

neighborhood and point formulations,
    63–65, 77, 213
Growth versus efficiency, 119

Heterogeneity, 297
Heuristic processes, 227, 237
  management paradigm, 289–291
Hyperbolic search, 78
Hypothetico-deductive process, 225ff

Ideological operations, 73, 279f
  ideologics, 303–312
  topological structures, 308
Impact programming, 177
Indeterminate problems, 17
Inductive processes, 44, 74, 102
Information, 200
  configurations, 213
  leverage, 211
  production functions, 204
  stocks (states), 249f, 251–253
  value of, 200, 256
Instrumentalism, 25
Iterative decision processes, 260–269

Judgmental data, 30, 224, 242

Learning-based decision processes, 265, 290
Levels of analysis, 189, 262–265
Leverage (of decisions), 90f
Linear programming, 239, 288

Management by objectives, 120
Management information systems, 240–269
  for service organizations, 150–161
Market clearance, 270
Markov process, 237
Mechanistic decision-making, 24ff, 89
  versus rhetorical, 37
Maturity index (of decisions), 90
Metahypothetical analysis, 226
Method-audit scheme, 174–185, 290
Mission analysis, 146ff, 178
Modality shifts, 264, 267
Model base, 237, 242
Model-building technology, 186–197,
    211–214
Moderately stochastic problems, 17–20,
    77f
Modularity (in decision analysis), 291, 298

Natural growth curve, 75
Network analysis, 155ff, 190–194
Nodal decision authority, 280–285
Normative decision predicates, 33

Objectivity (in decision analysis), 25, 28
Opportunity cost, 125, 147, 251–259, 280
Optimality, 1, 77f, 232
Optimal scale of plant, 118, 270–273
Organizational structure, 274–287, 290

Parametric analysis, 189ff
Parsimony, 239
Platonic system bias, 45
Preemption (analytical), 211
Prescriptivity (of models), 207ff
Probability distributions, 98ff
  for error analysis, 198–206
  superimpositional, 297
Problem contexts, 12–24
  definitions, 15
  distribution across organization, 13
Production function (generic), 74
Productivity, 140, 160ff
Profit centers, 119ff, 142
Program budgeting, 178–182
Propriety (of decision-makers), 110

Quadratic search, 78
Qualitative specification, 192–281
Quality of model formulations, 207ff

Range formulations, 78
Rationality, 47, 148
Reactivity, 34–37, 120
Realism, 24, 28
Real-time control, 290
Reductionism, 25

Reflectivity (of models), 207
Reflexivity, 157, 212
Relational analysis, 189–194
Relativistic decision criteria, 95–106
Return (rate of), 140, 144–152, 280
Rhetorical decision processes, 25ff, 37
Risk formulations, 82–85, 260–262

Satisficing, 1
Scenario-building, 45, 227
Search functions, 78ff
Set formulations, 61–70, 130–133
Sequential decision processes, 213, 290–301
Severely stochastic problems, 21ff
Shock models, 18
Speculative processes, 41, 256–260
Spread (of decisions), 90
State-variable, 189
Stochastic simulation, 44
Strategic decision-making, 8, 60–76, 132ff,
  138
Surrogation, 145
Syncretic solutions, 280
System properties, 54–56, 102

Tactical programming, 10, 76–85, 150–166
Time-series analysis, 237
Trade-off technology, 65ff, 113, 256–260
  with regard to decision structure, 268–271
Trajectory analysis, 86–89, 125–128

Utility analysis, 127, 133–140, 167–171

Value-added pricing, 142
Variance, 103ff, 141, 193, 298ff

Zero-base budgeting, 178
Zero-sum game, 158, 169